ANGLO-NORMAN STUDIES XI

PROCEEDINGS OF THE BATTLE CONFERENCE
1988

Photograph courtesy of Christine Mahany

ANGLO-NORMAN STUDIES

XI

PROCEEDINGS OF THE BATTLE CONFERENCE

1988

Edited by R. Allen Brown

THE BOYDELL PRESS

© by contributors 1988, 1989

First published 1989 by The Boydell Press, Woodbridge

The Boydell Press is an imprint of Boydell & Brewer Ltd
PO Box 9, Woodbridge, Suffolk IP12 3DF
and of Boydell & Brewer Inc.
Wolfeboro, New Hampshire 03894-2069, USA

ISBN 0 85115 526 X

ISSN 0261-9857

British Library Cataloguing in Publication Data
Battle Conference: 1988
  Proceedings of the Battle Conference, 1988.
  – (Anglo-Norman studies, ISSN 0261-9857; 11).
  1. Western Europe. Normans, history
  I. Title II. Brown, R. Allen (Reginald Allen),
  1924– III. Series
  940′.0441
  ISBN 0-85115-526-X

Printed and bound in Great Britain
by The Camelot Press PLC, Southampton

CONTENTS

ILLUSTRATIONS

St Pancras Priory, Lewes

SAS – Sussex Archaeological Society; FEMA – F. E. M. Anderson; ESRO – East Sussex Record Office; EG – Emil Godfrey; c. – Copyright.

PREFACE

The eleventh annual Battle Conference, which was held from 22 to 27 July 1988, at Pyke House, Battle, was the last to be directed by Professor R. Allen Brown. He died on 1 February 1989, after a long and heroic struggle against cancer. The Battle Conferences have been rightly described as one of the 'great historical enterprises' which he inaugurated and inspired. For more than a decade they have brought together scholars from many parts of Europe and North America, as well as the Middle East and Japan, to take part in an interdisciplinary forum for the presentation and study of the latest research in Anglo-Norman and late Old English history. Papers on archaeology, architecture, literature and language have all been prominent alongside those on every aspect of history. A notable feature has been the practical study of arms and armour, accompanied on one occasion by a demonstration of the way in which fully armed Norman knights could charge on horseback up the hill at Battle. Over the years the conferences have become a centre of warmth and friendship as well as good scholarship. Allen Brown gave them an impetus that will ensure their survival. Our sense of loss now is great; but the Battle Conferences will continue in future years as a fitting memorial to him.

The papers in this volume were all read in the course of the eleventh conference. Allen Brown himself attended almost to the end, and it was appropriate that the news of his appointment by the French government as 'Chevalier de l'Ordre des Arts et Lettres' came through on the last day. During the excursion to Lewes he led the participants, undeterred by thickets of brambles, to the summit of both mottes. The visit to Lewes Priory was kindly organised and led by Dr F. E. M. Anderson, to whom especial thanks are due. Mrs Gillian Murton and her assistants at the East Sussex County Council, and Mr Peter Birch and his staff at Pyke House, again gave invaluable support and help in organising the conference and providing for the comfort of the participants. Allen Brown was able to complete all the editorial work for this volume of the proceedings, apart from the final stages of seeing it through the press. Any difficulties which might have arisen at this stage have been smoothed over by the calm efficiency of the editorial staff under the direction of Dr Richard Barber at the Boydell Press.

Clare Hall, Cambridge *Marjorie Chibnall*

ABBREVIATIONS

Antiqs. Journ.	*The Antiquaries Journal* (Society of Antiquaries of London)
Arch. Journ.	*Archaeological Journal* (Royal Archaeological Institute)
ASC	*Anglo-Saxon Chronicle*, ed. D. Whitelock *et al.*, London 1969
Battle Chronicle	*The Chronicle of Battle Abbey*, ed. Eleanor Searle, Oxford Medieval Texts, 1980
BIHR	*Bulletin of the Institute of Historical Research*
BL	British Library
BN	Bibliothèque Nationale
BT	*The Bayeux Tapestry*, ed. F. M. Stenton, 2nd edn, London 1965
Cal. Docs. France	*Calendar of Documents preserved in France* ..., i, 918–1216, ed. J. H. Round, HMSO, 1899
Carmen	*The Carmen de Hastingae Proelio of Guy bishop of Amiens*, ed. Catherine Morton and Hope Munz, Oxford Medieval Texts, 1972
De gestis pontificum	William of Malmesbury, *De gestis pontificum Anglorum*, ed. N. E. S. A. Hamilton, RS 1870
De gestis regum	William of Malmesbury, *De gestis regum Anglorum*, ed. W. Stubbs, RS 1887
Domesday Book	*Domesday Book, seu liber censualis* ..., ed. A. Farley, 2 vols, 'Record Commission', 1783
Dudo	*De moribus et actis primorum Normanniae Ducum auctore Dudone Sancti Quintini Decano*, ed. J. Lair, Société des Antiquaires de Normandie, 1865
Eadmer	*Historia novorum in Anglia*, ed. M. Rule, RS 1884
EHD	*English Historical Documents*, i, ed. D. Whitelock, London 1955; ii, ed. D. C. Douglas, London 1953
EHR	*English Historical Review*
Fauroux	*Recueil des actes des ducs de Normandie (911-1066)*, ed. M. Fauroux, Mémoires de la Société des Antiquaires de Normandie, xxxvi, 1961
GEC	*Complete Peerage of England, Scotland, Ireland, Great Britain and the United Kingdom*, 13 vols in 14, London 1910-59
Gesta Guillelmi	William of Poitiers, *Gesta Guillelmi* ..., ed. R. Foreville, Paris 1952
Historia Novella	William of Malmesbury, *Historia Novella*, ed. K. R. Potter, Nelson's Medieval Texts, London 1955
HMSO	Her Majesty's Stationery Office, London
Huntingdon	Henry of Huntingdon, *Historia Anglorum*, ed. T. Arnold, RS 1879
Journ. BAA	*Journal of the British Archaeological Association*

Jumièges	William of Jumièges, *Gesta Normannorum Ducum*, ed. J. Marx, Société de l'histoire de Normandie, 1914
Lanfranc's Letters	*The Letters of Lanfranc Archbishop of Canterbury*, ed. H. Clover and M. Gibson, Oxford Medieval Texts, 1979
Med. Arch.	*Medieval Archaeology*
MGH	*Monumenta Germaniae Historica*, Scriptores
Monasticon	William Dugdale, *Monasticon Anglicanum*, ed. J. Caley, H. Ellis and B. Bandinel, 6 vols in 8, London 1817-30
ns	New Series
Orderic	Ordericus Vitalis, *Historia Ecclesiastica*, ed. M. Chibnall, Oxford Medieval Texts, 1969-
PRO	Public Record Office
Procs. BA	*Proceedings of the British Academy*
Regesta	*Regesta Regum Anglo-Normannorum*, i, ed. H. W. C. Davis, Oxford 1913; ii, ed. C. Johnson, H. A. Cronne, Oxford 1956; iii, ed. H. A. Cronne, R. H. C. Davis, Oxford 1968
RS	Rolls Series, London
ser.	series
Trans.	Transactions
TRHS	*Transactions of the Royal Historical Society*
VCH	Victoria County History
Vita Eadwardi	*The Life of Edward the Confessor*, ed. F. Barlow, Nelson's Medieval Texts, London 1962
Vita Herluini	ed. J. Armitage Robinson in his *Gilbert Crispin abbot of Westminster*, Cambridge 1911
Wace	Wace, *Le Roman de Rou*, ed. A. J. Holden, 3 vols, Société des anciens textes français, Paris 1970-73
Worcester	Florence of Worcester, *Chronicon ex Chronicis*, ed. B. Thorpe, English Historical Society, London 1848-49

ST PANCRAS PRIORY, LEWES:
ITS ARCHITECTURAL DEVELOPMENT TO 1200

Freda Anderson

Despite its importance as a market in the reign of the Confessor, its 1300 hides in the Burghal Hidage, its two moneyers and two mints, its strategic position in the centre of Godwin country, Lewes appears to have played no part either in the struggle between the Godwins and the King, or in the events of 1066. Nor, artistically speaking, is there much to report. The political and social changes brought about by the Conquest are well known, but this is not true of the remarkable architectural and sculptural developments that occurred after 1066, the vast majority of which were the result of the establishment of the Cluniac priory of St Pancras.

The narrow High Street of this small town runs from west to east along a high ridge whence steep narrow lanes descend to the low-lying area of Southover where the priory was built. At the east end of the High Street, School Hill descends to Lewes or Cliffe Bridge, over which lies the suburb of Cliffe.

Lewes is situated on the River Ouse, which is tidal with a gradient so slight that much of Lewes is below the level of the high tides.[1] At the end of the eleventh century when the priory was founded, the whole valley was probably a tidal inlet. Within the flood plain, there were higher areas that escaped and the priory was on one of these. It is referred to frequently as an 'insula'.[2] From this it would seem that, at times, anyway, the priory was surrounded, or partly surrounded, by water. It was not, of course, another Lindisfarne, nor was it likely to have been cut off completely from Southover; access was always possible across Hilly Fields, to the west, but one wonders whether priory structures at the Southover level were affected by flooding; the exterior wall, the Great Gateway complex were most at risk. The Ouse debouched into the sea at Seaford and the trade of the town depended on transport up the Ouse to Cliffe Bridge. Later in the medieval period, a shingle bar built up across the entrance to Seaford harbour, impeding navigation, but trade in the twelfth century is unlikely to have been affected adversely. Caen limestone for the twelfth-century priory reached the monastery by this route and in the thirteenth century, and probably before that, the prior had his own ships and traded

---

[1] P. F. Brandon, 'Origin of Newhaven and the Drainage of the Lewes and Laughton Levels', *Sussex Archaeological Collections* 109, 1971, 94–106. I am grateful to Dr and Mrs Colin Brent for their assistance over problems of the Lewes Levels and course of the Cockshut.
[2] C. T. Clay, *Early Yorkshire Charters, viii: The Honour of Warenne.* Yorkshire Record Society, Extra Series, 6, 1949, 58. Charter of William of Warenne II, '. . . in insula in qua monasterium aedificatum est . . .'.

1

directly with Caen.[3] The Tournai marble for the lavatorium, however, is not likely to have arrived by this route; the material probably went to London, using Wissant, or perhaps Antwerp, as the export port.[4]

The Ouse has two tributaries: the Winterbourne and the Cockshut. The more northerly, the Winterbourne, dries up in summer, as its name suggests, and its course can be seen most easily in the grounds of Southover Grange, the Fountains Hall of the priory. The Cockshut is historically much more important, although its present stagnant and weed-filled condition makes this hard to believe, together with the fact that its course in 1988 seems to be well south of the priory ruins. But this course was changed drastically between 1824 and 1847; before this, the Cockshut branched out into an Upper and Lower Cockshut, joining up again west of the so-called Pool – osier beds for the basket trade – that lay south-west of the present Cockshut Road.[5] The Upper Cockshut flowed through the priory grounds and flushed the twelfth-century reredorter, as the Cockshut, too, was tidal; how well this system worked is another matter. The course of this tributary also affected the architectural development of the priory.

The first Cluniac priory founded in England, with its unique dedication to St Pancras, by a reluctant Abbot Hugh of Cluny, was established by William of Warenne I and his Flemish wife, Gundrada, some time between 1078 and December 1081.[6] The circumstances in which this took place are, to say the least, unclear; this is not, however, the occasion to discuss these difficulties.[7]

Lanzo was the first prior and following normal Cluniac practice, he came with a few companions only, three in fact. This small group was responsible for the earliest architectural developments on the site. As elsewhere, Winchester for instance, the monks used Quarr limestone from the Isle of Wight. Only at Battle, as early as the eleventh century, were masons using Caen limestone. (There is some unreliable evidence that Warenne knew what was going on at Battle. It is alleged he grew so frustrated with Abbot Hugh's delays, that he contemplated switching his foundation to Marmoutier.[8])

One of the most fascinating questions concerning this early work is this: what buildings, if any, did Lanzo find on the site when he arrived? At least one. The foundation charter specified a church dedicated to St Pancras.[9] We do not know whereabouts on the site it was, nor its size and design. There is evidence from the same unreliable source quoted above, that Warenne rebuilt this church in stone from wood; if accurate, this would have to be between 1067 and 1077.[10] I shall call this church Lewes A.

[3] B. M. Crook, 'A General History of Lewes Priory in the Twelfth and Thirteenth Centuries', *Sussex Archaeological Collections* (henceforth Suss. Arch. Coll.) 81, 1940, 68–96. M. A. Lower and W. D. Cooper, 'Further Memorials of Seaford', *Suss. Arch. Coll.* 17, 1865, 143.
[4] The suggestion of Antwerp was made to me by Mr J.-Cl. Ghislain.
[5] G. A. Mantell, *A Day's Ramble In and About the Ancient Town of Lewes*, London, 1846, 65.
[6] Clay, 54, No. 2.
[7] Clay, 54, No. 2 and 59–62.
[8] Clay, 59–62. The reference to Marmoutier is contained in the later and suspect foundation charter. M. D. Knowles, *Monastic Order in England*, CUP, 1940, 154.
[9] Clay, 54, No. 2. '. . . Donamus . . . ad locum Cluniacum ubi preest domnus Hugo abbas . . . ecclesiam Sancti Pancracii cum his que ad eam pertinent'.
[10] Clay, 59–62.

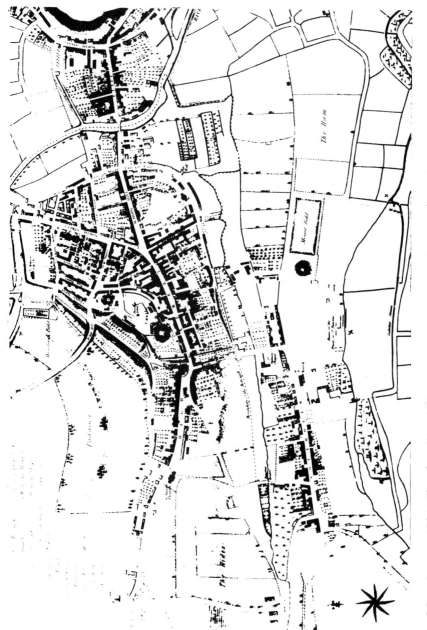

1 Map, Lewes, 1824; Figg (see list of Illustrations for acknowledgements)

Before *c.* 1100, these monks had added a cloister, dorter, reredorter and refectory; remains of the last three can be traced on the site. To this list, two further ecclesiastical buildings may be added. In a charter dated between 1091 and 1099 by its witnesses, William of Warenne II recounts how he returned to England after his father's death in 1088 and confirmed his parents' donations to the priory, in the chapterhouse. This building, therefore, would have been erected between 1078 and 1088.[11]

More important still, the same charter records that the Earl, soon afterwards, when 'the church of St Pancras was completed', was asked by Lanzo and the monks to have it dedicated.[12] Thus a second church was in existence at a date later than 1089 but before 1099; I shall call this church, Lewes B. Its relationship to Lewes A is quite undefined; it might have been an extension of Lewes A and not a new building.

After this first period of expansion, there was no further building campaign until the mid-twelfth century. This time Caen limestone was the chief material used. A charter of William of Warenne III is not only genuine but datable to 1147. In it the earl confirmed his gifts to the priory and his responsibility for the dedication of the church.[13] This church is clearly a new construction. I shall call it Lewes C.

Nothing survives of this church except its south-west tower, but we know a good deal about it from two sources. The first of these is John Portinari, an Italian, the leader of the demolition gang employed by Thomas Cromwell at the Dissolution. Two of Portinari's letters to his employer, together with a schedule of measurements of Lewes C, have survived.[14] Their gloating vandalism is depressing reading, but the information Portinari provides is invaluable.

The second source is a plan drawn at the time of the great discoveries of 1845. The priory was dissolved in 1538 and its post-Dissolution history is typical of that of other large monasteries. Two Renaissance mansions were built. One, Lords Place, was on the site itself, using the prior's house as its centre; the other was Southover Grange, already mentioned. The first was pulled down between 1678 and 1688;[15] the second, dated 1572, was the work of a certain William Newton and survives, despite a Victorian reconstruction between 1870 and 1874. The site was pillaged for its fine ashlar and deteriorated both in quality and extent. Then in 1845, came the decision to make a cutting across the site for the construction of the Lewes–Brighton railway. Within days of work beginning, two lead cists containing bones were dug up; the

[11] Both Clay and Salzman regard the list of donations as fabrications. Clay, 63–6 and L. F. Salzman, ed. *The Chartulary of the Priory of St Pancras at Lewes*, Sussex Record Society 40, 1934, xxi. But on other matters, the charter may contain valuable information; the architectural details it supplies here seem acceptable.

[12] Clay, 63–6, '. . . Postea vero non post multum tempus cum perfecta fuisset ecclesia Sancte Pancratii invitatus sum a priore Lanzone et a cunctis fratribus eiusdem ecclesie et rogatus ab eis ut eam facerem dedicare . . .'

[13] Clay, 84–5, No. 32; 97–8, Nos 49, 50.

[14] The Portinari documents can be found most easily in two articles by St John Hope: 'The Architectural History of the Cluniac Priory of St Pancras', *Suss. Arch. Coll.* 34, 1886, 75–6; 'The Cluniac Priory of St Pancras at Lewes', *Suss. Arch. Coll.* 49, 1906, 75–83.

[15] I am grateful to Mrs Judith Brent for this information.

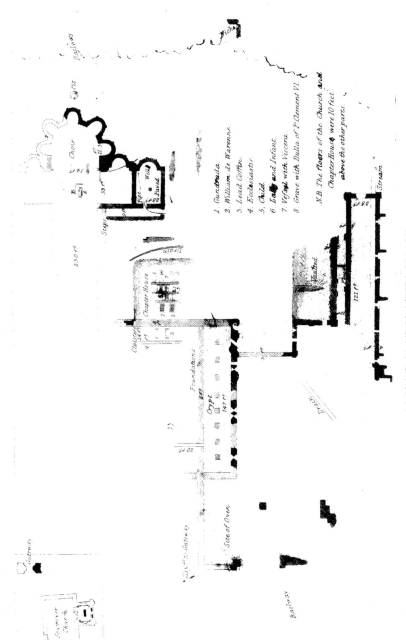

GROUND PLAN OF LEWES PRIORY

1. Gundrada.
2. William de Warenne.
3. Lead Coffin.
4. Ecclesiastic.
5. Child.
6. Infant and Infant.
7. Vessel with Viscera.
8. Grave with Bulla of P. Clement VI.

N.B. The floors of the Church and
Chapter House were 10 feet
above the other parts.

2 Parsons Plan, 1845

names of William and Gundrada were engraved engagingly, on their lids. The graves of the founders or, more accurately, their reinterments, had been discovered. The original place of their burial is contentious; at least, three different sites are documented.[16] The excitement caused by these dramatic finds was at national as well as local level -- a splendid account appeared in the Illustrated London News -- and this interest led to the first excavation of the site, conducted by M. A. Lower.[17]

The Parsons Plan drawn by the architect, J. L. Parsons, shows both what was discovered and what was already known. In the second category, prints of the priory ruins, together with the writing of antiquaries like Horsfield and Mantell, establish that the twelfth-century reredorter, part of what is called on the plan the 'Crypt' and part of the twelfth-century dorter and the feature to the west called the 'Niche' were still above ground.[18] The reredorter was believed to be the refectory, in spite of the fact that the Cockshut was flowing through it, thus, some different name had to be found for the genuine frater; the neutral 'Crypt' was adopted. No mention of the 'Niche' is found in any of the records, but it clearly antedated the 1845 excavations and will be dealt with in detail later.

The chief discoveries made by Lower were the east end of Lewes C, the twelfth-century chapterhouse and more details of the frater.

With regard to Lewes C, three apsidal chapels were uncovered; from Portinari's schedule two more can be added to make an eastern apse of five chapels. A short east transept was found, plus the possible remains of a turret, together with a strange feature that upsets the symmetry of the layout, a south chamber. A careful study of the shading indicates that this chamber antedated the construction of the rest of the east end and lies under the east transept; it is cut off from the new work by a solid wall.

Its measurements are hard to assess accurately, but they appear to have been as follows. The width is given as 28 ft [8.5 m.]. The total length is not given, but must have been more than 33 ft [10.05 m.] and to this the depth of the apse must be added. Thus, we have an east–west measurement of, say, 35 to 40 ft [10.66 to 12.19 m.]. This is not very small. Lower records 'the square basis of a pillar' in the centre, of Sussex marble, and in the corner, the base of the column it supported. It was 2½ ft [0.76 m.]. The apse was painted; Lower mentions the survival of a figure in 'sacerdotal' robes.[19] It was clearly an important building. Its possible identity is considered later. Unfortunately, Portinari does not refer to it.

Three new features of the frater were revealed; FY, i.e. another double-splayed window to the west of the other group; eight square bases within the frater, together with the foundations of a parallel north wall, 6 ft [1.82 m.] thick. An underground passage, the 'Lantern', was re-opened; it had been

---

[16] *Liber Monasterii de Hyda*, ed. Edwards, RS 45, 1886, 299. Orderic iv, 181–2. Hope, *Suss. Arch. Coll.* 34, 100–4; 102, lines 32–3 (fifteenth-century charter).

[17] M. A. Lower, 'Report on the Antiquities Lately Found at Lewes', *Journal of the British Archaeological Association* 1, 1846, 346–57.

[18] T. W. Horsfield, *The History and Antiquities of Lewes and its Vicinity*, Lewes 1824. G. A. Mantell, *A Day's Ramble*; 'A Few Remarks on the Discovery of the Remains of William de Warren and his wife Gundrad, etc', *Archaeologia* 31, 1846, 430–7.

[19] Lower, 'Report'.

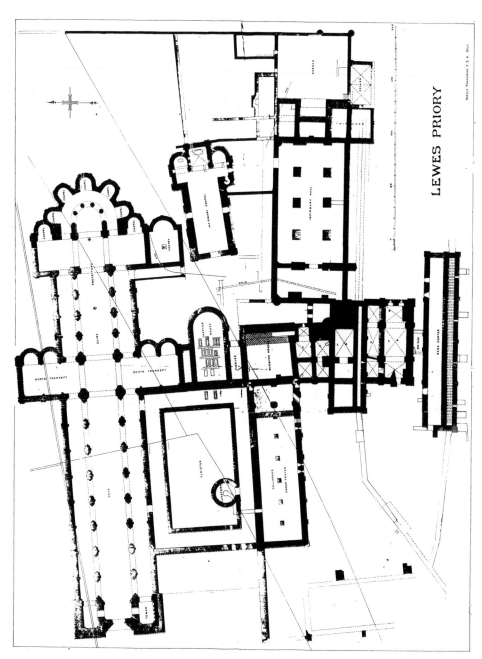

LEWES PRIORY

HAROLD BRAKSPEAR, F.S.A. DELT.

3 Brakspear Plan, 1906

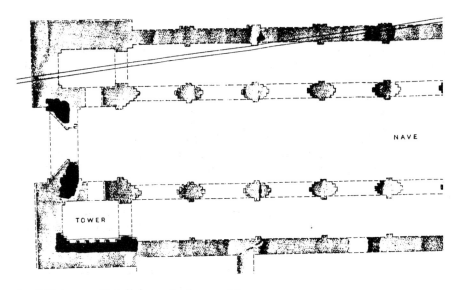

4   SW tower. Detail from Brakspear Plan

known to the older antiquaries in their youth.[20] It ran due north from the north wall of the frater and ended in a domed chamber, with a corbelled roof under the twelfth-century cloister. A wall joining the frater to the eleventh-century reredorter was also discovered. The passage, 9 ft [2.74 m.] outside the south chamber portal, should also be noted. Both features are important and will be discussed again later.

What the plan does not show are the marked differences of level. Lewes C is on much higher ground from the other buildings mentioned. These differences are one of the most notable features of the site and they have been exacerbated by spoil-heaps from the Lower excavation and subsequent ones. The site has not been fully or scientifically excavated, unfortunately, nor have any excavations, including those of Lower, been properly recorded. The archaeological work that has been carried out may be summarised as follows. St John Hope excavated the dorter area in 1882 and he and H. Brakspear, the infirmary range in 1900–2. John Blaker, the then owner of the site, for it was in private hands until bought by the Lewes District Council in 1945, discovered the south-west tower of Lewes C, in 1849–50. Brakspear found the site of the lavatorium in 1902–3.[21] These finds appear together for the first time on the Brakspear Plan of 1906. The importance of this plan, for good or ill, cannot be exaggerated; all subsequent plans, including that currently on sale, are its derivatives.

The discovery of the south-west tower, collated with the Portinari schedule, provided the length of Lewes C: 420 ft [128.01 m.]. Portinari gives the width at the entrance as 69½ ft [19.20 m.] and at the crossing, 150 ft [45.72 m.]; the

[20] W. Figg, 'On "The Lantern" in the Cluniac Priory of St Pancras, Lewes', *Suss. Arch. Coll.* 7, 1854, 150–7.

[21] For all these finds; Hope, *Suss. Arch. Coll.* 34 and 49.

height was 63 ft [19.20 m.]. But the plan must be regarded very critically. Neither the nave nor the north side of Lewes C has been excavated. The nave lies under the nurseries of Southover Growers, a market-garden. So the arrangement of the internal arcades and moulding of their piers are fanciful; the number of transeptal chapels is unestablished. All the same there can be no doubt that Lewes C was a smaller version of Cluny III with its five apsidal chapels at the east end and double transepts.[22] There are differences, of course. Portinari's measurements make it impossible for Lewes C to have had a nave with double aisles like Cluny III. More interestingly, perhaps, the profile of Lewes C from the west crossing eastwards is more reminiscent of a large Gothic church than a Romanesque one; yet like Cluny III it retained its Romanesque east end throughout its ecclesiastical life. This 'Gothic' profile will be discussed again later.

Further evidence of the architectural parallels between these two great churches is provided by the south-west tower. There is a remarkable correlation between the measurements of its surviving north pier and those given by Portinari for the eight crossing piers. It is clear that the ground plan of Lewes C was laid down in one manoeuvre. This resembles the perimeter construction of Cluny III, propounded by Salet.[23] This similarity is not likely to have been coincidence. We know from the Customary of Farfa and its detailed references to Cluny II that Cluniac houses sought the advice of the mother-house on architectural matters.[24] Cluny III was dedicated in 1131; contacts were maintained between Lewes and Cluny III during the time when work on Cluny III was in progress. The second important feature, the dating of the bases, will be discussed in the context of the general dating of the twelfth-century work.

There is some later evidence that makes it likely that the west façade of Lewes C was never finished. An entry in the thirteenth-century Annals for 1268 contains part of the bequests of Prior Foville.[25] He gave 200 marks for the completion of the two towers at the front of the church. How far the monks had got with the work on these towers is not stated, but it seems possible that the north-west tower had hardly started; it may well be that this splendid church had a lop-sided west front throughout its existence.

The appearance of the lavatorium at the south-west corner of the cloister is another important feature of the Brakspear Plan. It is one of that group of independent lavatoria, of which Much Wenlock is the best-known.[26] But the Lewes example is unique in being of Tournai marble. Moreover, all the evidence, in the form of 36 pieces of sculptured material, indicates that the lavatorium was carved in the Lewes workshop.[27] The re-opened north–south passage, the 'Lantern', had its domed chamber immediately under the lavatorium. This fact led Hope and others to believe that this chamber was part of

[22] K. J. Conant, *Carolingian and Romanesque Architecture 800–1200*, Harmondsworth, 1959, 112. [Plan of Cluny III]

[23] F. Salet, 'Cluny III', *Bulletin Monumental* 126, 1968, 235–92.

[24] *Cluniac Monasticism in the Central Middle Ages*, ed. N. Hunt, London 1971, 56–76.

[25] Hope, *Suss. Arch. Coll.* 34, 85 and note 20.

[26] W. H. Godfrey, 'English Cloister Lavatories as Independent Structures', *Journal of the British Archaeological Association* 106, Supplement, 1952, 91–7.

[27] F. E. M. Anderson, 'The Tournai Marble Sculptures of Lewes Priory', *Suss. Arch. Coll.* 122, 1984, 85–100. Also my unpublished PhD London thesis, 'The Romanesque Sculptures of Lewes Priory', 216–55.

5   SW tower, SE pier   6 SW tower, base (a)   7 SW tower, base (b)
8   SW tower, base (c)

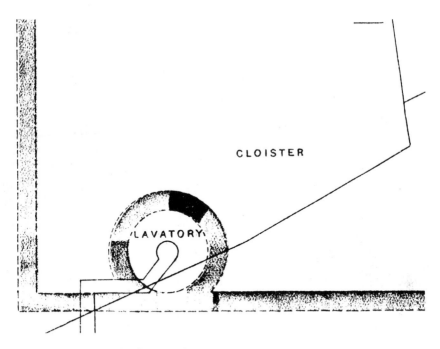

9 SW cloister. Detail of lavatorium from Brakspear Plan

10 Interior, twelfth-century reredorter

11   Exterior, Worcester Abbey reredorter

the complex above and provided its water supply. Various factors make this impossible. The chamber is too small to house a pump; the passage is not a drain; the surviving material is Quarr limestone again, making an eleventh-century date more probable than one in the twelfth. Further, the antiquaries who used to crawl through the passage as small boys, all testify to its total darkness; the present aperture in the roof, through which the alleged pipes would have gone, is modern. The proximity of the two structures is thus fortuitous only. The hypothesis that the chamber was a punishment cell for monks offending against the rules of dress is discussed by Figg, in a surprisingly impressive manner.[28]

South of the cloister, Hope's first excavation in 1882 provided new information about the eleventh- and twelfth-century dorters and reredorters, although at times one feels he created as many problems as he attempted to solve. The twelfth-century reredorter is not one of these. It has lost its upper storey and its interior longitudinal wall; extraneous windows abound, inserted presumably after the Dissolution, when the building became a malt-house. It was 158 ft [48.15 m.] long, divided into two areas, 14 ft [4.26 m.] wide in the north and a narrow space, 5¾ ft [1.75 m.], to the south. The latter provided the cubicles above, over the drain below. The brackets for the support of these cubicles may still be seen, together with the original window openings. As was stated earlier, the reredorter was flushed by the Upper Cockshut; the entrance to the culvert still survives at the east end. Emil Godfrey pointed out the parallels with the reredorter at Worcester.[29]

---

[28] Figg, *Suss. Arch. Coll.* 7.
[29] I am grateful to Mrs Godfrey for the gift of his slides of Worcester Abbey.

12   Interior, Worcester Abbey reredorter

13   Interior, twelfth-century dorter undercroft

The twelfth-century dorter was the usual upper-storey building and nothing of it survives. It was supported by a newly constructed undercroft and joined to the reredorter by a still existing bridge, 24 ft [7.31 m.] wide and 10 ft [3.04 m.] long. The undercroft is fundamentally a long hall, running east and west; it is divided into two aisles of unequal width, the north aisle being narrower. The materials used were Sussex marble for the first two courses with Caen stone for those above. Each aisle had three bays of blind arcading, the central wider than the other two. The hall was vaulted; probably, barrel vaulting with transverse arches was the method used. The north-west bay differed from the rest by being converted into a small chamber by the addition of a portal.

There are many interpretational problems in connection with this undercroft. For instance, the central bay on the north side has a springer that rises very little, even allowing for raised ground levels in modern times; to this should be added the fact that the chamber to the north of this arch has no apparent means of access. Two depressions, oval in shape, were found in the floor and they are not graves; their presence makes the problem more difficult still.[30] At a later date, that could hardly have been earlier than the thirteenth century, the hall was reduced in size. Both the east bay and the entrance to the north-west chamber were blocked in, for reasons that are obscure. The entrance was reduced in size, but this may have been caused by the need to deal with falling masonry; the present curving and ugly obstruction is post-1856 and was almost certainly an attempt at dealing with the same problem.[31] But the earlier reductions in size were for different and still unexplained reasons.

These twelfth-century problems seem almost elementary when we turn to those surrounding the eleventh-century reredorter and dorter. The Brakspear Plan is impossible to read accurately and St John Hope never published proper details of his finds. Matters are made worse by the present state of the terrain. A 'hill' has been created with a downward path running from east to west, from spoil-heaps. This 'hill' confuses the eye. The reredorter may be considered first. Inspection makes a ground-level location very probable, despite its unorthodoxy. The eastern chamber, known today as UXI, shows six single-splayed windows of Quarr stone, all blocked in, but not necessarily at the same time or for the same reason. The three on the east resemble the cubicles of the twelfth-century reredorter and may have been blocked in when the late twelfth-century infirmary was built to the east. Those to the north may have been filled in, when the new dorter was built, while the wall to the west has blind arcading similar to that of the undercroft. On the south side the culvert that flushed the reredorter has survived, but the function of the two stone pillars along its edge is yet another problem to be solved. Hope thought the eleventh-century reredorter was blocked in when the twelfth-century dorter was created, as a foundation for its upper floor. But this cannot be true

---

[30] Anderson, PhD, Vol. 3, 41.

[31] In 1856, John Cave published a set of 17 printed photographs; these included the interior of the undercroft minus the obstruction. Anderson, PhD, Vol. 2, 157. (From the Barbican House Library, Lewes.)

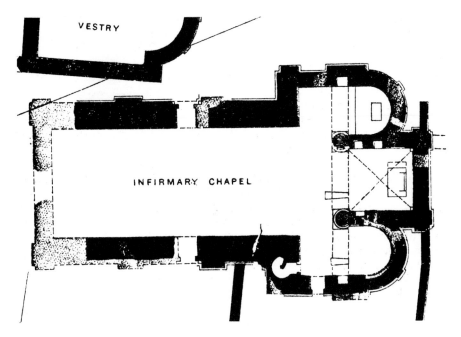

14 'Infirmary Chapel.' Detail Brakspear Plan

15 UXI, south wall

16   UXI, east wall

17   UXI, west wall

18 UXI, north wall

19   Wall F, 1987

of UXI, which was filled in with earth only, and has been dug out twice by excavation.

At least the siting of the reredorter is relatively clear. But even the site of the eleventh-century dorter is a matter of conjecture. It certainly lay to the north of the reredorter and is also likely to have been a ground-level building, contrary to normal practice. The wall joining the eleventh-century reredorter to the frater shown on the Parsons Plan, but omitted from the Brakspear Plan, might have been its western termination. The dorter would then have run east, to end at some indeterminable position amongst the confusion of details Hope provided, but never explained. There are, at least, two objections to this hypothesis. The first is the presence of two arches of very different height between the vice at the east end of the frater; they are shown very clearly on the 1737 print, to be discussed later. The second is the existence of an upper storey to the western end of the reredorter. It appears on all the surviving prints of the priory and it may well be of Quarr limestone, too.

The frater, or, as it is better to call it, Wall F, so that its function is not prejudged, is in many ways the strangest feature of the entire site. Hope's 1882 excavations revealed another vice, an internal example this time, at the north-east angle of the complex subtended by Wall F. But the 1906 plan makes unwarranted alterations to some of its internal features. The eight square bases have become five and a half and a fancy pier to the east behind a dividing wall are together both inventions. The western double-splayed window, FY, has disappeared and the length of the wall has been shortened. The south side of Wall F has acquired spurious buttresses. All these additions must be disregarded.

Yet even with these rectifications, Wall F is still an oddity. Hope called it the 'Frater Undercroft', implying its erection as a unit. But it is not possible to believe that the following components could have been put up together. From west to east along the south side, there are two double-splayed windows, FA and FB, a wide gap, FC, another double-splayed window, FD, a set of steps, FE, a skew passage FF and an external vice, FG. No self-respecting Norman mason could have created such an architectural hotchpotch.

Fortunately, we can trace the earlier appearance of the wall from prints. The first, a Buck print, is dated 1737.[32] From west to east, it shows two openings, a long stretch of blank masonry, followed by five more openings. Two substantial arches of differing heights link Wall F with the putative position of the eleventh-century dorter and have already been noted.

A second print of 1765, or 1761, shows, again from west to east, a large gap in the wall, with an ecclesiastical structure arranged rather too artistically behind; directionally, the church of St John-sub-Castro perhaps. From these two prints, we do not have to look for a medieval explanation for FC; the gap was made between 1737 and 1761/5.

A third print dated 1785 shows the ruins from the west with Wall F on the north. East of FC there are four openings, plus a clear outline of one of the substantial arches shown on the 1737 print. One of the most interesting features of this print is that, as in 1988, there are four openings east of FC, whereas in 1737, there were five. Therefore, between 1737 and 1785, one, FX, was blocked up. Its outlines may be picked out between FE and FF.

The 1785 print also shows differences between FG today and then. It was noticeably lower in height than any of the other openings and possessed what seems to be a relieving arch. In 1988, FG is higher; it has been straightened on the west and its original rounded arch cut off. This vice of Quarr limestone makes it clear that there was an upper storey and that an eleventh-century date is acceptable.

The skew passage, FF, is puzzling. The entrance is at right-angles to Wall F, but the passage is cut obliquely through it. The present mishmash of greensand and modern mortar makes any sort of dating impossible. But the skew effect can have no architectural function; both to north and south, the passage opens on to clear ground and there were no structures to be avoided. The angle may have been the result of some deficiency or weakness in the wall itself.

The presence of four steps within the opening FE is another odd feature of Wall F. They do not appear on the 1785 print, but this may be merely the angle of its sightlines. Equally, they may be post-1785. The steps are documented in 1845 when they are shown in a drawing, some 4 ft [1.21 m.] above the ground.[33] The level has risen by at least this amount since 1845, partly by the construction of the tennis-courts and partly by conservation work. It seems, therefore, that FE was originally a window, probably double-splayed; the steps were added in the eighteenth, or early nineteenth century. But, why? We can only guess. Perhaps, the owner of the site wanted a romantic place to display his classical statuary.

[32] From the work of Mrs Joan Counihan, this print must be one of Buck's earliest. I am grateful to her for the information.

[33] The drawing, the work of the Rev. Gaunt of Isfield, may be found in the Barbican House Library, Plate 39.

THE SOUTH VIEW OF LEWIS PRIORY & CASTLE, IN THE COUNTY OF SUSSEX.

20   Wall F, 1737

21   Wall F, 1737. Detail

22   Wall F, 1761/5

23   Wall F, 1761/5. Detail

24   Wall F, 1785

25   Wall F, 1785. Detail

26   Wall F, south face, FG

27   Wall F, south face, FF and FX

28   Wall F, south face, FE   29   Wall F, south face, FD

There were at least five double-splayed windows: FA, FB, FD, FE and FY, the missing window shown on the Parsons Plan in the middle of the railway cutting. The blocked opening, FX, may have been a sixth. FD and FE are strikingly different in height, but FA and FB are a pair. Their importance is enormous. On the south side, FA shows three-and-a-half regularly placed Quarr stone voussoirs and FB, two. They show an ashlar technique and resemble closely the voussoirs of the eleventh-century reredorter. But on the north side FA displays clumsy, irregular voussoirs of greensand, with another large fragment in a position that suggests there was an upper band of stones placed more laterally. FB is difficult to assess because its present voussoirs are not the original facing. Fortunately, a print of 1845 shows FB with voussoirs similar to those of FA. These voussoirs are not set in an ashlar technique; they resemble most closely, Late Saxon work. Among many other comparative examples, one may cite the Barrow arch in Shropshire and the arch over the nave entrance to the tower in Morland, Westmorland.[34] For some reason, the south face of Wall F was improved, but not the north.

Therefore, Lanzo and his companions found, at least, one Late Saxon building on the lower ground of the site and perhaps, more. FD and FE would also have been attached to a structure. FY, discovered by the rail-workers and then re-buried, for it does not appear on the 1737 print, is another window without its supporting structure. What these buildings were used for and who erected them remains a mystery. Whether the rectangular building to the

[34] These examples are taken from H. M. and J. Taylor, *Anglo Saxon Architecture* 2, Cambridge 1965, Plates 375 and 532.

south-west tower.[49] From this it would seem that the monks were not expecting the completion of Lewes C to be effected very rapidly.

This hypothetical timetable fits the available facts reasonably well. But it has been presented in a rigid and over-simplified manner; in practice, there would have been delays of all kinds between one stage and the next. It is also too easy to forget the unglamorous cellarer's block and the west cloister range about which nothing is known. But the size of the enormous oven, visible on the 1737 print with its 'squared spiracles', reminiscent of Glastonbury, or even Fontevrault, should make us think that the cellarer's buildings were very substantial.[50]

The interest, importance and often unique qualities of Lewes priory have been unknown to architectural historians of the Romanesque period for too long. It will be apparent from the foregoing analysis that much remains unexplained and conjectural. No more than a beginning has been made on finding acceptable solutions to the architectural problems of the Cluniac priory of St Pancras, Lewes.

[49] Rigold, *Bases*, Plate 119.
[50] Horsfield, *Lewes*, 248; presumably, he was referring to air-vents. In 1988, two non-aligned masonry stacks, covered with ivy, stand each side of the railway-line. They may be the narrow stacks shown on the 1737 print.

ACKNOWLEDGEMENTS   I have corresponded with Dr Richard Gem over St Pancras and I should like to thank him for his comments and criticisms.

I am grateful to the following for the use of their material; Sussex Archaeological Society, East Sussex Record Office, Mrs Emil Godfrey, Yorkshire Record Society.

I should also like to thank Phillimore for permission to quote from Rigold's article on Romanesque Bases.

WACE AND WARFARE*

Matthew Bennett

Kar custume est de tel ovrainne
Que tels i pert que puis guainne.
(B 8,866–7)[1]

That's the way of this kind of work
Some lose, some gain.

The 'work' to which Wace is referring is war. I begin with this pragmatic
comment because it sums up his attitude to warfare. The unpredictability of
war was a truism apparent to its practitioners. His military, aristocratic
audience would have known exactly what he meant.[2] Wace is very knowledgeable about many aspects of warfare. Most of his two largest works, the *Roman
de Brut* and the *Roman de Rou*, are concerned with campaigns, battles and
brave deeds. This was the contemporary fashion – presumably what his
audience wanted to hear – but also part of the poet's popularising and
propagandising purpose. His tracing back of legitimate authority from Henry
II to Brutus, the legendary Trojan conqueror after whom Britain is named,
necessarily involved the description of how successive wars were waged. It
does not really matter that Wace was a faithful copyist of earlier sources in this
context, for he often has additional and original information to add on military
matters. It does not matter that his phoney chronology spans three millennia,
for he makes almost no attempt to look beyond his experience of contemporary warfare.[3]

I use the word 'experience' deliberately. Recently, it has been suggested
that his use of the word 'vaslet' to describe himself may indicate that Wace had
a military training in his youth. Certainly, we know very little about his early
life. If he was born around 1100 and produced his literary works *c.* 1150 to
c. 1175, we only have an insight into the last third of his life. What did he do
for the other 50 years? He certainly lived, in the words of the Chinese curse, in
'interesting' times. In his mid-thirties began the sporadic but long-drawn-out
civil war for the English Crown, which led to the conquest of Normandy by her

* Thanks are due to RAB for setting me to read Wace in 1980 and Professor Bernie Bachrach for
suggesting this particular topic – in the suitable setting of the castle at Caen in 1987.
[1] Ed. I. Arnold, 2 vols SATF Paris, 1938, 1940. The sentiment is utterly conventional. Cf. the
words of a knight to the Countess of Leicester when pulling her out of a ditch at the battle of
Fornham St Genevieve in 1174, from *Jordan Fantosme's Chronicle* ed. R. C. Johnston. Oxford
1981, l. 1,071. The translations of the *Brut* are my own. Those of the Rou which follow often owe
much to Edgar Taylor, *Master Wace, his Chronicle of the Norman Conquest*, London 1837,
although this only covers the section from the Third version concerning William's life.
[2] See my article 'Poetry as History? The Roman de Rou of Wace as a source for the Norman
Conquest', *ante* V, 1982, 21–39, for Wace's potential audience.
[3] Except, perhaps, when describing the Normans' adoption of French horses and weaponry as
better than their own (Wace II 555–6).

old enemy, Anjou. What did he see of warfare? What did he know of it? Did
he do any soldiering himself? Did he suffer the pangs of hunger, blows in
battle, the elation of victory and the humiliation of defeat he describes so
vividly? Had he seen lands burnt and devastated, villages left smouldering
ruins, peasants scattered and townsmen massacred? Had he taken part in such
commonplace but gruesome activities in the course of war? Well, I don't
know, perhaps he had just an academic interest in warfare – as I do – but
which nevertheless enabled him to write most convincingly about it.[4]

What does Wace have to tell us about warfare? Well, there is a mass of
material to be mined from both his main works. Admittedly this is based
largely on other authors: his *Brut* on Geoffrey of Monmouth, the *Rou*, much
more a work of synthesis, on several Anglo-Norman historians writing from
immediately after the Conquest into his own times. I am not attempting to
compare his account with his sources to show exactly where he left them for his
own invention. His 'inventing' used to be held against him, but if we see it
rather as a contribution to the history of his own period, then it becomes
valuable information. Of course, it is in the nature of Wace's kind of poetry to
indulge in conventional expressions and descriptions which can detract from a
real appreciation of warfare. But, nonetheless, he has some genuine insights to
give us.[5]

Wace's knowledge will be examined under four main headings. First,
strategy: involving a discussion of geography, time spent travelling; the
descriptions, sites and garrisons of castles; and sieges by which strategic goals
were largely achieved, including how long they took and methods employed.
Closely associated with strategy is the second topic of logistics, that is, getting
the necessary men, horses and materiel to the point where they are needed.
Wace is very interested in ships and the sea, which played such a large part in
the warfare of Britain, and keen to display his knowledge on the subject. The
poet's vocabulary boasts his arcane knowledge as much as his graphic descriptions of fleets and tempests. Wace's language of warfare forms the third topic.
It is rich and often idiosyncratic in the stress it lays upon aspects of warfare not
often encountered in contemporary epic poetry. Which leads on to the final
section on tactics: the organisation of the army on the march and in battle; the
deployment of forces; tricks and stratagems employed; and descriptions of the
mêlée and the weaponry used. Especially interesting is the attention Wace
pays to infantry tactics, although writing in a genre which usually concentrates
on chivalric achievement.

An understanding of geography is essential to a proper appreciation of
military strategy. It must be said that Wace rarely gives details of topography
or the movement of armies that would allow us to reconstruct campaigns from
his evidence alone. This is partly because such details were not considered
necessary in the poetic genre within which he worked. Partly because he
probably knew little of British geography, or indeed that of France south of

---

[4] This whole paragraph must be speculative. Bennett, *ante* 1982, 22 provides a conventional
biography, Dr Elisabeth van Houts makes the suggestion that because Wace calls himself 'vaslet',
he had received a military education, in 'The Ship List of William the Conqueror' *ante* X, 1987,
159–83, esp. 163 & fn. 22.
[5] See Wace, 3, 99–117–168 for Holden's comments on his use of sources.

Paris.[6] He is largely dependent on his sources except where he occasionally brings them up to date, preferring Dover to Richborough as the most desirable point to enter Britain, for example.[7] But in his account of Belin and Brenne's campaign in Italy he gives a reasonable itinerary, entirely missing from his source. Their route is along the old Via Flaminia to Bologna where they turn south to cross the River Arno on their way to Rome (B 2,865–74).[8] Later the brothers use spies and peasant guides – a realistic touch, especially in mountainous areas – to outwit the Romans (B 2,985–94). Elsewhere Wace makes reference to the importance of spies in finding out an enemy's strategic intention. So, the pagan pirates Wanis and Melga are aware of how poorly Britain is defended when they make their attack (B 6,076–94). Rollo sends spies (or scouts) to gather information on the desirability of invading the Bessin: and the defenders reply in kind, enabling them to surprise the Normans (Wace II 567–82).

On this, his home territory Wace displays far wider knowledge. His account of the young duke William's rapid response to the rebellion of William of Arques provides both a realistic route and motivation. Receiving the news while hunting near Valognes (not far from Cherbourg) he takes the shortest possible route across the mouth of the Vire. Riding on through Bayeux and Caen he makes as if to go to Rouen: but this is a feint. At Pont Audemer, on the Risle, he swings left, crosses the Seine at Caudebec, and gallops via Ivetot on to Arques. William of Poitiers has a similar headlong ride, but with none of these details.[9] Wace's knowledge of Norman geography is used to good effect in his descriptions of the campaigns and actions of Val-ès-dunes, Varaville, and at Caen before 1106. He details the route of the French army in 1057, as it devastated the lands of the Bessin, for example.[10]

This sort of intentional devastation was a key part of mediaeval strategy, designed to cause widespread economic damage and to undermine a lord's political authority.[11] If he was unable to protect his subjects, they were incapable of providing his wealth. Like many of his contemporaries, Wace was keenly aware of this. When count Helias of Maine attacks Normandy in 1101, he drives the peasants from the fields and the merchants from the roads (Wace III 11,135–42). Cassibelan ravages the lands of an unlucky subject, so that

[6] Rosemary Morris, 'Aspects of Time and Place in French Arthurian Verse Romances', *French Studies* XLII, 1988, 257–77, outlines the romancers' approach to geography. Their tendency to transport their characters from Britain to Brittany, without mentioning the sea, is, of course, not indulged in by Wace.

[7] Cf. *Brut* (hereafter, B), 5,109–13 and Geoffrey of Monmouth *Historia Regum Britanniae*, ed. A. Griscom, London 1929, trans. L. Thorpe, Penguin 1966, 115 etc.

[8] They cross the Alps at Mt Genevre and Mt Cenis, capture Turin and Ivrea and then advance by way of Vercelli, Pavia and Cremona, Milan, Piacenca and Bologna, which sounds a bit confused unless this represents two separate lines of advance. The demands of metre and rhyme may also have distorted a reasonable itinerary.

[9] Wace III, 3,529–48: cf. *Gesta Guillelmi* 56–7, which gives no route, though emphasising the speed of William's movement. Wace has this episode out of chronological order, possibly in order to show the young duke triumphing over increasingly dangerous foes. A discussion of Wace's knowledge of geography may be found in M. de Boüard, 'A propos des sources du "Roman de Rou"', *Recueil de travaux offert à M. Clovis Brunel*, Paris 1955, i, 178–82 (Memoires et documents publiés pas la Société de l'Ecole des Chartes, xii).

[10] See below for a discussion of Varaville and Mortemer.

[11] C. Allmand, *The Hundred Years War* CUP, 1988, 54–6 provides a neat summary of *chevauchée* and its impact.

seeing the destruction Androgeus calls on Caesar for aid (B 4,383–95). King Arthur leaves nothing outside castle walls during his invasion of France (B 10,126–8). (I make no excuse for the confusion of chronology that must result from choosing examples so widely separated in time. Wace is describing the same type of warfare, irrespective of the era. For the same reason I use his names rather than their 'historical' counterparts, because many inhabit an imaginary world.) Rollo ravages around Bayeux to force the city's submission (Wace II 575–9); the English ravage the Cotentin, with dire results for themselves (Wace III 1,103–10); the Danes ravage Yorkshire, with King Aethelred powerless to hinder them (Wace III 1,249–56). It is an activity as commonplace as war itself.

All this devastation is far from senseless, and Wace is aware of its more immediate strategic goals. Duke William puts pressure on the French in 1054 by driving off the flocks and herds and dispersing their foragers (Wace III 4,832–40). King Harold, on the other hand, refuses his brother Gyrth's advice to pursue a scorched-earth policy during the Norman invasion. Instead, anger at the destruction of his lands leads him into overhasty battle – and defeat – just as William intended (Wace III 6,925–48). That an entire Christian society can be destroyed by such activities, is exemplified by Wace in the story of Gurmund, King of the Africans. The Saxons invite him to bring his army of 160,000 [*sic*] men over from Ireland. His ravages largely eradicate British Christianity.

Dunc pristent la terre a destruire;	They they took charge of the land and destroyed it,
Deus, quel dolur e quel injuire	God, what sorrow and what injury
De bone terre e de gentil,	they did to the fine folk and good land,
Que turné esta tel issil!	What a blow of fate was this ravaging,
Saisne les Alfricans cunduient,	The Saxons led the Africans,
Maisuns ardent, viles destruient;	burning houses and destroying towns.
Les chevaliers e les vilains,	Knights and villains,
Les clers, les muines, les nuneins,	clerics, monks and nuns
Batent e chacent e ocient;	they hunted, beat and murdered.
La lei Damnedeu cuntralient.	They did great damage to the Christian faith.
Mult veïssiez terre eissillier,	There you might see many lands devastated,
Femmes hunir, humes percier,	women violated, men speared,
Enfanz en berz esbüeler,	babies disembowelled in their cradles,
Aveirs saisir, preies mener,	riches seized, flocks led off,
Turs abatre, viles ardeir.	towers brought low and towns burnt.
(B 13,473–87)	

Significantly, Wace tells us, the name of the island was now changed from Britain to England, after its new rulers. The poet knows that war is a terrible thing.[12] Indeed, wise and strong generals like King Arthur have the power to

---

[12] Compare *Historia Regum Britanniae* where Cirencester is just captured and burnt, 264, with Wace's dramatic account: 13,533–624. The poet also makes the scene in which the mother of Belin

restrict plundering (B 9,897–904). And a Norman expedition led by Richard II pays for all food and fodder taken in the lands of his ally, the king of France (Wace III 2,169–76).

Destruction and harrying cannot hold a land, merely reduce it to obedience. The instruments of successful rule are castles. Even centuries before Christ, Belin holds Northumberland by controlling its castles and its ports (B 2,423–30). This is not meant to be a radical redefinition of when the castle first appeared in England. It is, rather, another example of the timelessness of the realities of war according to Wace. Indeed, he tells us that Swein of Denmark conquered England precisely because there were no castles, in contrast to Normandy which was well protected with them (Wace III 1,289–1,300). This might seem strange, since earlier British kings had defended London well. According to the *Brut*, Elidur built the Tower and Lud the city walls (B 3,585–6 and 3,745–50).[13] Caesar constructed the Tour d'Odre at Boulogne, where he cowered for two years secure from the Gauls (B 4,201–24). In contrast, Brutus is able to construct a tower at Tours (hence the city's name) in a mere dozen days (B 931–53). That this is not mere exaggeration is witnessed by the building of Hastings castle in a week in 1066. Wace imagines this as a prefabricated castle in barrels, reflecting the historical reality not of the Conquest, but of his own time.[14] The point is, that to Wace warfare was inconceivable without the castle. He also knew well how this fortification should be used.

He stresses that a well-defended castle is a well-provisioned one: such as Tillières, constructed by Richard II.

juste l'ewe ki Arve ad nun	near to the river called the Avre
fist e ferma une maisun.	he had a hall built and fortified.
Tant i ad fait e tant ovré,	Much was done here, much work
ke de paliz, que de fossé	of palisading, and ditching
que de mortier, que de quarel,	of masonry and mortar
ke il i ad fait un fort chastel,	until there was a strong castle
ne crient mangunel ne perrieres,	invulnerable to all kinds of stonethrowers,
metre li fist cest nun: Tuillieres.	constructed there with the name of Tillières.
Quant Ricard dut d'iloec partir	When Richard had to leave that place,
e le chastel out fait guarnir	the castle was well provisioned
de blé e de char e de vin. . . .	with wheat and meat and wine
(RIII 1,459–69)	

It is also garrisoned with brave knights who drive off an attack by Odo, count of Blois, with great élan.[15] This is part of the offensive use of the castle, which is best represented by Duke William's *Gegenburg* at Arques:

and Brenne prevents a battle between them into a real purple passage, which seems to express a genuine horror of civil war (B 2,712–830).

[13] This seems to be Wace's original observation.
[14] See Bennett, 1982, *ante* 37, fn. 81 citing *Pipe Roll 17 Henry II*, 29.
[15] The Brut has a parallel passage when King Arthur constructs a 'chastelet' on the Aube, 11,640–6. Wace is fond of attributing similar military actions to his heroes.

de fossé et de heriçun	from a ditch and barrier
e de pel fist un chasteillun,	of stakes made a small fort
al pié del tertre en la valee,	at the foot of the hill in the valley,
ki garda tute la cuntree;	which protected the whole country.
n'i pristrent puis cil del chastel	Then those in the castle could take nothing,
ne buef ne vache ne veel.	not a bull, cow or calf.
(RIII 3,443–8)	

'The finest knights in Normandy' are gathered for this little castle's defence and to enforce the blockade.

However well defended, castles are susceptible to siege, of course. Legendary Tintagel is accessible only through Merlin's magic which disguises Uther Pendragon as its real lord (B 8,621–32, 8,691–736). Those commanders without the great wizard's assistance have to resort to battering and assault. This can be a very long-winded business, though, as Gurmund discovers at Cirencester.

Perieres firent e berfreiz	They construct stonethrowers and siege towers,
Sis asaillirent plusurs feiz,	and make many assaults.
Lur enginz as murs traire,	Their engines shoot at the walls;
Mes ne poient engin faire	but they cannot make one,
Que cil dedenz ne cuntrefacent,	which those inside do not defeat.
Mariens e cleies entrelacent,	Wood and wattle are well interlaced,
Kernels refunt, portes afaitent,	crenellations repaired, doors constructed,
Le jor ovrent, la nuit se guaitent;	open during the day, watched at night;
Bretesches e murs apareillent.	the walls are well provided with wooden covers.
Quant li un dorment, li un veilent.	When one (guard) sleeps another remains alert.
As defenses pieres atraient,	Stones provide materials for the defenders.
E nequedent forment s'esmaient,	All the same, they were much afraid,
Kar il ne sevent ne ne veient	because they do not know, nor can they see,
Engin par quei defendu seient.	how they can engineer the place's defence.*
Cil defors suvent les assaillent	Those outside attack often,
E pur els prendre se travaillent,	and strive to take the town,
mes cil se peinent del defendre;	but no effort can overcome the defence,
Nes pot Gurmund par force prendre,	nor can Gurmund take it by force.
(B 13,541–58)	

---

*There is a pun here on 'engines' and trickery or ingenuity which does not quite come off in English.

Very rarely does an assault succeed. Duke William's capture of Alençon in this way is exceptional.

Lores fist venir esquiers	Then he had the squires come up,
e les homes as chevaliers	together with the knights,
les uns fist aler assaillir,	the latter to conduct the assault,
les altres le fossé emplir:	the former to fill the ditch.
les covertures des maisons	The coverings of houses,
e les lates e les chevrons	planks and pieces of wood
e quantque il ont prof trové	and anything that could be found
ont el fossé amoncelé,	to pile into the ditch,
pois mistrent feu devers le vent,	were set on fire before the wind.
li bois fu secs, li feu esprent.	The wood was dry, the fire flamed,
Que par le feu qu'il aluma,	So by the fire which blazed
que par l'assaut qu'il lor dona,	and which attacked them
li uns sont ars, li altre pris,	here one was burnt, another taken,
e tels i a, honte ocis.	and those caught up in it died a
	miserable death.

(Wace III 4,333–46)

Here the non-noble troops have a valuable rôle to play; and this emphasis on their importance is something that is peculiar to Wace, and which I shall return to. Taking a castle 'Sanz periere e sanz mangonel' as Richard II does at Mirmande is an extraordinary circumstance (Wace III 2,177). The best, and most usual plan, is to starve the defenders out. This is how Arthur forces the Parisians to come to terms (B 9,976–10,008).

Here we touch on the next topic of my talk: logistics. Even an army in the field, if surrounded and cut off from supplies, is driven to surrender, like Cassibelan's Britons to Caesar.

Quant faim e sei tant les destreint	Weakened by hunger,
Que senz arme e sanz fer les veint?	what could they do without weapon
	or blade?
Ja ne verrez tel fortelesce,	In truth no fortress,
Tant i ait gent de grant prüesce,	full of men of great valour,
Ki tant seit fort e grefs a prendre.	strongly defended and hard
	to take,
Que famine vient de vitaille	brought to famine by lack of food,
N'i estuet altre kis assaille.	needs any other assault.

(B 4,675–82)

Wace was aware that hunger is the greatest weapon in war. Whether he knew his Vegetius or not, he certainly understood the practical application of the Roman theorist's ideas.[16] So Arthur, on his Irish campaign, sweeps up all the cows and oxen in the country to feed his men and to deprive the enemy of

---

[16] Both episodes appear in the *Historia* but Wace expands them greatly. The application, by mediaeval commanders, of Vegetius' time-honoured principle of starving the enemy rather than fighting him, is succinctly described in John Gillingham, 'Richard I and the Science of War in the Middle Ages' in *War and Government in the Middle Ages. Essays in Honour of J. O. Prestwich*, ed. John Gillingham and J. C. Holt, Ipswich 1984, 78–91, citing the valuable comments of Wace's vernacular contemporary, Jordan Fantosme, ed. Johnston 83–5.

sustenance (B 9,669–72).[17] Knowing how many mouths he has to feed is of key importance for a general, of course, but Wace does little better than most mediaeval authors when dealing with numbers. He is vague on the size of hosts, saying that he does not know whether Arthur raised 400 or 4,000 Danish warriors from that country (B 9,990–2). Sometimes he does give a total for the knights in an army, though. There were apparently 2,000 in the army of Angusel, king of Scots, Arthur's opponent, but they were accompanied by 'numberless foot' (B 11,038–40). Sometimes his numbers reach the ubiquitous mediaeval 60,000 = a great many. It simply was not fashionable to count. Even his figures of seeming exactitude, like the 696 ships of Duke William's invasion fleet, supposedly passed down from Wace's father, are dubious (Wace III 6,423–6). But the lack of 'accurate' numbers does not affect the poet's ability to describe logistical operations clearly, especially those involving ships, sailing and amphibious landings.

Wace has a knowledge of ships and an expert's vocabulary which he is eager to share, regarding sails and sheets, halliards and hawsers. Clearly fleets play a big part in getting armies to and from Britain (or England). His interest ranges from Caesar's invasion attempts through Arthur's invasion of France, to, of course, the 1066 landings. He gives the correct number of ships (according to *De Bello Gallico*) for Caesar's first invasion, and underestimates for his second. The size of the fleets does not interest Geoffrey of Monmouth, though Wace borrows his vivid description of the holing of vessels by shore defences (B 4,243–59). In most sources little time is spent discussing how ships get from A to B. Not only does Wace provide vivid descriptions of embarking and disembarking, but also of storms which made sea travel so perilous. First, here is Arthur's army embarking for the conquest of Gaul:

Puis vint passer a Suthamtune;	Then they went to Southampton;
La furent les nefs amenees	there the ships were brought together,
E les maisnees assemblees.	and the households assembled.
Mult veïssiez nes aturner,	There you might see many ships made ready,
Nés atachier, nés aancrer,	ships tied up and ships at anchor,
Nés assechier e nés floter,	beached ships and ships afloat,
Nés cheviller e nés cloer,	pegged ships and tarred ships,
Funains estendre, maz drecier,	ropes stretched and masts raised.
Punz mettre fors e nés chargier,	Gangplanks are brought out and the ships loaded.
Helmes escuz, halbercs porter,	Helmets, shields and hauberks are carried,
Lances drecier, chevals tirer,	lances raised and horses drawn aboard.
Chevaliers e servanz entrer.	Knights and their servants enter,
E l'un ami l'altre apeler,	each friend calling to another,

---

[17] Wace also displays his knowledge of the reality of Irish warfare – as essentially a cattle raid – just as he accurately describes their warriors' vulnerability (see below). See Robin Frame's account of 'War and peace in the medieval Lordship of Ireland' in *The English in Medieval Ireland*, ed. James Lydon, Dublin 1984, 118–41.

Mult se vunt entresaluant	wishing to exchange greetings,
Li remanant e li errant.	those remaining and those leaving.
Quant as nés furent tuit entré	When the ships were all loaded,
E tide orent e bon oré,	and the time and tide were right,
Dunc veïssiez ancres lever,	then you might see anchors raised,
Estrens traire, hobens fermer,	painters pulled in and haliards made fast,
Mariniers saillir par cez nés,	the sailors leap about the boats,
Deshenechier veilles e trés;	loosing sails and canvas,
Li un s'esforcent al windas,	some set about the capstan,
Li altre al lof e al betas;	others see to the sheets and luffing.
Detriés sunt li guverneür,	In the stern stand the captains,
Li maistre esturman li meillur.	the best master steersmen.
(B 11,190–214)	

There are several descriptions of landings, but none so full or effective as the disembarkation of the Normans in 1066.

Li dus out grant chevalrie	The duke had a great chivalry
e mult out nes en sa navie,	and many ships in his fleet;
moult out archiers, mult out servanz,	many archers, many sergeants,
homes hardie e combatanz,	brave and warlike men,
carpentiers e engigneors,	carpenters and engineers,
boens fevres e boens ferreiors,	good smiths and metalworkers.
les nes sunt a un port tornees,	The ships steered to one port
totes sunt ensenble aunees,	and reached shore together.
toutes sont ensemble acostees,	All lay together,
toutes sont ensemble aanchres,	all anchored together,
ensemble totes asechierent,	all beached together,
e ensemble les deschargierent,	and were all unloaded together.
. . .	. . .
Donc veïssiez boens mariniers,	Then you might see good sailors,
boens servanz e boens esquiers	good sergeants and good squires,
sailir fors e nes deschargier,	sally forth and unload the ships,
ancres jeter, cordes sachier,	cast the anchors and haul the ropes,
escuz e seles fors porter,	bear out shields and saddles,
destriers e palefreiz tirer.	lead out the warhorses and palfreys.
Li archier sunt issu,	The archers disembarked,
al terrain sunt primes venu,	the first to set foot on land,
donc a chascun son arc tendu,	each with his bow bent,
coivre e tarchais al lez pendu;	his quiver and bowcase hanging at his side.
tuit furent res e tuit tondu,	all were shaven and shorn,
de corz dras furent tuit vestu,	and all clad in short tunics,
prez d'assaillir, prez de fuïr,	ready to attack, ready to flee,
prez de torner, prez de gandir;	ready to turn about and ready to skirmish.
	They scoured the whole shore,
le rivage ont tuit poralé,	but not an armed man could they
nul home armé n'i ont trové.	find there.

Quant issu furent li archier	When the archers had gone out,
donc issirent li chevalier,	then the knights disembarked,
tuit armé et tuit haubergé,	all armed and armoured,
escu a col, elme lacié;	their shields at their shoulder and helmets laced,
ensenble vindrent al gravier,	they formed up on the shore,
chascun armé sor son destrier,	each mounted on his warhorse.
tuit orent ceintes les espees,	All had their swords girded on,
al plain vindrent, lances levées.	and rode onto the plain with lances raised.
Li baron orent gonfanons,	The barons carried gonfanons,
li chevalier orent penons;	the knights had pennants.
joste les archiers se sunt mis,	They placed themselves next to the archers,
le terrain ont avant porpris.	on the ground which had been seized.
(RIII 6,465–76: 481–508)	

The details of this account, the sort of information entirely omitted from William of Poitiers, are not, of course, historical. But they bear witness to Wace's powers of observation and ability to interpret military activity.

Not all sea crossings were as fortunate as Duke William's. It is another mark of Wace's attention to detail that he re-creates some ferocious storms.

Une turmente grant leva;	A great tempest arises,
Li tens mua, li venz turna,	the weather changes, the wind shifts,
Tona e plut e esclaira;	– thunder, rain and lightning –
Li ciels neirci, li airs trobla;	the heavens darken, the starlight fades,
La mer mella, undes leverent,	the sea heaves, winds rise,
Wages crurent e reverserent.	waves swell and crash.
Nefs commencent a perillier,	Now ships are in peril,
Borz e chevilles a fruisser;	timbers and pegs break,
Rumpent custures e borz cruissent,	joints burst and timbers creak,
Veilles depiecent e mast fruissent;	sails tear and masts snap.
Ne poeit hom lever la teste,	No man might raise his head,
Tant par esteit grant la tempeste.	so great was the storm.
Les nefs furent tost departies	The ships were all scattered,
E en plusurs terres fuïes.	and fled to many different shores.
(B 2,479–92)	

Wace conjures this storm for the Danish fleet which is pursuing Brenne back to Northumbria. The passage shows both his knowledge of technical terms and of the effects of bad weather on ships of his time.[18]

On land Wace makes frequent reference to horses. Warfare is inconceivable without them. First there are the destriers – warhorses – essential for chivalric warfare. Rollo, on his arrival in Gaul, is quick to adapt to cavalry tactics (Wace II 555–6). The English at Hastings are derided for their ignorance of

---

[18] For literary influences see J. Griswald 'A propos du thème descriptif de la tempête chez Wace et chez Thomas d'Angleterre', in *Mélanges de langue et de litterature du Moyen Age et de la Renaissance offerts à Jean Frappier*, 2 vols 1970, i, 375–89.

mounted warfare (Wace III 8,603–5). Horses have a valuable rôle in logistics too, carrying provisions and all the army's gear. The best descriptions of this are in the passages on the French forces at Varaville in 1057 and at Mortemer, three years earlier. In the first case Wace uses the evocative word 'coe' or tail to depict the long, straggling line of march that the baggage train creates (Wace III 5,191–8).[19] When King Henry of France hears of the defeat of the other half of his pincer movement at Mortemer, all is confusion as his men break camp.

pernent palefreis e destriers,	They seized the palfreys and warhorses,
trossent roncins, chargent sommiers,	harnessed the hacks and loaded the packhorses,
loges alument e foillies,	burnt their shelters and bivouacs,
mult les aveient tost voïes;	emptied them of everything,
les herneis enveient avant,	and sent the gear on ahead,
detriés les vait li reis gardant.	– the king went forward with caution.
(Wace III 4,959–64)	

Above all, Wace is aware that money provides the sinews of war. He attributes the success of Henry I over Robert Curthose in the fight for Normandy, rather bitterly, to its power. Money means men: 'moult out deniers, grant gent mena' and Henry's huge wealth is carried 'od grant tonels, od grant charei' (Wace III 10,854/7). In contrast:

Li dus n'aveit gaires deniers,	The duke had hardly any money,
ker il despendeit volentiers,	because he spent it so freely,
tot erent ses rentes faillies	all his rents were exhausted
e despendues ses aïes;	and his feudal dues expended.
n'i poeient pas foisoner	They could not possibly suffice
a bien despendre e a doner.	a generous expenditure and gift-giving.
(Wace III 10,883–8)	

Money provides for provisions, troops and transport, buys off the duke's 'soldeiers' (Wace III 10,899–904) and eventually undermines all his support. Robert has nothing to give but promises.

Quant li dus doner ne poeit,	When the duke could give no more,
ou ne poeit ou ne voleit,	– couldn't or wouldn't –
par pramesses se delivrout,	he delivered himself of promises.
mult pramateit e poi donout.	He promised much and gave little.
(Wace III 10,931–6)	

Wace, ever the realist, assesses that Henry won because 'most of the knights and the best of the barons' defected to the better paymaster (Wace III 11,159–62).

---

[19] The image of an animal's tail dragging behind is one that might strike anyone who had seen a line of march. The modern British Army uses the term 'teeth' to describe frontline troops and 'tail' their innumerable, essential supports.

This idea, of 'gain' as the chief motivation for war, leads us on to the section I have called the language of warfare. We have already seen distinctive uses of vocabulary specific to warfare. Some would claim, Hans-Erich Keller amongst them, that a great deal of this vocabulary is specific to Wace.[20] Certainly the poet lays great emphasis on ransoms, booty and on pay for the 'soldeier'. This word has caused controversy when translated as mercenary owing to the modern, derogatory connotations of the term. To men of rank and status it could be insulting, as Robert Curthose made clear to his father. But it need not be, for lesser men, and its literal translation of soldier serves us well.[21] A wise general, like duke William, ensures that pay and gifts are kept up to such men, during periods of inaction. The long wait for a good wind at St Valéry epitomises the problem.

Donc vindrent soldeier a lui,	Then soldiers came to him
e uns e uns, e dui e dui,	one by one, and two by two,
e quatre e quatre, e cinc e siés,	and four by four, by fives and sixes,
or set, or oit, or nof, or diés;	by sevens, eights, nines and tens;
e li dus toz les reteneit,	and the duke retained them all,
mult lor donout et pramateit.	giving them much and promising more.
Plusors vindrent par covenant	Many came according to an agreement
que il aveient fait avant;	which they had made beforehand.
plusors del ducs terres voleient	Many wished for the duke's lands,
s'Engleterre prendre poeient;	should he conquer England.
alquanz soldees demandoent,	Some required pay,
livreisons e dons coveitoent,	and allowances and gifts.
sovnet les estoveit despendre,	Often it was necessary to distribute these,
ne poeient longues atendre.	to those who could not afford to wait.
(Wace III 6,403–16)	

Wace celebrates the great booty following Richard I's defeat of the Germans at Rouen (Wace II 3,291–9; 3,357–62). Horses and equipment are the immediate prizes; their masters languish in prison awaiting ransom. This gleeful passage following Mortemer sums up the poet's attitude:

N'i out gaires si vil garçon	There was hardly a boy, no matter how lowly,
que n'en menast Franceis prison	who did not lead a Frenchman to prison,
e bes destriers, ou dous ou treis,	with a fine warhorse, or two, or three,

---

[20] *Étude descriptive sur le vocabulaire de Wace*, Deutsche Akademie der Wissenschaften zu Berlin, Veroffentlichungen des Instituts fur Romanische Sprachwissenschaft Nr. 7, Berlin 1953. See also A. Bell. 'Notes on Gaimar's military vocabulary' in *Medium Aevum* XL, 1971, 93–104, who concludes that Wace's military vocabulary is much richer but not as exceptional as Keller believes.
[21] Orderic, V, 98 uses the term 'Mercennarius' as a derogatory one. Cf. the French 'soldeier' at Hastings who overcomes his fear to dispatch two opponents (Wace III 8,295–328).

estre l'autre menu herneis;	apart from all the lesser gear.
n'out chartre en tote Normendie	Nor was there a dungeon in all Normandy,
que de Franceis ne fust emplie.	which was not full of Frenchmen.
(Wace III 4,909–14)	

Even when prisoners are ransomed, their equipment was kept by their captors. This provided an incentive – especially for the lower ranks in the host. These 'non-noble' warriors include squires, sergeants and footsoldiers of all sorts. Wace lays especial emphasis on the value of infantry, whom he often calls the 'gelde'. This word has the dual implication of someone who is a paid warrior and also suggests a sense of corporate identity.[22] He includes the English, fighting on foot in their traditional manner at Hastings under this heading. And, although some of his characters make derogatory reference to such troops, on the whole they are shown to play an important part in war and battle. Richard I's victory over the French on the Rive Béthune (arr. Seine-Maritime) is achieved through their efforts:

Franchoiz furent plusor et cil de Normandie.
mez a l'eve se tindrent, quer de gelde iert garnie,
d'archiers et d'escuiers qui n'espernerent mie; . . .
Archiers trove et villainz donc la terre est planiere,
a chenz et a milliers garnissent la riviere,
qui porte arc et qui hache, quil grant lance geldiere;
moult occient chevauls et devant et derriere. . . .
Li roi vit son damage, puiz retrait sa baniere.
(Wace II 3,928–30; 37–41; 45)

The French were in greater numbers than the Normans,
but they were checked at the stream, because the footmen defended it,
with archers and squires, who gave them no mercy . . .
There were archers and peasants on the level ground,
in their hundreds and thousands lining the riverbank,
here a man carried a bow, here an axe, here a long pike,
they killed so many horses in the front and rear ranks . . .
When the king saw his losses, he led off his troops.

In the same battle, esquires are described as armed with pikes, coming to the rescue of the knights (Wace II 3,898). There are lesser men yet; 'li garçon et l'autre frapaille' who appear at Hastings and are used by Arthur in a battle against the Romans, made to stand on a hill and to look more warlike than they actually are (Wace III 7,941–94; B 12,309–14).[23]

Wace also uses some interesting vocabulary associated with the organisation and command of an army. A large force is described as an 'ost' or 'esforz'; a smaller group as a 'compagnie' or 'maisniee' (both having connotations of

---

[22] See F. Godefroy *Lexique de l'Ancien Français*. Paris 1901, 255, where 'gelde' can mean either a unit of soldiers or a craft association, and 'geldon' a spearman or a peasant levy.
[23] This is another example of paralleled behaviour between two great commanders. Either that, or a good idea used twice.

group loyalty); tactical units are the 'conrei' (squadron) and 'conestablie' (troop). This is effectively a hierarchy of units and Wace stresses the importance of leadership. 'Chevetaines' (captains) command companies and below them are constables. Unlike his Latin sources he sees no need to employ archaic and anachronistic terminology like legions, cohorts and centuries to describe his 'contemporary' warfare. In fact, he only uses the word 'legiun' in the context of a Roman force (B 3,179–83; 5,275). Wace employs a wide range of words to describe deployment for battle and manoeuvres of the opposing troops. Alexander Bell has pointed out the relative paucity of Gaimar's language in this area. This greater variety may be indicative of greater poetic skill; but I consider it to be a product of a greater interest in the subject and a wider knowledge.

Finally, there is another group of words which ties in the last topic: description of weaponry, especially non-chivalric equipment. He describes axes: 'hache', often 'noresche' (Scandinavian) and 'besague': pikes, 'gisarme' and 'truble' which is a combination of these two (rather like a halberd). He uses many words associated with an archer's equipment: 'coivre' and 'tarchais' to carry their arrows, and the 'talevas', a shield to keep them out. He has also other missile weapons, the 'funde' or sling and 'plumee' (which may be a lead-weighted javelin) both associated with siege and street fighting.

Before we leave this section on the language of warfare I would like to include a passage in which Wace sets out the ethos of the chivalric warrior. This is largely through the words he puts into the mouth of Neél (Nigel) vicomte of the Cotentin when repelling a Breton invasion in 1033, during the reign of Robert the Magnificent.

Neel e Auveré oïrent	Nigel and Alfred heard
l'asemblee ke Bretun firent,	of the Breton muster
cels de Avrencein asemblerent	and assembled the men of the Avrencin,
e tuz cels k'il porent manderent,	and anyone else they could call upon,
gent a pie e gent a cheval.	men on foot and on horse.
'Baruns,' funt il, 'franc natural,	'Barons,' he cried, 'freeborn men,
or verrum ki bein le fera	it is well known that you fight well,
e ki sun seignur amera;	and love your lord.
gardez ui cest jurn vostre honur,	Look to your honour this day
gardez le pru vostre seignur.	and protect your lord's reputation.
Pur malvaise gent cil nus tienent,	They will hold us cheap,
ki pur le lostre el nostre vienent;	those who come to take our reputation from us,
de la preie acoillir se peinent,	Who strive to gather and carry off the flocks.
se il, noz oilz veant, l'en meinent,	If this robbery happens before our eyes,
ke nus ne escuums noz aveirs,	and we do not recover our riches,
grant reprovier iert a nos eirs.	great blame will attach to our heirs.
Fierement les envaïssiez,	Attack them fiercely,
sis avrez tost estolteiez;	if you wish to rout them utterly.
ferez chevaliers e chevals,	Strike knights and horses,

ferez seignurs, ferez vassals,	strike lords, strike vassals,
tuez quanque tuer porreiz,	kill all of them which you may kill,
je mar humme i esparnierez.'	woe to any man of you who shows mercy.'
E cil crient: 'Alum, alum!	And they cry, 'Let's go, let's go!
Ke faites vu? Trop demorum!'	What are you doing? We have waited long enough!'

(Wace III 2,641–64)

All Neel's rousing speech seems to suggest is that 'Up and at 'em' is sufficient instruction to conduct a battle. In fact, as Wace shows, orders, and the co-ordination of forces known as tactics, are vitally important. He has clear ideas of how best to set out men for a battle. (I know battles were rare in reality; but they are very common in poetic description.) As I have already pointed out he is interested in the arms and armour of footmen, which has tactical implications. For example, there are the 'Haches, darz, gavelocs, gisarmes' of Arthur's infantry (B 11,140). These are similar to the 'English arms' which Harold describes at Hastings, when encouraging his men:

'e vos avez haches agues	'and you have sharp axes,
e granz gisarmes esmolues;	and large, glittering halberds;
contre vos armes, qui bien taillent,	against your arms, which cut so well,
ne qui que les lor gaires vaillent;'	they will hardly avail;'

(Wace III 7,771–4)

Wace makes the point that 'the English did not know how to joust, nor to carry arms on horseback' (Wace III 8,603–4) – something which clearly counted against them at Hastings. He follows this fairly conventional comment with a most original observation. 'It seems to me that it is not possible for a man to strike good blows with a two-handed axe and protect himself at the same time' (Wace III 8,607–13). Both remarks show that Wace really thought about warfare at the basic level of hand-to-hand fighting. Infantry weapons were good in the hands of brave, well-trained men, even those of low social rank; cavalry tactics were better but could be thwarted by good foot. I can think of no contemporary who expresses this conflict so clearly.

William wins at Hastings, according to the Norman sources, by a combination of the feigned flight of his knights (of which more later) and his powerful archers. Wace is aware of the significance of the missilemen, and not just at Hastings. In Arthur's battle against the emperor Lucius, arrows 'fall like hail' (B 12,547–8). His conquest of Ireland is made easier by the natives' ignorance of the weapon, while his own archers shoot most thickly. The Irish are further hampered by their lack of armour (B 9,681–8) and indeed are quite unaccustomed to battle (B 8,113–14).[24] Wace naturally assumes that his heroes – Briton or Norman – do have that advantage. He says very little about military training, although he is not unusual in that. When knights are in mock battle at Cassibelan's court, in celebration of his recent defeat of Julius Caesar, his

---

[24] Wace's assessment of the Irish is supported by the *Song of Dermot and the Earl*, ed. G. H. Orpen, Oxford 1892. This vernacular text of a generation later describes their lack of armour most tellingly in their first battle against the English, ll. 664–85, esp. 672–5.

nephew Hireglas is accidentally killed. Now, Wace distinguishes the 'bohorde', a safer form of mounted joust between the chevaliers, from the 'escrimie' or fencing, which the younger warriors ('bachelers' and 'damoiseaux') take part in. The day ends with a fencing match in which Hireglas' opponent loses his temper and kills him (B 4,334–62).[25]

These are individual exercises in arms, of course. What is missing from Wace, as from most mediaeval sources, are descriptions of training in a body. Knights were accustomed to acting in concert in the hunting-field from an early age. In the twelfth century we first have evidence for tournaments, including the mass mêlée which involved manoeuvre by troops of horse and foot.[26] Clearly such expertise must have been required for such a ruse as the feigned flight. Wace describes this on several occasions, not just at Hastings, and although the feasibility has recently once again been doubted, he obviously believed it possible.[27]

Another favourite ploy of the author's is the ambush. These are usually mounted from woods, as the word 'enbuschement' suggests. They occur frequently in the *Brut*, with some influence from Geoffrey of Monmouth, as in the case of Androgeus' treacherous attack on Cassibelan (B 4,596–8; 608–14). The French knights accompanying a supply train destined for rebellious Arques is lured into ambush by a feigned flight (Wace III 3,475–98). Or a valley may serve as a hiding-place, as it does for vicomte Nigel's attack on the Bretons already cited (Wace III 2,669–70).

Wace's finest description of an army-sized ambush is Duke William's attack on the French rearguard at Varaville.

Li reis aveit Dive passee,	The king had crossed the Dive,
l'eve qui cort par la contree,	the river which runs through that country,
ensemble od lui le plus de l'ost,	together with the majority of his army,
qui se penoent d'aler tost,	which had taken care to move quickly.
mais longue esteit la rote arriere,	But line of march behind was long
continuel tote et entiere.	and all together.
Li dus vit que la force ert soe	The duke saw that he could gain an advantage,
vers cels qui erent en la coe;	over those in the army's tail.
quant il entra en Garavile,	He pressed his men on from village to village,
sa gent enprés de vile en vile,	and when he came to Varavile,
Franceis trova qui se teneient,	he found those of the French there
qui la rieregarde faiseient.	who formed the rearguard.

○

[25] See *Orderic* ii, 29 for the 'real-life' death of Hugh de Giroie in javelin practice.

[26] Juliet Vale. *The Tournament 1100–1300*, Boydell & Brewer, 1986.

[27] J. M. Carter doubts the likelihood of the feigned flight in the eleventh century but will admit it in the twelfth. See: *The Anglo-Norman Anonymous*: The newsletter of the Haskins Society, 6, 1988, 7–8. Certainly Wace believed it possible, since he used it often eg. II 161–4, 3,231–5 etc. He makes the feigned flight at Hastings a tactic the Normans were so well versed in that they are able to put it into operation as it 'suits them (Wace III 8,175–88).

La veïssiez fiere assemblee,
maint colp de lance e d'espee,
de lances fierent chevaliers
e od les ars traient archiers,
e od les pels vilains lor donent,

mult en confundent e estonent,
en la chaucie les enbatent,
mult en i tuent e abatent,
e li Norman tot tens creisseient,
qui grant torbes acoreient.
Donc veïssiez rote haster,

l'un Franceis l'autre avant boter,
Mult lor ennoie la chaucie
qu'il trovent longe e enpeirie,
e il esteient encombré,
de co qu'il aveient robé;
mult en veissiez desroter
e trebuchier e fors voler,

qui pois ne porent relever
ne en la dreite veie entrer;
al pont passer fu grant la presse

e la gent d'aler mult engresse.
Viez fu li pont, grant fu li fais,

plances trebuchent, chient ais;
la mer monta, li flo fu granz,

sor le pont fu li fais pesanz,
li pont trebucha a chai
e quantqui out desus peri;
maint en chaï enprés le pont,
qui devala el plus parfont.
Al pont chaeir fu la criee,

mult dolerose e esfree,
mult veissiez herneis floter,
homes plungier e affondrer;
nus ne s'en pout vif escaper
s'il ne fu bien doit de noer.
Qant il orent al pont failli

n'i out si proz ne si hardi

qui n'eust poor de perir,
ker il n'aveient ou gandir;

Then there was a fierce battle –
many blows of lance and sword.
The knights struck with their lances,
the archers shot their bows,
and the peasants gave them what
    with their pikes,
stunning and utterly confounding them,
killing them and driving them
down the causeway in pursuit.
The Normans increased in numbers
hastening to form a large force.
Then you might see the French
    troops routed
pressing one on another.
The causeway hindered them,
being long and in bad repair,
and they were encumbered,
by everything they had plundered.
Many were seen breaking the line,
stumbling and hastily leaving the
    route,
who could not retrace their steps
or get onto the right track again.
On crossing the bridge the press was
    great,
everyone was eager to reach it.
The bridge was old, its burden was
    heavy,
its boards broke, planks split,
the sea rose and the current was
    strong.
The heavy weight on the bridge
caused it to crash and shatter,
and everyone upon it perished.
Many fell in close by the bridge
where the water was deep.
As the bridge collapsed into the
    water there a cry was heard,
of great sorrow and terror.
Much harness was to be seen floating,
men plunging and sinking.
No-one could escape alive,
if he did not know how to swim well.
When they heard that the bridge had
    fallen,
there was no-one, no matter how
    brave or bold,
who did not fear for his own life,
lest he should not be spared.

Normant detriers les vont pernant,	They see the Normans pressing on from behind
n'il ne poent aler avant,	but they may not go forward.
par les rivages vont tastant,	They cast along the river banks,
quez et passages vont querant,	seeking for fords and crossings,
armes e robes vont getant,	throwing away arms and plunder,
co peise lor qu'il en ont trebuchant,	because the weight of it causes them to stumble.
e li uns l'autre traïnant,	One leads another,
e li Normant d'iloc les traient,	the Normans press upon them there
qui nes esparnent ne manaient.	sparing none nor showing any mercy.
Tuit cil qui furent aresté,	All those who were trapped,
qui ne furent al pont passé,	and unable to cross that bridge,
furent retenu e lié,	were captured and bound,
ou ocis furent ou neié.	or killed, or drowned.
(Wace III 5,191–256)	

The vividness of this description is unique to Wace. Only he mentions the broken bridge and its disastrous impact on the fleeing French. It does not matter if this bridge never existed; we still have a powerful and accurate portrayal of an army in rout. And ambushes were important in warfare; they were much feared and often employed. Henry I's decisive victory at Tinchebrai was the result of an outflanking charge by a hidden group of cavalry.[28]

If open fields were more common as battlefields, this was because it was easier to muster men for purposes of control and morale. Wace usually employs the term 'conrei' meaning both an army's deployment and its smaller units to describe a battle line. It is normally composed of three divisions and composed of 'eschielles' (squadrons) commanded by the 'seigneurs' and 'chevetains' and the smaller units of 'conroi' and 'mesnee'. He places great emphasis on the importance of banners on the field of battle. The gonfanon is both a symbol of authority and a guide. So, when in the battle against the Bretons, vicomte Nigel leads the way:

e Auveré serreement	and closely ordered, Alfred
dut mener tute l'autre gent;	led all the other men,
lez lui fist un penun porter	near to him a banner borne,
ou lur gent pussent recuvrer.	upon which their troops could rally.
(Wace III 2,673–6)	

The death of a standard bearer signalled defeat, as Rollo points out when, in fighting the French.

Roullant fu ocis, qui l'enseigne portout,	Roland was killed, he who bore the standard,
qui tenoit les mesnies et les autres quiout.	who commanded the households and led the rest.
(Wace II 547–8)	

---

[28] The battle has been most recently discussed (and illustrated) by Jim Bradbury, *The Medieval Archer*, Woodbridge 1985, 42–3.

Wace makes a great point of the importance of Turstan fitz Rou's exemplary behaviour with William's standard at Hastings (Wace III 8,673–80 etc.).[29] Other field commands are given by horns (B 452) and trumpets (Wace III 7,999–8,000). The latter instrument is used to recall Brutus' forces from pursuing the 'French' (B 1,044–5). This suggests that Wace envisaged commanders having a tighter control over their knights than is normally supposed (unless we presume this mythical exaggeration). At night no sound is to be made until the battle cry for attack is shouted (B 9,085–8). This again speaks volumes for the control Wace thought commanders could exercise.

In battle the poet also stresses control, disciplined manoeuvre and good close order to fight effectively. He is not alone in this; many contemporary works recognise these military virtues, although they are often best expressed in the vernacular.[30] Harold exhorts the English at Hastings to keep good, close order to prevent the Normans from penetrating their ranks (Wace III 7,757–69). So much are his Latin sources agreed upon, but Wace adds a barricade, of which more later. William's forces are also carefully arrayed:

Cil a pié aloent avant,	Those on foot led the way
sereement, lor ars portant,	in serried ranks, bearing bows.
chevaliers emprés chevalchoent,	The knights rode close,
qui les archiers aprés gardoent;	protecting the archers from behind.
cil a cheval e cil a pié,	Those on horse and those on foot,
si com il orent commencié,	just as they had begun,
tindrent lor eirre e lor compas,	kept their order and the same pace,
sereement, lor petit pas,	in close ranks and at a slow march,
li un l'autre ne trespassout	So that no-one might overtake another,
ne n'apreismout ne n'esloignout,	nor get too close nor too far apart.
tout aloent serreement	All advanced in close order;
e tuit aloent fierement;	and all advanced bravely.
(Wace III 7,685–96)	

For the final Norman charge at Hastings, with Duke William closely surrounded by his knights, Wace provides a classic description.

jost lui vit son gonfanon,	You might see near to him, his banner,
plus de mil armez environ,	and more than a thousand armed men around him,
qui del duc grant garde perneient	who took good care of the duke,
e la ou il poigneit poigneient	and struck where he struck.
sereement, si com il durent,	In the closest order they could achieve,
vers les Engleis ferir s'esmurent.	they hurled themselves against the English.
Od la force des boens boens destriers	With the weight of the good warhorses,

[29] See my more detailed comments on this in *ante* 1982, 33.
[30] See the comments of J. F. Verbruggen, *The art of warfare in western Europe during the Middle Ages*, Oxford 1977, 16–17.

e od cels cols des chevaliers,	and the blows of the knights,
la presse ont tote derompue	they broke the enemy ranks
e la turbe avant els fendue;	scattering the mob before them.
li boens dus avant les conduit,	The good duke led from the front.
maint en chaça e maint s'en fuit	Many fled and many pursued.
(Wace III 8,759–70)	

What happened if close order was given up is exemplified in the *Brut*. A group of British knights charge out of a wood, surprising the emperor Lucius' men; but overtaken by enthusiasm they are thrown back by Romans in good order.

Breton puineient a desrei,	The Bretons charged in disorder
Ne vuleient estre en cunrei,	they did not wish to retain their formation.
. . .	. . .
Petreïeus fu mult engrés,	(The Roman commander) was unrelenting,
Ses bons humes tint de sei pres.	He kept his good men very close to
(B 11,957–8; 65–6)	him.

I shall close this section with what I suspect is, to Wace, a perfect battle array. It is the one Belin and Brenne adopt in their final battle against the Romans, when they have to reorganise their men for the decisive blow.

Lur gent firent raseürer,	Their troops were allowed to recuperate,
Chevals restreindre, homes armer,	to harness horses and arm the men.
Puis unt fait conreiz de lur gent	Then to form up in battle array,
Par mil, par cinquante, par cent;	by thousands, by fifties and by hundreds.
de plus hardiz, des plus aidables	The toughest and most useful men
Firent maistres e conestables	were made leaders and constables
A chescune eschielle par sei,	over each of their squadrons
Quis face tenir en conrei.	which take their place in the battle line.
Les plus hardiz combateors	The best fighters
Mistrent avant as fereors;	were placed in front as strikers.
lez cels firent destre e senestre	Those on the right and left flanks
Arbelastiers e archiers estre.	were crossbowmen and archers.
Le mielz de lur gent e le plus	The better and the larger part of their army
Descendirent des chevals jus,	dismounted from their horses[31]
En mi le champ furent a pied	and, in the middle of the field, on foot
Ordeneement e rengied.	drew up their ranks in good order.
Cil unt par mi trenché lur lances	They cut their lances down,

---

[31] The tactical significance of dismounting knights to fight on foot in the twelfth century is best expressed and discussed by Bradbury, *The Medieval Archer*, 39–57. The battle of Lincoln, where King Stephen fought on foot with a Scandinavian axe, and the Welsh foot played a large part in his defeat, seems directly relevant to Wace's interpretation of Hastings and other battles. Orderic vi, 542.

E querpies lur conuaissances, | and abandoned their heraldic devices.
Cil en irrunt le petit pas | They advanced at a slow march
Ferir sur la grant presse el tas, | to fight through the mêlée in a body.
Ja uns d'els ne desrengera | So that no one should lose his place
Ne pur home guenchira. | nor any man turn in flight.
Dunc unt grailles e corns soné | Then trumpets and horns were heard to sound

Si sunt al ferir aturné. | as they set themselves to fight.
(B 3,115–38)

I hope I have shown that Wace had a profound knowledge of warfare, which he was eager to share with his audience. True, there is much that is conventional in his descriptions, which we can find in the *chansons de geste* and elsewhere. But there is a great deal of unique material and significant insights in the poet's work which make them worthy of careful study for the military information they contain. His vision of how war should be pursued in the mid- to late twelfth century is comprehensive and packed with relevant detail. Without forgetting the main purpose of his mythical and historical epics, is there an element of didacticism in his work?

I have already stressed Wace's interest in the non-knightly component of contemporary armies. He has much to say about the value of infantry – at Hastings and Val-ès-Dunes, in the numerous defences of Normandy and in the many battles of the *Brut*. He is also interested in defences which make them more effective in battle: the river Semillon, the barricade at Hastings, the 'plashing' of woods by the Irish.[32] Indeed there are themes which suggest that he had a great interest in 'li communes', troops raised from town and villages, such as his own Caen. It is the term used for the peasant rebellion against Richard I, and it is as though Wace wants to make the point of the military viability of such troops.

Admittedly, the fighting he describes at Caen is a classic chivalric encounter (Wace III 10,945–11,054); but he sets the French defeat at Mortmer in a town. The French are depicted as being trapped in their lodgings, barricaded in and smoked out by the Norman forces (Wace III 4,867–902). Seen in this light, the barricade at Hastings makes more sense. After all, it is composed of window frames and other bits of wood (Wace III 7,793–805). Where were these to be found on an open battlefield? Rather they represented the materials to hand in a built-up area. Did Wace's knowledge of warfare have something to do with a town militia? Had he witnessed the attack on Bayeux and Caen by Robert of Gloucester in 1138?[33] This is mere speculation, of course, but it is worth speculating to try to identify the source of Wace's military knowledge. We do not know that he was a fighter, whether as a knight serving in a household or playing a rôle with the night watch. But he certainly knew his military onions; something that his audience, then and now, should appreciate.

---

[32] The technique of 'plashing' or cutting trees to make the edge of woods into an impenetrable defence was a peculiarly Irish activity. Wace's use of the word 'plaissier' is, as far as I know, the earliest description of this activity. Cf. *Song of Dermot and the Earl*, 1,588–97, where ditches are also used to impede the English army's movement.

[33] *Historia Novella*, 73.

JOHN LELAND AND THE ANGLO-NORMAN HISTORIAN

Caroline Brett

John Leland the antiquary died in 1552. The great contributions which he
made to learning were in the fields of topography and bibliography. Between
about 1533 and 1547 he spent much of his time in travel around England and
Wales, equipped with a royal commission to investigate monastic, cathedral
and college libraries, just before, during and after the Dissolution of the
Monasteries. His journeys resulted in several volumes of notes on the manuscripts he found and also on the landscapes through which he passed. He had
begun his working life as a classical scholar and thought of himself as a notable
Latin poet, but, apparently with patriotism as his main propelling force, he
developed a strong interest in every aspect of his country's past. He planned a
whole series of historical works, of which more will be said later, but in fact all
that he published in his lifetime were a few short pieces of a polemical nature.
He completed in manuscript a biographical dictionary of British writers from
the beginnings of history to his own time, the *Commentarii de Scriptoribus
Britannicis* (hereafter *Commentarii*). His other historical and topographical
work remained in note form. It was all finally published in the eighteenth
century, when the manuscripts had collected in the Bodleian Library. The
material on history and manuscripts is known as the *Collectanea* and the
topographical notes as the *Itinerary*.[1] Leland's work on any particular subject
will often be divided among these three 'works', so that they have to be taken
as a single whole.

Leland has usually been regarded as the founder of scientific antiquarian
study in Britain but the contrast between his aims and his actual achievement
has led to greatly conflicting assessments of him. Some claim that he was
overrated, the esteem of his contemporaries being based on his own exaggerated estimate of his abilities.[2] The real importance of his career lies partly
in its timing. The short lists which he left of books in one hundred and
thirty-seven monastic libraries are a crucial last-minute glimpse of the contents
of the libraries just before they were permanently scattered. Also important
was the influence which his blueprint for his own works was to have on the

---

[1] On Leland's life, see May McKisack, *Medieval History in the Tudor Age*, Oxford 1971, 1–25;
T. D. Kendrick, *British Antiquity*, London 1950, 45–64; James P. Carley, 'John Leland and the
contents of English pre-Dissolution libraries: Glastonbury Abbey', *Scriptorium* xl, 1986, 107–20.
His historical works are: Thomas Hearne, ed., *Ioannis Lelandi Antiquarii De Rebus Britannicis
Collectanea*, 2nd edn, 6 vols, London 1770; Antony Hall, ed., *Commentarii De Scriptoribus
Britannicis, Auctore Ioanne Lelando*, 2 vols, Oxford 1709; Lucy Toulmin Smith, ed., *The Itinerary
of John Leland in or about the years 1535–1543*, 5 vols, London 1906–10. I am at present preparing
a new edition and translation of the *Commentarii*.
[2] Honor McCusker, *John Bale Dramatist and Antiquary*, Pennsylvania 1942, 54.

next generation of scholars. Yet these are rather vague and general matters. It is difficult but worthwhile to try to define the importance of Leland in relation to a single period of history like the Anglo-Norman (1066–1154). What did Leland in fact do to improve the availability of information on this period, and did his work affect the way in which its history was interpreted?

The answers are not as clear as they might be. Leland viewed history very much as a unity and never concentrated on the Anglo-Norman period particularly. Some of his innovations concerned the Anglo-Norman period but others as well, and one has to discuss the whole at the risk of digression. Another difficulty is that 1066–1154 was not a period which had ever become obscure and neglected or stood in need of 're-discovery', as had the Anglo-Saxon age. There was a great change in the way it was thought of in the sixteenth century, but it is hard to assign responsibility for the re-interpretation and novel use of sources to a man who produced as little in the way of explicit historical thinking as Leland. To try to understand Leland's rôle one has to review the whole context: the state of historical knowledge and thought through the sixteenth century. Within the general picture Leland is often just an indicator, not an instigator of the developments which were taking place. Yet one can show at least a few instances in which his work had decisive effects, and further research may in time show more.

I should like to divide the discussion into two unequal parts, and deal first with the question of the availability of genuine information about the Anglo-Norman period in the sixteenth century, and afterwards, more briefly, with changing interpretations and historical methods.

In the early 1500s, how well-off for source-material was the scholarly inquirer who wished to know about Anglo-Norman history? One may say at once that information was plentiful in quantity but dubious in quality. History was scarcely yet legitimate as an academic discipline for the Renaissance humanist scholar, but a functional sense of the past more precise and structured (and of course more artificial) than is usually found today was strongly present. In a time which revered antiquity and sought precedents for every action, this was essential. Noblemen had to know their ancestors' claims to the land, corporations the origins of their privileges. Leland's *Itinerary* itself is evidence for the vast fund of informal but quite detailed information about the past on which the inquirer could draw – particularly the Anglo-Norman past, since individuals and institutions prided themselves on origins in that period. The *Itinerary* is full of such remarks as 'I head there of an old mariner that Henry I gave great privilege to the town of Scarborough', or 'The castle (of Sheriff Hutton) . . . as I lernid there, was builded by Rafe of Raby the first Earl of Westmorland of the Nevilles'.[3] It is rarely possible to trace the immediate sources of such remarks. All this 'knowledge' was essentially local, and its more formal aspect had been the production of a number of local 'antiquarian' histories of high quality, incorporating records as well as narrative, in the later Middle Ages. The work of Thomas Rudborne on the history of Winchester, or of John Rous on the earls of Warwick, are examples.[4]

[3] Toulmin Smith, ed., *The Itinerary*, i, 60, 65.
[4] Henry Wharton, ed., 'Thomae Rudborne historia maior de fundatione ecclesiae Wintoniensis', in *Anglia Sacra*, 2 vols, London 1691, i, 179–286; Thomas Hearne, ed., *Joannis Rossi Antiquarii*

Local history hung on a framework of national history, pegged by the reigns of kings and the occasional incursions of royal and baronial politics on the local scene. But this national history itself was in a somewhat poor condition at the end of the Middle Ages. Since the great twelfth-century synthesising histories of England, successive British and world histories had been written – by Ralph of Diceto, Roger of Wendover, Matthew Paris, Gervase of Canterbury, Ranulf Higden and others – but each of these drew on only a proportion of the existing sources, randomly 'selected' by their availability to the author, and had the effect of further diluting and contaminating the stock-pot which the history of Britain was becoming. History-writing had a centrifugal tendency. National or universal histories – especially Ranulf Higden's *Polychronicon*, the most successful one of the later Middle Ages – would be circulated and continued with local annals in various churches, but local information was not in turn gathered into the general histories. The general history of the Anglo-Norman period available to the reader of *c.* 1500 was William of Malmesbury and his contemporaries watered down and provided with accretions through several successive stages. It was freely available, since the *Polychronicon* and a combined version by Caxton of the London chronicles had been printed several times by the early sixteenth century, but for depth and accuracy it left much to be desired.[5]

The difficulties in the way of remedying this situation were more practical than theoretical. The materials for history were all present, chiefly in the monasteries, but there was no central organisation of studies, or any systematic way of bringing the scholar and his materials together. There could be no cumulative progress in historical study as long as manuscripts were copied on individual initiative and at random and bibliographies and catalogues did not circulate. There were several attempts at bibliography in the later Middle Ages. From the historian's point of view the most important was by Henry Kirkstead of Bury St Edmunds (*c.* 1346–78), a list of ecclesiastical authors and their works combined with a list of libraries where the books could be found. There was also the *Granarium* of John Whethamsted, twice abbot of St Albans 1430–65 – a dictionary of ancient and mediaeval historians and their works, which Leland discovered and used. In the mid-fifteenth century a historical concordance, *De Concordantiis Historiarum Angliae*, existed and was used by Thomas Rudborne.[6] But none of these was at all widely distributed: each represented an individual effort, soon dissipated. The last, in fact, is lost altogether and the subject-matter of the first two was too general for English history to be intensively covered.

Warwicensis Historia Regum Angliae, 2nd edn, Oxford 1745; see Antonia Gransden, *Historical Writing in England, ii, c. 1307 to the Early Sixteenth Century*, London 1982, 394–8, 309–27, and, on late mediaeval local history generally, 342–424.

[5] E. Gordon Duff, *Fifteenth Century English Books*, Oxford 1917, 27–9, 46–7 (nos 97, 102).

[6] Henry of Kirkstead's *Catalogus Scriptorum Ecclesiae* is partly printed in Thomas Tanner, *Bibliotheca Britannico-Hibernica . . .*, ed. David Wilkins, London 1748, xvii–xliii. On the authorship see R. H. Rouse, ' "Bostonus Buriensis" and the author of the *Catalogus Scriptorum Ecclesiae*', *Speculum* xli, 1966, 471–99. On Whethamstede's *Granarium* see E. F. Jacob, 'Verborum florida venustas: some early examples of euphuism in England', *Bulletin of the John Rylands Library* xvii, 1933, 264–90. Rudborne: Wharton, ed., *Anglia Sacra*, i, 244–5.

This was the approximate situation in 1500. The sixteenth century brought upheavals into which historiography was drawn, to be transformed inevitably, though incidentally. The printing press offered the means of overcoming the problem of distribution of materials, but before it could go far in that direction the Dissolution of the Monasteries began to effect its own chaotic redistribution. With monastic assets confiscated and libraries open to all takers, it was as if the whole country suddenly filled with whirling papers. Many books vanished but many others caught the light for the first time in centuries as they passed rapidly to successive new owners; later, in the reign of Elizabeth I, when the political struggles had died down, something like a centralised organisation of historical studies did appear. It was not a government initiative of the kind which Leland hoped for in the 1530s; it was a gradual accumulation of manuscript-resources in the hands of those who were most interested, a small, personally connected group of scholar-statesmen of a kind which had not previously existed. Archbishop Matthew Parker was the pioneer, and Sir Robert Cotton, founder of the Cottonian library, the prime example.[7]

John Leland was at the centre of the process, his writings capturing the moment of the great redistribution. Whether it would have taken a different course without him is doubtful: the scale of the processes tended to brush individual efforts aside. But we should certainly know far less of it without him. Leland's scholarly interests were universal and hardly anyone was ever as well placed as he to achieve the impossible. He travelled with a royal commission, sometimes in company with the king's official inspectors and valuers of monastic property, which intimidatingly underlined the fact that he could examine and remove manuscripts at his own discretion. Moreover, he continued his travels when the monasteries had been dissolved and the libraries lay about unprotected.[8] With these opportunities it is natural that he should have been the one to propose a completely new fusion of national and local history. He wrote to King Henry VIII in 1546 of his intention to write a 'county history' with a separate book for every shire in England and Wales, combining topography with explanations of the origins of every name and feature of the landscape, natural and man-made. He also proposed a book 'on the British nobility', which would list all the people who held rank and office in Britain from the beginning of history to the present – a dictionary of national biography, genealogically based.[9] These aims were wildly disproportionate to one man's capacities, and Leland was soon to fall victim to insanity and premature death, but, as F. J. Levy writes, 'that the plan was in its essentials the correct one can be deduced from the fact that almost all the antiquarian research of the sixteenth century followed it'.[10] The force behind the plan was the new nationalism of Tudor England. Just as local family, ecclesiastical or

---

[7] McKisack, *Medieval History*; F. S. Fussner, *The Historical Revolution. English Historical Writing and Thought 1580–1640*, London 1962.

[8] Anthony à Wood, *Athenae Oxonienses*, ed. Philip Bliss, 4 vols, London 1813–20, i, 198; Toulmin Smith, ed., *The Itinerary*, i, xxxvii–xxxviii, ii, 148; James Gairdner, ed., *Letters and Papers, Foreign and Domestic, of the Reign of Henry VIII, 1509–47*, 21 vols in 33, London 1862–1910, vii, 637.

[9] *Itinerary*, i, xlii.

[10] F. J. Levy, *Tudor Historical Thought*, San Marino, California 1967, 129.

civic standing had earlier depended on a knowledge of the local past, so the new national self-awareness would have to include an awareness of the past of the whole nation, accessible to all. Leland took it for granted that the past would prove creditable: 'I trust that this your realm shall so well be known, once painted with his native colours, that the renown thereof shall give place to the glory of no other region'.[11]

The main limitation in Leland's aims was that he was not a lawyer, and did not have the time or the training to set to work on the public records. Apart from that, he was interested in every physical and literary relic of the past. How he developed these aims and acquired the initial knowledge from which to decide his course remains obscure. In the humanist school where he was first educated, St Paul's in London, the only history in the curriculum was classical history, studied as a rhetorical exercise.[12] The situation was similar at Cambridge and Oxford, where he went successively, although some of the college libraries owned manuscripts of the best Anglo-Norman historians.[13] Leland must have been inspired by his patriotism, combined with national rivalry. He was spurred into historical studies by the fact that in Italy and Germany scholars were much further advanced than in England; that the German Trittenheim had published a biographical dictionary of ecclesiastical writers which ignored many British writers and travestied others; that (according to Leland) German scholars were raiding British libraries for neglected works which they could pass off as their own countrymen's productions, and that an Italian, Polydore Vergil, had the temerity to work on a history of England which questioned some cherished national myths, especially that of King Arthur.[14] Polydore's history was published in 1534, when Leland was beginning his travels; it may have been a direct incentive to him to pursue his research, but he probably also had some advance knowledge of it, since it was mainly written much earlier, in 1512–13.[15]

It is interesting to compare the works of Polydore Vergil and John Leland. Polydore is generally acclaimed as the first Renaissance historian of England while Leland is characterised as having a 'medieval mind'.[16] But Renaissance thought only gradually worked its way into the various disciplines which historical writing involves, and its initial impact was mainly literary. Polydore writes a polished narrative, rarely interrupted by references to source-material, which makes his book a mine of information but singularly unhelpful to any historian wishing, like Leland, to build further on it. Polydore in fact went to some trouble to collect source-material. He based his account of the Anglo-Norman period mainly on William of Malmesbury and Matthew Paris, which

[11] *Itinerary*, i, xlii–xliii.
[12] Levy, *Tudor Historical Thought*, 43–6.
[13] For instance Henry of Huntingdon, Ailred of Rievaulx and Ralph of Diceto at Clare College, Cambridge: H. Luard, 'A letter of John Bale to Archbishop Matthew Parker', *Cambridge Antiquarian Communications* iii, 1864–8, 157–73 at 166–7.
[14] Johannes Trithemius, *De Scriptoribus Ecclesiasticis*, Paris, 1512. For Leland's strictures on Trittenheim, see, for instance, Hall, ed., *Commentarii*, i, 179–80; on his rivalry with Polydore, Denys Hay, *Polydore Vergil, Renaissance Historian and Man of Letters*, Oxford 1952, 79; Edwin Greenlaw, *Studies in Spenser's Historical Allegory*, Baltimore 1932, 11–15.
[15] Polydore Vergil, *Anglicae Historiae Libri Vigintiseptem*, Basel 1534; Hay, *Polydore Vergil*, 79.
[16] Kendrick, *British Antiquity*, 49, 83.

was a reasonable choice from the point of view of accuracy, but for which his reasons were as much literary as strictly historical. He approved of these two because they were writers who had already exercised some critical skill and judgment in shaping their data into a logical narrative with interpretation and explanation provided – in other words, they were real historians. From their quality as writers he inferred that their data could be trusted. The other monastic chronicles of mediaeval England he dismissed as 'bald, uncouth, chaotic and deceitful'.[17] This was a source-criticism which threw out the baby with the bath-water. Polydore Vergil had not fully grasped the idea of relying on contemporary evidence only as a guiding principle of history.

Admittedly, Leland had not done so in the least. As has been said, he saw the past as a dimension of the present, and therefore undifferentiated in itself. His motive was to rehabilitate the lesser historians and writers of mediaeval England and to prove that England had as many men of learning as Italy could boast. In doing so, he accepted much anachronistic evidence, but also worked his way through quantities of national and local chronicles, some misattributed, some anonymous, some undated, and very often arrived at logical and sensible datings and localisations for them on internal evidence. The resulting work in the *Collectanea* and writers' biographies in the *Commentarii* made the task of finding the best contemporary authorities far easier for historians of the later sixteenth century and after, when the contemporary method had become established. Leland's own bibliographical work was not published in its own right until 1709, but the bulk of it was incorporated into the *Catalogus Scriptorum Britanniae* by John Bale, his one-time assistant and friend, who did his vociferous best to ensure Leland's posthumous reputation and pass on the benefits of his scholarship.[18] Bale was a Protestant convert who spent much of his life embroiled in religious controversy. He published his *Catalogus* in Basel in 1557 while in exile in Queen Mary's reign. Based on Leland, the list contained many misconceptions not in its source (for instance, Bale tended to multiply the number of works ascribed to authors by repeating them under different titles); however, it also contained comment on some works not known to Leland, and made Leland's findings usefully available.[19]

In Leland's source-criticism, his lack of a sense of anachronism is evident when he deals with the Anglo-Norman period. For instance, notes from fifteenth-century genealogical rolls purporting to go back to the Norman Conquest, shown to him on his travels by aristocratic hosts, take up a good deal of space in the *Itinerary*.[20] In the *Commentarii*, in his biography of Wimond, first prior of St Frideswide's, Oxford, he cited three sources: the account of Wimond's appointment from the *Gesta Pontificum* of William of Malmesbury, a statement from an unidentified chronicle of St Frideswide's which contradicts this, and a dating of 1111 for the appointment from the fifteenth-century Thomas Rudborne.[21] In the *Collectanea* he made excerpts from the *Historia Regum* by Gervase of Canterbury, who flourished under

[17] Gransden, *Historical Writing*, ii, 434; Hay, *Polydore Vergil*, 86.
[18] John Bale, *Scriptorum Illustrium Maioris Brytanniae . . . Catalogus*, 2 vols, Basel 1557.
[19] For examples relating to William of Malmesbury see *De gestis regum*, i, cxvi–cxvii.
[20] For example *Itinerary*, i, 237–8, 307–14, ii, 1–26.
[21] Hall, ed., *Commentarii*, i, 192.

Richard I and John, and noted the story that William I had all the charters and movable property of the English monasteries seized in 1070. This is a historical interpretation (first found in Matthew Paris under 1072) of indications in the Anglo-Saxon Chronicle and some charters that there was plundering that year and that it was probably then that knight-service was imposed on the monasteries.[22] In itself, however, it has no authority, although it was used by other sixteenth-century historians including Polydore Vergil and (following him) John Bale.[23]

On the credit side, Leland usually made intelligent deductions about the date and place of composition of his sources. He identified the anonymous *Eulogium Historiarum*, a fourteenth-century universal chronicle, as a Malmesbury work, as its modern editor has done on the same internal evidence.[24] He deduced the dates of Gervase of Canterbury correctly and identified the various stages of continuation of his *Historia Regum*; he was not to know that the manuscript of the *Historia Regum* which he used had been anonymously rewritten (perhaps by John of London) from 1065 onwards, since the original manuscript did not come his way.[25] Leland's dating methods were not always fine enough to enable him to deduce dependence correctly: for instance, he thought that Henry of Huntingdon drew on Alfred of Beverley, rather than the other way round.[26] Still, on the whole Leland's *Commentarii* represent a notable achievement in imposing order on a chaotic mass of material, studied in difficult circumstances. For the period 1066–1154, Leland had identified William of Jumièges, 'Florence' of Worcester, the *Historia Novorum* of Eadmer, the *De Gestis Regum*, *De Gestis Pontificum* and *Historia Novella* of William of Malmesbury, the *Historia Regum* attributed to Simeon of Durham and other important Northern historical works in the same manuscript, Henry of Huntingdon, Alfred of Beverley and Ailred of Rievaulx; almost the only major narrative historical works which he missed were those with a continental transmission, Orderic Vitalis and the *Gesta Stephani*. He had also worked outwards from references in the better-known writers, especially William of Malmesbury, to build up a knowledge of many more obscure writers of theological, hagiographical and devotional works. However, there are some puzzling omissions or lapses. Leland did not know *De Nugis Curialium* by Walter Map. This survives in only one manuscript, but that was from Ramsey Abbey, which Leland visited. His neglect was continued into the nineteenth century, until at last the work was published in 1850.[27] More importantly, Leland missed or ignored manuscript 'E' of the Anglo-Saxon Chronicle from Peterborough, an important historical source to 1121, while making notes at

---

[22] Hearne, ed., *Collectanea*, i, 256–77 at p. 262; see *EHD*, ii, 155, 863, 960–70.

[23] Bale, *Catalogus*, i, 166–7.

[24] Hearne, ed., *Collectanea*, ii, 302–14; Frank Scott Haydon, ed., *Eulogium Historiarum siue Temporis*, 3 vols, RS ix, 1858–63, i, xxxiii.

[25] William Stubbs, ed., *The Historical Works of Gervase of Canterbury*, 2 vols, RS lxxiii, 1879/80, ii, vii–x.

[26] Hearne, ed., *Collectanea*, iii, 223; Antonia Gransden, *Historical Writing in England c. 550 to c. 1307*, London 1974, 212.

[27] Oxford, Bodleian Library, ms. Bodley 851; M. R. James *et al.*, edd. & transl., *Walter Map De Nugis Curialium, Courtiers' Trifles*, Oxford 1983, xlv-xlix; Thomas Wright, ed., *Gualteri Mapes De Nugis Curialium*, London 1850.

Peterborough from the chronicle of Hugh Candidus (d. *c.* 1175) which was partly derived from it.[28] Likewise, at Ely he neglected *Liber Eliensis*, a collection of hagiography, charters and local annals recognised as a valuable source for the Anglo-Norman period, and merely made notes from the text known as *Chronicon Abbatum et Episcoporum Eliensium*, which is an abbreviated version of the middle book of the original *Liber Eliensis*.[29] The fact that the quick lists of books which Leland made for most of the monastic libraries which he visited often exclude books known today as the most interesting products of those libraries has led to speculation that the monks hid their best books from him. It is perhaps more probable that he visited many monasteries only after other raiders or collectors had already had the pickings of their collections.[30] We are hampered in that the chronology of his journeys is not clear in detail, on account of the disordered state of his notes. This is a problem which reappears when one discusses what specific manuscripts (as opposed to works) Leland may have seen and rescued from destruction.

From Leland's notes and book-lists we can often identify surviving books with manuscripts which he saw, but that any manuscript actually passed through his ownership can be ascertained only by indirect evidence, although we know that he took many for the Royal Library and others for himself and that this was an important aspect of his work.[31] Most of the evidence for what Leland owned comes from John Bale's *Index Britanniae Scriptorum*, a notebook, not published in his lifetime, containing a list of authors and their works annotated with the sources of Bale's knowledge of them; 176 works bear the comment 'from the library of John Leland'.[32] But these notes were made in Leland's lifetime, and what happened to individual manuscripts in his collection after his death is far from clear. Years later, in 1560, when Bale had come back from exile on the Continent, he wrote a letter to Archbishop Matthew Parker, encouraging him to try to recover historical manuscripts, and giving a list of those works whose whereabouts he knew.[33] Leland's executor had been Sir John Cheke, who had himself died; the latter's executors had only a few of the works which Leland had once owned.[34] Bale's letter is nevertheless useful as an illustration of the direct line of descent of Leland's initiative through

---

[28] Hearne, ed., *Collectanea*, i, 2–18; on Hugh see Thomas Duffus Hardy, *Descriptive Catalogue of Materials Relating to the History of Great Britain and Ireland*, 3 vols in 4, RS xxvi, 1862–71, ii, 412–13; F. Liebermann, 'Über ostenglische Geschichtsquellen des 12., 13., 14. Jahrhunderts, besonders den falschen Ingulf', *Neues Archiv der Gesellschaft für ältere deutsche Geschichtskunde* xviii, 1892/3, 225–67, at 227–32.

[29] Hearne, ed., *Collectanea*, ii, 588–610; E. C. Blake, 'The *Historia Eliensis* as a source for twelfth-century history', *Bulletin of the John Rylands Library* xli, 1958/9, 304–27, at 306 and n. 5.

[30] C. E. Wright, 'The dispersal of the monastic libraries and the beginning of Anglo-Saxon studies. Matthew Parker and his circle: a preliminary study', *Trans. of the Cambridge Bibliographical Society* i, 1949–53, 208–37, at 216–17; N. R. Ker, *Medieval Libraries of Great Britain. A List of Surviving Books*, 2nd edn, London 1964, xi–xii.

[31] Ker, *Medieval Libraries*, xi–xiii; Carley, 'John Leland and the contents of English pre-Dissolution libraries', 108. Annotations in Leland's hand have made it possible to identify some manuscripts which he owned: see Daniel J. Sheerin, 'John Leland and Milred of Worcester', *Manuscripta* xxi, 1977, 172–80.

[32] Reginald Lane Poole & Mary Bateson, edd., *Index Britanniae Scriptorum quos ex variis bibliothecis non parvo labore collegit Ioannes Baleus cum aliis*, Oxford 1902.

[33] Luard, 'A letter'.

[34] McKisack, *Medieval History*, 6–7.

Bale to Archbishop Parker, who planned a national effort to gather historical evidence and solicited Bale's advice for the project. Parker finally got royal support for his historical work in 1568, and began to collect his famous library of manuscripts (now in Corpus Christi College, Cambridge) and to publish some of the sources which Leland had discovered and written of in the *Commentarii*. But he did not immediately publish any Anglo-Norman works, although in the case of some of the texts which he did publish (notably Asser's Life of King Alfred) it was clearly Leland's research which had led him to them.[35] The Anglo-Norman histories found their first publishers in the 1590s among the scholars of the other principal line of descent from Leland, passing through John Stow and William Camden to the Elizabethan Society of Antiquaries. Among members of this circle, Lord William Howard first published the Worcester world-chronicle in 1592, Henry Savile the works of William of Malmesbury and Henry of Huntingdon in 1596 and Camden himself the *Gesta Normannorum* of William of Jumièges in 1603.[36] These men were themselves collectors of manuscripts: Savile, for instance, owned two of the manuscripts which he used for his edition of Henry of Huntingdon.[37] The similarity of the Elizabethan antiquaries to Leland lay more in their interest in origins, physical remains of the past, and place-names; it cannot be shown that their work on Anglo-Norman history was indebted to Leland's research and manuscript-discoveries.

Looking at Leland's involvement with some individual Anglo-Norman authors will give the best idea of some of the problems in tracing his part in their text-history. In the case of the greatest Anglo-Norman historian, William of Malmesbury, Leland can hardly be said to have played a major part in preserving his works for posterity. When one tries to trace which manuscripts of the works he used, the results are dismal. His book-lists reveal that he saw manuscripts of *De Gestis Regum* in five different places (St Paul's and the Austin friary in London, and at Faversham, Kirkham and Glastonbury); not one of these can be identified with any of the thirty-two manuscripts which survive, nor has anyone traced the copy of the *De Gestis Regum* and *Historia Novella* which we know (thanks to Bale) that Leland owned.[38] By comparing the copious extracts Leland made from the work with all the surviving manuscripts one might reach a solution, but the results would be of only limited interest, since William was evidently never in danger of being forgotten.[39] The real importance of Leland's work on William of Malmesbury is that he alerts us to the existence of lost works by the author, the Lives of Saints

[35] Wright, 'The dispersal', 220; Simon Keynes & Michael Lapidge, transl., *Alfred the Great. Asser's Life of King Alfred and Other Contemporary Sources*, Harmondsworth 1983, 223.
[36] William Howard, ed., *Chronicon ex Chronicis, ab initio mundi usque ad annum Domini 1118 deductum auctore Florentio Wigorniensi monacho . . .*, London 1592; Henry Savile, ed., *Rerum Anglicanum scriptores post Bedam praecipui*, London 1596; William Camden, ed., *Anglica, Normannica, Hibernica, Cambrica a ueteribus scripta, ex bibliotheca G. C.*, Frankfurt 1603. On the editors and the Society of Antiquaries see McKisack, *Medieval History*, 61–5 and 155–69.
[37] Diana Greenway, 'Henry of Huntingdon and the manuscripts of his *Historia Anglorum*', *ante* ix, 1986, 103–26 at 103 n. 1.
[38] Hearne, ed., *Collectanea*, iv, 47, 54, 6, 36, 153; *De gestis regum*, i, lxvi–xci; Poole & Bateson, edd., *Index*, 136.
[39] The extracts are at *Collectanea* i, 136–50; iii, 234–43; Hall, ed., *Commentarii*, i, 89.

Patrick, Indract and Benignus, extant at Glastonbury before the Dissolution.[40] Leland took enough notes from them to give a fair idea of their content, but was unable to rescue the manuscripts because of the timing of his visits, which we can for once deduce from his notes. The first time he went to Glastonbury, before 1539, the monastery was running normally; by the time he visited it again it had been dissolved and was partly in ruins.[41] This clearly illustrates the limitations of his work.

Of the *Historia Anglorum* by Henry of Huntingdon a little more can be said. Leland saw a copy of it in the Dominican priory of Lincoln, a copy which is later found in the Royal Library (British Library ms. Royal 13.B.vi). It is reasonable to assume that Leland took it for the King's collection. He may have taken another copy for himself from elsewhere, for Bale's *Index* states that he owned one and in 1560 Bale's letter to Matthew Parker included the information that a copy of Henry of Huntingdon was with Sir John Cheke's executors. The copy from which Leland took notes in his *Collectanea* was, so he stated, from Southwick, and can now be identified (thanks to an *ex-libris*) as British Library ms. Arundel 48. If this was the one which Leland owned, it must have passed from Cheke to Thomas, Earl of Arundel (1592–1646), one of the most noted private manuscript-collectors of his time – by what intermediate stages we do not know.[42] A further Henry of Huntingdon manuscript noted by Leland was at the Carmelite convent of Lincoln and is now British Library ms. Egerton 3668. However, manuscripts seen by him at Clare College, Cambridge, and at Eynsham cannot now be identified, while many surviving ones with well-established early provenances were never noted by him.[43]

In the case of some rarer, less popular historical works, Leland's rôle was more important. One was the *Historia Regum* attributed to Simeon of Durham, a work neglected from the twelfth century to the sixteenth, which survives in full in a single manuscript, now Cambridge, Corpus Christi College, 139, from Sawley, Yorkshire. The sixteenth-century history of this manuscript, which also contains works by Stephen of York, Thurstan of Fountains, Ailred of Rievaulx, John of Hexham and the so-called 'Nennius', indicates how complex the process of rescue could be.[44] Leland's notes from it show that it had come into the possession of Thomas Soulemont (d. 1541), an antiquary and the French-speaking secretary of Henry VIII. Leland borrowed it, took notes from the texts and wrote biographies of 'Nennius', Stephen of York and Simeon of Durham for his *Commentarii* on the basis of his notes.[45] Later,

---

[40] Hearne, ed., *Collectanea*, iii, 273–6; Hall, ed., *Commentarii*, i, 196; Carley, 'John Leland and the contents of English pre-Dissolution libraries', 119.

[41] Carley, 'John Leland and the contents of English pre-Dissolution libraries', 110; E. H. Bates, 'Leland in Somersetshire, 1540–1542', *Proceedings of the Somersetshire Archaeological and Natural History Society* xxxiii, 1887, 60–136.

[42] J. R. Liddell, ' "Leland's" lists of manuscripts in Lincolnshire monasteries', *EHR* liv, 1939, 88–95, at 90; Poole & Bateson, edd., *Index*, 166; Luard, 'A letter', 166; Ker, *Medieval Libraries*, 119, 181; J. Forshall, *Catalogue of the Manuscripts in the British Museum, ns, i, Part I, The Arundel Manuscripts*, London 1834, i–ii.

[43] On the manuscripts see Greenway, 'Henry of Huntingdon', 122–5.

[44] David N. Dumville, 'The sixteenth-century history of two Cambridge books from Sawley', *Trans. of the Cambridge Bibliographical Society* vii, 1977–80, 427–44.

[45] Hearne, ed., *Collectanea*, iii, 347–68 and 45; Hall, ed., *Commentarii*, i, 74–5. On Soulemont see *Dictionary of National Biography, s.v.*

between 1559 and 1567, Archbishop Parker's Latin Secretary, John Joscelyne, wrote a memorandum on who was known to own various historical works.[46] The Sawley manuscript (identifiable by the unique series of works which it contains) was said to belong to Parker, having been acquired from Nicholas Wotton, dean of Canterbury (d. 1567) and from a prebendary of Westminster called Pekyns (d. 1554). After passing through the hands of these joint or successive owners, the manuscript ended safely in Parker's bequest of manuscripts to Corpus Christi College. Leland, without even owning the manuscript, had put Simeon on the scholarly agenda by his laudatory biography of him in the *Commentarii*, reproduced by Bale and quoted in full in the first edition of Simeon in 1652. Leland's strictures on Roger Howden for reproducing Simeon's work without acknowledgment were also repeated in later works, including the Rolls Series edition of Roger.[47]

More immediately valued by sixteenth-century scholars for controversial purposes were two other works in whose transmission Leland was involved, Eadmer's *Historia Novorum* and the collected letters of Lanfranc. Only two mediaeval manuscripts of the Eadmer work survive, both early, one from Christ Church, Canterbury, and the other from Haughmond Abbey in Shropshire.[48] Leland stated in the *Commentarii* that he had seen the work at Haughmond. Bale's *Index* cites the *Historia* 'from the library of John Leland', implying that Leland had actually acquired a copy.[49] But it is difficult to join up these references with the next indications of work on Eadmer, by Matthew Parker and his circle. In 1567 Parker asked Nicholas Robinson, bishop of Bangor, for a transcript of the *Historia* from a manuscript available in his diocese. This might be assumed to refer to the Haughmond manuscript, still *in situ*, of which Parker may have learned through Leland's resumé. The Christ Church manuscript also had a known owner in 1567: one Henry Johns of Cambridge, from whom Parker borrowed and eventually bought it. Nothing more is known of Johns, or of whether his manuscript was formerly owned by Leland.[50] The links are thus not clear, but there are some grounds for thinking that Leland had a share in preserving one or both manuscripts of Eadmer's full account of the political career of Anselm. The evidence concerning Lanfranc's letters is unfortunately even vaguer: a single reference in Bale's *Index* to the 'decretal letters' of Lanfranc being in Leland's library. If this meant the single surviving complete collection of Lanfranc's letters, from Canterbury (now BL ms. Cotton Nero A.vii), it would be a most important statement; unfortunately this is not certain.[51]

The local, composite and anonymous works which Leland found in monastic libraries are of course even more difficult to identify and trace to their later

[46] British Library ms. Cotton Nero C.iii, fos 208v–212v; printed in Thomas Hearne, ed., *Roberti de Avesbury Historia de Mirabilibus Edvardi III*, Oxford 1720, 269–98.

[47] Roger Twysden, *Historiae Anglicanae Scriptores X*, 2 vols, London 1652 (the foreword by John Selden quotes Leland at i–ii); William Stubbs, ed., *Chronica Magistri Rogeri de Houedene*, 4 vols, RS li, 1868–71, i, xxvi.

[48] Eadmer, ix–x. The manuscripts are now respectively, Cambridge, Corpus Christi College, ms. 452, and BL Cotton ms. Titus A. ix.

[49] Hall, ed., *Commentarii*, i, 180; Poole & Bateson, edd., *Index*, 64.

[50] Eadmer, xii–xv.

[51] Poole & Bateson, edd., *Index*, 279; on the manuscripts of Lanfranc's letters see *Lanfranc's Letters*, 15–25.

owners. He made excerpts from large numbers of local chronicles, saints' lives and cartularies, noting material relevant to his main interests, the history of the landscape, of learning, and of the nobility. Many of the sources are unidentified and of historical value only for the later Middle Ages, but one may single out a chronicle compiled at Durham by Prior John Wessington between 1416 and 1446, containing a series of thirty charters from the pontificate of Ranulf Flambard which shed an interesting light on northern politics under Henry I. The summaries of the charters made by Leland were the most accessible (and the only printed) version of them until H. H. E. Craster published them in 1930.[52] Craster was of the opinion that Leland's notes were taken from at least two of the three manuscripts of the chronicle which now exist, and that he may have owned the one now in the Bodleian Library.[53] This last proposition is doubtful, since the only evidence is that the manuscript was later owned and annotated by both John Stow and John Dee, who each obtained a number of Lelandian manuscripts. But that Leland saw the manuscript is clear.

On occasion Leland made notes from monastic cartularies extensive enough to enable one to identify the manuscript in question – for instance the fourteenth-century Ramsey cartulary in the PRO, the late-thirteenth-century Barnwell *Liber Memorialis* (BL ms. Harley 3601) and either the *Registrum Album* (BL ms. Add. 14847) or a closely similar cartulary, Cambridge, University Library, ms. Ff.2.33 (s.n. 1200) (*c*. 1300), from Bury St Edmunds.[54] All these contained series of notes of Anglo-Norman royal charters, partly reproduced by Leland. However, Leland's main concentration of material from charters is more difficult – if not impossible – to trace to its various sources. This is a large section of his *Collectanea* devoted to a list of English and Welsh religious houses, giving the names of their founders, in most cases some of the witnesses to the founding charter, and sometimes other information from charters, the arms of the monastery and, finally, comments by Leland himself.[55] Much of the material naturally relates to the Anglo-Norman age. It is clear that Leland intended it as raw material for his planned book on the British nobility. He always singles out the lay witnesses to the charters and makes comments on their relationships, tenure of office and similar matters. Strangely, although most of the religious houses in the country are covered, the information recorded is so laconic and highly selective that he could scarcely have made much use of it. It is also too brief for specific sources to be identified. From the *Itinerary* one may see that Leland visited or at least passed most of the houses on his list, but often oral information or commemorative tablets rather than actual muniments would have been enough to give him the information which he recorded. The tantalising possibility of

[52] H. H. E. Craster, 'A contemporary record of the pontificate of Ranulf Flambard', *Archaeologia Aeliana* 4th ser. vii, 1930, 41–50.

[53] H. H. E. Craster, 'The Red Book of Durham', *EHR* xl, 1925, 504–32, at 510–14.

[54] Hearne, ed., *Collectanea*, ii, 580–8; William Henry Hart, ed., *Cartularium Monasterii de Rameseia*, 3 vols, RS lxxix, 1884–93; *Collectanea*, ii, 433–7, iii, 324–6; John Willis Clark, ed., *Liber Memorandorum Ecclesiae de Bernewelle*, Cambridge 1907; *Collectanea*, i, 223–6; D. C. Douglas, *Feudal Documents from the Abbey of Bury St Edmunds*, London 1932, nos 63, 67, 75, 173.

[55] Hearne, ed., *Collectanea*, i, 25–123.

derivation from now lost manuscripts is present and deserves to be fully investigated, but unfortunately the independent pieces of information in Leland are too vague and limited to allow much historical argument to be built on them. One example is his note on St Petroc's priory at Bodmin in Cornwall. He heads it: 'These following things are copied from ancient charters of donations.' What immediately follows is a patently legendary account of the founding of the priory by St Petroc and its refounding by King Æthelstan, but then there is a note on how, at the Norman Conquest, the priory was robbed of its possessions by the count of Mortain and restored by Bishop William Warlewast of Exeter and by Algar, dean of Coutances.[56] No identifiable mediaeval source for this information now exists, but the rôle of Robert of Mortain seems to be confirmed by the entry in Domesday Book stating that he held land formerly belonging to St Petroc; and a late mediaeval source, William of Worcester's *Itinerary* of 1478–80 (which Leland did not know), tells the same story, making it seem probable that a genuine local source did exist.[57] Yet the information is no more than a footnote to local history.

Despite its inadequacies, Leland's list of monasteries was very influential in that it inspired the detailed study of monastic records which led to the production of the *Monasticon Anglicanum* in 1655–73. Leland's notes were available to John Speed, author of a *History of Great Britain* published in 1611, who included at the end of his account of Henry VIII a list of monasteries and their founders for which Leland was the main source. Tanner's *Notitia Monastica* of 1695 built further onto Leland's nucleus, while the definitive *Monasticon* by Roger Dodsworth and William Dugdale made use of quantities of original records but still fell back on Leland's *Collectanea* for its texts of many documents for which manuscripts were available, including some Bury St Edmunds charters and even excerpts from the *Narratio de Standardo* by Ailred of Rievaulx.[58]

An intriguing subject which deserves further investigation is the relationship between Leland's work and that of the heralds, whose task it was to check that the nobility were correct in their use of arms and titles, and who carried out visitations to this end which began to be fully recorded in 1530. During the sixteenth century the records gradually came to include fuller genealogies, and charter-evidence preserved by the monasteries began to be used to verify them.[59] This development was very much in line with Leland's interests; one of his poems shows that he was acquainted with Thomas Wriothesley, who headed the College of Arms in 1530; and the record of the visitation of the northern counties in that year includes accounts of the foundation and arms of

---

[56] Hearne, ed., *Collectanea*, i, 75–6; see also Toulmin Smith, ed., *The Itinerary*, i, 175, 180; Hall, ed., *Commentarii*, i, 62.

[57] *Domesday Book*, i, 121b; Charles Henderson, *Essays in Cornish History*, edd. A. L. Rowse & M. I. Henderson, Oxford 1935, 219–22; John H. Harvey, ed. & transl., *William Worcestre Itineraries*, Oxford 1969, 86–7.

[58] *Monasticon*, iii, 139–40; vi, 209. On the line of descent of Leland's monastic material see David Knowles & R. Neville Hadcock, *Medieval Religious Houses, England and Wales*, 2nd edn, London 1971, 1–3.

[59] Anthony Richard Wagner, *Heralds and Heraldry in the Middle Ages. An Inquiry Into the Growth of the Armorial Functions of Heralds*, London 1939, 101.

a number of monasteries, which overlap with Leland's list of monasteries in the *Collectanea*.[60] If, as this implies, Leland was co-operating with the heralds, we must rate his originality lower or – perhaps – his influence higher than before. But heraldry has perhaps been underrated as an occupation which inspired genuine historical work. William Camden, who fulfilled the scheme of Leland's *Itinerary* in his *Britannia* of 1586, and William Dugdale, of the *Monasticon*, were both Kings of Arms as well as antiquaries.[61]

To sum up the discussion of Leland's part in the increased availability of the sources for Anglo-Norman history, one can say that, as far as the rescue of individual manuscripts went, his work was of limited effect. His own manuscripts were scattered on his death and it took Matthew Parker's initiative of 1568 (backed by the Crown) to begin to co-ordinate the work of individual collectors in preserving source-material. It was more indefinably, as an inspiration and a guide, that Leland's work was vital. He produced reference-lists of sources and of monasteries which gave his followers a good foundation to build on; he introduced the idea of a national history which would be the sum of local histories, and thus potentially brought a great deal more varied source-material than ever before within the historian's domain. The follower who most resembled him was John Stow of London, a spare-time historian who acquired some of Leland's papers and collected a great deal more manuscript-evidence in order to produce the kind of history which Leland himself might have written – in *The Chronicles of England*, of 1580, a book crammed with badly co-ordinated data but scrupulously referenced to an impressive number of authorities, including many cartularies and local chronicles. Of course, this kind of work was not yet recognised as history; it was chronicling or antiquarianism. In true history some principle of selection and co-ordination had to be applied. But in going on to discuss some of the principles which informed historiography of the Anglo-Norman period in the sixteenth century, it hardly needs saying that the gathering of fresh material by people like Leland and Stow was a precondition of advances in historical thought.

Cumulatively, the events of 1485 to 1557 were historiographically comparable to the Norman Conquest. For the first time since the twelfth century, historians were conscious of being present at the beginning of a new era, and this led to a new periodisation and new interpretations for practically the first time since William of Malmesbury. William, from the vantage point of the 1120s, had seen the Norman Conquest as a judgment on the English for their crass materialism and corruption; the Normans themselves, fierce, treacherous and ambitious, acted as the scourge of God. However, in time, God's anger abated and this was signalled by the Battle of Tinchebrai in 1106: 'it was doubtless by (God's) provident judgment . . . that Normandy should be subjected to England on the same day as the Norman army had come to subject her' forty years before.[62] The last word in William's history and the implication of the works of his near-contemporaries Gaimar and Geoffrey of

---

[60] James P. Carley, 'John Leland in Paris: the evidence of his poetry', *Studies in Philology* lxxxiii, 1986, 1–50 at 29–34; British Library ms. Harley 1499, fos 43–82.
[61] Walter H. Godfrey *et al.*, *The College of Arms*, London 1963, 85–6, 54–5.
[62] *De gestis regum*, ii, 198.

Monmouth was that the Normans were now integrated into the island's British and English past. Essentially, there was no further thought on the meaning of the Norman Conquest or on how it fitted into a long-term pattern in British history until the late fifteenth century and the arrival in power of the Tudor dynasty. The interpretations which arose then did not contradict the moral view (which has persisted at least subliminally to the present day), but added new ideas alongside it. Soon after 1485, John Rous expressed a belief that a turning-point had been reached with the accession of Henry VII. He interpreted the period since the Norman Conquest as one of territorial expansion for the English crown followed by decline, and he hoped that Henry would vindicate all his predecessors' claims just as his ancestry consolidated them.[63] This was propaganda, but it did suggest a new historical construction. Later, during the Reformation and through into Elizabeth's reign, the Protestant reformers, led in this matter by John Bale, propounded a historical view of the whole period since the apostolic era as a gradual decline from pure religion; the year 1000 marked the beginning of the reign of the Beast of the Apocalypse and an acceleration in the decline, and the Norman Conquest was a turning-point, since with it there began the direct intervention of the papacy (or Antichrist) in British affairs.[64] At the end of the sixteenth century, with threats of rebellion or invasion by Catholic powers receding and the powers of the Crown increasing, the emphasis in interpretation shifted from a religious to a legal and constitutional one. Now there began the great debate as to the legal consequences of the Norman Conquest – whether or not it represented a fundamental interruption in the 'immemorial' common law by which the English believed themselves to be ruled.[65] One construction of mediaeval history saw English constitutional 'liberty' taken away by the Conqueror to be gained back after a long struggle with King John and definitively confirmed by Henry III.[66] Thus interpretations shifted, but at almost any point during this century of violent change those scholars who were not actively trying to destroy the past were aware of its irrevocability and were trying to preserve its traces in a way roughly comparable to William of Malmesbury's collecting and codifying of Anglo-Saxon history in the Anglo-Norman period.

By assisting in this task, Leland provided material for the new religious and legal interpretations of the Anglo-Norman period rather than taking part in them himself. Now and then his writings provide a straw in the wind, occasional comments typifying or foreshadowing coming trends.

To take the religious interpretation first, an anti-clerical and anti-papal interpretation of mediaeval English history was being developed at least as early as the 1530s by William Tyndale and by those whose task it was to find precedents for Henry VIII's rejection of papal authority.[67] Leland, a fanatical royalist, took part in the process by writing an anti-papal dialogue entitled

---

[63] Hearne, ed., *Joannis Rossi Antiquarii Warwicensis Historia*, 218–19 and *passim*.

[64] Levy, *Tudor Historical Thought*, 89–92.

[65] A. J. Pocock, *The Ancient Constitution and the Feudal Law. A Study of English Historical Thought in the Seventeenth Century*, Cambridge 1957, 42–3; David Douglas, *The Norman Conquest and British Historians*, Glasgow 1946, *passim*.

[66] John Hayward, *The Lives of the III Normans, Kings of England*, London 1613, 100–2.

[67] Levy, *Tudor Historical Thought*, 78–84.

Antiphilarchia, which relied mainly on biblical arguments but brought in the historical viewpoint: 'The Normans', he wrote, 'many times refused the yoke of the Roman church as a violent constraint born out of tyranny'.[68] 'The story is well known', he continues, but in fact Tyndale and (later) Bale tell it with an emphasis quite different from his. To them, the only thing consistently characterised is the treachery and pride of the pope's representatives, such as Anselm and Becket, who headed a fifth column against their lawful rulers. The Anglo-Norman kings are foils to these villains and are presented in ambivalent terms. Bale approved William the Conqueror's refusal of fealty to Pope Gregory VII, but disapproved of his carrying out the Conquest with papal support, and used his illegitimate birth as a metaphor for this.[69] Oddly, considering their low opinion of monks, both Bale and John Foxe (in his *Acts and Monuments* of 1563) censured the Norman kings for sales of benefices and exactions from the Church.[70] Theirs is a church-centred view; one receives the impression that Leland's, if he had fully expressed it, would have been much more king-centred. Among notes of his on a Life of Thomas Becket he comments: 'King William, who conquered England, knew how to control his clergy: his brother Odo and Stigand, archbishop of Canterbury, are examples'. In another place he draws a hand pointing to the information in Matthew of Westminster's *Flores Historiarum* that Henry II sided with Emperor Frederick against Pope Alexander and had all adults in England abjure the pope's authority.[71] Leland knew that his kings were heroes; it was the monks about whom he found it hard to decide, giving neutral references in his *Commentarii* even to the reformers' *bête noire*, Anselm.[72] Leland valued every man of learning, but in his neutrality on this point he was being overtaken by events even as he wrote.

Bale's *Acts of the English Votaries* was an anecdotal polemic rather than history; Foxe's *Acts and Monuments*, as far as Anglo-Norman history was concerned, was a standard chronicle with pieces of anti-papal explication added here and there. It was Matthew Parker who first developed a really systematic argument, based on historical sources, against Roman Catholicism, in his *De Antiquitate Britannicae Ecclesiae*.[73] For his Anglo-Norman section he relied on Eadmer and the correspondence of Lanfranc and Anselm; as argued above, Leland may indirectly have provided him with the former. But by concentrating on the Anglo-Saxon period and idealising it as a time when English religion was pure compared to that of the Continent, Parker was implicitly voting against the Norman Conquest itself and feeding a developing pro-Saxon, anti-Norman strain in English historiography which would have been foreign to Leland.[74]

---

[68] Cambridge University Library ms. Ee.5. 14, s.c. 1068, p. 341.
[69] Bale, *Catalogus*, i, 166–7; idem, *The First Two Parts of the Acts or Unchast Examples of the English Votaryes*, London 1551, part 2, fo. xxv.
[70] Bale, *Catalogus*, i, 166–7; Josiah Pratt, ed., *The Acts and Monuments of John Foxe*, 8 vols, London 1877, ii, 140–1, 154.
[71] Hearne, ed., *Collectanea*, iii, 425, 385 (translation mine).
[72] Hall, ed., *Commentarii*, i, 178–80.
[73] Matthew Parker, *De antiquitate Britannicae ecclesie et priuilegiis ecclesiae Cantuariensis cum archiepiscopis eiusdem 70*, London 1572.
[74] Levy, *Tudor Historical Thought*, 114–23; Douglas, *The Norman Conquest*, 15–16.

Tending to add to this was the legal interpretation of the Norman Conquest which was beginning tentatively in the sixteenth century with Polydore Vergil, who was perhaps the first in modern times to allege that the Normans imported a legal system which was fundamentally unjust and irrational as well as harsh, since it was in a language which the people could not understand.[75] Little as he liked Polydore, Leland seems to have agreed with this view, to judge from an aside in his *Commentarii* to the effect that the Normans were eventually induced to make their laws 'less tyrannical' by the admixture of old Anglo-Saxon law (which, Leland thought, was itself derived from pre-Saxon British law).[76] Complaints of the oppressiveness of Norman law of course went right back to the Anglo-Saxon Chronicle, but it was not until the end of the sixteenth century that it was argued about rather than complained of. Leland contributed nothing directly to the debate, but did help to create the required conditions for it by bringing more source-materials and documentary evidence into the historical field. By the early seventeenth century Sir Henry Spelman, the pioneering legal historian, was using monastic charters as well as public records and chronicles to discuss how the Norman Conquest had changed the nature of land tenure in England, and the forms of English government in general.[77] It was in the field of law that the concept of past society as an organic unity, which differed fundamentally and irretrievably from the present, was first developed.

It would be nonsensical to assign to Leland a real causal rôle in this. Printing, Renaissance cultural aspirations, and the new techniques of Tudor government had created a new breed of secular political theorist who would have sought out the records, however easy or difficult they were to find, and drawn the conclusions. The processes in which Leland was involved had by now left him far behind, and this was a kind of study of the past which he would not have envisaged.

Study of the past had increased greatly in pace over the sixteenth century but was still an aspect of many disciplines rather than a pursuit in itself. 'History' proper was still a literary form with limited subject-matter, designed to teach morality or, more recently, political wisdom. Chronicling was a popular pursuit designed to fill a gap in people's minds with indiscriminate information about the past.[78] The history of religion was for theological controversy, while the history of law and the constitution assisted in the working-out of contemporary political questions. Antiquarianism, meanwhile, was supposed to provide a past aspect for all things present: it was the antiquary who sought for the greatest breadth and quantity of information, but not the greatest depth, since he took an itemising approach rather than a narrative or argumentative one, asking little of his sources but that they should exist.

[75] Vergil, *Anglica Historia*, 1570 edn, 154–5.
[76] Hall, ed., *Commentarii*, i, 13.
[77] Henry Spelman, 'The original, growth, propagation and condition of feuds and tenures by knight-service, in England', 'Of the ancient government of England', 'Of parliaments', in *Reliquiae Spelmannianae. The Posthumous Works of Sir Henry Spelman Kt. Relating to the Laws and Antiquities of England*, ed. Edmund Gibson, Oxford 1698, 1–48, 49–56, 57–66.
[78] Levy, *Tudor Historical Thought*, 167–285 *passim*.

Since the sixteenth century the different branches of historical study have only slowly come together. The universal, indiscriminate interest in the past which characterises antiquarianism is usually contrasted with the attitude of the true historian, who seeks to impose constantly renewed and revised patterns on the past. The mantle of the 'real historian' has tended to fall on the legal and constitutional historian since his brilliant seventeenth-century début, especially in Anglo-Norman studies. The central current of the ever-new interest in this period has been in the evolution of government and its legitimacy, at first producing ideas strongly coloured by the political situation of the historian's own time and even seeking to affect it. Recently historians have become more detached, but are still fascinated, in a bureaucratic world, by the beginnings of bureaucracy.

Now, however, it seems that we may be taking part in a new merger of 'antiquarianism' and history, as historians make new efforts to use the totality of available information and impose order on it by new techniques. To paraphrase some comments made by Professor Warren Hollister in 1982, we have moved by stages away from a generalised constitutional history seen in terms of king against barons and central government against traditional liberties; we have moved through a more individualised history concentrating on specimen cases, to the method whereby every individual case is valued for the light it can shed on the whole, and statistical techniques help to give structure to the results.[79] A new awareness of the diversity of the nation makes local history vital; genealogy regains its importance as it is recognised that family ties among the aristocracy often played a veiled but vital part in political manoeuvres. Charter-attestations in obscure cartularies are vital for establishing nobles' relationships with the king at various times, as well as with their local church. The generalisations inherited from a legal tradition have been broken through by new patterns. As for the material side of antiquarianism, Leland's tentative suggestions in the *Itinerary* on the date of Ripon Cathedral, or his attempts to find the vestiges of the Empress Matilda's castle at Faringdon, have developed into a scientific discipline.[80] It may be stretching a point to claim this generation's progress in Anglo-Norman history as a revival of Leland's antiquarianism and undifferentiated enthusiasm for the past, but I imagine that although Leland might not have understood all that is going on, he would surely have liked it.

[79] C. Warren Hollister, 'Recent trends in Anglo-Norman scholarship: the new political history', *Albion* xiv, 1982, 254–7.
[80] *Itinerary*, i, 80–1, 126.

THE GROWTH OF CASTLE STUDIES IN ENGLAND AND ON THE CONTINENT SINCE 1850*

Joan Counihan

Now that the study of castles – or *castellogie* – has become a respectable and established subject in its own right, it is difficult to imagine how little it was so regarded in the early part of the nineteenth century. Then detailed studies of castles were scarce, or covered in a chapter or two, perhaps, in large volumes devoted to mediaeval architecture generally. In spite of the work of many enthusiastic and energetic antiquarians in the eighteenth and early nineteenth centuries, the whole business of antiquities was in something of a muddle. A great deal was written about a great number of interesting objects or places by, very frequently, gentlemen of means and leisure but with not an enormous amount of background knowledge of their subject. So, as we shall see later, much of what they had written fell into disrepute and gave the study of antiquities a bad name. But however ridiculous the conclusions they may have come to in many instances – they had one good point in common. Many of them drew beautifully. Whatever they may have *said* about the hundreds of ivy-clad ruins which caught their eyes, at least they have passed down to us very useful images of how ancient ruins looked more than two hundred years ago. We have only to look at those 1737 prints of castles, abbeys and stately homes by Samuel and Nathaniel Buck, still on sale in souvenir shops, to notice how lovingly the architectural detail is recorded. Then between 1799 and 1805, Edward King produced his *Munimenta Antiqua or Observations on Antient Castles* in four massive volumes.[1]

Though King, who was born about 1735 and died in 1807, was working before the time-limit of this paper, his influence must have been considerable in the years following his death. His books are enormous in size and beautiful in presentation. They are packed with learned material in Greek and Latin and full of detailed drawings, and he devoted the whole of volume three to Norman and Saxon buildings of all kinds. Even in his day, though it was recognised that much of what he wrote was full of factual mistakes, his drawings and plans were invaluable to the architect and historian and have been valued as such ever since.

* I would like to thank Maylis Baylé for having given me the idea for this paper and for all her assistance in suggesting source material on De Caumont and others. I also have to thank Dr T. D. Barry of Trinity College, Dublin, for his help in enabling me to examine the Orpen correspondence on the Irish motte question at the National Library of Ireland. And lastly, my thanks to Mr Bernard Nurse, the Librarian of the Society of Antiquaries, London, for much practical assistance in my research.

[1] Edward King, *Munimenta Antiqua or Observations on Antient Castles* including remarks on the whole progress of Architecture, especially vol. III, London 1804.

It seems to me that the detailed study of castles is and always was of equal interest to the historian, the archaeologist and the architect and that an archaeological historian such as Mrs Armitage[2] was the ideal person to write about the subject. She had long discussions in print at the turn of the century about the origins of Norman castles in the British Isles and made frequent attacks on people, such as Clark in England and Westropp in Ireland whom she considered were not suitably qualified to make many of the assumptions they did make. She complained, for example, about Mr Westropp's lack 'of any reference to the Continental writers who have made a special study of these earth-works'.[3] (This was with reference to the dispute over Irish mottes, of which more later.) She based much of her method of study on various continental archaeologists and antiquarians and it was they, she considered, who were the pioneers in early earth-work and castle studies.

In a letter, written in 1911 to Goddard Orpen, the Irish historian, she comments: 'I am afraid the "great historical insight" with which you credit me is really due to Dr. Sophus Müller, the great Danish archaeologist, as I have acknowledged whenever I have quoted him. In his great work *Vor Oldtid* he has a chapter on the Danish earthworks, including mottes, which I have found most illuminating . . . It is fortunate that I am able to read Danish easily, as I have found Steenstrup's *Normannerna* of great help in determining the nature of Danish earthworks, although Steenstrup is not an archaeologist.'[4]

In tracing the growth of systematic, scientific and careful work on the study of earthworks and early castles which evolved bit by bit from the mass of antiquarian material published on the continent and in the British Isles from before 1850 and onwards, I have concentrated mainly on the French and Scandinavian sources Mrs Armitage used herself in her work. She did, it is true, consult several German writers but, for obvious reasons, I have had to draw the line somewhere and have concentrated on the authors she most quoted. There were two other Scandinavians, as well as the two mentioned above, who did much by their writings and their actions to organise anti-quarian material in a methodical manner. One of them, J. J. A. Worsaae (1821–85), travelled much over Europe as an archaeologist and remarked in his book, *Recollections*, published in 1858 that the Scandinavian countries had so well organised their museums at the beginning of the nineteenth century compared with the German, English, French and Southern European countries because the latter had their interests in archaeology absorbed by their numerous Roman monuments, while national monuments were neglected. He saw a connection between the early development of archaeology in Northern Europe and the fact that this region had not been included in Rome's sphere of influence.[5] This is borne out by the work of C. J. Thomsen (1788–1865) a Danish archaeologist and numismatist. He had a distinguished career as inspector of museums and it was he who promoted the Three Age System which was explained in his *Guide to Northern Archaeology* published in

---

[2] *Ante* viii, 1985.
[3] E. S. Armitage, *The Antiquary* xiii, 1906, 291.
[4] E. S. Armitage, letter to Goddard Orpen, 14 September 1911, in the possession of the National Library of Ireland, ms. 17784.
[5] Bo Gräsland, *The Birth of Prehistoric Chronology*, Cambridge University Press 1987, p. 15 (Gräsland's précis).

England in 1848. As Bo Gräsland writes in his book, *The Birth of Prehistoric Chronology*: 'The three main periods – Stone, Bronze and Iron Ages – is a chronological system – not now much used and which may to-day appear to be commonplace and self-evident. In actual fact it superseded a view which . . . was little better than total confusion.'[6] In fact Mr Gräsland summed up the work done in Scandinavian countries as playing: 'a predominant part in the process which transformed archaeology from the unsystematic collecting of curiosities into a leading science in cultural history.'[7]

As we have seen, the influence of Sophus Müller (1846–1934) and Japetus Steenstrup (1813–97) on the development of castle studies during the end of the nineteenth century was significant but good work was being done too in France earlier that century on mediaeval buildings – castles included. A surprising number of eminent French archaeologists and historians were born round about the start of the nineteenth century, many of whose works Mrs Armitage consulted in the preparation of her final book on castles. The one who stands out for industry and initiative is Arçisse de Caumont. He was born at Bayeux in 1802 and before Mrs Armitage (born 1841) was out of the nursery had begun writing a series of beautifully illustrated books on the *History of Art in the west of France up to the seventeenth century* (published in 1830) followed by *The History of Religious Architecture in the Middle Ages* (1841). Then from 1850 to 1862 he produced three volumes of his famous *Abécédaire ou Rudiment d'Archéologie* filled with his detailed drawings. The books are rather charmingly presented as catechisms, with questions and answers and intended 'for the teaching of that science in Colleges, Seminaries and Houses of Education of both sexes'.[8] Volume two contains his observations on civil and military architecture. Drawings of all our old friends are there – Le Plessis Grimoult; Falaise; Nogent-le-Rotrou; Château Gaillard; Langeais and Dover, to name but a few. I must mention here that the eagle-eyed Mrs Armitage, in discussing her visit to Fulk Nerra's Langeais in her own book, makes the remark: 'it somewhat shakes one's confidence in de Caumont's accuracy that in the sketch he gives of this keep he altogether omits this doorway.'[9] This doorway being one which she had seen with her own eyes on the first floor but is non-existent in de Caumont's sketch.

De Caumont groups his material on castles into five classes:
1. Fortresses constructed from the fifth to the eleventh century exclusively
2. *Châteaux-forts* of the eleventh and twelfth centuries
3. Those of the thirteenth century
4. Those of the fourteenth and fifteenth centuries
5. Those at the end of the fifteenth century and of the sixteenth[10]

But as well as travelling about Europe (including England) making sketches and observations to put into his books, he founded, at the comparatively tender age of twenty-one, the Société Française d'Archeologie and the Société des Antiquaires de Normandie. He died in 1873 very much mourned by his

---

[6] Bo Gräsland, *The Birth of Prehistoric Chronology*, p. 28.
[7] Bo Gräsland, *The Birth of Prehistoric Chronology*, p. 28.
[8] Arçisse de Caumont, *Abécédaire ou Rudiment d'Archéologie*, 3rd edition vol. 2, Caen 1869, title page.
[9] E. S. Armitage, *Early Norman Castles*, London 1912, note 3, p. 353.
[10] Arçisse de Caumont, 376.

colleagues. His place as Director of the Société des Antiquaires de Normandie was taken that year by François Guizot (1787–1874) a distinguished historian much consulted by Mrs Armitage. Then there was Viollet le Duc (1814–79). Whatever our feelings might be about the things he did in the process of restoring castles, there is no denying his industry. He produced from 1854 to 1869 in ten volumes his massive *Dictionnaire d'Architecture Française du XI au XVI siècles*, filled once more with detailed drawings of a high order. In fact many of his illustrations were used to good effect in Camille Enlart's lengthy *Manuel d'Archéologie Française* which came out in two parts in 1902 and 1904. These cover all aspects of French architecture from Merovingian times to the Renaissance. Though we in Great Britain might wonder when archaeology is called archaeology and when it is called architecture or the study of antiquities, in France there is far less distinction between these subjects. In part two of his *Manuel*, Enlart has a number of chapters on the origins of castles and their successive use over the centuries. In this book several of the castles are illustrated by photographs including an early photo of Fulk Nerra's keep at Langeais taken in 1900. He, like several of his French contemporaries, refers frequently to Edward King's *Munimenta Antiqua*. In his bibliography for the castle section of the *Manuel* he lists J. H. Round's article on the *Castles of the Conquest* and George Neilson's article on *Motes in Norman Scotland*,[11] both of these first-class according to Mrs Armitage. As she made many references to and comments on Enlart's work in her own book, there is no need for me to say more. But as it was published some years after Clark's *Medieval Military Architecture*, which is also listed in his bibliography, he must have been to some extent influenced by Clark's theories. In fact, Mrs Armitage, in a tart little foot-note *à propos* of the German author Köhler's book on English, French and German castles, says: 'No continental writers are entirely to be trusted about English castles; they generally get their information from Clark and it is generally wrong.'[12] Between the first half of the nineteenth century and its last decades, interest in earthworks and early castle-sites had decidedly been quickened; but there were still many years before *castellogie* became a subject as we now know it. At the beginning of the twentieth century there was much discussion about the exact meaning of terms; about the exact time of the arrival in this country of the first castle and about many things which we now take for granted. Mrs Armitage, for example, had much to say in her chapter on Anglo-Saxon fortifications about the meaning of the words *castel*, *castellum*, *burh*, *burgus* and *wic* etc.[13] The days of the enthusiastic but unscientific amateur were still there. It was usually only the comfortably-off who could afford to indulge in barrow-digging or follow antiquarian pursuits. One or two of these, such as General Pitt-Rivers, a landowner and retired army man, or George Neilson, procurator of police in Glasgow in 1891 but also a charter scholar and expert palaeographer, set about castle-studies and archaeology in a thoroughly scientific manner. Mrs Armitage certainly approved of them both.

[11] Camille Enlart, *Manuel d'Archéologie Française*, 2, Paris 1904, 560–1.
[12] Armitage, 358, note 4.
[13] Armitage, 24, 25 and Appendix D 383.

In 1895 she had started writing for the *Yorkshire Archaeological Journal* and corresponding with General Pitt-Rivers about his findings on his own Rivers estate. She reviewed his book on his excavations in Cranbourne Chase that year, and a few quotations from this article[14] summarise well her outlook on the subject of archaeology and how much in advance of her day was her thinking on the subject. For example, in writing of the General himself: 'Fortune is not often so kind as to place an ardent archaeologist in a district teeming with prehistoric remains, and to endow him with ample means and leisure for the task of exploration. But to these advantages General Pitt-Rivers unites others which are (as the French would say) quite otherwise important: a long training in minute observation; a unique experience in the excavation of earthworks; a military eye which sees points in the construction of a rampart which would be hidden from an ordinary observer; and above all a scientific mind which refuses to generalize without accurate data, and which will spare no pains to get the data accurate.' Then later on in the review she has one of her digs at the speculative archaeologist of her day: 'The third volume of General Pitt-Rivers' work contains an account of his excavations in Bokerly Dyke and the Wansdyke, the latter a famous earthwork, as long as the Roman Wall, stretching from Portishead on the Severn to Chisbury Camp in Wiltshire, the former a shorter length of earthwork, in the main parallel with the Wansdyke but further to the south. The late Dr. Guest, of whose great learning such scholars as Dr. Freeman and Mr J. R. Green always spoke with bated breath, thought he had determined the origin of these earthworks, which he called the "Belgic ditches". But the spade has little respect for great reputations. It has tossed Dr. Guest's theories into the air, for in the hands of General Pitt-Rivers it has conclusively proved that Bokerly Dyke was not earlier than the reign of Honorius, and Wansdyke, though the *terminus a quo* of its possible date is not so decisively fixed, is certainly Roman or post-Roman.' Then a final observation from her on the state of archaeology ninety years ago: '. . . the science is still in its infancy in England and it must be confessed that the infancy is a long one. How is it that a boy who collects butterflies or a girl who goes out with her botanical case, is supposed to be pursuing a scientific taste, while a man who cares for such things as earthworks and old stones is still generally regarded with a half-smile as a foolish though harmless trifler? . . . Surely the reason of this indifference is that the realm of archaeology has so long been the realm of guess-work, the happy hunting-ground of those who took little heed to observe, and not much to read the observations of others, but whose delight it was to sail paper-boats of theory over the ocean of the unknown. The instances above alluded to of Dr Guest and the Belgic ditches shows that even the rise of the new historic school was not accompanied with the rise of an archaeological school founded on exact observation.' She corresponded with Pitt-Rivers on and off until his death in 1900, meeting him at his museum at Farnham in June 1897, where she had gone on a visit accompanied by her daughter, Clarice. They exchanged books and pamphlets and he advised her about a piece of pottery she had found in

---

[14] E. S. Armitage, *Yorkshire Archaeological Journal* xiii, 1895, 35–43.

the ancient camp at Almondbury near Huddersfield, which she was glad to find he considered of Norman origin.[15]

George Neilson (1858–1923) in his article on the *Motes of Scotland* in the *Scottish Review* of 1898 did for Norman Scottish castles what Goddard Orpen (1852–1932) was doing for the origin of Irish Norman castles. The results of Orpen's research appeared in his book – *Ireland Under the Normans* (Oxford, Clarendon Press, 1911) – but for some years earlier he had joined forces with J. H. Round and Mrs Armitage in the fierce arguments which went on in the pages of various learned journals in 1904 to 1906. Mr T. Westropp, another of those comfortably-off prolific authors – a leading light in, and later to become President of, The Royal Society of Antiquaries of Ireland – was in the opposition. He was seconded by Mr T. Davis-Pryce of Nottingham and letters to the Editor of *The English Historical Review* flowed fast and furious. In fact the poor man, Mr R. L. Poole, got quite worn out with it all. It had stemmed from a long two-part article Mrs Armitage had written in *The English Historical Review* in 1904 on *The Early Norman Castles of England*, which was followed later by a paper by Orpen on *Mote and Bretashe Building in Ireland*.[16] Mrs Armitage's article and the arguments which followed it have already been discussed in my earlier paper (*ante* viii, 1985) but Orpen's paper on Irish mottes and Mrs Armitage's support for him stirred up a different kind of hornets' nest. She wrote a two-part article in *The Antiquary*, September 1906 on *The Norman Origin of Irish Mottes* containing a list of these mottes – which later appeared in her book in 1912. She and Orpen seem to have come to the same conclusions about the arrival of the first Norman mottes in Ireland though, as far as I know, they were working separately. The Norman invasion of Ireland coming a hundred years after the conquest of England puts the date of the building of the first Norman castles on a different time-scale. The country-side, too, was already covered with hillocks and raths which the Irish had looked upon as being exclusively Irish. Mrs Armitage understood their feelings: 'One can easily sympathise with the feelings of those who, having always looked upon these mottes as monuments of ancient Ireland, are loath to part with them to the Norman pirate.'[17] Behind the scenes Westropp had been writing to Orpen: 'I know of nothing done about the recording of ancient earthworks. Such a scheme is easy to carry out in Great Britain but in Ireland, even in a single Munster county (where forts swarm in every townland and the sites of hundreds, not only of levelled, but even of existing forts never appear, even on large scale maps) it seems a Herculean task. It would need a man in every parish. I am more and more borne down with the sense of our being mere beginners in nearly every branch of fieldwork in Ireland . . . If I could leave a complete survey for Limerick and Clare I would be more than content; but forts and dolmens seem to spring up like mushrooms even in places one fancied one had worked out – and as for the hills!!'[18] Then in obvious

---

[15] E. S. Armitage, letters to General Pitt-Rivers, in the possession of the Salisbury and South Wilts. museum.

[16] Goddard Orpen, *EHR* xxi, 1906, 417–444.

[17] E. S. Armitage, *The Antiquary* xlii, 1906, 333.

[18] T. J. Westropp, letter to Orpen, 14 May 1906, in the possession of the National Library of Ireland, ms. 17784.

exasperation over Mrs Armitage's latest article he writes: 'The exclusively Norman theory of motes entirely fails to account for the mote and bailey structures in Bosnia, Austria, Germany and the *Ohio valley* where even Mrs Armitage can scarcely postulate a Norman settlement.' He goes on: 'After studying the fields and records and finding the motes absent from so many sites of castles and early manors and so many of the latter without motes, the theory that the Normans used and adapted earlier motes and bailies (as they certainly did in the low forts) fits in with the facts. So far from excluding the making of motes and bailies by the Normans in Ireland I have always held it as true. I merely maintain that it is impossible to hold the *exclusive* theory and that *each* case rests on its merits.'[19] Finally a letter from R. L. Poole, editor of *The English Historical Review*, to Mr Orpen about the latter's offer of an article on the subject: 'Let me begin by a statement of what has already happened on the "motte" question. No sooner had Mrs Armitage's first article appeared than I was besieged by insistent letters from a Mr Davis Pryce of Nottingham, who seemed desirous of defending the Celtic races from the slur cast upon them by Mrs Armitage's aspertion that their boasted earthworks were merely Norman. Now I will confess that I am sorry that Mrs Armitage ventured upon this controversial field. She had not really worked it out, and in fact she only adduced the Celtic evidence (I think in a footnote) as corroboration of her general theory. But I am inclined to think it would have been better to let her argument stand upon the evidence she had fully examined. I say this quite irrespectively of the question whether on the Celtic evidence she was right or wrong. Mr Davies Pryce wrote to me, I suppose, a dozen or more times. I rejected one article from him, and finally accepted a short statement, to which by agreement a reply by Mrs Armitage was added, and lastly an "editorial" note reproducing the substance of Mr Pryce's rejoinder. With that the specific discussion was terminated . . . But unless I have misread the purport of your letter, your proposed article will not at all come within the forbidden lines. You proceed not from ground plans but from place-names;. and your primary argument is not archaeological but philological. I shall therefore be very grateful if you will be so good as to let me see your article. I have difficulty in dealing with the general subject, not only because I am not *ex professo* an archaeologist, but also because I am bound, editorially to "keep open mind". But I do not hesitate to confess to you that Mrs Armitage appears to me to have made out her case in principle, even though exceptions may have to be admitted. Her hypothesis that particular methods of fortification belong to particular stages in civilisation seems to harmonise with the evidence better than any other. So, personally, I am delighted that you should execute a flanking movement in her support.'[20]

An interesting letter to Orpen of about this time from A. G. Chater, Hon. Secretary of the Committee of Ancient Earthworks and Fortified Enclosures, raises a point about the use of the word 'motte': 'I think the spelling *motte* is more largely used in England and seems to be gathering ground, while *mote* is

---

[19] T. J. Westropp, letter to Orpen, 17 August 1906, in the possession of the National Library of Ireland, ms. 17784.
[20] R. L. Poole, letter to Orpen, 23 April 1906, in the possession of the National Library of Ireland, ms. 17790.

more general in Ireland and Scotland – no doubt by the use of the more modern French term it is intended to avoid confusion between m.o.t.e. and m.o.a.t; but either form must be more or less artificial as far as this country is concerned, since it does not appear that the peasantry, in all events the greater part of England, ever called this type of fortress "a mote". We almost always have the word *castle* attached to these works. Probably the committee's classification will continue to call them "moated mounds" in pursuance of the policy of using descriptive terms and avoiding theory.'[21]

During the following ten years or so, many of the participants in these paper battles died and the First World War interrupted lives and much archaeological work. It was during that war, in 1916, that John Murray, the publisher, saw fit to remainder Mrs Armitage's great book on castles and she was never given the opportunity to make the corrections she had already prepared for future editions. It was to be fifty-five years before Gregg International Publishers Limited brought out a long-overdue facsimile edition.

Gradually, though, public interest had been growing in the maintenance and excavation of old sites and buildings. Publication of the *Victoria County Histories* must have had, and still does have, influence in keeping research going. As we know, Mrs Armitage herself wrote a good chapter on the Yorkshire earthworks in *The Victoria History of the County of York* which was published in 1912. In time the Ancient Monuments Branch of what later became the Department of the Environment took over the care of a great number of castles and HMSO published very useful booklets on them. Allen Brown wrote several of these and was also part-author of *The History of the King's Works* (published 1963) along with Arnold Taylor, who had been responsible for the care of Welsh castles since 1946 and subsequently became Chief Inspector for Ancient Monuments until his retirement in 1972. Since then both Allen Brown and Arnold Taylor have published detailed and serious books on castles (as opposed to several coffee-table picture books which appeared from time to time) – Allen Brown's splendid *English Castles* (reprinted by Batsford in 1976) and Arnold Taylor's *Studies in Castles and Castle-Building* and *The Welsh Castles of Edward I* both brought out by the Hambledon Press in 1986. As well as these, Derek Renn's very useful *Norman Castles in Britain* was published in 1968, so that within the last twenty years books dealing exclusively with castles have supplemented the good work originally done by Mrs Armitage in *her* book on castles in 1912.

But there is one more step to record in the history of *castellogie* and that is the formation of the bi-annual Château Gaillard Conference, which concerns itself largely with the study of castles. Its formation in 1962 was almost accidental. A number of delegates, headed by Professor de Boüard of Caen, had been attending a conference at Les Andelys to mark the completion of the restoration and conservation of the castle of Château Gaillard. Before the final meeting broke up, it was suggested that the members should nominate a permanent committee and continue to meet every two years to have a conference on some aspects of *castellogie*. Since then, the Château Gaillard

---

[21] A. G. Chater, letter to Orpen, undated, in the possession of the National Library of Ireland, ms. 17790.

Conference has been held at a different place every two years with papers on every facet of castle-studies given during its sessions. In 1970, for example, Jean le Patourel gave a talk on *The Moated Sites of Yorkshire* and Grant Simpson with Bruce Webster spoke on *The Distribution of Mottes in Scotland* in which they confirmed the value of George Neilson's article on Scottish motes written seventy-two years before. 1974 saw Robin Glasscock's paper on *Mottes in Ireland* augmenting the work done by Orpen and Mrs Armitage in the early 1900s. In 1978 Robert Higham, in talking about *Early Castles in Devon*, reflected once more on the use of the words *motte* and *ringwork*. And so the study of and growth in knowledge of the history of castles expand from year to year. *Castellogie* itself is no longer the Cinderella among the scientific and archaeological subjects that it once was. Why then is it so important that the study of castles should be taken seriously? I let Allen Brown have the last word on this: 'Of all the buildings the castle is the most characteristic of the feudal Middle Ages by belonging uniquely to them, and thus affording those who seek it direct access to a past by no means wholly vanished and still with much to give.'[22]

[22] R. Allen Brown, *English Castles*, London 1976, 224.

THE LOGISTICS OF FORTIFIED BRIDGE BUILDING ON THE SEINE UNDER CHARLES THE BALD

Carroll Gillmor

The Frankish military response to the Northmen under Charles the Bald consisted primarily of fortified bridge construction to inderdict the passage of Norse ships on the fluvial systems of West Francia. Previous scholars, namely Ferdinand Lot and Fernand Vercauteren, provided chronological narratives of this process,[1] while Kurt Ulrich Jäschke undertook a three-way comparison of the West Frankish military measures with the fortified burghs of Alfred the Great and the defence works of Henry I of Saxony.[2] Departing radically from these approaches this study on the logistics of the entire bridge-building process promises to develop data on the expenditure of material resources on the project, and will illuminate the complexity of this Carolingian administrative effort with an analysis of texts on the organisation of the labour for this project. The methodology of this study involves the integration of several different kinds of evidence, specifically, the written texts, archaeological findings, historical climatology and modern comparative data on human and animal efficiency. This interdisciplinary approach, when combined with similar studies of this kind,[3] will provide the basis for an environmental history of Early Mediaeval Europe.

[1] Ferdinand Vercauteren, 'Comment s'est-on défendu, au IX siècle dans l'empire france contre les invasions normandes?' *Annales du XXXe Congres de la Fédération archéologique et historique de Belgique*, Brussels 1936, 117–32. Ferdinand Lot, 'Le pont de Pîtres', *Recueil des Travaux historiques*, Geneva 1970, ii, 535–61. Marjorie N. Boyer, *Medieval French Bridges*, Medieval Academy of America, Publication No. lxxxiv, Cambridge, Mass. 1976, 21–7.

[2] See Kurt-Ulrich Jäschke, *Burgenbau und Landesverteidigung um 900, Uberlegungen zu Beispielen aus Deutschland, Frankreich und England*, Vorträge und Forschungen, Sonderband xvi, Konstanzer Arbeitskreis für mittelalterliche Geschichte, Sigmaringen 1975.

[3] The interdisciplinary approach to ancient and mediaeval military history has found increasing acceptance in recent years. See Donald Engels, *The Logistics of the Macedonian Army*, Berkeley 1978. On the logistics of invading Asian mounted forces see Denis Sinor, 'Horse and Pasture in Inner Asian History', *Oriens extremus* xix, 1972, and Rudi P. Lindner, 'Nomadism, Horses and Huns', *Past and Present* xcii, 1981. Especially important for this study are Bernard S. Bachrach's articles, most notably 'The Cost of Castle Building: The Case of the Tower at Langeais, 992–994', in *The Medieval Castle: Romance and Reality*, ed. Kathryn Ryerson and Faye Powe, Dubuque, Iowa 1984, 47–62. See also his 'Animals and Warfare in Medieval Europe', in *L'uomo di fronte al monde animale nell' alto medioevo*, in *Settimane di studio del Centro italiano di studi sull'alto medioevo* xxxi.1, Spoleto 1985, 707–64; 'On the Origins of William the Conqueror's Horse Transports', *Technology and Culture* xxvi, 1983, 505–31; 'The Angevin Strategy of Castle Building in the Reign of Fulk Nerra, 987–1040', *American Historical Review* lxxxviii, 1983, 533–60. Also, Carroll Gillmor, 'War on the Rivers: Viking Numbers and Mobility on the Seine and Loire, 841–886', *Viator* xix, 1988, 79–109; 'The Naval Logistics of the Cross-Channel Operation, 1066', *ante* vii, 1984, 105–31. Most recently, Richard P. Abels, *Lordship and Military Obligation in Anglo-Saxon England*, Berkeley 1988, and James F. Powers, *A Society Organized for War: The Iberian Municipal Militias in the Central Middle Ages, 1000–1284*, Berkeley 1988.

The fortified bridges of Charles the Bald represent a turning-point in the history of mediaeval bridges and fortifications. Not until the 860s were bridges built on extensive fluvial systems for the unique military purpose of fluvial defence. Charles the Bald seems to have stumbled upon the idea of the fortified bridge[4] during a military operation in 862, when he found a way to stop the Northmen by cutting off their retreat on the Marne with a hastily fortified bridge, and then decided to expand on this discovery with a project to build a fortified bridge at Pont de l'Arche to prevent further Norse incursions on the Seine.[5] Until that time, bridges had functioned in combination with roads to facilitate overland transport.[6] Not a simple repair job on the old wreckage, the new bridge on the Marne was rebuilt differently (*secus*) from its original construction.[7] The sense of the passage in the *Annales Bertiniani* indicates that the king repaired and fortified the partially destroyed bridge on the Marne, since the renovated bridge successfully cut off the Norse retreat downstream from Meaux.

Although the fortified bridge was to be different from previous structures, the extent of the construction project would have depended on whether there was a bridge already on the site. If there were, it would have to be rebuilt into a fortified bridge; if not, a new structure would have to be built from scratch. A Roman bridge did not exist on the site, for the Roman road on the right bank of the Seine ran well to the east of Pont de l'Arche.[8]

Nevertheless, Pont de l'Arche was an enticing site for a bridge for commercial or military purposes. In choosing a site to interdict the Norse advance up the river, the king and his advisors did not have to weigh the merits of

---

[4] Operations against the Northmen before 862 suggest that Charles the Bald accidentally discovered the idea of the fortified bridge on his Marne operation, for guards on the banks and a fluvial barrier appeared in separate military actions but not in combination before 862. During the first Norse invasion of Paris in 845 the king attempted to deploy *custodes* along the banks to deter the Northmen. See Ferdinand Lot and Louis Halphen, *Le Règne de Charles le Chauve*, Paris 1909, 131–3. In 852 Charles the Bald and his brother, Lothair, managed to stop a band of Northmen on the Seine by placing obstacles (*obsidiones*), possibly a pontoon bridge or a line of logs, across the river. See Lot, 'Godefrid et Sidroc sur la Seine (852–3)', *Recueil des travaux historiques* ii, 687 n. 6, and Jules Lair, 'Les Normands dans l'île d'Oscelle 855 à 861', *Société Historique et Archéologique de Pontoise et du Vexin* xx, 1897, 14–15.

[5] The king acknowledged that the Marne campaign inspired this enterprise in the *Adnuntiatio* that he addressed to the magnates assembled at Pîtres in June of 864, in *Capitularia Regum Francorum*, MGH Legum Sectio II, 2 vol. Berlin 1883–97, ii, 311: 'de istis operibus, quae contra Dei et Sanctae eius ecclesiae et nostros communes inimicos Nortmannos incepimus, sine defectu et lassatione viriliter laboretis scientes, qualiter nobis placuisset, si istas firmitates hic factas habuissemus, quando in tali angustia, sicut experti estis, ad Meldis contra eos communiter laboravimus'. Charles the Bald urged the continuation of diligent labour in the construction of the works at Pitres, emphasising how the existence of fortifications would have prevented the great invasion of 856. As an example, he reminded them of their successful common effort against the Northmen at Meaux, referring to this operation on the Marne.

[6] Boyer, *Medieval French Bridges* 21ff.

[7] *Annales Bertiniani*, *Annales de Saint-Bertin*, ed. Félix Grat, Jeanne Vielliard and Suzanne Clemencet, Paris 1964, s.a. 862, 88: 'pontem ad insulam secus Treiectum reficit et Normannis descendendi aditum intercludit'.

[8] For the route of the Roman road along the right bank of the Seine see Sprüner-Mencke, *Hand-Atlas für die Geschichte des Mittelalters und der neueren Zeit*, ed. 3. Gotha 1880, Gallia; Nicholas Hammond, *Atlas of the Greek and Roman World in Antiquity* Park Ridge, N.J. 1981, no. 23.

several alternatives. The strategic-geographical location of Pont de l'Arche at the confluence of the Seine and two of its tributaries, the Andelle and the Eure, had been recognised earlier by the Northmen. In 856 they had used a stronghold on the site as a place to await reinforcements.[9] After the Northmen had departed from the Seine basin in 862, the king selected a location near to Pitres for the construction of his fortified bridge, just downstream from the confluence of the Seine and the Eure, the present-day Pont de l'Arche.[10] Two strategic objectives could be achieved from this place. To control navigation on the Seine, it was of vital importance to place the bridge downstream from the tributaries. These smaller waterways sometimes flowed parallel to the Seine. Combined with the transport of ships a short distance overland, these streams would enable the Northmen to regain access to the Seine by repeating the portage manoeuvre that the Norse chieftain Weland had devised for the expulsion of the Northmen from Jeufosse in 861.[11] Moreover, a bridge downstream from the Eure would maintain the geographical separation of the Northmen, preventing the Seine group from ascending this tributary to Chartres, where they could link up with the Northmen operating in the Loire region.[12]

Logistical calculations of the material resources required to build this structure and an analysis of the complexity of this administrative effort are dependent on whether the project was completed or not. Although no remnants of the physical structure at Pont de l'Arche have survived, hints of its appearance can be obtained from written sources. Under the year 869 of his chronicle, Ado of Vienne provided the most complete description of a fortified bridge, which Lombard-Jourdan has identified with the present Pont au Change in Paris.[13] The fortified parts of this structure were the bridgeheads,

---

[9] MGH, Capit. ii, 303: '. . . super fluvium Sequanam in locum, qui Pistis dicitur, ubi . . . aliquandiu sedes fuit Nortmannorum, . . .' In 856 a stronghold already existed at Pîtres. Cf. *Chronicon Fontanellense*, ed. Jules Laporte, *Société de l'histoire de Normandie, Mélanges*. Rouen 1951, p. 89. 855 (856), 89: '. . . Pistis castrum quod olim Petremamulum vocabatur, . . .' Since the incipit of the record of the 862 assembly mentioned a Norse headquarters at Pitres, Charles was probably referring to their occupation of the site in 856.

[10] *Annales Bertiniani*, s.a. 862, 91: '. . . locum, qui Pistis dicitur, ubi ex una parte Andella et ex altera Audura Sequanam influunt, . . .'. Cf. Lot, 'Le pont de Pîtres', 537 n. 5.

[11] Lair, 'Les normands dans l'île de Jeufosse', 9–39, and Gillmor, 'War on the Rivers', 84.

[12] Vercauteren, 'Comment', 123, evidently referred to Sidric's temporary partnership with Bjoern in 856–7. See Lot, 'La grande invasion normande de 856 a 862', in *Recueil des travaux historiques* ii, 714–5.

[13] Ado of Vienne, *Chronicon*, MGH, Scriptores ii, 323: 'rex Carolus aliquot annos adversus Danos atque Northmannos variis eventibus dimicans, pontem mirae firmitatis adversum impetum eorum super fluvium Sequanam fieri constituit, positis in utrisque capitibus castellis artificiossissime fundatis, in quibus ad custodiam regni praesidia disposuit'. Lot, 'Le pont de Pîtres', 550 n.3, identified Ado's description with the bridge at Pont de l'Arche without explaining why Ado would have had occasion to travel to the lower course of the Seine, but Anne Lombard-Jourdan, *Aux origines de Paris: la genèse de la rive droite jusqu'en 1223*, Paris 1985, 36, maintained that the fortified bridge Ado described was the one in Paris which ultimately helped to defend the city against the Northmen in 885–6. Ado's reference under the year 869 to a completed or nearly finished structure cannot be linked with a forged diploma of 861 of Charles the Bald which refers to a bridge at Paris. In this diploma of 14 July 861 (in *Recueil des Actes de Charles II le Chauve*, ed. Georges Tessier et al., 3 vol. Paris 1943–55, no. 485) which was forged from an authentic document and was confirmed by Charles the Simple in 909, Charles the Bald donated an unspecified bridge to the church of Paris, without making reference to the construction of a

which were built as strongholds for the stationing of garrisons.[14] The structure must have been completed by 877, when the Capitulary of Quiersy provided for the garrisons and maintenance of the fortified bridges on the Seine and the Loire.[15]

Information about the kinds of materials used in remodelling the bridge at Pont de l'Arche for fluvial defence appears in the capitulary of the 869 assembly at Pitres, where Charles received annual contributions for continuing the fortified bridge and making additional modifications in rampart construction. Included among the new developments was the first reference to wood and stone, the building materials for a walled enclosure, and implicitly for the bridge as well.[16]

---

fortified bridge. Edouard Favre, *Eudes comte de Paris et roi de France*, Paris 1893, 24 & n. 3, explained that it would be difficult to accept a suggestion that the bridge which barred the Seine in 886, was constructed in July of 861, since at the date of the diploma, the bridge was already completed, 'post expletionem vero ejusdem pontis'. Furthermore, at the end of 861, Weland ascended the Seine and established winter quarters upstream from Paris at Melun (*Annales Bertiniani*, s.a. 861, 86) and then s.a. 862, 89, he descended the Seine with his fleet to Jumièges. Again s.a. 866, 125, the Northmen reached Melun and attacked the *scara* commanded by Robert the Strong. In Favre's judgment these facts cannot be reconciled with defence works so extensive as the bridge of Charles the Bald. In 869 the *Annales Bertiniani*, 153 (below n. 16) noted that Charles began the construction of a *castellum* at St Denis, but not until the capitulary of Quiersy in 877 are fortifications expressly mentioned at Paris itself (the Ile de la Cité). Also, if construction at St Denis began in 869, Ado's description in 869 of a completed bridgehead cannot coincide with the beginning of fortified bridge construction there. The 877 capitulary emphasises the restoration and maintenance of the *castellum* at St Denis, which doubtless was intended to be the first line of defence for the Paris area. The beginning of fortified bridge construction at the Ile de la Cité therefore cannot be assigned to a specific year, but may have been among the public works which the king mentioned in the Edict of Pîtres in Capit. ii, 327: 'fideles nostri in istis quae in Sequana fiunt, et in aliis operibus laborant'. Moreover, 861 cannot have been the first year of Charles the Bald's fortified bridge construction, for the king himself acknowledged at the 864 general assembly at Pîtres (above n. 5) that the bridge repair operation on the Marne in 862 inspired the construction of the bridge at Pont de l'Arche.

[14] Lucien Musset, 'La Seine Normande et le commerce maritime du IIIe au XI e siècle', *Revue des Sociétés Savantes de Haute Normandie, Lettres et Sciences Humaines* liii (1969), 8. That the bridgeheads were intended as fortifications is indicated by the *Annales Bertiniani*, s.a. 862, 91: '. . . in Sequana munitiones construens, ascendi vel descendendi navibus propter Nortmannos aditum intercludit', and s.a. 864, 113: 'Karolus . . . firmitates in Sequana, ne Nortmanni per idem fluvium possent ascendere ibidem fieri iubet'. See also the *Cartulaire de l'Yonne*, ed. Max Quantin, Auxerre 1854–60, i, 87–90: '. . . in loco qui Pistas vocatur, quo nos generalis necessitat traxerat instituendi munitiones'.

[15] MGH, Capit. ii, p. 361: 'De civitate Parisius et de castellis super Sequanam et super Ligerim ex utraque parte, qualiter et a quibus instaurentur; specialiter etiam de castello Sancti Dionysii'.

[16] *Annales Bertiniani*, 869, 153. The term *castellum* which denotes a walled enclosure, also describes the bridgeheads and is confirmed by the archaeological remains. See map in J. M. Hassall and David Hill, 'Pont de l'Arche: Frankish Influence on the West-Saxon Burgh?' Arch. Journ. cxxvii (1970), 103. Also, Brian Dearden, 'Charles the Bald's Bridgeworks at Pitres: Recent Investigations at Pont de l'Arche and Igoville', *Conseil d'Administration du Centre de Recherches Archéologiques de Haute Normandie*, forthcoming, fig. 3. In 869 Charles the Bald began work on a *castellum* at St Denis of wood and stone that was to encircle the monastery. The passage of the *Annales Bertiniani*, s.a. 869, 153, that described the *castellum* at St Denis, gave an indication of its physical appearance: 'castellum in giro ipsius monasterii ex ligno et lapide conficere coepit.' Since it was to be constructed in a circle, the *castellum* apparently denoted a walled enclosure for the monastery. See Bernard S. Bachrach, 'Early medieval fortifications in the "west" of France: a revised technical vocabulary', *Technology and Culture* xvi, 1975, 565, proposed a similar definition for *castellum* after examining the military terminology of Ademar of Chabannes nearly a century later. *Castellum* denoted a walled enclosure as distinct from a *castrum* which possessed a tower in

The site of the fortified bridge at Pont de l'Arche has had a continuous history of bridge and fortification construction. In the early thirteenth century the original bridge of Charles the Bald was replaced by Philip Augustus with another structure that provided the present place name and survived into modern times. Under the direction of the French Ministère de Culture and Professors David Hill, Jane Hassall, and Brian Dearden of the University of Manchester, recent archaeological work on the site has yielded new evidence. In his 1971 article, Hill suggested that the outlines of former structures may reflect the configuration of the ninth-century works.[17] On the right bank is the outline of a mediaeval enceinte; on the left bank are the remains of what appears to be an earthwork which has been surveyed by Dearden. The perimeter of these outlines measures slightly more than 600 metres each; the area enclosed by these outlines is simply too large for them to have functioned effectively as fortified bridges. Dearden thinks they may have been enclosed areas to function as refuges for the local populations, and that the size of the actual bridgeheads resembles those of Paris (pers.com. 22 July 1988). The measurements of the Paris bridges as provided in Anne Lombard-Jourdan's study will be used in logistical calculations for constructing the bridgeheads.[18]

The picture of the completed bridge is of a structure with stone bridgeheads and a wooden span. The logistics of building the fortified bridge at Pont l'Arche involves the integration of written and archaeological evidence. Moreover, historical climatology and modern comparative data on human and animal efficiency offer the potential for determining the logistical requirements of the project, specifically, the nutritional needs of the workers and oxen, and the length of time needed for felling and transporting timber to the construction site.

The amount of timber necessary to drive the pilings and build the span of the bridge at Pont de l'Arche largely depends on the width and depth of the Seine. Based on the outlines of the bridgeheads which presumably terminated at the banks of the Seine and Eure, the ninth-century bridge at Pont de l'Arche extended for 400 metres.[19] Comparatively recent researches in historical climatology suggest that the climate of the Early Middle Ages was not fundamentally different from today's,[20] so the maximum flood stage of the modern river can indicate the probable height of the bridge. At Pont de l'Arche the present depth of the river ranges from a shallow 3.7 metres, to a

addition to a wall built around a hill. Lombard-Jourdan, *Aux origines de Paris*, 37, explained that a *castellum* also could refer to a bridgehead. See the text of Ado of Vienne above n. 13 and the 877 Capitulary of Quiersy n. 15.

[17] Hassall and Hill, 'Pont de l'Arche', 194, investigated the outlines of two enceintes at Pont de l'Arche. Provided that the foundations of these enceintes were actually built under Charles the Bald, their outlines indicate the ninth-century width of the Seine at the point where the bridge spanned the river: 430 metres across from bank to bank as compared with the 200 metre width of today.

[18] Lombard-Jourdan, map. p. 197.

[19] The distance across the Seine is measured from along the suggested line on the maps which appear in Hassall and Hill, 'Pont de l'Arche', p. 193, fig. 4 and Dearden, 'Charles the Bald's Bridgeworks at Pîtres', fig. 2.

[20] Thomas M. L. Wigley, *et. al.*, eds, *Climate and History: Studies in Past Climates and their Impact on Man*, New York 1982.

maximum flood stage of 7.7 metres.[21] For purposes of these computations the depth of the Seine will be rounded off to 10 metres. The type of soil and the river flow partially determine what kind of bridge could be built on the site. At Pont l'Arche the right bank of the Seine possessed typical rendzine soil, while the left bank was comprised of alluvial deposits.[22] The river flow at Pont de l'Arche at the river's shallowest point in March 1876 was 2,180 cubic metres per second, while the deepest water of July 1874 measured 65,000 cubic metres per second.[23]

Without written or archaeological evidence to indicate the finer details of the bridge's appearance which would provide the basic guidelines for its construction, especially the configuration of the span, more indirect methods are required to suggest how the bridge must have looked. The Roman military engineering tradition, including the construction of bridges such as the one Julius Caesar ordered built across the Rhine, was readily available to Charles the Bald. In 840, the year of his succession, Bishop Freculph of Lisieux presented Charles with a specially revised edition of the *Epitoma rei militaris* of Vegetius with a preface indicating that the work might prove useful to him as the frequency of the Viking raids increased.[24] Although Charles the Bald had access to this information, it is quite another matter to prove that he read the work and applied its contents to the resolution of a military problem. The technology and labour skills for constructing such a bridge were clearly available in Carolingian times, since in 789 Charlemagne had ordered the construction of a fortified bridge across the Elbe.[25]

Modern comparative data that approximate ninth-century conditions can suggest plausible details of the design of the bridge. During the American Civil War the Quartermaster General Herman Haupt built a number of wooden trestle bridges so that Union armies could cross the numerous rivers in the South. The particulars as to how these bridges were constructed subsequently appeared in military field manuals of the Army Corps of Engineers from the mid-nineteenth to the early twentieth century.[26] These works were written to meet the logistical requirements of armies in remote areas with unskilled conscript labour. The conditions under which these bridges were constructed

---

[21] *La Reconstruction du Pont de Pont de l'Arche sur l'Eure et la Seine*. Ministère des Travaux publics, Paris 1956, fig. 14, p. 14, indicated that the depth of the Seine ranged from 2.67 to 7.70 metres.

[22] An Atlas entitled *Les bassins de la Seine et les cours d'eau normands*, Agence Financière de Bassin Seine 1973.

[23] M. A. de Preaudeau, *Manuel hydrologique du bassin de la Seine*. Ministère des travaux publiques, Paris 1884, 97.

[24] Rosamond McKitterick, 'Charles the Bald (823–877) and his library: the patronage of learning', *EHR* xcv (1980), 31. Also, Bachrach, 'The Practical Use of Vegetius' *De Re Militari* during the Early Middle Ages', *The Historian* xlvii, 1985, 242, on Charles the Bald; the article is mainly concerned with the reign of Fulk Nerra.

[25] *Annales Regni Francorum*, ed. Fridericus Kurze, Hanover 1895, s.a. 789, 85: 'cum ad Albiam pervenisset, castris in ripa positis amnem duobus pontibus iunxit, quorum unum ex utroque capite vallo munivit et inposito praesidio firmavit'.

[26] Herman Haupt, *Hints on Bridge Construction*, n.p. 1842, and his *Military Bridges*, New York 1864. Also, *Manual of Military Field Engineering*, United States Infantry and Cavalry School, 3rd ed., Kansas City, Mo. 1897, and *Engineer Field Manual*, Professional Papers of the US Army Corps of Engineers, No. xxix, Washington DC 1912.

bore remarkable similarities to labour skills and technology available in the ninth century. The Civil War bridges were built with the unskilled labour of the conscripted troops, utilising materials that could be obtained on the spot and tools of no greater technological complexity than axes, augers, and rope. In comparing the military bridge construction of the Civil War with that of ninth-century Francia, the most notable difference was that axes of the Civil War era were made of steel, while those of the ninth century were of iron.

Wooden bridges were comprised of several parts, each having a distinctive name. In the operational terminology of timber bridge building, the principal component of the bridge was the trestle, a four- to six-legged support. The bay or span denotes the distance of empty space between the trestles. The superstructure consisted of balks and transoms. Balks, sometimes also called stringers, were the supporting beams for the floor that were placed perpendicular to the direction of the river. The ends of the balks rested on crosspieces of the supports called transoms; on the balks were laid the poles forming the floor.[27]

The trestle was made on shore and floated to its place on the bridge and then secured to the river-bed. The trestle was erected with the assistance of a raft that was held at a measured distance from the last trestle by a pole on each side. For uneven bottoms the six-legged trestle was preferred;[28] the legs of the trestles were previously cut to correspond with the irregularities of the river-bed – differences that were accurately determined by taking levels or soundings. After being floated into place, the trestle had to be set into position along the line of the projected bridge. After the first or any trestle had been set, the workers floated a raft against it and tied it securely and then brought the next trestle to be set up to the other end; the workers then forced the legs under the raft at a distance. Workers raised a trestle to vertical position by attaching ropes to the top and bottom poles. The lower ropes were slackened as the upper ones were tightened. As soon as the trestle rested in place another raft was brought up, tied, and another trestle placed into position until the bridge was completed. Building a trestle bridge in this way had several advantages. Work could be commenced in any number of places at the same time; no accurate soundings were required so long as poles were sufficiently long; different squads could work at the same time.[29]

The setting of the trestles into the river-bed could have been accomplished by constructing an A-frame with a platform large enough for two men to work. The apex of the frame would be placed around the log to be driven and the workers would strike alternate blows with their hammers. The weight of the men standing on the platform helped to drive the pile into the bottom.[30]

The construction of a trestle bridge at Pont de l'Arche would have required a considerable amount of timber. A computation of the number of trees needed to build the bridge will be compared with the available timber resources of the immediate area to determine the diminution of the available

[27] *Manual of Military Field Engineering*, 149.
[28] *Manual of Military Field Engineering*, 157–8, and *Hints on Bridge Construction*, 62. *Engineer Field Manual*, 182.
[29] *Manual of Military Field Engineering*, 159.
[30] *Manual of Military Field Engineering*, 165.

timber reserves. A trestle bridge built on the model of Quartermaster General Haupt would have required 1,500 oaks about 12 metres long and 30 centi-metres in diameter.[31] The forest distribution for this number of trees with a chest-high diameter of 30 centimetres would have been six per .4047 hectares, or a total of about 100 hectares, according to tables generated by the forest industry in Wisconsin for a tree farm operation. In the virgin forest of ninth-century West Francia, the random growth of trees would have increased the area; however the tall, thin oaks which are most desirable for a trestle bridge must grow in a limited space, so the wood-cutters would have had to search for groups of oaks growing in this manner.[32]

An indication of the forest cover in ninth-century West Francia can be obtained from information developed by Higounet and Musset on the location of forests in northern France.[33] Precise figures on the areas of these forests do not exist, but it is possible to compare the approximate extent in hectares of the forests in the Seine basin with the timber requirements of the trestle bridge. The Seine basin downstream from Paris contained about 1,500 hec-tares of forest,[34] so the timber requirements for building a trestle bridge would not have reduced significantly the available timber reserves.

The physical structures eventually became a reality through the availability of abundant building materials nearby, and the animal power to convey them to the site. The first steps in the logistics of bridge construction involved felling the trees and transporting them to the construction site. On several occasions Charles the Bald ordered workers and ox-carts to be brought to the site, but no numbers appeared in the *Annales Bertiniani* or the capitularies.[35] Even so,

---

[31] *Manual of Military Field Engineering*, 1897, 154; *Engineer Field Manual*, 1912, 181: 'trestle bridge is not limited as to length; bays are usually 3.7–4.5 metres long depending on the traffic and the available material. A six-legged trestle consisted of four vertical and two bracing legs each at 15 cm. diameter; one transom measuring 3.9 metres; two foot pieces at 1.37 metres; and ten oak pins.' About 50 trestles would have been required to span the ninth-century bridge based upon a post-Civil War field engineering manual which recommended the construction of a trestle bridge for spans 7.6 metres and over, or about eight metres between the trestles. The 400 metre width of the ninth-century bridge would require 50 trestles; the vertical legs would need 200 trees; two bracing legs 50 trees; and 50 transoms, each requiring a tree. Finally, the 50 foot pieces would have required an additional 25 trees, allowing two per tree. The total number of trees for the trestles alone would have numbered approximately 325. The crosspiece or balks that were positioned perpendicular to the transoms would have to be 9.4 metres long and 15 cm. wide to reach across a 7.6 metre span. Each of the fifty trestles required six balks to make the bridge 2.74 metres wide, adding up to a total of 300 balks. Small poles ranging from 10 to 15 cm. in diameter and 3.7 metres long would have to be laid on top of the balks at right-angles to form the floor. With a floor 400 metres wide and the poles cut in half allowing six halves per metre, the number of poles would have been 1200.

[32] For this section, some data will be applied from my article, 'The Logistics of the Cross Channel Operation, 1066'. R. Zon and R. D. Garver, *Selective Logging in the Northern Hardwoods of the Lake States*, Oshkosh, Wisc. 1927, 9; *The Building and Trials of the Replica of an Ancient Boat: the Gokstad Faering*, National Maritime Museum, Greenwich 1974, i, 51.

[33] Charles Higounet, 'Les forêts de l'Europe occidentale du Ve au XIe siècle', *Settimane di Studio del Centro Italiano di Studi sull'alto medioevo*, Spoleto 1966, xiii, 343–97; Lucien Musset, 'Les forêts de la basse Seine,' *Revue archéologique* xxxvi, 1950, 84–95.

[34] Musset, 84. For a map of the lower Seine forests, see Higounet, Index, 76–9.

[35] *Annales Bertiniani*, s.a. 862, 91: 'Karolus, horum pater, omnes primores regni sui ad locum qui Pistis dicitur, ubi ex una parte Andella et ex altera Audura Sequanam influunt, circa iunii kalendas cum multis operariis et carris convenire facit, et in Sequana munitiones construens, ascandendi vel descendendi navibus propter Nortmannos aditum intercludit'. Charles ordered the

the numerical strength of the labour force can be indirectly estimated. Construction on the bridge began in 862, the year of the first general assembly at Pîtres. The 864 Edict of Pîtres referred to traffic crossing the bridge the previous year,[36] indicating that the wooden bridge had been completed, but the stone bridgeheads had yet to be built. The following computations will attempt to show the amount of work that could have been accomplished in building the wooden parts of the bridge in the summer of 862, allowing three months of reasonably good weather.[37]

– The entire bridge took approximately fifteen years to build from its inception in 862 until the 877 Capitulary of Quiersy. Without a reasonably sure way of estimating the numerical strength of the work force, the calculations that follow will endeavour to determine what a force of thirty workers and thirty teams of oxen could have accomplished in building the wooden parts of the structure in the summer of 862. The length of time required for cutting down 1,500 trees of approximately 30 centimetres in diameter has to be derived from modern comparative data which were developed before the early 1930s, when the widespread use of the power saw took over logging operations. The cost of bridge building is expressed in annual working days (AWD), what a worker could accomplish in a single day. Wood-choppers, using modern steel axes, are seldom able to put in more than 7.5 hours of effective work per day and frequently do less.[38] Within this amount of time, an experienced cutter could produce one cord of pine (spruce), and the equivalent number of pine trees with a 30 centimetre diameter would be about five.[39] Modern steel axes have

foremost men of his kingdom to assemble at a place called Pîtres (three kilometres from Pont de l'Arche) where from one side the Andelle and from another the Eure into the Seine, about the beginning of June with a large number of workmen. Also, s.a. 866, 127: 'Karolus hostiliter ad locum qui dicitur Pisti[s] cum operariis et carris ad perficienda opera, ne iterum Nortmanni sursum ascendere valeant, pergit'; and s.a. 869, 153, see above n. 16. Dr Simon Coupland recently sent me an unpublished paper refuting the existence of Charles the Bald's palace at Pîtres as argued in Lot, 'Le pont de Pîtres', 554 n. 4, and M. Cochet, 'Note sur les restes d'un palais de Charles le Chauve', *Mémoires de la société des antiquaires de Normandie* xxiv, 1858–69, 156–65.

[36] The Edict of Pîtres refers to the destruction of a *heribergum* which the king had ordered the previous year, 863. The *heribergum* may have been intended as a temporary quarters for the workers. In 864 the king was concerned primarily about the destruction of the *heribergum* by individuals who, crossing back and forth continuously on the bridge, probably used the *heribergum* as a temporary lodging place and refuge from the Northmen. MGH, Capit. ii, 327–8: 'Et quoniam fideles nostri in istis, quae in Sequana fiunt, et in aliis operibus laborant et heribergum nostrum, quod praeterito anno hic fieri iussimus, homines de illa parte Sequanae in istas partes venientes et de istis partibus in illas partes euntes destruxerunt per occasionem, quia in illo contra debitam reverentiam manere coeperunt, et nunc istud heribergum non sine labore et dispendio fidelium nostrorum fieri fecimus: volumus et expresse mandamus, ut, sicut nec in nostro palatio, ita nec isto heribergo aliquis alius sine nostra iussione manere praesumat nec illus aliquis destruat'. See Lot, 'Le pont de Pîtres', 555n.

[37] Francois L. Ganshof, *Frankish Institutions under Charlemagne*, trans. Bryce and Mary Lyon, New York 1970, 67.

[38] N. C. Brown, *Logging – principles and practices in the United States and Canada*, New York 1934, 99. C. Todes, *Labor and Lumber*, New York 1931, 125, compared the efficiency of the new power saw with two hand fallers in a seven-hour period.

[39] Brown, *Logging*, 100, reported that a two-man felling crew in virgin Douglas fir could cut about 4–5 trees per day. A. Koroleff, *Pulpwood Cutting, Efficiency of Technique*, in Canadian Pulp and Paper Assn, Woodlands Section, Montreal 1941, table 4, p. 16, gave a cutting time of eleven minutes for an eight-inch-diameter spruce.

to be sharpened only once a day to retain a cutting edge on pine,[40] while mediaeval iron axes dulled much faster and probably had to be sharpened several times a day. In contrast with pine the hardness of oak prevented a cutter from felling more than three 30-centimetre-diameter trees per day.[41] The cutting of oaks to obtain the 1,500 trees needed for the various parts of the bridge is 500 AWD, or 17 days for 30 workers. The flooring of the bridge averaged about 10 centimetres for each pole. 4,092 half-poles would be needed to cover 430 metres of 2,043 poles. At half the diameter of the regular trees, 140 of these thin trees could be cut in a day for a total of 14 days' cutting time, so that the total cutting time for all of the trees would be 31 days.

Once the timber was cut, it had to be transported overland by ox-cart a variable short distance to the river, where the logs easily could have been floated downstream to the construction site. Conservative estimates for the later Middle Ages have established that the transport of heavy loads, such as logs, cost approximately one-third of an AWD per 1,000 kilograms per 1.6 kilometres.[42] A 12-metre wet oak log at 30 kilograms per 197 cubic centimetres would weigh 1,200 kilograms,[43] and 1,500 of them would weigh 1.8 million kilograms. The transportation of this quantity of oak would have cost the equivalent of 600 AWD. However, these calculations are based on standards of the fourteenth century. In the ninth century, the technology of overland transportation was less than half as efficient. Upon calculating an average distance of 2 kilometres for the transportation of the materials at a cost of one-third of an AWD per 1.6 kilometres per 500 kilograms, the carrying capacity of an ox-cart *c.* 1000 AD,[44] the result is the equivalent of 1,200 AWD for oak, or forty days for thirty teams of oxen.

The cost to northern Frankish society of providing for the nutritional maintenance of these workers and oxen during the ninety days of summer, would have been substantial in view of the subsistence agrarian economy. In the climate of northern France hard-working men require about 3,500 calories daily, or about 2 kilograms of unmilled wheat equivalent.[45] During the tenth and eleventh centuries the estimated average ratio of seed grain to consumable was 2:1,[46] and the average agricultural worker produced a surplus of *c.* 950 kilograms of consumable wheat on 6 hectares (158 kilograms per hectare) of average arable land. However, for yearly sustenance the agricultural workers required a caloric equivalent of about 730 kilograms of unmilled wheat equivalent and thus only 220 kilograms of true surplus were produced.[47] To

---

[40] Koroleff, *Pulpwood Cutting*, 23.

[41] J. F. Fino, *Forteresses de la France médiévale*, 3rd edn, Paris 1977, 83, explained that two wood cutters could fell a tree in times ranging from 25 minutes to 2.5 hours for trees with diameters varying from forty centimetres to one metre. Fino based his information on the military manual of E. Legrand-Girard and H. Plessix, *Manuel complet de fortification*, Paris 1909, 198.

[42] L. F. Salzman, *Building in England down to 1540: a documentary history*, Oxford 1952, 119, provided this estimate, but then cited considerable evidence that the costs were greater.

[43] *Manual of Military Field Engineering*, 154.

[44] Bachrach, 'The Cost of Castle Building', 51.

[45] Gillmor, 'War on the Rivers', 91 n. 37.

[46] Georges Duby, *Rural Economy and Country Life in the Medieval West*, trans. C. Postan, London 1968, 25–7.

[47] Concerning the seed grain quantities per hectare, see the data provided in B. H. Slicher Van Bath, *The agrarian history of western Europe, AD 500–1850*, trans. O. Ordish, London 1963, 137, and Duby, 24, 128.

provide the calories needed for the workers for three months, a total of 5,400 kilograms of unmilled wheat equivalent was required, or about 34 hectares of average arable land for surplus. Moreover, if each peasant produced a surplus of 220 kilograms, 25 peasants would have been needed to produce the 5,400 kilograms of unmilled wheat equivalent to sustain the workers during the summer of 862. Each agricultural worker tilled 4.67 hectares to obtain 730 kilograms for his own sustenance and the total hectares needed to sustain the workers for the summer would have been 7.4. An ox consumes 12 kilograms of fodder per day, so that over the forty days of pulling timber to the construction site, the necessary forage per ox would be 480 kilograms.[48]

In tracing the stages of construction, the year 862 seems to have been spent in building the wooden trestle bridge; half of 863 was mainly devoted to transporting stone. Based on these computations the construction of the stone bridgeheads cannot have begun until 864. Indeed in that year the king held the next general assembly at Pont de l'Arche, and expressly ordered the construction of the bridgeheads.[49] Built between 864 and 877 the bridgeheads entailed the far greater difficulties of moving stone and the production of mortar.

Since nothing remains of the physical structures of the bridgeheads, an interdisciplinary methodology and comparative data on mediaeval stone fortifications can determine what would constitute a militarily defensible bridgehead. The height and thickness of a militarily defensible bridgehead can be derived from comparisons with the intact remains of early stone fortifications in the Loire valley, particularly those of Fulk Nerra which first appeared around the year 1000. Professor Bachrach's methodology for determining the cost of castle building at Langeais will furnish valuable data for explaining the logistics of fortified bridge construction at Pont de l'Arche. A stone wall less than 3.5 metres high would be useless and it would have to be at least 1.3 metres thick, as exemplified by the stone castle at Langeais.[50] The approximate size of the bridgeheads will be derived from comparable structures at Paris. Lombard-Jourdan hypothesised that the bridgeheads of the Pons Major measured about 25 metres by 5 metres, providing the broadest frontage running parallel to the river bank, presumably to position the largest number of men possible along the fortified embankment. The quantity of stone needed for the bridgeheads clearly would be derived from the 60 metre perimeter of a single bridgehead. Both bridgeheads would have required about 550 cubic metres of stone excluding the foundations.[51] Limestone is abundant in the immediate area but no quarries have been discovered to date.

The stone had to be transported by ox-cart over flat terrain. At one-third of a working day per 1.6 kms per 500 kilograms a single team of oxen could have pulled 500 kilograms in three hours, 3.2 kilograms in six hours, and 4.8 kilograms in nine hours. This progression, however, assumes that the oxen worked at the same pace for the entire work day and does not make allowance

[48] Bachrach, 'The Cost of Castle Building', 51.

[49] *Annales Bertiniani*, s.a. 864, 113: 'firmitates in Sequana, ne Nortmanni per idem fluvium possint ascendere, ibidem fieri iubet'.

[50] Bachrach, Personal Correspondence, August 1982.

[51] 120 metres around the periphery of both bridgeheads multiplied by 3.5 (the height of the bridgeheads) = 420 × 1.3 = 546 cubic metres.

for the onset of fatigue towards the end of the day. Even so, if bridge building was done primarily during the ninety days of summer, the 1,250 loads could have been hauled by sixteen teams of oxen.

The use of mortar on this site has been documented archaeologically by the excavations by Hassall and Hill.[52] The production of lime, the ingredient which imparts viscosity to mortar, was a time-consuming process. Limestone, abundant in this area of the Seine basin, was placed in a cylindrical cavity or kiln set into the ground, where the cooking process lasted about a week. As the container boiled, lime accumulated on the inner walls of the kiln. After removal from the kiln, the lime was mixed with particles or fragments of carbon, which was most easily obtained from ash of the wood used in the kiln fires.[53] Extensive production of lime at Pont de l'Arche would have reduced further the forest cover of the immediate area.

The remains at Pont de l'Arche are insufficient to estimate the ratio of stone to limestone in the bridgeheads so a working model will be hypothesised applying the data developed by Bachrach in his study on Langeais. Using the example of Langeais for what may have been the general practice in northern France, Bachrach estimated that the ratio was at least one part mortar to three parts stone,[54] so, if we have *c.* 550 metres of fill, then 25 per cent of the fill (the space occupied by the mortar) equals 138 cubic metres.

Mortar is comprised of three parts sand to one part lime. One cubic metre of mortar weighs 667 kilograms; one cubic metre of sand weighs 1,600 kilograms.[55] Twenty-five per cent of 138 cubic metres of mortar equals 35 cubic metres of lime, so 75 per cent of 138 equals 104 cubic metres of sand. If one cubic metre of lime weighs 667 kilograms, then 35 cubic metres of lime weigh 23,345 kilograms. If one cubic metre of sand weighs 1,600 kilograms, then 104 cubic metres of sand weigh 166,400 million kilograms.

The production of lime in a kiln would have consumed rather substantial quantities of average green wood, as one cubic metre of lime requires 7.20 cubic metres of average green wood;[56] since the structure required 35 cubic metres of lime, it needed 252 cubic metres of average green wood. The transportation costs for this amount of wood were considerable in relation to the size of the structure. One cubic metre of average green wood weighs 530 kilograms.[57] The total weight of 252 cubic metres of this wood is 133,560 kilograms. Computed according to the figures for ox-cart transport, about 147–294 trips would have been needed to move the wood to the lime-burning site. For each kilogram of lime that was produced, two kilograms of limestone

---

[52] Hassall and Hill, 'Pont de l'Arche: Frankish Influence on the West-Saxon Burgh?', 195, noted the pink mortar on the site.
[53] Alfred B. Searle, *Limestone and its Products*, London 1935, 150–1, discusses the mixed feed kiln and its fuel requirements, which is summarised by Bachrach, 'The Cost of Castle Building', 59 n. 28.
[54] Bachrach, 'The Cost of Castle Building', 56.
[55] Bachrach, 'The Cost of Castle Building', 48, derived from his data that 75 cubic metres of lime weigh 50,000 kgs; 225 cubic metres of sand weigh 360,000 kgs.
[56] Bachrach, 'The Cost of Castle Building', 48, that 75 cubic metres of lime require 540 cubic metres of average green wood.
[57] Bachrach, 'The Cost of Castle Building', 48, that 540 cubic metres of average green wood weigh 286,000 kgs.

were required.[58] The fortified bridge at Pont de l'Arche would have required 276 kilograms of lime.

These computations, based largely on modern comparative data, clearly reflect the magnitude of the costs both to Frankish society and the natural environment through the use of timber and stone resources. Moreover, the reorganisation of labour necessitated by the ineffectual operation of the traditional military obligation further emphasises the complexity of the administrative effort behind this project. Charles the Bald changed the existing military organisation to collect a work force, provide for permanent garrisons, and maintain these structures under hazardous frontier conditions. To this end, the traditional mobilisation procedures as contained in the 864 Edict of Pitres will be compared with the texts on bridge construction in the *Annales Bertiniani* for 868–9, when the exigencies of the bridge-building project required significant reforms of the military structure to expedite the collection of a work force. The points of comparison include the bridge-building obligation, the process of streamlining the property qualification of peasants from irregular combinations to standardised groups of manses, the role of the magnates in these changes, and the provision for military colonists of fiscal lands to serve as garrisons.

The mobilisation of work forces depended on two sources: military obligations and manorial labour services. Of all the capitularies containing military regulations on fortified bridge construction, the 864 Edict of Pitres elaborated most extensively on the details of the project. To build the new structure and still retain an offensive capability, the Edict retained the traditional distinction between the two types of armies that were mobilised according to the nature of an operation: a force of those liable for military service under their counts for offensive warfare (*expeditio exercitalis*), while threats to the entire kingdom, now largely confined to the Seine basin,[59] required military service from all inhabitants (*defensio patriae*).[60] In addition to reaffirming the traditional

---

[58] Bachrach, 'The Cost of Castle Building', 56.

[59] The locations of authenticated diplomas in *Recueil des Actes de Charles II le Chauve*, indicate that the king's itinerary, particularly after 856, steadily converged around the area of Paris, a trend which corresponded to the increasing intensity of the Norse invasions. Carlrichard Bruhl, *Fodrum, Gistum, Servitium Regis*, Kölner Historische Abhandlungen, xiv, Cologne 1968, 50–1, pointed out a shift in the king's preference for residences from royal *palatii* to *civitates*, and especially royal abbeys. The internal strife resulting from the Norse invasions and the threat of attack by Carolingian rivals, he argued, forced the king to buy the support of the magnates with alienations from the fisc. Owing to the diminution of the fisc the king increasingly exercised the right of visitation on church property. Jan Dhondt, *Etudes sur la naissance des principautés territoriales en France (IXe _ Xe siècle)*, Bruges 1948, 10–13, 26–9, for the widely accepted view that Carolingian power depended on the amount of land in the royal fisc and that the dismemberment of the Carolingian Empire is largely to be explained by the steady diminution of the fisc through alienations to the magnates. Dhondt studied fiscal alienations by thoroughly investigating Carolingian royal diplomas which appeared pp. 270–6 of his work, 'Tableau des donations foncières royales en France occidentale (760–965)'. Dhondt, 259, added this table only as 'une note provisoire', clearly underestimating its importance for future discussions of this question. For an evaluation of Dhondt's methodology, see Jane Martindale, 'The Kingdom of Aquitaine and the Carolingian Fisc', *Francia* xi, 1983, 131–6, and *passim*, and on 162, she emphasised the more promising enterprise of tracing the destinites of lands which remained in the royal fisc.

[60] MGH, Capit. ii, p. 321. This article was quoted from an 829 capitulary of Louis the Pious: ii, p. 7. Also, the 847 Capitulary of Meersen ii, 71, III: Adnuntiatio Karoli, *c.* (5), and the text

regulations for mobilising the grades of combatants within the military hierarchy, the Edict enacted logistical measures to build bridges for fluvial defence. Especially important, the Edict reiterated the procedure for mobilising part of the work force. Below the holders of small parcels, those who combined their manses to send one of their number to serve in the army,[61] were the impoverished whose total lack of military equipment prevented them from participating in campaigns. Rather than giving a formulaic repetition of long-standing regulations,[62] the Edict stipulated that those who were unable to go into the army or to function as helpers were obliged in accordance with ancient custom to build new cities and bridges as well as points of access across swamps, and to perform guard duty in the marches.[63] Thus, the lowest rung of the military hierarchy, the poorest agricultural workers, were to provide a vital part of the labour for the fortified bridge. Military regulations could be enforced to mobilise impoverished men, the lowest-ranking and least desirable personnel, for the primary task of bridge construction; their only asset was their labour. By contrast, the labour services or *corvées* of the free manses provided manpower better suited to the job of building bridges because of cartage, a traditional labour service of the free manses requiring the agricultural labourers to provide draught animals and carts which could haul building materials to the site for three or four days a week.[64]

appended to *c.* (5). See Boyer, *Medieval French Bridges*, 20–1, that bridge building was traditionally the job of the local inhabitants. The best discussions of traditional Carolingian military organisation are still the articles by Francois L. Ganshof, 'Charlemagne's Army', in *Frankish Institutions under Charlemagne*, trans. Bryce and Mary Lyon, New York 1970, 60–7, and 'L'armée sous les carolingiens', *Ordinamenti militari in occidente nell'alto medioevo* in Settimane di Studio del Centro Italiano di studi sull'alto medioevo, xv. 1, Spoleto 1968, 109–30.

[61] MGH, Capit. ii, 321. References to combinations of manses are also found in Charlemagne's capitularies. See MGH i, p. 134; i, p. 137.

[62] Janet Nelson, 'Legislation and Consensus in the Reign of Charles the Bald', in *Ideal and Reality in Frankish and Anglo-Saxon Society: Studies presented to J. M. Wallace-Hadrill*, ed. Patrick Wormald, Oxford 1983, 209, for additional examples in the Edict of Pitres of modifying or adding to older capitularies.

[63] MGH, Capit. ii, p. 321: 'ut illi, qui in hostem pergere non potuerint, iuxta antiquam et aliarum gentium consuetudinem ad civitates novas et pontes ac transitus paladium operentur et in civitate atque in marca wactas faciant'. Bridge building for those unable to perform military service here is derived from a traditional obligation and the custom of other peoples, who might possibly be identified with the Anglo-Saxons. This view seems to be implied by Abels, *Lordship and Military Obligation in Anglo-Saxon England*, 72. In an immunity charter for the episcopal see of Metz, Charlemagne in 775, MGH, Diplomata Karolinorum, ed. Engelbert Muhlbacher, Berlin 1906, p. 132, enumerated the exempted military obligations in order of importance: 'Illud addi placuit scribendum, ut de tribus causis – hoste publico, hoc est de banno nostro, quando publicitus promovetur, et wacta vel pontos compenendum – illi homines bene ingenui immunes esse videntur.' See Jäschke, *Burgenbau*, p. 79 & n. 515. For the military obligation of bridge building in Anglo-Saxon England, see William Henry Stevenson, 'Trinoda Necessitas', *EHR* xxix, 1914, 689–703; Eric John, 'The Imposition of Common Burdens on the Lands of the English Church', *BIHR* xxxi, 1958, 117–29, and his *Land Tenure in Early England*, Leicester 1960, pp. 64–79. C. Warren Hollister, *Anglo-Saxon Military Institutions*, Oxford 1962, 59–60. Also, Nicholas P. Brooks, 'The Development of Military Obligations in Eighth and Ninth Century England', in *England before the Conquest. Studies in Primary Sources presented to Dorothy Whitelock*, ed. Peter Clemoes and Kathleen Hughes, Cambridge 1971, pp. 69–84. Patrick Wormald, 'The Ninth Century', in *The Anglo-Saxons*, ed. James Campbell, Oxford 1982, 154.

[64] The principal sources for ninth-century Carolingian *corvées* are the *polytyptiques* or inventories of the monasteries. The most important compilation for the Seine-Loire area is the *Polytyptique de l'Abbe d'Irminon*, ed. Auguste Longnon, Paris 1885, of 806–29, which contains the inventories

➝ Between the Edict of Pîtres and the reforms of 868–9 the traditional mobilisation procedure for bridge building proved unworkable. The Norse occupation of the bridge at Pont de l'Arche in 865[65] clearly indicates the absence of an effective garrison during early construction of the fortified bridge. Apparently there was no force in the area of the bridge that could defend it; Norse control of the site in 865–6 showed that a partially built fortification could not be left without a permanent garrison. Acting on the counsel of his *fideles*, the king abandoned Pont de l'Arche to the Northmen and transferred fluvial defence upstream, to Auvers on the Oise and Charenton at the confluence of the Seine and the Marne. An alternative to the defence structures at Pont de l'Arche, the immediate strategic objective of this transferral was the protection of the Paris region.[66]

The problem of effectively mobilising men and materiel largely explains why the 868–9 reforms took the direction they did. The precise nature of these changes will be compared with the features of the old military obligations of the work force. To expedite the construction operation, in 868 the king sent a directive to the magnates to undertake the construction of a *castellum* at Pont de l'Arche. Measuring the planned dimensions of the *castellum*, the king gave to individual magnates of his kingdom a survey by the foot so as to determine their assessments for rampart construction. The king measured the *castellum*, and then ordered the magnates to be responsible for building an assigned section of it, a measure similar to the more extensive text of the *Burghal Hidage*.[67] In 869 Charles refined and further developed the procedure to ensure completion of the project. To obtain the necessary data on which to base military reforms, the king ordered a survey of all lands within his kingdom to determine assessments for raising a work force, expressly for the military purpose of fortified bridge construction at Pont de l'Arche.

he (Charles the Bald) sent his letters throughout the realm ordering that bishops, abbots, and abbesses should take care to bring written lists concerning their honors, and how many *mansi* each has, and moreover that royal vassals should list in writing the benefices of the counts and counts the fiscs of vassals, and they should deliver the written lists of the churches at the aforesaid *placitum*.[68]

of all possessions of the abbey of St Germain-des-Près. See also the commentary by Benjamin Guerard, *Polyptyque de l'abbé d'Irminon*, Paris 1844, and Jean Durliat, 'Le polyptyque d'Irminon et l'impôt pour l'armée', *Bibliotheque de l'Ecole des Chartes* cxli, 1984, 183–201. For an assessment of Durliat's work, see Jean-Pierre Devroey, 'Polyptyques et fiscalité à l'époque carolingienne, une nouvelle approche?' *Revue belge de philologie et d'histoire* lxiii, 1985, 783–94. For the most recent discussions of the polyptychs, see Walter Goffart, 'Merovingian Polyptychs, Reflections on two Recent Publications', *Francia* ix, 1981, 57–77, and John Percival, 'The Precursors of Domesday: Roman and Carolingian Land Registers', in *Domesday Book: A Reassessment*, ed. Peter Sawyer, London 1985, 5–27.

[65] *Annales Bertiniani*, s.a. 865. 123.

[66] *Annales Bertiniani*, s.a. 865, 122. Vercauteren, 'Comment', 124.

[67] *Annales Bertiniani*, s.a. 868, 150: '. . . et castellum mensurans pedituras singulis ex suo regno dedit.' Nicholas Brooks, 'The unidentified forts of the Burghal Hidage', *Med. Arch.* viii, 1964, 74–90. David Hill, 'The Burghal Hidage, The Establishment of a Text', *Med. Arch.* xiii, 1969, 84–92, and his *An Atlas of Anglo-Saxon England*, Toronto 1981, p. 85.

[68] *Annales Bertiniani*, s.a. 869, 152–3: 'Et antequam ad Conadam pergeret, per omne regnum suum litteras misit, ut episcopi, abbates et abbatissae breves de honoribus suis, quanta mansa

This passage reflects a continuation of Carolingian usage, but it also diverges significantly from tradition. Charlemagne had ordered the *missi* to compile detailed inventory statements (*brevia*) of his landed capital, and the chancery developed a formulary especially for these inventories. A detailed comparison of the text in the *Annales Bertiniani* with these earlier surveys, notably the *Brevium Exempla*,[69] clearly shows that the 869 passage did not adhere to the form of the earlier inventory, for the narrative passage expressed assessment units as manses. In 869 Charles the Bald clearly was following the precedent of these *brevia* in concept rather than form, in requiring lists of landed wealth to support his military building project.

Carolingian rulers often ordered the compilation of lists and surveys of their landed property, but F. L. Ganshof was inclined to doubt that most of the numerous reports, lists and returns, were actually used; instead, he thought the documents were piled up in the various royal residences, forgotten, and eventually discarded.[70] In agreement with Ganshof, Jane Martindale explained that 'very few of the returns compiled – if they were ever compiled – have survived to the present day.'[71] Ganshof suggests that many landed surveys were not put to practical use, and Martindale doubts whether many of them were ever compiled in the first place, but James Campbell thinks the 864 Edict of Pitres exemplifies the effectiveness of Carolingian administration with a detailed questionnaire on markets and, of course, the 869 text in the *Annales Bertiniani* on the landed surveys for bridge construction.[72] Fortified bridge construction at Pont de l'Arche obviously constitutes an exception to the conclusions of Ganshof and Martindale. The provisions for garrisons and maintenance in the 877 capitulary of Quiersy indicate that the survey was both compiled and implemented even though perhaps not all of the returns were received. Moreover, further archaeological investigation may provide additional evidence in support of this conclusion in that the outlines of the structures may prove to be the earthworks of Charles the Bald, thereby providing an example of how vital archaeological evidence is for a study of this type.

In addition to the passage from the *Annales Bertiniani* of 869, a capitulary of Quiersy also in 869 orders the mobilisation of workers and ox-carts for construction at Pont de l'Arche, but does not mention the compilation of this survey.[73] The text from the *Annales Bertiniani* may indicate a reference to a

---

quisque haberet, futuras kalendas mai deferre curarent, vassalli autem dominici comitum beneficia et comites vassallorum beneficia inbreviarent et praedicto placito breves aedium inde deferrent . . .' For a translation and commentary on this passage, see Robert S. Hoyt, *Feudal Institutions: Cause or Consequence of Decentralization?*, New York 1961, 18–20.

[69] MGH, Capit. i, 250–6. Ganshof, *Frankish Institutions under Charlemagne*, 35–6, and Georges Duby, *Rural Economy and Country Life in the Medieval West*, Trans. Cynthia Postan (n.p. 1968), pp. 361–6. Klaus Verhein, 'Studien zu den Quellen zum Reichsgut der Karolingerzeit', *Deutsches Archiv für Erforschung des Mittelalters* x, 1953–4, 313–94; xi, 1954–5, 373–5, on the *Brevium Exempla* as a forerunner of some subsequent inventories.

[70] Ganshof, *Carolingians and the Frankish Monarchy*, London 1971, p. 134.

[71] Jane Martindale, 'The Kingdom of Aquitaine and the Carolingian Fisc', 154.

[72] James Campbell, 'The Significance of the Anglo-Norman State in the Administrative History of Western Europe', *Histoire comparée de l'administration (IVe–XVIIIe siècles)*, Munich 1980, pp. 128–9.

[73] Capitula Pistensia in MGH, capit. 869, no. 275: Adnuntiatio, c. 4, which thanks the magnate for the defence of Holy Church, a reference to their contributions for fortified bridge construction.

lost capitulary or, possibly, the details of the mobilisation may have been omitted from the 869 capitulary of Quiersy. Once the bridge was completed there was no need to retain all of these documents. Moreover, the storage of such vast numbers of documents would not have been feasible given the itinerant habits of the Carolingian kings.[74]

In several ways the details of this mobilisation procedure differed from earlier regulations in the Edict of Pîtres, especially regarding changes in the mobilising authorities. Following the precedent of an 829 capitulary of Louis the Pious, the Edict assigned responsibility for mobilisation to the counts and *missi*[75] whose task was to determine the number of free men in each county by compiling lists of persons according to the number of manses each had.[76] Instead of collecting the information by royal officials, in 869 King Charles sent written orders directly to the ecclesiastical lords that they should themselves draw up in writing the descriptions of their own lands. The 869 regulation on the duties of royal vassals and the counts is particularly significant. The vassals were responsible for the listing of the counts' benefices, while the counts reported on the benefices of the vassals. The lists of the vassals and the counts would serve as checks on each other, but no such duplication of lists was imposed on the ecclesiastical lords. If taken literally, the burden of mobilising workers for bridge building fell only on the ecclesiastical lords, leaving no stated purpose for the written reports about the military obligation of the benefices held by the counts and vassals. In accordance with earlier regulations, the counts and vassals served on horseback because the extent of their land holdings placed them at the top of the military hierarchy,[77] and the lists of benefices were to provide an accurate estimate of the potentially available forces.

With the reforms of 869 Charles entrusted the supervision of fortification construction to the ecclesiastical lords whereas before all of the magnates were obligated.[78] Assigning the task of rampart construction exclusively to the

---

[74] Still the best work on early medieval itinerant kingship is Bruhl, *Fodrum, Gistum, Servitium Regis*, 42–3, for the reign of Charles the Bald. The hazard of transporting documents on pack horses is exemplified by the tragic loss of baggage by Philip Augustus at Fréteval in 1194, an event which demonstrated the need for a stationary archive for the storage of documents. On this, see John W. Baldwin, *The Government of Philip Augustus*, Berkeley 1986, 405*ff*.

[75] MGH, Capit. ii, p. 321: '. . . comites vel missi nostri diligenter inquirant, quanti homines liberi in singulis comitatibus maneant, qui per se possunt expeditionem facere . . .' Renewal of *Conventus apud Marsnam Primus*, 847 in MGH, Capit. ii, 71, *c.* (5), and the *Capitulare Missorum Silvacense*, 853 in ii, 274. Insertion of *comites* into the text of the Edict of Pîtres indicates that the counts were now equal to the *missi* in determining the potential numerical strength of the forces to be mobilised.

[76] Lists of those required to perform military service first appeared in the capitularies of Louis the Pious. See *Capitula ab episcopis in placito tractanda*, Dec. 828 or early 829 in MGH, Capit. ii, 7; *Capitulare missorum*, dated early 829, ii, 10; *Capitulare pro lege habendum Wormatiense*, August 829, ii, 19–20.

[77] Ganshof, 'A propos de la cavelerie dans les armées de Charlemagne', *Academie des Inscriptions et Belles Lettres. Comptes rendus des séances*, 1952.

[78] MGH, Capit. ii, p. 321. The magnates were in charge of mobilising workers and building materials in the traditional manner from the start of bridge construction. See *Annales Bertiniani*, s.a. 862, 91: 'omnes primores regni . . . cum multis operariis et carris convenire fecit'. In 864 Hincmar wrote two letters concerning the works at Pîtres. Unfortunately the *Regesta* of these letters in Flodoard's *Historia Remensis Ecclesiae* which are edited by Ernst Perels in MGH, Epist.

higher clergy may have been in part an attempt to remove them from service in the field, a reaction to the trend of rapid militarisation of the clergy during the Norse invasions.[79] Moreover, through direct supervision of bridge construction, Charles could verify the accuracy of the lists of ecclesiastical holdings himself, while delegating to the vassals and counts the inspection of the lists of each other's holdings.

In comparing the royal order of 869 with the Edict of Pitres, the greatest difference emerges with the mobilisation of the landed and impoverished peasants. The earlier practice of the Edict required that at the time of mobilisation the magnates would name from compiled lists those who had to participate in expeditions, as distinct from those who functioned as helpers, and, finally, determined the members of the poorest class – those who actually performed the manual labour on the fortifications as a military obligation. This traditional arrangement lasted until 869, when Charles the Bald stipulated in writing the obligations in manpower and equipment which were to be brought to Pont de l'Arche. The purpose of the registers drawn up by the ecclesiastical lords, especially those for the smaller property holders, was to provide a more accurate estimate of the forces which were available – essential information which Carolingian kings before Louis the Pious had lacked for planning their campaigns. In fulfilling the manpower requirement,

(Charles the Bald) commanded that one free man[80] from each hundred *mansi* and one cart with two oxen from each thousand *mansi* be sent to the aforesaid general assembly at Pitres together with other tribute.[81]

The king's order improved significantly on the old system. The measure was intended to facilitate mobilisation by placing the logistical requirements equally on specified numbers of manses. By expressing military service in

viii.1, Berlin 1939, are the only evidence of their existence. See p. 165: 'Item Weniloni Rotho-magensi de operariis et opera, quam faciebat ad Pistas in Sequana', as well as: 'Item de opera pontis, quem rex cum ipso ac ceteris nonnullis fidelibus suis faciebat ad Pistis in Sequana'. Nelson, 'The Church's Military Service in the Ninth Century: A Contemporary Comparative View?', *Studies in Church History* xx, 1983, 22, emphasised the practical operation of the ecclesiastical military obligation, but without reference to the 869 military reform. See Hoyt, *Feudal Institutions*, 19–20.

[79] In his discussion of the militarisation of the clergy, Friedrich Prinz, *Klerus und Krieg im früheren Mittelalter*, Monographien zur Geschichte des Mittelalters, ii, Stuttgart 1971, 115–46, and his 'King, Clergy and War at the time of the Carolingians', in *Saints, Scholars and Heroes: Studies in Medieval Culture in Honor of Charles W. Jones*, ed. M. King and W. Stevens, Collegeville, Minn. 1979, ii, 301–29, has surprisingly little to say about Hincmar's ideas on the involvement of the higher clergy and ecclesiastical institutions with warfare, especially in view of Hincmar's egregious opinion in the *Annales Bertiniani*, s.a. 866, 131, that the death of Robert the Strong at Brissarthe in 866 was evidence of divine judgment for his possession of lay abbacies, especially St Martin of Tours. On the battle at Brissarthe, see Lot, 'Une année du règne de Charles le Chauve, annee 866', in *Recueil des travaux historiques* ii, 449–54, and Karl F. Werner, 'Zur Arbeitsweise des Regino von Prüm', *Die Welt als Geschichte* xix, 1959, 106, 110–11, that the accounts of the battle of Brissarthe and the siege of Angers in 873 were isolated reports which Regino of Prüm incorporated into his *Chronicon*.

[80] Jan Niermeyer, *Mediae Latinitatis Lexicon Minus*, Leiden 1960, 479: *haistald*.

[81] *Annales Bertiniani*, s.a. 869, 152–3: 'et de centum mansis unum haistaldum et de mille mansis unum carrum cum duobus bobus praedicto placito cum aliis exeniis, quae regnum illius admodum gravant, ad Pistis mitti praecepit, quatenus ipsi haistaldi castellum quod ibidem ex ligno et lapide fieri praecepit, excolerent et custodirent.'

terms of a definite number of fiscal assessment units,[82] the 869 reform clearly was directed at the removal of the irregular combinations of manses[83] which must have contributed to the previously inaccurate numerical estimates of manpower. Reflecting earlier military regulations, the Edict ordered a representative from each numerically variable group of manses to perform military service. With the 869 assignment of fortification building to the ecclesiastical lords, military service was regularised for the smaller property holders on ecclesiastical *honores*. Instead of the variable number of manses which previously contributed a representative, now each 100 manses had to provide a free man who drove to the site with other free men in a cart which contained building materials. The 869 reform possibly had an effect on the military obligation of some ecclesiastical estates. The polytyptique of Irminon, Abbot of St Germain-des-Près, *c*. 830, indicated that peasants on ecclesiastical estates made a payment in silver or in sheep in lieu of military service. The 869 reform strongly suggests that the obligation of cartage for bridge building was intended to replace the peasant exemptions from military duties on the ecclesiastical *honores*.[84]

An analysis of the effectiveness of fluvial defence on the Seine suggests that permanent garrisons contributed the vital complement to the physical structures. Without them, fortified bridges on the major waterways easily might have been occupied by the Northmen. The task at hand is to examine the military organisation for an explanation of how the king maintained guards on the bridge sites. Earlier Carolingian military history abounds in precedents for permanent garrisons. Charlemagne had sent groups of landed vassals to serve in this capacity, especially in Saxony, the Spanish March, and Italy.[85] However, Charles the Bald was so preoccupied with building the physical structures that measures for the garrison, maintenance, and repair were not formally enacted until 869 and 877.

Efforts to provide effective garrison forces were not made until the reforms of 869, which provided that the free men were to maintain the bridges by performing the duties of garrison and repair once the construction was completed. The text of the *Annales Bertiniani* 'ipsi haistaldi castellum . . . excollerent et custodirent,' suggests free men were sent there as military

---

[82] Hoyt, *Feudal Institutions*, 20, interpreted the manses of this passage as fiscal assessment units rather than parcels of land for agricultural exploitation. Also, Durliat, 'Le polyptyque d'Irminon et l'impot pour l'armée', 183, 197.

[83] Ganshof, *Frankish Institutions under Charlemagne*, p. 63.

[84] Polytyptique de l'abbaye de Saint-Germain-des-Prés, 218, 230: a *colonus* paid four silver *sous* for military service; 158, 161: *lides* paid from two to twelve sheep for a military service exemption. Cf. Durliat, 'Le polyptyque d'Irminon et l'impôt pour l'armée', 197.

[85] Ample early Carolingian precedent exists for sending military colonists, *Königsfreie* or *Wehrbauer*, to garrison frontier areas. Pier Silverio Leicht, 'Il feudo in Italia nell'età Carolingia', in *I problemi della civiltà carolingia*, Settimane di Studio del Centro italiano di studi sull'alto medioevo, i, Spoleto 1954, 73; Eduard Hlawitschka, *Franken, Alemannen, Bayern und Burgunder in Oberitalien*, Freiburg im Breisgau 1960, 32; Ganshof, *Frankish Institutions*, 154, n. 13; 64 & 156 n. 33; Theodor Mayer, 'Die Königsfreien und der Staat des frühen Mittelalters', in *Das Problem der Freiheit in der deutschen und schweizerischen Geschichte*, Lindau 1963, 49–51; Karl Bosl, 'Freiheit und Unfreiheit', *Vierteljahrschrift für Sozial und Wirtschafts-geschichte* xliv, 1957, 204; Heinrich Dannenbauer, 'Die Freien im karolingischen Heer', in *Aus Verfassungs-und Landesgeschichte: Festschrift Theodor Mayer* i, Lindau 1954, 49–64; Leyser, 'Henry I and the Beginnings of the Saxon Empire', 5–6; Eckhard Muller-Mertens, *Karl der Grosse, Ludwig der Fromme und die Freien*, Forschungen zur mittelalterlichen Geschichte x, Berlin 1963, 61–6, 74–8; J. Schmitt,

colonists.[86] The area around Pont de l'Arche had been devastated by the Northmen, especially during their occupation of the site in 865. Charles the Bald therefore needed a group of men who would not only guard the bridge, but also restore the productivity of the land in the immediate vicinity. An estimate of the manpower required to garrison the bridge can be derived from archaeological remains of the bridgeheads and comparative data from the *Burghal Hidage*. As explained above, the outlines of the bridgeheads provide their perimeter as approximately 120 metres. The *Burghal Hidage* specifies that a garrison should contain one man for every 1.21 metres[87] so that the total garrison force needed for Pont de l'Arche would be about 100 men.

The 877 capitulary of Quiersy mentioned further regulations about the ramparts. Since these measures appeared simply as chapter headings, it is possible that they were simply proposals which would be elaborated on in the future. In chapter 26 Charles spoke of a *castellum* which was then being constructed around Compiege; in chapter 27 he intended to make provision for the organisation of personnel to inspect the fortifications in the Paris region, especially St Denis, as well as the strongholds in the Loire basin.[88]

The sources do not mention free men (*haistaldi*) again after their first and only appearance among the logistical reforms of Charles the Bald, but there is some indirect evidence of the continuous presence of garrisons at the fortified bridges. They surely must have been effective in the Seine basin, for there were no Norse fleets operating on the Seine between the appearance of 100 Norse ships in the estuary in 876[89] and 885, when the Northmen rowed upstream for the siege of Paris. That a fortified bridge was garrisoned is suggested by the itinerary of the invasion fleet in 885. Although their ships had entered the Seine on 25 July, the Northmen did not reach Paris until 24 November, a rather lengthy period of four months for the 234 km. excursion from Rouen to Paris. In 885 what appears to be a fortified bridge near Pontoise on the Oise, drew the attention of a Scandinavian contingent which besieged it in November.[90] Although the garrison did capitulate, the Oise fortress drew some troops away from the main force which was headed for Paris, or slowed the advance towards Paris. The garrisoned bridge at Pontoise must have hindered the Norse advance for several weeks, permitting more progress to be made on the defence preparations at Paris, where the Franks repelled the Norse advance. By providing workers and garrisons, the military reforms of Charles the Bald enhanced the effectiveness of the fortified bridges against the Norse invasion of the Seine in 885–886.

Untersuchungen zu den Liberi Homines der Karolingerzeit, Europäische Hochschulschriften, Reihe iii, lxxxv, Berne 1977, 110–35; Timothy Reuter, 'Plunder and Tribute in the Carolingian Empire', *TRHS* xxxv, 1985, 87–8.

[86] *Annales Bertiniani*, s.a. 869, 153: '. . . ipsi haistaldi castellum quod ibidem ex ligno et lapide fieri praecepit, excolerent et custodirent.'

[87] The number of men is derived from comparison with the Anglo-Saxon practice of the Burghal Hidage. See Hill, 'The Burghal Hidage: The Establishment of a Text', 84. For the application of this data to the size of the Norman garrison at Pevensey, see Bachrach, 'Some Observations on the Military Administration of the Norman Conquest', *ante* viii, 22.

[88] For the 877 capitulary of Quiersy on the maintenance of bridges, see MGH, Capit. ii, p. 361: 'De civitate Parisius et de castellis super Sequanam et super Ligerim ex utraque parte, qualiter et a quibus instaurentur; specialiter etiam de castello Sancti Dionysii.'

[89] *Annales Bertiniani*, s.a. 876, 207.

[90] *Annales Vedastini*, ed. Bernhard de Simson, MGH SSrG, Hanover 1909, 57–8.

CHARLES THE BALD'S FORTIFIED BRIDGE AT PÎTRES (SEINE): RECENT ARCHAEOLOGICAL INVESTIGATIONS

Brian Dearden

The site of Charles the Bald's river fortifications at Pîtres (figure 1) was firmly associated with that of the river crossing point at Pont-de-l'Arche by Lot (1905), who gave a detailed review of the evidence. The site was also noted by Hassall and Hill (1971).

Near the north bank of the Seine the abraded remains of an earthwork can still be seen at Igoville, known locally as 'Le Fort', opposite to the town of Pont-de-l'Arche (marked as 'Approximate centre of visible remains of earthwork' and 'Land boundary and earth bank' on figure 2).

In 1971 a small excavation was carried out by David Hill and Jane Hassall, with the kind permission of the landowner M. Paul Lambert, and M. de Boüard of the Ministère de Culture, Rouen, before the extension of M. Lambert's factory. This investigation took advantage of a small settlement pit (marked 'E' on figure 3), that existed in the northern rampart of 'Le Fort'.

The pit measured about 4 × 3 metres, and this was cleaned up to make a rectangular excavation. Features to be observed especially in the north face (see figure 4), indicated that the pit had been dug through a complex timber structure, conserved as soil shadows of former timber joists, and large voids formed by horizontal tree trunks burning *in situ*, firing the surrounding clay into *briquetage*. The timbers were of two types:– the large unworked logs, some split in half, and also worked and squared joists. The east and west sections of the excavation indicated that this structure had been inserted into a hole dug into the rampart of 'Le Fort'. At the time of this work, it was not possible to investigate the lateral extent of the timbers. During this and a further sondage made to the western rampart (marked '2' on figure 3), a small amount of pottery was recovered. This was not in a satisfactory state of stratification however, due to the later demolition and spreading of the bank. A small amount of pottery was identified from the eighth–ninth centuries, with a build-up during the tenth to thirteenth centuries.

The current investigations.

In 1987 site investigations were recommenced by the author in consultation with David Hill, and in this the co-operation of Mlle Claude Varoqueaux, Directeur des Antiquités Historiques, Le Petit Quevilly (Rouen), and also of the landowners is acknowledged. The work is necessary for record purposes, due to the encroachments of industrial development in the area.

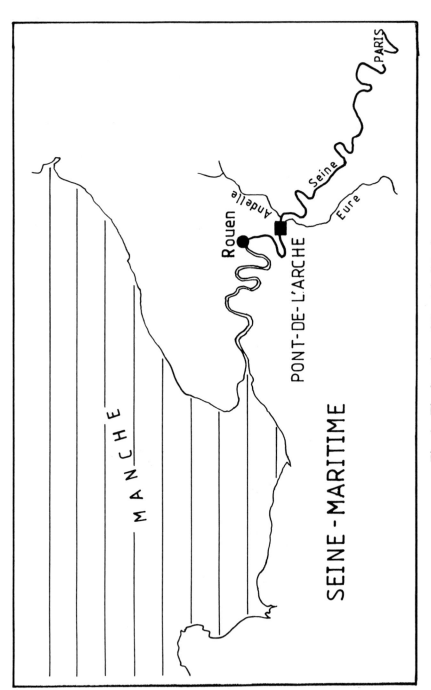

Fig. 1   The location of Pont-de-l'Arche

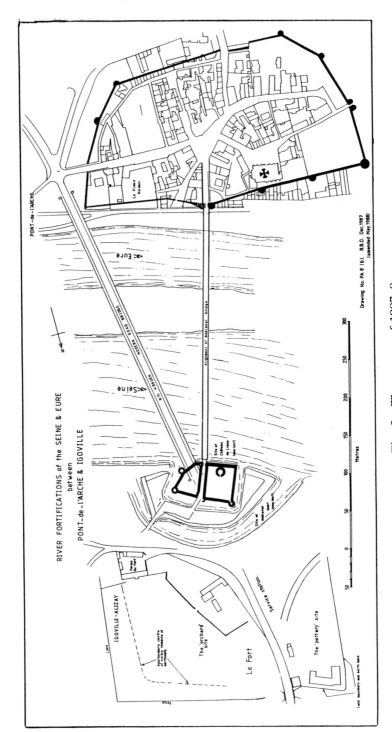

RIVER FORTIFICATIONS of the SEINE & EURE
between
PONT-de-l'ARCHE & IGOVILLE

Fig. 2   The survey of 1987–8

Le FORT – Igoville.

N15 < Rouen

E

CONTOURS SURVEY.

Heights are above the national datum
and refer to the B.M. 19·86m. altitude
located on the church at Pont-de-l'Arche

0   50
Scale – metres

Drg. No. P.A. 20.   BBD   May 1988

Fig. 3   The contours survey, 1988

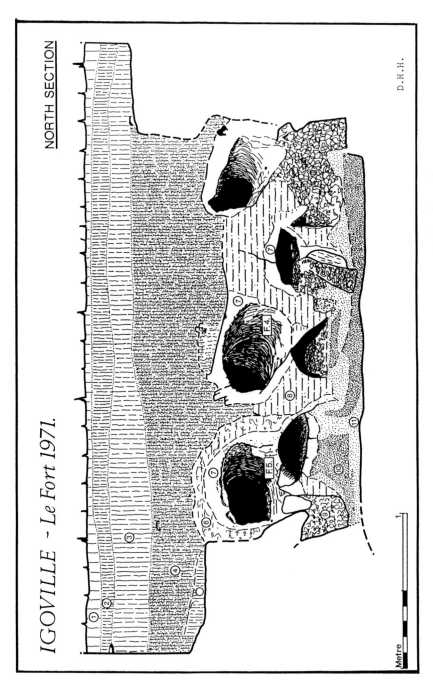

Fig. 4   Le Fort, Igoville. Excavation of pit, 1971. North section

A plane survey of the whole site, on both banks of the Seine and at the confluence with the Eure has now been carried out (figure 2). Onto this has been imposed the former mediaeval bridge (the immediate successor to Charles the Bald's bridge), the mediaeval fortifications of Pont-de-l'Arche (still largely existing), and the former Château de Limay, which guarded the northern bridgehead. I am indebted to the Dept des Ponts et Chaussées and to the archive of Evreux for the details of these monuments that are shown in black on the plan. On the north side of the Seine can be seen the position of the vestiges of the earthwork referred to above, and the unusual sub-rectangular plan of this becomes apparent. The northern rampart lies roughly parallel with the Seine, while the east and west wings are angled towards the east.

During the spring of 1988 a contours survey of the remains of the ramparts at Igoville has been made (figure 3), and a start made on the geo-physical examination of the site. The magnetometer tests tend to indicate that there is a considerable area that has been subjected to burning along the northern rampart, perhaps associated with the burnt timbers reported by Hassall and Hill (above). This extends roughly from the centre to the north-west corner of the northern rampart.

The investigations are continuing, and during the autumn of 1988 it is hoped to complete the geo-physical examinations of the site, and make a start on excavation work to locate and empty a part of the northern ditch to Le Fort.

A short review of the site (Dearden & Hill 1988) is also forthcoming.

References

Dearden Brian and Hill David 1988: 'Charles the Bald's bridgeworks at Pîtres: Recent investigations at Pont-de-l'Arche and Igoville. An interim report.' Forthcoming in the annual report of the *Centre de Recherches Archéologique de Haute Normandie Caen.*

Hassall Jane and Hill David 1971: 'Pont-de-l'Arche: Frankish Influence on the West Sussex Burh', *Arch. Journ. cxxvii.*

Lot F. 1905: Le Pont-de-Pitres, 'Mélanges Carolingians (suite)', *Le Moyen Age* 2e s. Tome IX 1905.

THE STRUGGLE FOR BENEFICES IN
TWELFTH-CENTURY EAST ANGLIA

Christopher Harper-Bill

The demand of the papal reformers of the late eleventh century that the Church should be free to fulfil its divine mission, unfettered by secular domination and interference, was directed not only against the tyranny of emperor, kings and princes. Equally abhorrent was the control exercised by laymen over the local churches established on their estates by their ancestors; such proprietorship was unacceptable whether it was at the hands of magnates, lesser lords of single manors or groups of townspeople. It is undeniable that the novel idea that it was sacrilegious for a layman to hold ecclesiastical property or to confer office within the church elicited a widespread response, just as did the simultaneous assault on clerical marriage. It has been suggested that by 1200 a quarter of English churches had passed into the hands of the religious orders, and in those which remained in lay hands, untrammelled lordship had been reduced, in theory at least, to little more than the right of presenting a priest, who must be suitable, for institution by the diocesan bishop.[1] The main argument of this paper, however, which is based on evidence from the diocese of Norwich in the century before the Fourth Lateran Council, is that there has been a tendency to exaggerate the extent to which the laity relaxed their grip on ecclesiastical patronage; that the religious, to whom so many local churches were surrendered, assiduously imitated their lay predecessors in the effort to extract therefrom financial profit, to the extent even that they sanctioned heredity succession to benefices when it was to their advantage; and that the advowson itself came to be regarded by monks, canons and nuns as a marketable commodity.

The vast majority of the innumerable charters which record the donation by lay lords of their churches to monasteries give little indication of the sentiments which lay behind the gift, beyond the statement that it was made for the salvation of the donor and his kindred. The general climate of opinion is well illustrated by the sermon of Bishop Herbert Losinga, woven around the text 'Alms extinguish sin as water does fire', and by the exhortation of Roger de Clare to his men to contribute to the new works at Stoke by Clare, in which he expressed the pious hope that God would repay their offerings one-hundred-

---

[1] For a most valuable treatment, see B. R. Kemp, 'Monastic Possession of Parish Churches in England in the Twelfth Century', *Journal of Ecclesiastical History* xxxi, 1980, 133–60; differences of emphasis in this paper should not obscure the debt which I owe to this article. For a recent and good regional study, see J. E. Burton, 'Monasteries and Parish Churches in Eleventh- and Twelfth-Century Yorkshire', *Northern History* xxiii, 1987, 39–50.

fold.[2] Occasionally, however, it is possible to catch a glimpse of individual motives. In the 1120s, at the impressive funeral service for his wife, William d'Albini, weeping and bewailing, gave to his monks of Wymondham who interred her the manor and church of Happisburgh.[3] At about the same time Gunnora Bigod, with the consent of her husband Robert of Essex, on the day that their son was born and because of their delight at his safe delivery, gave four churches to the Cluniacs of Thetford.[4] William II of Wormegay in the early years of Henry II's reign granted the church of Westbriggs to Castle Acre, where his father was buried, and the same community received the church of South Creake from Ralph de Bellofago for the soul of King Henry I, who had raised him.[5] In joy as in sorrow the Anglo-Norman knightly class turned to the cloister, and their conjunction in prayer was often cemented by the grant of a parish church.

The paramount motive for gifts was, of course, the desperate quest for salvation through masses. An early example of the establishment of a chantry, in the second decade of the twelfth century, is provided by Hubert de Mountchesney's grant to Abingdon Abbey of Edwardstone church, in which two monks were to be placed to pray for him; the endowment and the obligation to liturgical intercession were subsequently transferred to the newly founded priory of Earls Colne.[6] Many donations were made in return for admission to the cloister and the consequent near-guarantee of eternal bliss. Stoke by Clare received the church of Little Thurlow from Robert *pincerna* when in the 1140s he became a monk, and Rede from William of Rede on condition that he might on his deathbed assume the habit of religion, while Aubrey son of Ertald, co-grantor of Little Bradley church, was not only to participate in all the prayers and spiritual benefits of the priory but was to have the right to nominate whomsoever he wished for reception into the community.[7] In prompting such gifts considerations of feudal solidarity might supplement religious motivation. The barons and men of an honour might wish to link the churches established on their fees to the monastery founded by their lord, as did those of Bigod, whose gifts to Thetford were confirmed by Bishop Everard. The charter of Bishop Herbert confirming all grants, past or future, to this house by Roger Bigod and his tenants and conceding that they might be buried there is, in the light of the subsequent dispute about Roger's interment, almost certainly spurious, but it reflects most accurately the aspirations both of monks and of knights towards solidarity in almsgiving and burial.[8] A particularly fine example of honorial, monarchical and religious values, and also of sound historical sense, is provided by the grant by Ralph

---

[2] E. M. Goulburn and H. Symonds, *The Life, Letters and Sermons of Herbert de Losinga*, London 1878, ii, 26; *The Stoke by Clare Cartulary*, ed. C. Harper-Bill and R. Mortimer, Woodbridge 1982–4, i, no. 35.

[3] *Monasticon* iii, 330–1.

[4] T. Martin, *The History of the Town of Thetford in the Counties of Norfolk and Suffolk*, London 1779, 126.

[5] BL ms. Harley 2110, fos 46v, 87.

[6] *Cartularium Prioratus de Colne*, ed. J. L. Fisher, Colchester 1946, nos 14, 64–5.

[7] *Stoke by Clare Cartulary* ii, nos 273, 277, 289.

[8] PRO, E40/14810; Martin, *Thetford*, appx. no. vii; cf. M. Brett, *The English Church under Henry I*, Oxford 1975, 98–9.

son of Thorold to Binham Priory of the church of Little Ryburgh, given for the souls of Kings William I and II and Henry I, in whose time and with whose assent Peter de Valognes had founded the priory, for the same Peter who had enfeoffed Ralph's grandfather with his lands, and for the souls of King Henry II, Queen Eleanor and their children.[9]

These examples have been cited at length because it is certainly not the aim of this paper to deny that very many patrons of varying status, prompted by their own consciences or the advice of bishops or clerks, or in accordance with the will of their lords, did spontaneously surrender their churches to the religious, nor to question their assertion that their paramount motive was the confident hope of easing thereby their pathway to salvation. It is possible, indeed, that historians have placed rather too much emphasis on the parsimony of such grants, by arguing that once proprietorial rights had been curtailed because of the reception of reforming ideals, the laity had little to lose by granting a church to a monastery, thus as it were purchasing salvation with a debased currency;[10] for, as I hope to demonstrate, rights of ecclesiastical patronage continued to be highly valued by lay lords.

The programme of the reformers to release local churches from lay domination could be put into effect only because of the devotion of secular lords to specific monasteries. In the late eleventh century, and even a hundred years later, the most assiduous of bishops could impose no coherent pattern on the transfer of churches to religious patronage. Just as Norman lords might grant the tithes of their demesne wheresoever they wished,[11] so they might donate the churches on their estates to any house of monks, canons or nuns, with no regard for the physical distance between beneficiary and gift. The generosity of Robert Malet to Bernay and of the Clare family to Bec, Norman monasteries which had aided their enterprises by their prayers, were expressed by the foundation of daughter-houses at Eye and Stoke by Clare, to which were attached numerous churches.[12] There was no such community rooted in East Anglia to supervise the five churches given by Walter Giffard to Longueville, for the tiny cell of Great Witchingham was little more than a branch-office of the Norman mother-house, established to safeguard its financial interests.[13] As late as the reign of Henry II Nicholas de Stuteville, of the Norman branch of that family, gave the church of Kimberley to the Cistercian monastery of Valmont in the duchy, and King Richard soon after his accession granted Soham church to the abbey of Le Pin, near Poitiers, in gratitude for the services of its abbot as his almoner; the church was almost immediately appropriated to the Cistercian monks.[14] In 1198 Hugh de Gournay granted the five churches of Caistor on Sea and that of Cantley to the collegiate church of St Hildevert de Gournai for the increase of the canons' commons. His concern

---

[9] BL ms. Cotton Claudius D xiii, fos 121r–v, 164r–v.

[10] For example Kemp, 'Monastic Possession', 135; Burton, 'Monasteries and Parish Churches', 39–40.

[11] G. Constable, *Monastic Tithes from their Origins to the Twelfth Century*, Cambridge 1964, 82.

[12] *Stoke by Clare Cartulary* i, no. 136; *The Cartulary of Eye Priory*, ed. V. M. Brown, Woodbridge forthcoming, no.1.

[13] *Newington Longeville Charters*, ed. H. E. Salter, Oxford 1921, no. 100.

[14] *Bracton's Notebook*, ed. F. W. Maitland, London 1887, ii, 33–5, no. 39; Cambridge, Pembroke College, Soham charter A2 (26 October 1189), A4.

for proper religious observance is revealed by his stipulation that only those canons rising for matins each day should receive the extra allowance thus provided, the remainder to be distributed to poor clerks who did attend, but this pious provision was of little concern to East Anglian incumbents or parishioners.[15] Even the collapse of the Angevin empire did not put an end to grants of churches to overseas communities. In 1214 King John gave thirty marks from the crown's moiety of Holkham church to the abbey of San Martino del Monte in Viterbo, in a gesture obviously designed to win the favour of his new-found ally the pope, and Henry III subsequently granted the advowson to the Italian monastery.[16] In the 1230s the monks of Battle gave a portion of the revenues of Great Thurlow church to the hospital of St Ascentius at Anagni, probably in an attempt to secure a channel of ready access to the *curia*.[17] It is doubtful, however, if the consequences of such grants were any more damaging than those of gifts to far-distant communities within England. Battle abbey had received eight churches in the diocese of Norwich from William Rufus, and Lewes Priory held a large group of East Anglian churches granted to it by the lords of Warenne before the foundation of the convent at Castle Acre.[18] In the late twelfth century the accidents of feudal geography resulted in the donation by John Lestrange, who held fees in Norfolk but whose fortunes increasingly centred on the West of England, of the church of Hunstanton to Haughmond and that of Holme next the Sea to Lilleshall, both Shropshire monasteries.[19] It was almost inevitable that such distant houses should regard these possessions exclusively as a source of revenue.

Although they could not determine the destination of gifts, there can be no doubt that as the twelfth century progressed diocesan bishops achieved greater control over the process of transference. In the half-century after the Conquest lords normally made their grants as of right, and their charters recorded the conveyance of a piece of property. Thus, in the late eleventh century, Gilbert FitzRichard exhorted the barons and men of his honour of Clare to give as much as they could of their churches and tithes to the new monastic foundation within his castle walls, and although Bishop Herbert was present and blessed the enterprise, there is no hint that his will was paramount or his action constitutive.[20] Still in the mid-twelfth century lords of far lower status acted independently and in a proprietorial spirit. Richard son of Duet, for example, with the assent of his wife and mother, granted to the canons of Blythburgh in firm alms his church of Blyford, to be held of him and his heirs

[15] D. G. Gurney, *The Record of the House of Gournay, compiled from Original Documents*, London 1848–58, i, 164.
[16] *Rotuli Chartarum*, ed. T. D. Hardy, Record Commission 1837, 198b; *Calendar of Papal Letters*, i, *1198–1304*, ed. W. H. Bliss, HMSO 1894, 339.
[17] *Calendar of Papal Letters*, i, 165; see C. Harper-Bill, 'Battle Abbey and its East Anglian Churches', in *Studies in Medieval History presented to R. Allen Brown*, ed. C. Harper-Bill, C. J. Holdsworth and J. L. Nelson, Woodbridge, 1989, 164–5.
[18] *Battle Chronicle*, 98; *The Norfolk Portion of the Chartulary of the Priory of St Pancras at Lewes*, ed. J. H. Bullock, Norwich 1939, x–xii.
[19] BL ms. Add. 50121, fo. 28r; *The Cartulary of Haughmond Abbey*, ed. U. Rees, Cardiff 1985, no. 614.
[20] *Stoke by Clare Cartulary*, i, no. 55.

freely, quietly and in perpetuity.[21] By this time, however, some donors were acknowledging limitations in their role. Already before 1145 Roger de Vere had notified Bishop Everard that he had granted one-third of Little Walding-field church to Earls Colne Priory *in quantum ad laicam pertinet personam*.[22] Gilbert de Gant, earl of Lincoln, when in the 1150s he gave Haughley church to Lewes priory, humbly petitioned the archbishop of Canterbury and the bishop of Norwich to give their consent and confirmation.[23] The conflict of interpretation is seen clearly in the case of the gift by Gilbert earl of Clare to the monks of Stoke of the church of Bures between 1139 and 1143. The earl's charter stated that he had granted the church by the advice of God and of his barons; he felt no reservations in his power to act and there is no mention of episcopal consent. The confirmation of the gift by Bishop Everard, however, states that 'I have granted and canonically conceded the church of Bures to the monks of Stoke, Gilbert earl of Clare as advocate and lord of the foresaid place conceding this as far as was in his power, and the clergy of Norwich advising and consenting'; later in his *actum* he refers to the church as *donationem meam*.[24] It appears that by 1140 the doctrine enunciated at the Council of Westminster of 1102, that the religious should receive parish churches only from the diocesan bishop, was gaining ground.[25] It was accepted by some donors and ignored by others. One beneficiary at least, the convent of Stoke by Clare, was eager enough to receive a church from the founder's heir on his terms, but nevertheless thought it expedient to approach the bishop for confirmation, and he saw the grant in a very different light. Donors gradually came to recognise too that they might confer not ownership of churches, but merely the right of presentation. Manasser de Dammartin's charter recording the gift of Cotton church, for example, was carefully phrased: 'I will therefore that St Edmund and Hugh the abbot and his successors should possess fully and wholly in perpetuity whatever right I or my predecessors had in the advowson of the foresaid church'.[26] By the end of the twelfth century the limitations of lay proprietorial right and the need for episcopal initiative appear to have been generally recognised. In the 1190s Roger of Claxton notified John of Oxford that, as far as pertains to the advocate and a lay person, he has conceded and given the church of Claxton to the canons of Blythburgh in free and perpetual alms, and therefore humbly implores the bishop's benevolence that he may deign by his gift and authority to confirm the alms of this his donation.[27] The same bishop stated the transfer of the proprietorship of St Saviour's church at Norwich to the monks of the cathedral

[21] *Blythburgh Priory Cartulary*, ed. C. Harper-Bill, Woodbridge 1980–1, i, no. 118.

[22] *Colne Cartulary*, no. 71.

[23] *Lewes Cartulary, Norfolk Portion*, no. 65.

[24] *Stoke by Clare Cartulary*, i, nos. 21, 77. The confirmation of the grants of his predecessors by Earl Gilbert was made in the presence of Archbishop Theobald, but the gift of Bures does not appear to have been made on the same occasion.

[25] *Councils and Synods with other Documents relating to the English Church*, i, *AD 871–1204*, ed. D. Whitelock, M. Brett and C. N. L. Brooke, pt. ii, *1066–1204*, Oxford 1981, 677.

[26] *Feudal Documents from the Abbey of Bury St Edmunds*, ed. D. C. Douglas, London 1932, no. 193 (1156 × 1178).

[27] *Blythburgh Cartulary*, i, no. 202.

priory to be an episcopal grant, made at the petition and presentation of three lay patrons.[28]

The bishop also tightened his control over the financial exploitation of local churches by their new monastic patrons. In early charters of donation it is difficult to know precisely what had been given when a church was granted to a religious house. It is highly likely, for example, that Bishop William Turbe's confirmation of the appropriation of two churches and of pensions received from seventeen others reflects that proportion of their income originally granted to the monks of Eye by Robert Malet, their founder.[29] Many of the sixty or so 'grants' by John of Oxford of pensions from parish churches to various monasteries are certainly confirmations of revenues previously received, of which ratification was now urgently sought by the recipients once episcopal consent to pensions became mandatory if the religious were to have the right to enforce payment at law.[30] In the wake of the Third Lateran Council of 1179 monasteries habitually sought episcopal consent for new pensions.[31] Almost immediately after the church of Fincham was granted to Castle Acre, for example, John of Oxford imposed a pension of one mark to be paid by the parson to the monks, and the same bishop in 1188 granted an identical sum as a pension from the church of Holme next the Sea to Ramsey Abbey after the monks had by a final concord quitclaimed their right to the advowson to John Lestrange.[32]

The greatest profit might, of course, be achieved by a monastic house which was able to secure the appropriation of a parish church. As with pensions, many early *acta* recording such appropriations may in reality be confirmations of the *status quo*. This was explicitly stated to be the case when Bishop William Turbe, in a charter for Stoke by Clare, referred to the church of Gazeley *quam in proprios usus longo tempore possiderunt.*[33] The same bishop formally granted the appropriation of seven churches to Castle Acre, and by 1168 six churches had been given *in proprios usus* to St Benet of Holme.[34] Under Bishop John of Oxford the rate of appropriation increased; his surviving *acta* record such grants of over fifty churches to twenty-five religious houses. This

[28] *The Charters of Norwich Cathedral Priory* i, ed. B. Dodwell, Pipe Roll Society (henceforward PRS) ns xl, 1974, no. 142 (1188 × 1200).

[29] *Eye Priory Cartulary*, no. 44; cf. A. Saltman, *Theobald, Archbishop of Canterbury*, London 1956, nos 105–6.

[30] This ruling of Pope Alexander III was elicited by Roger bishop of Worcester, September 1167 × 1169; see M. G. Cheney, *Roger Bishop of Worcester, 1164–1179*, Oxford 1980, 80, 349; *Decretales Gregorii IX* (*Corpus Iuris Canonici*, ii, ed. E. Friedberg, Leipzig 1881), 3. 39. 8; *Regesta Pontificum Romanorum*, ii, ed. P. Jaffé, S. Loewenfeld et al., Leipzig 1888, no. 13162. For a further decretal to the archbishop of Canterbury and his suffragans following their request for guidance in 1175, see Jaffé–Loewenfeld, no. 13816. For examples of pensions which were almost certainly not new but which were now confirmed, see *Stoke by Clare Cartulary*, i, nos. 85–6, 88, 98; *St Benet of Holme, 1020–1210*, ed. J. R. West, Norfolk Record Society, ii–iii, 1932, i, no. 110.

[31] Canon 7 of Lateran III; cf. C. R. Cheney, *From Becket to Langton*, Manchester 1956, 115, 129.

[32] BL ms. Harley 2110, fo. 127v (1188 × 1198); *Cartularium Monasterii de Rameseia*, ed. W. H. Hart and P. A. Lyons, RS, 1884–93, ii, no. 315.

[33] *Stoke by Clare Cartulary*, i, no. 87.

[34] BL ms. Harley 2110, fos 123v–124r; *St Benet of Holme*, i, nos 91, 93, 96.

figure, because of the loss of documentation, is only an indeterminate proportion of the total. After 1175 it was rare for appropriation to be authorised without provision being made for a perpetual vicar who should serve the cure in person in return for a guaranteed decent income.[35] The ordination of vicarages was intended to ensure the provision of an effective pastoral ministry within the parishes. Most, however, were insufficiently endowed to guard against the ravages of inflation or the effects of agrarian crisis. The poverty of vicarages and the numerous pensions from parish churches are both manifestations of the universally accepted legal framework within which operated both monastic proprietors, avowedly intent on the exploitation of their churches, and diocesan bishops, despite their genuine concern for pastoral care. In the late twelfth century canon lawyers classified ecclesiastical benefices as pertaining to the domain of private rather than of public law; the protection of proprietary rights and financial interests took precedence over public welfare and the common good.[36] The crucial distinction between the holding of office and the ownership of property was blurred. The very word *beneficium* is derived from feudal vocabulary, being an early term for the fief, and the ecclesiastical benefice too came to be seen as a holding for which services must be rendered to the proprietor. In England the recognition that advowson cases, since they concerned property, pertained to royal rather than church courts did not entail any great damage to the interests of religion, since the two jurisdictions adopted an identical view of the benefice, which was seen overwhelmingly in material terms.

Thus far the picture is utterly conventional. Under the increasingly effective supervision of successive bishops, hundreds of parish churches in the diocese of Norwich were in the twelfth century transferred to monastic patronage; an approximate total of 270 is obtained merely by counting those to which reference is made in episcopal *acta*, and this figure again, due to the loss of monastic archives, is a gross underestimate. Incidentally to the main theme of this paper, from very many of these churches the monastic patrons drew some income, varying from a small pension to the greater proportion of the total revenues. The pattern of patronage in 1215 was very different from that in 1100. Yet concentration on this process of transfer, which Sir Frank Stenton called 'one of the most notable administrative achievements of the English middle ages',[37] has perhaps tended to obscure the very obvious fact that many advowsons were not surrendered by the laity. It is almost impossible to quantify, even for a later period, for the great surveys of ecclesiastical revenues of 1254 and 1291 were made for the purposes of taxation, and thus list only the financial interests of monasteries in parish churches; the assessors were not concerned with who held the right of presentation to unappropriated rectories. The 'Domesday Book' of Norwich, which was compiled probably

---

[35] I hope to deal more fully with early vicarages in Norwich diocese in a paper in *Proceedings of the Suffolk Institute of Archaeology and History*.

[36] I am here heavily reliant on F. Oakley, *The Western Church in the Late Middle Ages*, Ithaca 1979, 30–1; cf. G. Barraclough, *Papal Provisions*, Oxford 1935, 82–3.

[37] F. M. Stenton, 'Acta Episcoporum', *Cambridge Historical Journal* iii, 1929, 2; cf. Brett, *English Church under Henry I*, 230.

for Bishop Despencer at the end of the fourteenth century, includes the names of some but not all patrons at some unspecified date.[38] Some indication of the continuing lay concern with parochial advowsons in a period when lords had been deprived of the opportunity for overt financial exploitation of their churches is provided by the numerous feet of fines preserved in the Public Record Office. From the reign of King John there survive final concords recording the resolution of disputes between competing laypersons over the advowsons of twenty-five churches or fractions thereof, and between laymen on one side and religious corporations on the other relating to sixteen churches.[39] For the reign of Henry III the respective figures are 102 and ninety-two churches, although many of these advowsons were contested more than once.[40] These figures are cited merely to provide some indirect, and slightly later, evidence for the assertion that lay lords in the twelfth century retained a lively interest in the acquisition, recovery and retention of the *ius patronatus*.

It would, indeed, be surprising were it otherwise, for it is conventional wisdom that before the Gregorian reform lay lords viewed churches as appurtenances of their estates, and equally that in the later middle ages the gentry imposed their mark, filling the parish churches with chantries and converting them into family mausolea, treating them as vehicles for pomp and piety over which they exercised firm control. Is it conceivable that in the intervening period they abandoned interest *en masse*? The response in the twelfth century to the demands of the ecclesiastical reformers for the surrender of local churches to the religious was indeed remarkable, but it was neither universal nor un-regretted. Few laypeople in conflict with a monastery over the proprietorship of a church resorted to the means employed in the late 1150s by Avelina de Ria, who physically removed the church of Ranworth out of the fee of the abbot of St Benet's into her own,[41] but coercion and intimidation might be exercised in more subtle ways, and there is a note of realism in the *arenga* of an *actum* of Bishop Gray in favour of Hickling priory, in which he stated that episcopal confirmation of churches was designed to remove from benefactors the opportunity of rashly reclaiming what they had piously given.[42]

Some grants of parish churches to religious houses were, indeed, hardly the pious free-will offerings as which they masquerade in donors' charters or episcopal confirmations. The *acta* of William Turbe and John of Oxford, couched in common form, which confirm the Norfolk church of Deopham to the monks of Christ Church Canterbury are illuminated by a memorandum in the cathedral archives detailing a long and bitter dispute with the donor,

---

[38] C. R. Cheney, *English Bishops' Chanceries, 1100–1250*, Manchester 1950, 112–3.
[39] *Feet of Fines for the County of Norfolk, 1198*–1202, and *Feet of Fines for the County of Norfolk, 1202–1214, and of Suffolk, 1199–1214*, ed. B. Dodwell, PRS ns xxvii, xxxii, 1950–58; see index, *s.v.* Advowson.
[40] *A Short Calendar of Feet of Fines for Suffolk*, ed. W. Rye, Norwich 1885, 32–111 *passim*; *A Calendar of Feet of Fines for Suffolk*, ed. W. Rye, Ipswich 1900, 17–75 *passim*.
[41] C. Harper-Bill, 'Bishop William Turbe and the Diocese of Norwich, 1146–1174', *ante* vii, 151–2, and references there given. The original removal of the church was shortly before the accession of Henry II.
[42] Bodley ms. Tanner 425, fo. 41r.

Henry de Ria, who finally (1143 × 1152) was coerced by excommunication into granting the manor and church to the monks in recompense for another, the gift of his father, which had long been alienated.[43] Behind many gifts of churches must have lain a process of litigation, or at least accommodation. Such was certainly the case when Geoffrey son of Jordan abandoned his claim to Colveston church to the monks of Lewes (1161 × 1173); this was done only after it had been established before the bishop that the church which he claimed had in fact been a chapel of the monks' church of St Bartholomew, Ickburgh.[44] At the end of the twelfth century John Haltein's charter recording his 'gift' of the advowson of Herringby to the monks of Castle Acre as an act of piety for the salvation of his soul was in reality the culmination and result of an action in the *curia regis* in October 1196 concerning the church of Hellesdon, which the prior and convent quitclaimed to him in return for his grant to them of Herringby, which was almost immediately appropriated to the monks by the bishop. This appropriation was not, however, to take effect until the death of Robert Haltein, clerk, the donor's brother, who was to hold the church for an annual pension of 20s. Behind John Haltein's devout disclaimer that he was to retain nothing in Herringby church save the prayers of the monks lay his achievement of security for himself in another contested advowson and for his sibling in a lifelong source of income.[45]

From the later years of Henry II's reign the extant records of the *curia regis* detail numerous disputes between religious communities and laymen over advowsons. It would probably be an illusion to believe that the ever-widening purview of royal jurisdiction ensured that justice would be done. Jocelin of Brakelond relates how, when the church of Boxford fell vacant and a jury of recognition had been summoned, five knights came to Abbot Samson, tempting him to bribe them to give testimony in favour of Bury. He told them to testify according to their consciences and they maliciously deprived him by their oaths of his right in the church, which he only recovered later at great expense.[46] In the early years of the thirteenth century Bishop Gray wrote to the royal justices to inform them that Richard de Clare was unjustly harassing the monks of Binham over a moiety of St Peter's church at Great Walsingham; despite this episcopal testimony the earl won his case.[47] The ladies of Nuneaton were more successful in contesting an action brought against them by the earl's estranged wife, Amice countess of Clare. As part of a concerted campaign to recover her rights in Sudbury she first claimed in the episcopal court that the church of St Gregory pertained to her *maritagium*, and when the king's justiciar himself testified that her father had given the church to the nuns before her marriage, she resorted to the *curia regis*, and only when the verdict went against her there too did she abandon her claim by a final concord in July 1206 in return for reception into the confraternity of the Warwickshire

[43] Canterbury, Dean and Chapter Archives, register E, fo. 391v and Chartae Antiquae, D 10; Saltman, *Theobald*, 536–8.

[44] V. H. Galbraith, 'Osbert Dean of Lewes', *EHR* lxix, 1954, 296–7.

[45] BL ms. Harley 2110, fos 114v, 127r; *English Episcopal Acta* iii, *Canterbury 1193–1205*, ed. C. R. Cheney and E. John, London 1986, no. 406.

[46] *The Chronicle of Jocelin of Brakelond*, ed. H. E. Butler, London 1949, 60–1.

[47] *Bracton's Notebook*, iii, 251–5, no. 1238.

convent. That the nuns were not convinced that the matter was at an end is indicated by the inclusion of all this information in an episcopal *actum* of 1206 which recorded the institution of a parson at their presentation, and that their fears were justified is suggested by the countess's claim to the dependent chapel of St Peter in 1214.[48]

Religious communities were certainly not always successful in litigation over advowsons before the king's justices. In the twelve years before the turn of the century the abbot of St Benet of Holme quitclaimed to lay rivals the advowsons of three churches and a chapel and achieved security of tenure through final concords in two churches and the moiety of a third.[49] There are instances, moreover, where the quitclaim by a lay litigant was in reality only one side of a bargain. The surrender by Thomas Noel to the monks of Bury of his claim to the church of Nowton was counterbalanced by Abbot Samson's quitclaim to him of Hawstead (1182 × 1185).[50] When in 1186 Robert de Vallibus acknowledged the right of St Benet's to St Martin's church at Shottisham, the abbot recognised in turn that St Mary's in the same vill was an independent church in Robert's gift and not, as the monks had hitherto maintained, a chapel of St Martin's.[51] In 1188 Abbot Samson agreed to the partitioning with Robert of Coddenham of the advowson of Boxted, an arrangement which the abbot repeated ten years later with Robert de Scales at Wetherden; these arrangements were made in spite of mounting episcopal hostility to the division of churches into moieties or smaller fractions.[52]

East Anglian feet of fines from the reign of John suggest that the religious were more successful in such litigation in the early thirteenth century. Of sixteen actions thus terminated, eleven brought by laymen and five by monasteries, the religious obtained the advowson in every instance, most often for no financial outlay, the only recompense being the reception of the rival claimant into confraternity.[53] The attraction of such spiritual benefits certainly should not be discounted, and it is impossible to know how often the terse form of the final concord conceals a genuine change of heart, as in 1202 when the quitclaim by Robert son of Ertald to St John's abbey at Colchester of the advowson of Hemmingstone is explained by his letter to the bishop of Norwich, in which he stated that he had enquired diligently into the monks' rights, and because he did not wish to be in a state of sin or to go against the advice of his friends, he had demised to the convent whatever in the church pertained to him.[54] Such an example, however, may be balanced by another transaction by which a layman received an excellent bargain. When in 1203 Henry of Flegg quitclaimed to the prior of Hickling a moiety of Waxham church, Theobald de Valognes, his lord and founder of the monastery,

[48] BL ms. Add. ch. 47956, 47958; PRS ns xxxii, no. 464, *Curia Regis Rolls*, HMSO 1923– , vii, 66.
[49] *St Benet of Holme*, i, nos. 293, 297–300.
[50] *Feudal Documents*, nos. 220, 226.
[51] *St Benet of Holme*, i, no. 293.
[52] *Feudal Documents*, no. 232; PRS os xxiii, 17; *Jocelin of Brakelond*, 95; *The Kalendar of Abbot Samson of Bury St Edmunds*, ed. R. H. C. Davis, Camden third series, lxxiv, no. 118; cf. Cheney, *From Becket to Langton*, 130.
[53] PRS ns xxxii, nos. 34, 61, 81, 133, 248, 259, 279, 386, 441, 464, 484, 511, 545, 556, 561.
[54] PRS ns xxxii, no. 386; *Cartularium Monasterii Sancti Johannis Baptiste de Colecestria*, ed. S. A. Moore, Roxburghe Club 1897, i, 260.

reduced the annual service from his land from twenty to eight shillings.[55] Grants made at the very end of the twelfth century and confirmed by episcopal authority might be challenged at a later date and some financial recompense obtained for an ancestor's generosity. Between 1188 and 1198, for example, William Talebot gave to Castle Acre the church of St Michael at Fincham; in 1253 the prior had to bring an action against Adam Talebot, who had last exercised the right of presentation, and in return for recognition of the prior's right he received a payment of twenty marks.[56]

It emerges quite clearly that even after the Gregorian reforms had eradicated any hope of direct financial profit to be derived by laymen from proprietorship of a local church, the *ius patronatus* retained considerable value, for it remained a means to provide for younger brothers and sons or, in the case of magnates, for the ever-increasing number of clerks necessary to administer their affairs. In one instance there is a fairly precise indication of the value placed by a great family on an advowson, for when in 1205 a Clare tenant surrendered to his lord the patronage of Stansfield, the earl remitted to him the service of one knight's fee for his lifetime, and to his heirs that of half a fee.[57] There are numerous instances from the mid-twelfth to the early thirteenth centuries of the determination of the laity to retain their rights of patronage. In the 1160s Ralph de Playz agreed in the presence of the bishop that the monks of Castle Acre should receive an annual pension of 20s. from the church of Methwold Hithe, which they claimed, as long as they abandoned to him the advowson. In the last years of the century Roger Buzun agreed with the same convent that he should retain the advowson of Whissonsett, but that the clerks presented by him and his heirs should pay an annual pension of one mark to the monks.[58] In the 1190s Bishop John of Oxford granted an annual pension of 8s. from the church of St Lawrence, South Walsham, to St Benet of Holme and an annual benefice of six marks in Cretingham church to SS Peter and Paul, Ipswich, after the religious had agreed by final concords to abandon their claims to, respectively, Roger Bigod and Ernald de Coleville; these arrangements were certainly made with the consent of the lay patrons as the price, to be borne by their presentees, for their retention of the patronage.[59] At the turn of the century Robert FitzWalter entered into negotiations with Binham Priory and recovered from the monks the advowson of Bacton (Suffolk), which had been granted to them by his wife's father; in return they received a pension or benefice within the church of five marks, which throughout the thirteenth century their successors had the greatest difficulty in extracting from the incumbent.[60]

Even when a layman's ancestors had granted an advowson to a monastery, or he had lost it by legal process, he might still attempt to retain the effective exercise of patronage. In the late 1170s Roger of Tofts conceded that he had

[55] PRS ns xxxii, no. 34.
[56] BL ms. Harley 2110, fos 116r, 127v. .
[57] PRS ns xxxii, no. 439. This church was valued at £8 in 1291 (*Taxatio Ecclesiastica . . . AD 1291*, ed. T. Astle *et al.*, Record Commission, 1802, 120).
[58] BL ms. Harley 2110, fos 124v–125r, 127v.
[59] *St Benet of Holme*, i, nos 108, 299; PRO, E40/14020; PRS os xxiv, no. 25.
[60] BL ms. Cotton Claudius D xiii, fos 183r–184r.

previously granted Bircham Tofts church to the cathedral priory of Canterbury, but in order to resolve the dispute between them Prior Herluin agreed that Roger should have the right to present to the monks a suitable vicar, whom they should then present to the bishop and who would render to them an annual pension of 4s.[61] Around this time too Earl William de Mandeville obtained from the monks of Walden the concession that he might, for his lifetime, present his own clerks to seven churches in Essex and Suffolk which had been given to the community, on condition that both he and the incumbents should pay a pension.[62] At the conclusion of litigation about Hockering and Mattishall Burgh churches in 1204 the canons of St Mary Overy, Southwark, succeeded in retaining the advowson, but were granted an annual pension of six marks in return for their agreement always to present clerks nominated to them by the previous lay patrons and their heirs – an arrangement which still prevailed in the fourteenth century.[63]

There is much evidence to suggest, therefore, not only that laymen were anxious to retain ecclesiastical patronage, but also that some monastic houses at least had begun to think of the *ius patronatus*, which by itself should have conferred no financial advantage, in terms of economic calculation. It may indeed be that attempts by lay lords to recover churches alienated by their ancestors were prompted by the realisation that the religious had shown themselves as self-interested as their predecessors in their attitude to the parishes. The view of the local church as a piece of real estate ripe for exploitation, far from being undermined, was shared by the new monastic patrons, by the clerks who sought to benefit from their patronage, and even by diocesan bishops, whose assiduous efforts to provide for pastoral care were undermined not only by the canonical concept of the benefice but also by their desperate need to secure revenues for members of their own *familiae*.

Those instances of monastic aggression against the priests of churches in their gift, which are occasionally documented, were probably prompted by financial motives. The prior and convent of Castle Acre, for example, in the late 1150s attempted to eject the incumbent of Threxton church, who claimed that he had been canonically instituted at the presentation of the earl of Warenne before the monks acquired the church.[64] Some years later Bishop Roger of Worcester was delegated by the pope to hear the complaint of a Suffolk parson that he had been forced by the abbot of Bury to renounce his church by threat of expulsion from his patrimony, which he held of St Edmund.[65] More often, however, monastic patrons were inclined to cooperate with those clerks holding or seeking to hold their churches in arrangements which were mutually advantageous. This accommodation of interests may be seen both in the creation of non-residential vicarages and in the toleration of hereditary succession to ecclesiastical benefices.

[61] *English Episcopal Acta*, ii, *Canterbury 1162–1190*, ed. C. R. Cheney and B. E. A. Jones, London 1986, no. 90.
[62] BL ms. Harley 3697, fo. 19r.
[63] PRS ns xxxii, no. 61.
[64] *The Letters of John of Salisbury*, i, ed. W. J. Millor and H. E. Butler, revised by C. N. L. Brooke, London 1955, no. 80.
[65] Cheney, *Roger of Worcester*, 317, no. 1.

It has been clearly demonstrated that the twelfth-century vicarage might be something very different from that model defined by the canonists which was applied on numerous occasions by English bishops, including those of Norwich, long before the Fourth Lateran Council.[66] Some vicarages, indeed, appear to have been created merely as a means of inserting into the parochial structure another benefice, in the sense of a new source of income which did not entail direct pastoral responsibilities. In the mid-twelfth century the monks of Castle Acre, rectors of Witton church, presented the prior and convent of Bromholm, their daughter house, to the vicarage of the church, so that there was a corporate vicar as well as rector.[67] That a vicar might not be expected to reside is shown quite clearly by the arrangements made when Gervase of Norwich, parson of Castle Acre's church of Great Dunham, presented Roger the clerk to the perpetual vicarage of the church, with the stipulation that the clerk who was actually to serve the cure should be appointed with the parson's advice.[68] In the mid-thirteenth century it was testified in the *curia regis* that at the request of Bishop John of Oxford the parson of Thornham conceded to master Simon of Huntingdon the vicarage of the church, retaining for himself only 100s. as the *personatus*. Local witnesses stated that master Simon had been the bishop's proctor at the court of Rome, and the clear implication is that the parson, his revenue much reduced, continued to serve the church while a member of the episcopal *familia* drew a stipend as non-resident vicar.[69] Geoffrey, chaplain of John of Oxford, was in the 1180s presented to the church of Fulmodestone by Castle Acre Priory, to which he was to pay an annual pension of three marks. In 1202 a new parson was instituted, but Geoffrey, now archdeacon of Suffolk, was to retain the perpetual vicarage of the church.[70] In the early years of the thirteenth century the same archdeacon also obtained the perpetual vicarage of Hardley, having sued Roger of Gillingham, the parson, for the church itself; the agreement before papal judges-delegate which terminated the dispute stipulated that Geoffrey as vicar should pay the parson nine marks a year and should discharge the church's obligations to the bishop.[71] Geoffrey held other churches, and it is unlikely that he resided at either Fulmodestone or Hardley; the vicarages appear to have been expedients devised to increase his income. A further example of such a vicarage is provided by the church of Martham. Here another Geoffrey, dean of Norwich, was instituted as parson first at the presentation of the bishop and then in 1198, after a dispute between John of Oxford and the cathedral chapter, of the monks of Norwich. He immediately presented as vicar Adam of Walsingham, who was to pay him twelve marks a year as a pension. This Adam was a clerk of Archbishop Hubert Walter, who had adjudicated in the case between the bishop and his monks; although a local man, he was among the most frequent witnesses of the archbishop's *acta* and cannot have resided.[72]

[66] Kemp, 'Monastic Possession', 149–55.
[67] Cambridge University Library ms. Mm. ii 20, fo. 12v.
[68] BL ms. Harley 2110, fo. 126r–v (? 1178 × 1189).
[69] *Curia Regis Rolls*, xvi, no. 1659.
[70] BL ms. Harley 2110, fo. 127r.
[71] Historical Manuscripts Commission, *Report on Manuscripts in Various Collections*, 8 parts, 1903–13, vii, 180.
[72] *Norwich Cathedral Charters*, i, nos. 263–4; *English Episcopal Acta*, iii, nos 558–9.

The convolutions of the quest for benefices is best, if obscurely, illustrated by the complicated history of the two churches of Weasenham and that of East Lexham in the last eighteen years of the twelfth century.[73] The documents cannot be dated precisely, but the apparent sequence of events was that, following a dispute, William the priest was confirmed as perpetual vicar of the three churches while master Lambert, probably an episcopal clerk, was to receive from the monks of Castle Acre, the patrons, one mark a year while William the vicar lived, as a token of his expectative right. Master Lambert was subsequently instituted as parson, but some time later an agreement was reached before the bishop whereby Adam of Walsingham was to be instituted as parson, saving to Castle Acre its accustomed pension. Adam thereupon presented master Lambert to the vicarage of Lexham and John of Weasenham to that of Weasenham. There was some delay occasioned by the failure of the monks to give their consent to these transactions – quite possibly because they were bemused by them – but eventually Adam was instituted to the *personatus*, that is, as the episcopal *actum* states, to the pensions due from these churches. There can be few better illustrations of the treatment of the parish church by the holders of benefices constituted within it as a source of income which might be bargained in order to obtain the optimum results, or of the acquiescence of monastic patrons and diocesan in such manoeuvres.

One of the main aims of reforming prelates in sanctioning the donation of local churches to monasteries had been the elimination of a married priesthood and its corollary, hereditary succession to benefices. At the beginning of the twelfth century Archbishop Anselm had shown little sympathy for Bishop Herbert's lament that, were he to deprive all the married clergy of Norwich diocese, there would hardly be a church still served.[74] A century later Pope Innocent III instructed Bishop John de Gray that married clergy in his diocese might be ejected from their livings by papal authority, and as late as 1240 Pope Gregory IX wrote to Bishop William de Ralegh to fortify him in his efforts to circumvent the subterfuge employed by sons of parsons in obtaining their fathers' churches.[75] In the mid-twelfth century reference is made in an episcopal *actum* to the custom of the city of Norwich by which a parson held his church as had his ancestors,[76] and in 1194 the jurors in an advowson dispute in the *curia regis* stated that at Dunston 'they had never seen any parson presented to the church, but always the parsons held it, one parson after another from father to son, down to the last parson lately deceased'; he left only a daughter, to whom the king's justices adjudged the advowson.[77] The greatest of lay patrons, the king, presented his clerk master John of Bridport to the living of Hingham, previously held by his father.[78] The hopes of the reformers that the monastic acquisition of advowsons would end such practices

[73] BL ms. Harley 2110, fos 126v–127r.
[74] *Councils and Synods*, i, pt. ii, 683–4.
[75] *The Letters of Pope Innocent III (1198–1216) concerning England and Wales*, ed. C. R. and M. G. Cheney, Oxford 1967, no. 498; *Calendar of Papal Letters*, i, 190.
[76] Cambridge, Gonville and Caius College archives, X Ia.
[77] *Rotuli Curiae Regis*, ed. F. Palgrave, Record Commission 1835, i, 37–8; cf. Cheney, *From Becket to Langton*, 127.
[78] *The Book of Fees*, HMSO 1921–31, i, 280.

were not well founded. There is much evidence to suggest that the new cloistered patrons were prepared to sanction hereditary tenure of churches if by this means they might increase their own revenues.[79]

An example which spans the twelfth century and three generations is the church of Thornham. Bishop Herbert granted the service of 2s. 6d. rendered to him by Thurstan the deacon, the parson, to the monks of the cathedral priory. When Thurstan's son Elvric succeeded him in the church this annual pension was increased to 5s., and Thurstan's grandson William had to give the monks each year forty seams of grain.[80] In the 1140s Withgar, parson of Mendlesham, one of Battle Abbey's dower churches, wishing to provide for his children after him, asked that his son should be presented to the bishop for institution to the church; the abbot finally agreed, on condition that the annual pension to the monks should be increased from 10s. to 40s.[81] Between 1167 and 1183 the prior of Binham, with the consent of the abbot of St Albans, granted the church of Little Ryburgh to the two sons of Alan the parson, to be held for half a mark during their father's lifetime and thereafter for one mark.[82] Such presentations continued into the thirteenth century. Shortly before 1218 Fabian parson of Riston presented his son Roland to the vicarage of his church by means of letters of the prior and convent of Lewes, the patrons, to the bishop. That the Cluniac monks were prepared thus flagrantly to contravene the canons is perhaps explained by the claim of the Baynard family to the advowson and the desire to avoid for as long as possible a vacancy in the church which might be the occasion for litigation.[83]

Hereditary succession was certainly condoned by St Benet's Abbey in the time of Abbot William II (1153–68), who in two recorded instances presented sons to their fathers' churches. Thomas of Ludham was granted the churches of Ludham, Potter Heigham and St Michael-at-Plea, Norwich, as they had been held by his father, for 10s. a year; to Potter Heigham he was certainly instituted by the bishop. The Norwich church had also been held by Thomas's grandfather Stigand, who in the early twelfth century had, in association with his son, granted it to St Benet's.[84] Compliance with the fashion for monastic endowment had not in this instance disrupted hereditary tenure. Abbot William's brother held the church of St Lawrence, South Walsham, which had previously been occupied by their father and subsequently passed to Geoffrey's son Philip, himself a married man, who was instituted by the bishop at his uncle's presentation.[85]

In the light of these examples, a letter of Pope Lucius III (1181–5) to Abbot Thomas of St Benet's is of great interest.[86] The pope had heard from the abbot

[79] For evidence from another diocese, see B. R. Kemp, 'Hereditary Benefices in the Mediaeval English Church: a Herefordshire Example', *BIHR* xliii, 1970, 1–15; J. Barrow, 'Hereford Bishops and Married Clergy, *c.* 1130–1240', *BIHR* lx, 1–8.

[80] *Curia Regis Rolls*, xvi, no. 1659.

[81] *Battle Chronicle*, 240–4.

[82] BL ms. Claudius D xiii, fo. 165r.

[83] *Lewes Cartulary, Norfolk Portion*, no. 128.

[84] *St Benet of Holme*, i, nos 95, 183; cf. nos 76, 83.

[85] *St Benet of Holme*, i, nos 88, 145, 240.

[86] *St Benet of Holme*, i, no. 70; for another letter on this subject from Pope Clement III, see *ibid.*, no. 72.

that an evil custom had grown up through the negligence of his predecessors, whereby the sons of priests who held the abbey's churches obtained, during their fathers' lifetime, confirmation that they would enter into their churches upon their deaths; in return for this concession a pension was paid to the monks. The pope declared any such agreement and confirmation to be contrary to ecclesiastical discipline and uncanonical. Abbot Thomas may have been particularly scrupulous and have wished to use his parochial patronage to improve the standards of the clergy. It may, however, have occurred to him, in the 1180s, that the extraction of pensions in this way was a somewhat old-fashioned and unprofitable method of exploiting the financial potential of churches in his gift, which was made more difficult by the newly imposed necessity for episcopal consent. Writing at about this time the author of the Battle chronicle, recounting Abbot Walter's efforts to recover and increase the pensions from the abbey's East Anglian churches, stated the opinion of some *moderni* among the monks that he would have acted more prudently if he had sought to appropriate those churches, with all their profits, to the monastery, instituting vicars who would serve for a decent annual wage; by granting the churches to clerks who would pay pensions, he had accepted a small proportion of their considerable revenues when he could have had everything.[87]

It was to be a century and a half, however, before the monks of Battle completed by this means the maximisation of their ecclesiastical revenues in East Anglia, and in the meantime they were subject to those strong external influences on the exercise of their patronage which were experienced by all religious houses. The use of the papal plenitude of power in providing to benefices was rare in the twelfth century, although Walter, a papal notary, had before 1169 obtained a church in the gift of Bury St Edmunds, and it would be interesting to know by what means master Albert of Vercelli, parson of Rattlesden in 1200, had obtained the benefice which in that year he granted at farm to one of his parishioners.[88] In general, however, the intrusion of Italians into East Anglian rectories was initiated by the patronage and influence of Pandulf, papal legate and bishop-elect of Norwich during Henry III's minority, and was consolidated by the active presence in the diocese as archdeacon of John of Ferentino.[89]

More obvious in the twelfth century was the influence of the crown, both direct and indirect. As the royal administration in the course of the century grew ever more sophisticated, churches in the king's own gift proved increasingly inadequate as a source of income for the legion of royal clerks. A certain Geoffrey, who complained in Archbishop Theobald's court that he had been despoiled by one Gregory of the church of Beccles, which was in the gift of Bury St Edmunds, appealed to the apostolic see because, he alleged, he could say there things which he did not dare to mouth in England because Gregory was a servant of the king.[90] A fascinating series of decretal letters, preserved

---

[87] *Battle Chronicle* 250–2.
[88] *Papsturkunden in England*, ed. W. Holtzmann, Gottingen 1930–52, iii, 301–2, no. 161; Ipswich, Suffolk Record Office, Iveagh Deeds, box 324 part i (temporary reference).
[89] He was archdeacon of Norwich *c.* 1228–38; there is evidence of the activity of his kinsman James, dean of Holt, in several cartularies.
[90] *Letters of John of Salisbury*, i, no. 81.

only in a continental collection, indicate that after the collapse of the rebellion of 1173–4 Wimer the chaplain, sheriff of Norfolk and Suffolk, used his influence to obtain from the monks of Thetford the church of Holy Trinity, Bungay, ejecting therefrom a certain Thomas, clerk of the disgraced Bigod earl of Norfolk.[91] There is evidence of more direct royal pressure. Henry II granted the church of Wighton to Norwich cathedral priory, but at his request they installed in it Richard Brito, a royal clerk who was to hold it for his lifetime in return of an annual payment of one mark to the fabric fund.[92] Osbert de Camera, a prominent royal servant, was granted the church of Exning, in the gift of Battle abbey, and was succeeded therein by Richard de Camera, and a writ of Henry II gave notification that he had taken under his protection Eye Priory and its possessions, especially the church of Badingham, which at his petition the prior had granted to the same Osbert for a pension of one mark.[93] Jocelin of Brakelond, in his chronicle, has Abbot Samson relate how in 1161 he had gone to Rome to recover the lapsed rights of St Edmund to a pension from the church of Woolpit and had obtained a bull authorising the appropriation of the church when it fell vacant. On his return from this hazardous journey, however, he found that in his absence the church had been granted to Geoffrey Ridel, keeper of the king's seal, and when Geoffrey vacated it on his elevation in 1173 to the bishopric of Ely, at the king's request it was granted to master Walter de Coutances, in return for which concession Henry II conceded that on Walter's death or resignation, its revenues should be assigned to the convent for the use of sick monks.[94] The crown took every opportunity to extend its patronage. When Nicholas de Stuteville after 1204 threw in his lot with the king of France, King John presented to the vacant church of Kimberley, previously granted by Stuteville to Valmont, and the new rector was John of Brancaster, archdeacon of Worcester and a senior royal clerk who also held a benefice in the gift of Eye Priory.[95] Royal interests might equally well be served by indirect patronage. When in the early thirteenth century Richard de Clare claimed against the monks of Binham a moiety of St Peter's, Great Walsingham – an action which he subsequently won – Bishop Gray, despite his letter to the king's justices in support of Binham, in accordance with the decree of the Third Lateran Council himself collated the church after it had been left vacant for six months because of litigation. The beneficiary of this canonical act was Richard Marsh, the king's vice-chancellor.[96]

Competition for benefices in the diocese of Norwich was exacerbated by the fact that the cathedral was a monastic foundation, and the bishop therefore did not have at his disposal the rich prebends available to his colleagues at Lincoln, London and Salisbury. The problem was recognised in 1220 by Pope

[91] *Decretales Ineditae Saeculi XII*, ed. S. Chodorow and C. Duggan, Monumenta Iuris Canonici series B, Corpus Collectionum vol. 4, Vatican City 1982, nos 46, 51, 53, 65.

[92] *Norwich Cathedral Charters*, i, no. 31 (probably Easter 1176 or Christmas 1178).

[93] San Marino, California, H. E. Huntingdon Library, Battle Abbey Papers vol. 29, fo. 80r–v; *Eye Priory Cartulary*, no. 4.

[94] *Jocelin of Brakelond*, 48–9; *Feudal Documents*, no. 97.

[95] *Bracton's Notebook*, ii, 33–5, no. 39; *Eye Priory Cartulary*, no. 61.

[96] *Bracton's Notebook*, iii, 251–5, no. 1238.

Honorius III when he granted licence to Pandulf, because the benefices in his gift were few and of little value, to present clerks in his service to more than one living.[97] Conflict between bishop and chapter over their respective rights of presentation to parish churches annexed to the mother church of the diocese had been one of the issues which had contributed to the tension between the monks of Norwich and John of Oxford, and this dispute was only finally resolved in 1205 by Bishop Gray.[98] Lacking sufficient patronage of his own, the bishop desperately needed to tap the resources of others. Abbot Samson of Bury admitted that he was bound by his promise to provide revenue for an episcopal clerk and stated that he would grant a moiety of Hopton church to whomsoever the bishop should nominate.[99] It appears that similar pressure was placed upon other, less independent, religious houses as well as upon lay patrons.

It is surely significant that many of the earliest letters of institution, dating from the episcopate of William Turbe, are in favour of members of his *familia* who were presented to livings by various monasteries. When between 1146 and 1149 the incumbent of St Andrew's church at Lamas resigned, the bishop confirmed the grant of the benefice by the abbot of St Benet's to Nicholas the clerk, who frequently attested episcopal *acta*. Probably in 1150 the bishop granted in alms to Jocelin, his clerk, the church of Stalham, also in the gift of St Benet's. In full synod the prior and convent of Castle Acre presented Ralph, the bishop's clerk, to the church of Haverhill (1151 × 1173), and Ernald Lovel, one of the most regular witnesses of Turbe's charters, was granted the church of Honington by Robert de Valognes (1158 × 1173).[100]

From the time of John of Oxford evidence is more abundant. The clearest example of the use of parish churches in the gift of monasteries to provide for the bishop's staff is the grant by the prior and convent of Eye to Archdeacon Roger of Suffolk, who was frequently in his diocesan's company, of the stewardship (*procurationem*) of their appropriated living of St Leonard's, Dunwich, in return for a pension of twelve marks, hospitality for the prior and provision for a monk and a chaplain resident at the church (1190 × 1200).[101] It was far more common, however, for members of the *familia* to be presented by the religious to the *personatus* of their churches, and a new inducement to accept the bishop's clerks as incumbents was provided by papal rulings on the necessity for episcopal consent to pensions drawn from churches. There is reason to believe that Bishop John of Oxford granted pensions to monasteries when, and perhaps on condition that, members of his *familia* were presented. Thus between 1175 and 1186 Thomas, bishop's clerk, was granted Felmingham and St Peter-in-Conisford, Norwich, for annual pensions of five shillings and a pound of incense rendered to St Benet's, and Archdeacon Thomas (probably the same man) received the church of North Walsham from that house for a yearly payment of £1. When Geoffrey, the bishop's chaplain, was instituted to Fulmodestone it was stipulated that Castle Acre priory should

[97] *Calendar of Papal Letters*, i, 71.
[98] *Norwich Cathedral Charters* i, nos 263–4; cf. nos 177–8.
[99] *Jocelin of Brakelond*, 62.
[100] *St Benet of Holme*, i, nos 84, 89; BL ms. Harley 2110, fo. 125r; *Jocelin of Brakelond*, 61.
[101] *Eye Priory Cartulary*, no. 162.

been paid at St Botolph's day, 17 June, and at Michaelmas day in September. This is confirmed by a place-name such as Somercotes, an isolated settlement in the sea marsh, away from the parent village.[40]

A salt-works, therefore, consisted of an area of foreshore, the salt-house, of clay or cob with a timber roof covered with thatch or reed, and a heap, built up from the processed sandy silt, broken earthenware vats and other débris. It is the mounds of débris, the 'fittes' of Lincolnshire and the 'Red Hills' of Essex, that sometimes remain to serve as indications of the industry. In Lincolnshire they are conspicuously large, about twenty metres in diameter and up to seven metres high.[41] In Sussex, they range from six to forty metres in diameter, but generally they are under two metres in height. In Kent there are two which exceed 4.5 m. in height.[42] The salt-working sites along the river Adur, Sussex, have been examined by Holden and Hudson, and those in Lincolnshire have been assessed by Rudkin, Owen, Healey, and notably by Hallam.[43] It is a significant feature of this extraction process that spoil-heaps gradually had the effect of raising the level of the land, and of pushing the high-water mark and the newer salt-works nearer the sea. Apparently this was unconscious reclamation, with the reclaimed land being used, first for pasture, and even for settlement. The process is shown clearly on a map of 1595. This shows an area of the Fulstow–Marshchapel coastline in Lincolnshire.[44] It was a process which had started a long time before the Norman Conquest.

Twelfth-century documents refer not only to *salinæ*, spoil-heaps, and areas of sand shore (*greva*), but also illustrate that the foreshore was divided into strips. For example, the grant, in 1101–19, of the bishop of Norwich to the cathedral priory, gives lands in Purfleet and all his Gaywood salt-works, except those in which he had his *plumba* (lead pans), and except one other *salina*, held by Seman's mother.[45]

One spoil-heap, or mound (*hoga*), in Lynn, Norfolk, was sufficiently prominent to have acquired its own name by the time of a grant of *c.* 1182 – *de hoga de Len vocatur Belasi*.[46] Another late-twelfth-century document grants *salinam in marisco de Gaywoode . . . cum greva et cum hoga*.[47] Two other documents, among a large number cited by Hallam, serve to illustrate further the main elements in coastal salt-working. In the late twelfth century, Simon le Bret gave to Kirkstead Abbey *salinam*, with a toft and an area of shore for

---

[40] Rudkin and Owen, 81, 83; A. E. B. Owen, 'Salt, Sea Banks and Medieval Settlement on the Lindsey Coast', in N. Field and A. White (ed.), *A Prospect of Lincolnshire*, Lincoln 1984, 47.
[41] Rudkin and Owen, 76.
[42] E. W. Holden and T. P. Hudson, 'Salt-making in the Adur Valley, Sussex', *Sussex Archaeological Collections*, cxix, 1981, 128–9.
[43] Holden and Hudson, 117–48; Rudkin and Owen, 76–84; R. H. Healey, 'Medieval Salt-making', *South Lincs. Archaeology*, i, 1977, 4–5; H. E. Hallam, 'Salt-making in the Lincolnshire Fenland during the middle ages', *Lincolnshire Architectura; and Archaeological Society Reports and Papers*, ns viii, 1960, 85–112 and *Settlement and Society A Study of the Early Agrarian History of South Lincolnshire*, Cambridge Studies in Economic History, Cambridge 1965.
[44] M. W. Beresford and J. K. S. St Joseph, *Medieval England: An Aerial Survey*, 2nd edn, Cambridge 1979, 262–5 and Figs 111a–b.
[45] D. M. Owen (ed.), *The Making of King's Lynn*, British Academy Records of Social and Economic History, ns ix, London 1984, no. 2, p. 68.
[46] Owen, *King's Lynn*, 6, no. 63, p. 89.
[47] Owen, *King's Lynn*, no. 65, p. 90.

collecting sand and making salt – the dimensions of the land are given.[48] The same Simon, in 1195–1205, granted Dereham Abbey nine acres in the *greva* of Wrangle, *ad salinas faciendas*, and a *placia*, five perches by three perches, *ad domum faciendum*.[49]

An essential commodity in salt production was a sufficient supply of fuel, either wood or peat. As has been noted above, pre-Conquest charters contain grants of fuel and show how important this was. It is no surprise that similar grants are to be found in the twelfth century. For example, in about 1165, Mathew de Praeres gave St Edmund's Abbey land in Wainfleet, together with a grant of turbary in the Fen, for use in the boiling-houses: the area used by the salters for keeping their sand when the sea had saturated it with salt is mentioned.[50] In 1193, William de Roumara granted the canons of St Mary's Dereham, Norfolk, four spades-worth digging in the east marsh of Bolingbroke.[51]

With a scarcity of woodland, the demands made by the local population, and by the salt-workers, would have caused considerable inroads to be made on the peat resources of the fenlands of Norfolk and Lincolnshire. It has been suggested that much of the Norfolk marshland had already been cut for its turf by the twelfth century.[52] Given the concentration of known salt-works in Norfolk, near the salt-marshes of the Lower Bure and Yar, and around Sutton and Walsham, and near Ormsby, Rollesby and Filby, it is thought possible that salt-working in the area, through its demand for peat, may have contributed to the making of the Broads to the east of Norwich. In the same way, in the Netherlands, in the district around Zieriksee, salt production using salt peat caused a number of lakes to be formed.[53] This is one remarkable possible result of salt production. Another is totally unexpected, and has an important bearing on the understanding of settlement history for parts of Norfolk and Lincolnshire, where salt-working was undertaken. It has been shown above that débris resulting from salt production led to areas of land being reclaimed and used, first, for grazing. Arthur Owen, in an important, though neglected, paper on the mediaeval settlement of the Lindsey coast, has shown that there is a remarkable relationship between salt-making and settlement. He has shown that along the old coastline between Wisbech and King's Lynn, in the Marshland district of Norfolk, village sites coincide with extensive areas of salt-workers' mounds. Furthermore, not only does the old sea bank, notably near West Walton, incorporate mounds, but at least three mediaeval churches, West Walton, Terrington St Clement and Clenchwarton, south-west and west of King's Lynn, stand on conspicuous mounds: these are explicable only as salt-workers' mounds.[54] In south Holland, Owen has observed further

---

[48] Hallam, *Settlement and Society*, 5: *unam salinam Wrengela cum uno tofto et area sabularia de latitudine octo perticarum cum pertica xx pedum et in longitudine de sedic usque ad profundum mare ad coligendum sabilum et faciendum salem in arenis meis.*

[49] Hallam, *Settlement and Society*, 77–8.

[50] D. C. Douglas, *Feudal Documents from the Abbey of Bury St. Edmunds*, British Academy Records of Social and Economic History, viii, London 1932, no. 205, p. 173.

[51] Stenton, no. 526, p. 381.

[52] J. M. Lambert et al., *The Making of the Broads* . . ., Royal Geographical Society Research ser., iii, 1960, 76.

[53] Lambert, 83–4, 106.

[54] Owen, 'Salt, Sea Banks', 46.

examples at Tydd St Mary and Gedney, and in Lindsey, North Coates, Marshchapel, Grainthorpe, Conisholme and North Somercotes. The church sites at Skidbrook, Saltfleetby St Peter, Theddlethorpe All Saints, Croft, Thorpe St Peter and Friskney, all have features to suggest that they are disused salt-works. This consequence of reclamation is remarkable. More remarkable is the fact that it can be shown, without any doubt, from the archaeological work of Clarke and Carter, and the documentary analysis by Dorothy Owen, that King's Lynn was built over disused salt-works.[55] Hudson has now demonstrated that Bramber, Sussex, was built in a similar way: the houses of William of Braose's newly planted late-eleventh-century borough, granted to Battle Abbey, were described as having been built 'in the land of the saltern'.[56] The same William of Braose, who died between 1093 and 1096, is accredited with 58 salt-works in the Domesday Book. Before *c.* 1190 William gave five in Bramber to Sele Priory.[57] Lewes Priory received another four from William's son Philip before 1121, and Durford Abbey, near Petersfield, Hampshire, soon after its foundation *c.* 1160, was granted by William of Braose II a salt-works under Bramber castle and two shillings rent from another in the same place.[58]

These donations are a sufficient indication of the continuing fashion for wealthy families to endow monastic houses with operating salt-works. Monastic archives provide copious examples of such grants. The overwhelming majority, for the east and south coasts, are, like the ones cited above, for operating salt-works: only rarely are the grants specifically for creating salt-works. It would appear that, more often than not, the salt-works were let out for a salt-or, later, a money-rent, presumably because salt production was very seasonal and would have been impossible to carry out from the monastic centre.

Unfortunately, monastic archives are very poor in providing details of how salt-works were operated. Father Hockey, however, has shown that Quarr Abbey, on the Isle of Wight, received a tithe of salt from its founder's salt-works at Lymington, on the opposite side of Southampton Water, together with a further tithe from Robert de Widvill's workings and the salt from its own works at Pennington.[59] To house the salt a granary was built specially on the quay at Lymington: this salt was the only commodity regularly transported to Quarr from its mainland estates.[60]

Shaftesbury Abbey, Dorset, which surprisingly has no reference to salt-working recorded among its Domesday manors, would have needed salt in large quantities. The only property of this well-endowed nunnery which could have produced salt was its estate at Corfe, with land adjoining Poole Harbour. Part of this estate included one hide at Arne, surveyed *c.* 1170. This twelfth-century survey contains important evidence about the organisation of salt production.[61]

[55] H. Clarke and A. Carter, *Excavations in King's Lynn 1963–1970*, Society for Medieval Archaeology, Monograph ser., vii, London 1977, 411–13; Owen, *King's Lynn*, 5–6.
[56] T. P. Hudson (ed.), VCH, *Sussex*, vi, pt i, London 1980, 201.
[57] L. F. Salzman, *The Chartulary of Sele Priory*, Cambridge 1923, 17.
[58] Holden and Hudson, 136.
[59] S. F Hockey, *Quarr Abbey and its lands 1132–1631*, Leicester 1970, 90, 96.
[60] Hockey, 91.
[61] BL Harl. 61, f. 60v–61r; see Keen, 'Medieval Salt-working', 26 for an edition of the Arne entry.

The survey contains the names of twenty-two men and the widow Edith. The one hide was divided into sixteen parts held by fourteen individuals in units of one part, in ten entries, or one and a half in four instances: only three holdings had rent (*gablum*) due from them. In addition, four crofts are mentioned, one with sixpence rent, the others with a due of one plough-share. The majority of people had one *plumbum*. Two groups of four held one jointly, seven had two each. Three had three, while two people had four. In all, forty-four *plumba* are recorded. The rent for one *plumbum* varied. Two shillings and ten pence was the usual amount, though it was sometimes less, at 2s 1d or 2s 4d, and sometimes as high as three or four shillings: the total rental was £6 16s. In addition to the rent, the majority had to provide a *wikeworc*, or load of salt for each *plumbum*: the total number of *wikeworkes* was forty-six.

Darby notes the use of the word *plumbi*, 'leaden vats', in the Domesday Survey entries for Bromsgrove and Tardebrigge, and a reference to *fabrici plumbi* in the entry for Northwich and Tibberton, 'which could be the lead works for making the vats'.[62] Lead pans are referred to in later sources and were certainly used, as has been noted above, for boiling brine. In Droitwich they are known to have been used before the introduction of iron pans in the seventeenth century. At Arne the twelfth-century survey may be simply recording their numbers. However, it cannot be assumed that *plumbum* refers to a boiling-pan; it may rather refer to the furnace on top of which the pan was placed. As one *wikeworc*, or load of salt, was due to Shaftesbury Abbey for each *plumbum*, it would be necessary to assume that, if a furnace were implied, the number of pans to each furnace was the same for each one referred to. This would account for the consistent render of salt. There can be little doubt that lead boiling-pans were used at Arne. There remains still the interpretation of *wikeworc* in the twelfth-century survey. The surveys of Fontmell and Iwerne in the same document may provide a clue.[63]

Fontmell and Iwerne were the estates closest to Shaftesbury Abbey, and it is not surprising that the tenants there had particular manorial services to perform. The survey records that all the men of Fontmell had to carry twenty loads of herring from Wareham, and from Arne twenty loads of salt (*xx summas de sale*). In the survey of Iwerne it is recorded that Oswi carried salt from Arne and herring from Wareham. Six other men owed the same service, but the quantity of salt is not specified. Eighteen other men did the same work as Oswi, except that the carrying done was half that expected of Oswi: Godman carried one load of herring and another of salt.

Unfortunately the details are not precise enough to work out how the forty-six *wikeworkes* due to the abbey from Arne were divided among the men from Fontmell and Iwerne. If one *summa salis* was the same as one *wikeworc*, the closest total, of forty-five *wikeworkes*, is arrived at by the men of Fontmell carrying twenty, Oswi and six others one and a half each (10½ total), eighteen others three-quarters each (13½ total), and Godman one.

This possible arrangement may be satisfactory enough to suggest that one *wikeworc* was the equivalent of one *summa salis*. If this is correct, the

---

[62] Darby, *Domesday England*, 261.
[63] BL Harl. 61, f. 65r, 67r; see Keen, 'Medieval Salt-working', 27 for an edition of the Fontmell and Iwerne extracts.

suggestion that a *summa* generally consisted of eight level bushels, equivalent to a quarter, may provide not only an indication of the amount of salt carried to Shaftesbury, that is forty-six quarters, but also of the output of the salt-works at Arne.[64] Assuming that the amount due to the abbey was a tithe of the total production, the total output would be four hundred and sixty quarters.

However, a grant by Patrick, earl of Salisbury (1142–67), gave to the church of St Michael, Breamore, Hampshire, and to the prior and convent of the church, '4 wichwertes of salt, to wit 8 quarters of salt out of his salt-marsh' at Canford.[65] If this is a correct indication of local measures, it may indicate that the Arne *wikeworc* consisted of two quarters, not one. Shaftesbury Abbey, therefore, may have received ninety-two quarters of salt from a possible total production of nine hundred and twenty quarters.

In either case, it is impossible to establish if the amount of salt received from Arne provided the abbey's total annual requirement. One may note, however, that it was the practice on the bishop of Winchester's estate at Bishop's Waltham to keep an annual stock of about one hundred and sixty quarters.[66]

This paper, using as its base the Domesday evidence, has been biased towards the east and south coasts. But even here the evidence can be far from complete. New demands led to the search for new supplies. It is significant that when seven new monastic houses were founded between 1088 and 1150 in Cumbria, they were all granted rights to build salt-works, with the associated rights for obtaining peat and turf.[67] The low coastline and extensive areas of sand, with easy access to large peat deposits, provided ideal conditions, particularly around Morecombe Bay: these physical conditions determined the possible locations for salt-working.

While new salt-works and monastic houses were being established on the west coast, one may pause to reflect that, on the east coast, settlements had been established and churches had already been built, or were to be built, on top of derelict salt-works, and that, in Dorset, the men from Fontmell and Iwerne were carrying their loads of salt and herring northwards to Shaftesbury Abbey.

Acknowledgements

A special debt of gratitude is owed to Mr R. N. R. Peers, who has provided encouragement and support during the preparation of this paper. Thanks are due also to Mr D. Mills, who answered several questions on Anglo-Saxon linguistic matters, to Dr D. Roffe for the benefit of his extensive knowledge of Lincolnshire, and to Mr J. T. Munby for generously providing access to many of the volumes on his shelves.

[64] R. E. Zupko, *Dictionary of English Weights and Measures* . . ., 1968, 140, 153.
[65] E. A. Fry, *Dorset Inquisitions Post Mortem, From Henry III to Richard III. AD 1216 to 1485*, 1916, 85.
[66] Bridbury, 112.
[67] J. J. Martin, 'Collected notes on the salt industry of the Cumbrian Solway Coast', in K. W..de Brisay and K. A. Evans (ed.), *Salt: The Study of an Ancient Industry*, Colchester 1975, 71.

Table One   An analysis, by county, of the *Domesday Book* holders

Holder	LINCOLNSHIRE	NORFOLK	SUFFOLK	ESSEX	KENT	SUSSEX	HAMPSHIRE with Isle of Wight	DORSET	DEVON	CORNWALL	Total
King	9	96¼	1	5	29		4			3: 8*	147¼: 8*
Archbishop of Canterbury					34						34
Archbishop of York	2										2
Bishop of Bayeux	19	16½		1	19						55½
Bishop of Durham	14										14
Bishop of Exeter						1			25		26
Bishop of Lincoln	2										2
Bishop of London				4							4
Bishop of Thetford		24									24
Canons of St Paul's				3							3
Fécamp Abbey						100					100
Glastonbury Abbey							13*				13*
Horton Abbey									11:11*		†11 :11*
New Minster, Winchester							2				2
Milton Abbey							13*				13*
Old Minster, Winchester							3				3
Romsey Abbey							1				1
St Augustine's, Canterbury					48						48
St Benet of Holme		9½									9½
St Edmund's		3	1								4
St Etheldreda		26									26
St Étienne, Caen									2		2
St Guthlac's, Crowland	4										4
St Martin's, Dover					1						1 (but deprived of)
St Mary's, Barking				8							8
St Mary, Rouen									1		1
St Mary of Wilton							1				1
St Michael of the Mount									33*		33*
St Peter's, Jumièges							1				1
St Peter's, Peterborough	16										16
Count Alan	115	6½	2				2				125½
Count of Eu						49					49
Count Eustace		1¾		7							7¾
Count of Mortain						77+		44:16*	17: 2*	10	148+ :18*
Countess Judith	3										3
Earl Hugh	21		1								22
Earl Roger						9	2				11

* salt-worker

† a further 4 had to be taken by the Count of Mortain

Holder	LINCOLNSHIRE	NORFOLK	SUFFOLK	ESSEX	KENT	SUSSEX	HAMPSHIRE with Isle of Wight	DORSET	DEVON	CORNWALL	Total
Aelmer		1½									1½
Alfred of Lincoln	1										1
Almar		2¼									2¼
Alfred, the Breton									2		2
Ansketel						1					1
Arcy, Norman of	2										2
Baldwin, the sheriff									1		1
Baynard, Ralph		8		6							14
Baynard		1									1
Beaufour, Ralph of		¼									¼
Belet, William							14*				14*
Beuvrière, Drogo de la	1										1
Berner, the crossbowman		1½									1½
Bigot, Roger		6½+	2								8½+
Braose, William of						58+					58+
Cheever, William									1		1
Croan, Guy of	1+										1+
Drogo	1										1
Ecouis, William of		16½									16½
Eudo, son of Spirewic	2	½									2½
Ferrers, Hermer de		1									1
Gernon, Robert				2	3						5
Ghent, Gilbert of	7										7
Godric, the Steward		½									½
Hamo, the Steward				2							2
Heppo, the crossbowman	2										2
Hermer		11½+									11½+
Hugh, son of Baldric	4½										4½
Jocelyn, son of Lambert	1										1
Judhel									2		2
Malet, Durand	2										2
Malet, Robert		1½	1								2½
Mandeville, Geoffrey de			1	3							4
Montfort, Hugh de		9½		4½	8⅓						22⅓
Mortimer, Ralph of						6					6
Odo						1					1
Percy, William of	6										6
Peverel, Ranulf				1							1
Poilley, William de									1		1

Holder	LINCOLNSHIRE	NORFOLK	SUFFOLK	ESSEX	KENT	SUSSEX	HAMPSHIRE with Isle of Wight	DORSET	DEVON	CORNWALL	Total	
Pomery, Ralph de									4	: 4*	4	4*
Rabellus, the engineer		1									1	
Raismes, Roger of			2								2	
Ralph, the crossbowman			3								3	
Ranulph, brother of Ilger			1								1	
Reinbald		5½									5½	
Reynold, son of Ivo		2									2	
Robert, the bursar	6										6	
Robert, son of Corbucion		1		1							2	
Robert, son of Gerald						1					1	
Roald									2		2	
Swein of Essex			1	1							2	
Tallboys, Ivo	13+										13+	
Tetbald, son of Berner									1	: 3*	1	3*
Tosny, Robert of		11									11	
Valognes, Peter of	4										4	
Valognes, Peter of		8									8	
Vere, Aubrey de			3								3	
Verli, Robert de		1									1	
Vessey, Robert of	2										2	
Warenne, William of		21½+				11					32½+	
William, the deacon				1							1	
William, son of Stur							1				1	

APPENDIX ONE

The Domesday Salt-works

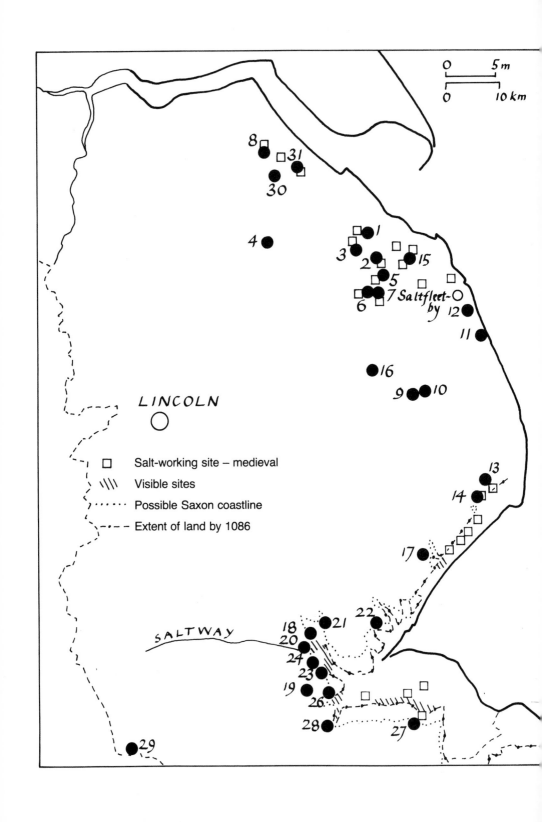

8 □
□ 31
30

4 ●

□ 1
3 □
2 □ □ 15
5 □ □
7 Saltfleet-○
6 by 12
11 ●

●16
9 ●●10

LINCOLN
○

□   Salt-working site – medieval
\\\   Visible sites
......   Possible Saxon coastline
- - -   Extent of land by 1086

13
14

17

22
18 21
20
SALTWAY
24
23
19
26
28
27
29

Fig. 1   LINCOLNSHIRE

NORTH RIDING

Bradley:	1 Tetney (13)
Haverstoe:	2 Fulstow (26)
	North Thoresby and
	'Audby' (21)
	3 North Thoresby (2)
	4 Rothwell (3)
Ludborough:	5 Covenham (7)
	6 Fotherby and
	Thorganby (4)
	7 (Little) Grimsby (1)
Yarborough:	8 Habrough and
	Newsham (1)
	30 Keelby (1)
	31 Stallingborough (6½)

SOUTH RIDING

Calcewath:	9 Calceby
	10 Haugh
	11 Mablethorpe
	12 Theddlethorpe with
	Wainfleet in
	Candleshoe (20)
Candleshoe:	13 Croft (1)
	14 Wainfleet (11)
Lowthesk:	15 Grainthorpe (6)
	16 Maidenwell (1)

HOLLAND

Wolmersty:	17 Leake (41)
Kirton:	18 Bicker (22 and
	1 waste)
	19 Cheal (1)
	20 Donington (27)
	21 Drayton (8½)
	22 Frampton (15)
	23 Gosberton (1)
	24 Quadring (2)
	25 'Stenning' (8)
	26 Surfleet (2)
	Drayton Hundred
	(1½)
	Kirton Hundred (2)
	Gosberton Hundred
	(2)
Elloe:	27 Fleet (2)
	28 Spalding
	(*area salinarum*)

KESTEVEN

Beltisloe:	29 (North) Witham (2)

The mediaeval salt-working sites have been plotted from B. Kirkham, 'Salt making sites found in North East Lincolnshire since 1960', in K. W. de Brisay and K. A. Evans (eds), *Salt: The Study of an Ancient Industry*, Colchester 1975, Fig. 24; visible sites and the possible Saxon coastline, from R. H. Healey, 'Medieval salt-making', *South Lincs. Archaeology* i, 1977, Fig. 1; the extent of land by 1086 from maps in H. E. Hallam, *Settlement and Society: A Study of the Early Agrarian History of South Lincolnshire*, Cambridge Studies in Economic History, Cambridge 1965.

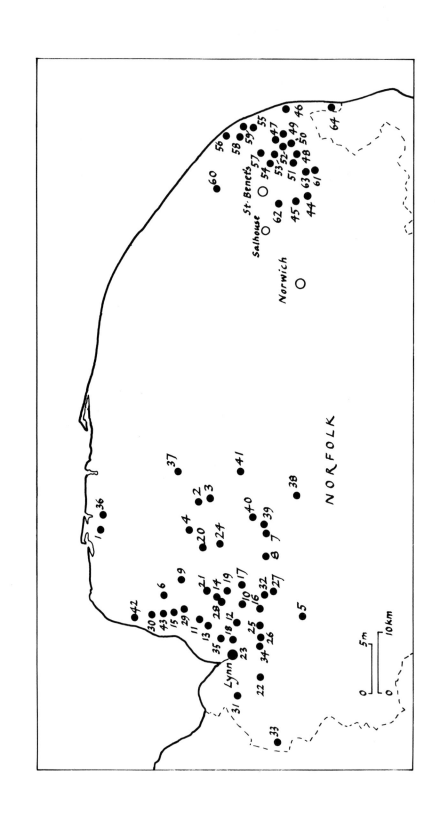

Fig. 2 NORFOLK

Names in [ ] brackets indicate those places for which salt-works are recorded only before Domesday.

WEST

Brothercross:	1 [Burnham] (1)
	2 Helhoughton (1)
	3 Raynham (1)
	4 Rudham (1)
Clackclose:	5 [Shouldham] (1)
Docking:	6 Shernborne (½)
Freebridge:	7 Acre (Castle) (½)
	8 Acre (West) (5)
	9 Anmer (1½)
	10 Ash Wicken with Bawsey (½)
	11 Babingley (5)
	12 Bawsey (1½)
	13 Castle Rising (12)
	14 Congham (½)
	15 Dersingham (2)
	16 East Winch (1½)
	17 Gayton (1½)
	18 Gaywood (21)
	19 Grimston (½)
	20 Harpley (½)
	21 Hillington (½)
	22 Islington (8½)
	23 Lynn (9½)
	24 Massingham (¼)
	25 Middleton (18)
	26 North Runcton (4⅓)
	27 Pentney (⅓)
	28 Roydon (3½)
	29 Sandringham (1)
	30 Snettisham (1 and 2 parts)
	31 Terrington (12½)
	32 West Bilney (½)
	33 West Walton (38)
	34 West Winch (2)
	35 Wootton (14)
Gallow:	36 [Burnham] (1)
	37 Fakenham (½)
Greenhoe (S):	38 Necton (1)
	39 Newton (½)
Launditch:	40 [Lexham (West)] (¼)
	41 Mileham (1)
Smethdon:	42 Heacham (1)
	43 Ingoldisthorpe (1)

EAST

Blofield:	44 Moor (1)
	45 North Burlingham (½)
Flegg (East):	46 Caistor (45)
	47 Filby (10½)
	48 Herringby (5½)
	49 Mautby (18¾)
	50 Runham (18½)
	51 Stokesby (3)
	52 Thrigby (½)
Flegg (West):	53 Burgh (2)
	54 Clippesby (¼)
	55 Hemsby (2)
	56 Ness (3 parts)
	57 Rollesby (½)
	58 Somerton (3)
	59 Winterton (½)
Happing:	60 Sutton (½)
Walsham:	61 Halvergate (1)
	62 (South) Walsham (3)
	63 Tunstall (1)

under Suffolk–

| Lothingland: | 64 Gorleston (3) |

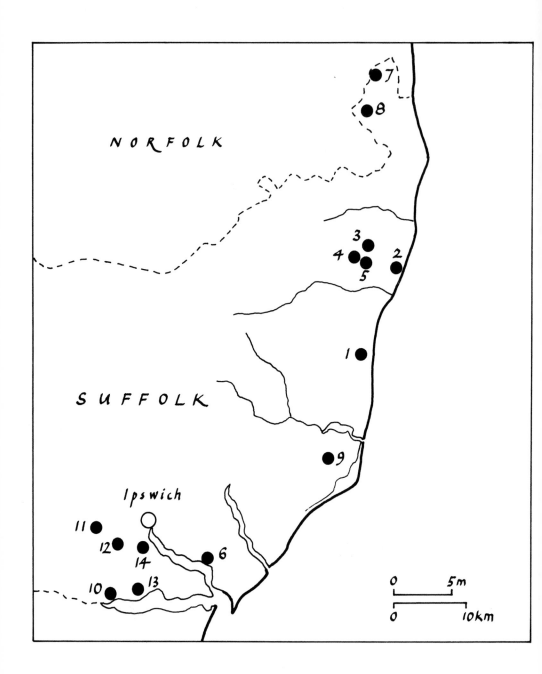

Fig. 3   SUFFOLK

Blything:	1	Bridge (1)
	2	[(Easton) Bavents] (1)
	3	[Frostenden] (1)
	4	Uggeshall (1)
	5	[Wangford] (1)
Colneis:	6	'Leofstanestuna' (1)
Lothingland:	7	Burgh (Castle) (3)
	8	[Fritton] (1)
Plomesgate:	9	Sudbourne (1)
Samford:	10	Brantham (2)
	11	Hintlesham (1)
	12	Pannington (1)
	13	Stutton (3)
	14	Wherstead (1)

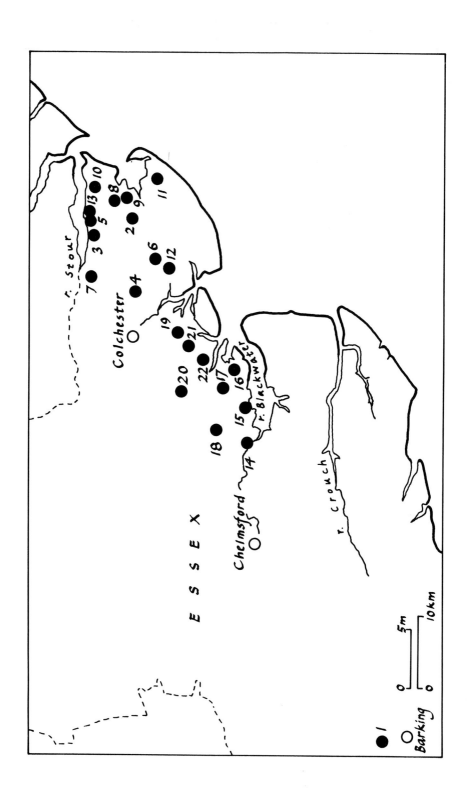

Fig. 4 ESSEX

Becontree:	1 Wanstead (1)
Tendring:	2 Beaumont (2)
	3 Bradfield (1)
	4 Elmstead (1)
	5 Jacques Hall (1)
	6 (Great) Bentley (1)
	7 (Great) Oakley (2)
	8 Lawford (1)
	9 Moze (3)
	10 Ramsey (1)
	11 The Naze (2)
	12 Thorrington (1)
	13 Wrabness (1)
Thurstable:	14 Heybridge (1)
	15 Goldhanger (1½)
	16 Tollesbury (3)
	17 Tolleshunt (13)
	18 Totham (7)
	Thurstable Hundred (4)
Winstree:	19 Langenhoe (1)
	20 (Layer) Marney (1)
	21 Peldon (1)
	22 Wigborough (6)

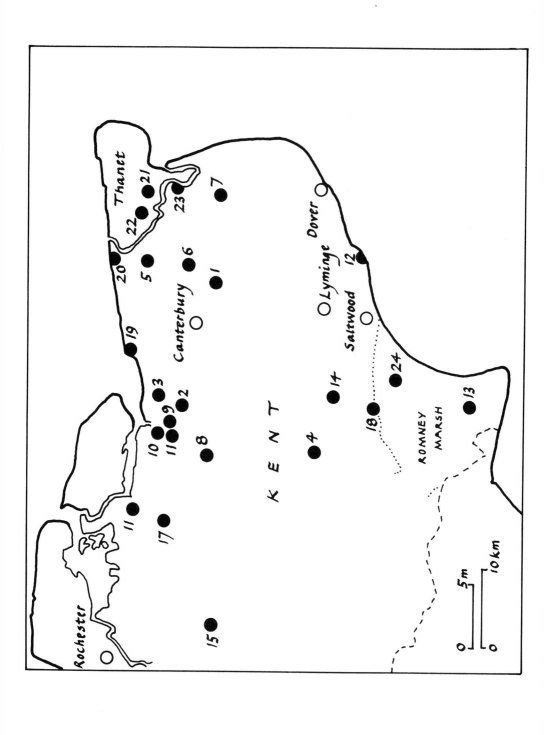

Thanet

21
22
23
20
5
7
6
1

Canterbury

Dover
12
Lyminge
Saltwood
24
13

ROMNEY MARSH

3
2
9
10 11
8

14
18

K   E   N   T

4

11
17

15

Rochester

5m
10 km
0
0

Fig. 5   KENT

Bridge:	1 Bekesbourne (1)
Boughton:	2 Boughton Blean (1)
	3 Graveney (4)
Chart:	4 Chart Magna (1)
Chislet:	5 Chislet (47)
Downhamford:	6 Wickhambreux (2)
Eastry:	7 Eastry (3)
Faversham:	8 Arnolton (2)
	9 Faversham (2)
	10 Oare (1)
	11 Ospringe (1)
Folkestone:	12 Folkestone (1)
Langport:	13 Langport (7)
Longbridge:	14 Mersham (2)
Maidstone:	15 Maidstone (2)
Milton:	16 Milton (27)
	17 Tunstall (1)
Newchurch:	18 Bilsington (10)
Reculver:	19 Northwood (7)
	20 Reculver (5)
Thanet:	21 Minster (1)
	22 Monkton (1)
Wingham:	23 Fleet (1)
Worth:	24 Eastbridge (8⅓)

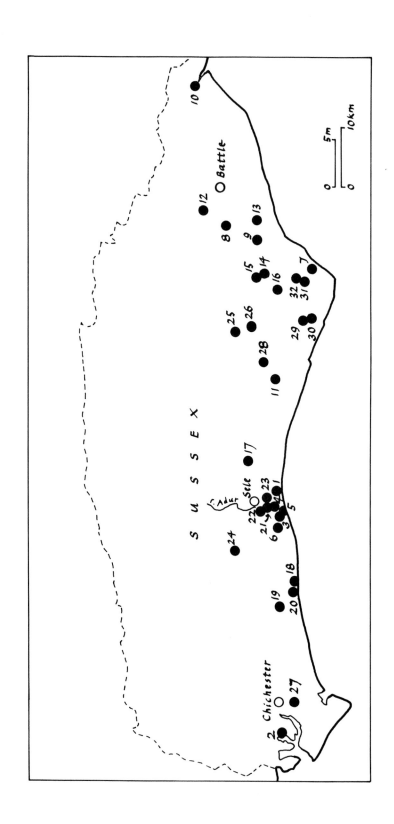

Fig. 6   SUSSEX

Aldrington:	1 Kingston (9)
Bosham:	2 Bosham (1)
Brightford:	3 Cokeham (1)
	4 Hoe (6)
	5 Lancing (23)
	6 Sompting (9)
Eastbourne:	7 Eastbourne (16)
Foxearle:	8 Ashburnham (3)
	9 Wartling (3)
Guestling:	10 Rye (100)
Holmestrow:	11 Rodmell (11)
Netherfield:	12 Netherfield (8)
Ninfield:	13 Hooe (34)
Pevensey:	14 Bowley (4)
	15 Hailsham (2)
	16 Wootton (5)
Poynings:	17 Saddlescombe (render)
Poling:	18 East Preston (3)
	19 Lyminster (2)
	20 'Nunminster' (West Preston) (2)
Steyning:	21 Applesham (2)
	22 Coombes (render)
	23 Wappingthorne (render)
	24 Washington (5)
Shiplake:	25 Laughton (16)
	26 Ripe (8)
Stockbridge:	27 Hunston (2)
Totnore:	28 Beddingham (4)
Willingdon:	29 Charlston (3)
	30 Dean (?West) (4)
	31 Ratton (2 fourth parts)
	32 Willingdon (11)

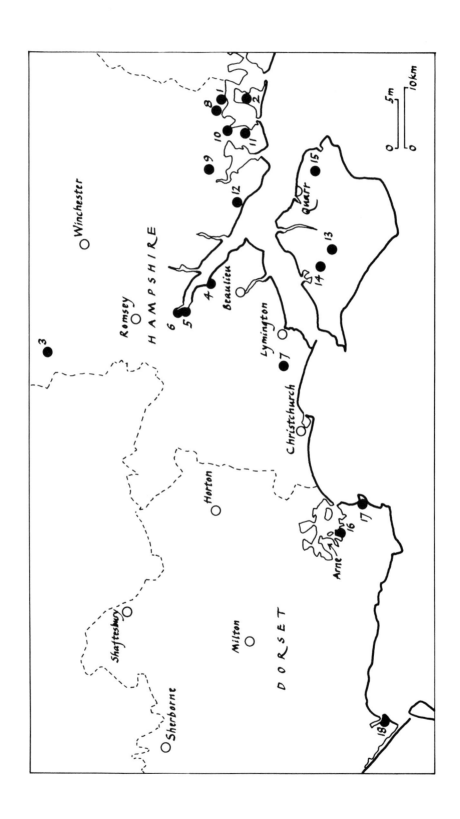

Fig. 7 HAMPSHIRE AND EAST DORSET

Bosmere:	1 Havant (3)
	2 Hayling Island (1)
Broughton:	3 (Nether) Wallop (1)
Redbridge:	4 Dibden (1)
	5 Eling (1)
	6 Totton (1)
Rowditch:	7 Hordle (6)
Portsdown:	8 Bedhampton (2)
	9 Boarhunt (9)
	10 Cosham (1)
	11 Copnor (1)
Titchfield:	12 Crofton (2)
Isle of Wight:	13 Bowcombe (1)
	14 Watchingwell (1)
	15 Whitefield (1)
Dorset–	16 Ower (13*)
	17 Studland (32)
	18 Weymouth (12)

* salt-worker

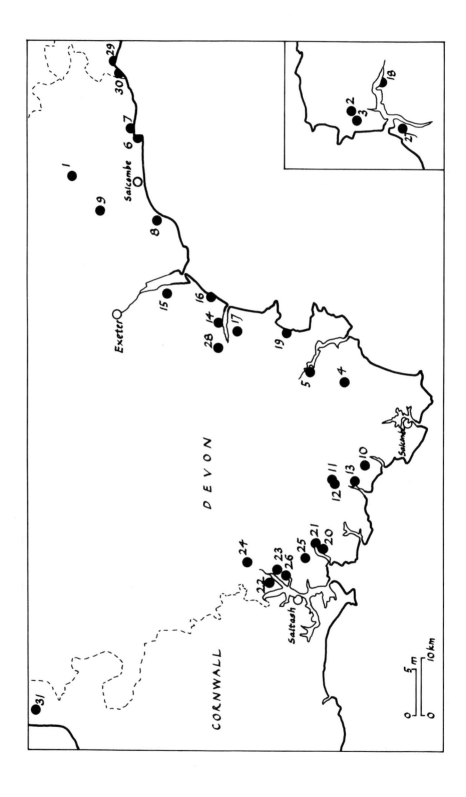

Fig. 8 DEVON, WEST DORSET AND CORNWALL

Axminster:	1 Honiton (4 and 2*)
Braunton:	2 Lobb (1)
	3 Saunton (1)
Coleridge:	4 Blackawton (1)
	5 Ashprington (1)
Colyton:	6 Beer (4)
	7 Seaton (11 and ?11*)
E. Budleigh:	8 Otterton (33*)
	9 Ottery St Mary (1)
Ermington:	10 Bigbury (1)
	11 Ermington (1)
	12 Hollowcombe (4)
	13 Orcherton (1)
Exminster:	14 Bishopsteignton (24)
	15 Kenton (8*)
	16 (Lower) Holcombe (4 and 4*)
	17 (Nether) Haccombe
	17 (Nether) Haccombe (1)
Fremington:	18 Hollowcombe (3*)
Haytor:	19 Paignton (1)
Plympton:	20 Alfermerston (Train) (1)
	21 Woodford (1)
Roborough:	22 Bere Ferris (7)
	23 Blaxton (1)
	24 Buckland Monachorum (1)
	25 Egg Buckland (1)
	26 Tamerton Foliat (1)
Shebbear:	27 Northam (2)
Teignbridge:	28 Whiteway (1)
Dorset–	29 Charmouth (16*)
	30 Lyme (27*)
Cornwall–	31 Stratton (10)

* salt-worker

APPENDIX TWO

The *Domesday Book* Entries for Salt-working

LINCOLNSHIRE

folio	Philli-more	Holder	Hundred	Manor	1086	Render	Total
338	1,34	King	Elloe	Fleet	2	2s	
338v	1,77		Yarborough	Habrough and Newsham	1	12d	
	1,85		Louthesk	Grainthorpe	6	6s	9
339v	2,6	Archbishop of York	Yarborough	Stallingborough	2		
340	2,30		Kirton	Bicker	1 waste		2
340v	3,6	Bishop of Durham	Haverstoe	Fulstow	11	2s	
	3,16		Ludborough	Covenham	2	3s	
341	3,47		Candleshoe	Wainfleet	2	8d	14
342	4,24	Bishop of Bayeux	Haverstoe	North Thoresby and 'Audby'	3		
342v	4,42		Haverstoe	North Thoresby and 'Audby'	16	16s	19
344v	7,34	Bishop of Lincoln	Kirton	Cheal	1	8d	
	7,36		Kirton	Gosberton	1	4d	2
345v	8,11	St Peter's, Peterborough	Kirton	Donington	16	20s	16
346v	11,6	St Guthlac's, Crowland	Kirton	Drayton	4	5s 4d	4
347	12,19	Count Alan	Haverstoe	Fulstow	8	8s	
347v	12,38		Haverstoe	(North) Thoresby	2	2s	
348	12,58		Drayton	—	½	8d	
	12,59		Drayton	—	1	16d	
	12,60		Kirton	Drayton	4½	6s	
	12,61		Kirton	Donington	9	12s	
	12,62		Kirton	Donington	2	32d	
	12,64		Wolmersty	Leake	26		
	12,64		Wolmersty	Leake	15		
	12,70		Kirton	Frampton	15	20s	
348v	12,71		Kirton	—	2	16d	
	12,75		Kirton	Bicker	20	30s	
	12,76		Gosberton	—	2	12d	
	12,89		Kirton	'Stenning'	6	8s	
	12,90		Kirton	Quadring	2	12d	115
349	13,7	Earl Hugh	Candleshoe	Wainfleet ⎫			
			Calcewath	Haugh, Calceby, Theddlethorpe & Mablethorpe ⎭	20	10s	

folio	Philli-more	Holder	Hundred	Manor	1086	Render	Total
349v	13,33		Louthesk	Maidenwell	1		21
350	14,1	Ivo Tallboys	Bradley	Tetney	13	12s	
351v	14,97		Elloe	Spalding	—	20s	13+
353	18,9	Robert of Tosny	Ludborough	Fotherby and Thorganby	4	2s	4
354	22,25	William of Percy	Ludborough	(Little) Grimsby	1	6d	
	22,26		Ludborough	Covenham	5	2s	6
355v	24,74	Gilbert of Ghent	Candleshoe	Croft	1	6d	
	24,75		Candleshoe	Wainfleet	6	3s	7
356	25,7	Hugh, son of Baldric	Yarborough	Stallingborough	2½	2s	
	25,12		Haverstoe	(North) Thoresby and 'Audby'	2	2s	4½
357v	27,16	Alfred of Lincoln	Haverstoe	Rothwell (North Thoresby and 'Audby')	1		1
359v	28,41	Jocelyn, son of Lambert	Candleshoe	Wainfleet	1	8d	1
360	29,20	Eudo, son of Spirewic	Candleshoe	Wainfleet	2	16d	2
360	30,9	Drogo de la Beuvrière	Yarborough	Keelby	1	12d	1
361v	32,1	Norman of Arcy	Yarborough	Stallingborough	2	3s	2
363	37,6	Robert of Vessey	Kirton	'Stenning'	2	2s 8d	2
363v	38,14	Robert the bursar	Haverstoe	Fulstow	6	6s	6
365	44,6	Durand Malet	Haverstoe	Rothwell (North Thoresby and 'Audby')	1		
	44,14		Haverstoe	('Audby') Rothwell	1		2
366v	56,1	Countess Judith	Beltisloe	(North) Witham	2	10s	
367	56,22		Kirton	Bicker	1		3
368	57,44	Guy of Craon	Kirton	Bicker	1	16d	
	57,54		Elloe	Spalding	*aream salinarum*	4d	1+
369	61,5	Heppo, the crossbowman	Kirton	Surfleet	2	12d	2
376	CN,22	Drogo	Haverstoe	Fulstow	claims 1		1

NORFOLK

folio	Philli-more	Holder	Hundred	Manor	TRE	1086	Total
111	1,15	King	Gallow	Fakenham	½	½	
120	1,72		S. Greenhoe	Newton	½	½	
122	1,88		Brothercross	Helhoughton	1	1	
126	1,132		Freebridge	East Winch	1½	1½	
	1,133		Freebridge	Wootton	20	14	
128	1,147		Gallow	Burnham (Overy)	1		
	1,152		Walsham	Halvergate		1	
129	1,155		Walsham	(South) Walsham	½	½	
134	1,201		East Flegg	Caister	39	39	
134v	1,202		East Flegg	Mautby	7	7	
	1,202		East Flegg	Mautby	4	4	
			East Flegg	Mautby	6½	6½	
			East Flegg	Mautby	¼	¼	
	1,203		East Flegg	Runham	10	10	
			East Flegg	Runham	2½	2½	
			East Flegg	Runham		2	
135	1,204		East Flegg	Thrigby	½	½	
136v	1,212		Launditch	Mileham	1	1	
138	1,217		West Flegg	Somerton	1½	1½	
283	1,31	(under Suffolk)	Lothingland	Gorleston		3	96¼
142v	2,4	Bishop of Bayeux	Freebridge	Snettisham		1	
			Freebridge	(Castle) Rising	12	12	
			Freebridge	Roydon	2	2	
			Freebridge	Roydon		1½	16½
146v	4,26	Count Alan	West Flegg	Somerton	1½	1½	
149	4,44		Freebridge	Islington	3½	3½	
			Freebridge	Islington		1	
149v	4,45		Freebridge	Ash Wicken and Bawsey		½	6½
151	5,1	Count Eustace	Freebridge	Massingham	¼	¼	
151v	5,2		Freebridge	Anmer	½	½	
			Freebridge	Anmer	1	1	1¾
153v	7,1	Robert Malet	Freebridge	Bawsey		1½	1½
159	8,13	William of Warenne	East Flegg	Filby	3	2	
160v	8,21		Freebridge	(West) Walton	1½	7	
			Freebridge	(West) Walton	7 .	7	
	8,22		Freebridge	(Castle) Acre		½	
	8,24		Freebridge	Gayton	1½	1½	
161	8,26		Freebridge	Congham		½	
	8,27		Freebridge	Grimston		½	
161v	8,30		Freebridge	Harpley		½	

folio	Philli-more	Holder	Hundred	Manor	TRE	1086	Total
163	8,47		Smethdon	Heacham		1	
163v	8,48		Freebridge	Snettisham		2 parts	
169	8,107		Brothercross	Rudham	1	1	21½ +
173	9,2	Roger Bigod	Freebridge	Pentney	⅓	⅓	
179v	9,88		Happing	Sutton	½	½	
180	9,90		East Flegg	Runham	2½	2½	
	9,91		East Flegg	Filby	2½	2½	
	9,92		West Flegg	Ness	3 parts	3 parts	
	9,93		East Flegg	Mautby	1	1	6½ +
191	10,2	William, bishop of Thetford	Freebridge	Gaywood	30	21	
195	10,30		West Flegg	Hemsby	2	2	
199v	10,73		Blofield	North Burlingham	½	½	
200v	10,82		West Flegg	Winterton	½	½	24
202v	12,6	Godric the steward	Walsham	(South) Walsham		½	½
206v	13,12	Hermer	Freebridge	Terrington	7	7	
207	13,13		Freebridge	Islington	½	½	
	3,14		Freebridge	North Runcton		4⅓	11½ +
209	14,4	Abbot of St Edmund's	Freebridge	Islington	1	1	
	14,5		Freebridge	Middleton		2	3
213	15,4	St Etheldreda	Freebridge	(West) Walton	22	24	
	15,6		Freebridge	Islington		2	26
216	17,1	St Benet of Holme	Walsham	(South) Walsham		2	
216v	17,10		West Flegg	Rollesby		½	
220v	17,61		East Flegg	Filby	1	1	
221	17,63		East Flegg	Caister	6	6	9½
222	19,3	William of Écouis	Freebridge	Islington		½	
	19,4		Freebridge	Middleton		8	
225	19,36		East Flegg	Stokesby	2	2	
225v			East Flegg	Stokesby	1	1	
	19,37		East Flegg	Filby	5	5	16½
226v	20,8	Ralph of Beaufour	Launditch	Lexham (West)	¼		¼
231v	21,9	Reynold, son of Ivo	Freebridge	West Winch	2	2	
	21,10		Freebridge	Ash Wicken	½		2
235	22,1	Ralph of Tosny	(S.) Greenhoe	Necton		1	
236	22,16		Freebridge	Acre	5	5	

folio	Philli-more	Holder	Hundred	Manor	TRE	1086	Total
	22,19		Freebridge	Lynn		5	11
237v	23,4	Hugh de Montfort	Brothercross	Burnham	1		
	23,5		Brothercross	Raynham		1	
238	23,11		Freebridge	Middleton	10	8	
238v	23,12		Freebridge	West Bilney	½	½	9½
245v	29,1	Eudo, son of Spirewic	Freebridge	Hillington	½	½	
	29,3		Freebridge	Babingley	9		
	29,4		Freebridge	Dersingham	1		½
251	31,22	Ralph Baynard	Clackclose	Shouldham	1		
251v	31,31		Freebridge	Terrington	5½	5½	
	31,32		Freebridge	Lynn		2½	8
256	34,1	Peter of Valognes	Freebridge	Babingley		5	
	34,2		Freebridge	Dersingham		1	
			Freebridge	Dersingham		1	
256v	34,4		Smethdon	Ingoldisthorpe	1	1	8
258v	35,1	Robert, son of Corbucion	Freebridge	Sandringham	1	1	1
262	38,4	Robert de Verli	Walsham	Tunstall		1	1
267v	51,3	Berner the crossbowman	Freebridge	Hillington	1	1	
268	51,4		Docking	Shernborne		¹/₁₂	1¹/₁₂
269v	55,1	Radellus, the engineer	Blofield	Moor		1	1
272	64,1	Almar	West Flegg	Burgh	2	2	
	64,4		West Flegg	Clippesby		¼	2¼
273	65,8	Reinbald	East Flegg	Herringby	4½	4½	
			East Flegg	Herringby		1	5½
	65,9	Aelmer	East Flegg	Runham	½	½	
			East Flegg	Runham		1	1½
274v	66,17	Hermer de Ferrers	Freebridge	Lynn		1	1
276	66,55	Baynard	Freebridge	Lynn		1	1

SUFFOLK

folio	Philli-more	Holder	Hundred	Manor	TRE	1086	Total
284v	1,58	King	Lothingland	Fritton	1		
289	1,118		Samford	Hintlesham	1	1	1
295v	3,77	Count Alan	Samford	Wherstead		1	
296	3,82		Samford	Brantham	1	1	2
299v	4,14	Earl Hugh	Blything	Uggeshall		1	1
317	6,143	Robert Malet	Plomesgate	Sudbourne	1	1	1
331v	7,6	Roger Bigot	Blything	Bridge		1	
342	7,106		Colneis	'Leofstanestuna'		1	2
402	27,10	Swein of Essex	Samford	Pannington		1	1
411v	32,6	Geoffrey de Mandeville	Samford	Stutton		1	1
414v	33,6	Ralph Baynard	Blything	Frostenden	1		
	33,7		Blything	Wangford	1		
419v	36,2	Robert Gernon	Samford	Stutton	2	2	2
425	39,17	Ranulf, brother of Ilger	Samford	Brantham	1	1	1
444v	68,1	Gilbert, the crossbowman	Blything	(Easton) Bavents	1		
445	69,1	Ralph, the crossbowman	Lothingland	Burgh (Castle)		3	3

ESSEX

folio	Philli-more	Holder	Hundred	Manor	TRE	1086	Total
6	1,27	King	Tendring	Lawford		1	
7v	1,31		Thurstable	—		4	5
9v	3,5	Bishop of London	Becontree	Wanstead	1	1	
10	3,7		Winstree	Layer (Marney)	1	1	
11	4,2		Thurstable	Totham		1	
	4,3		Thurstable	Totham	1	1	4
13v	5,10	Canons of St Paul's	Thurstable	Heybridge	1	1	
	5,11		Tendring	The Naze	3	2	3
18	9,8	St Mary's, Barking	Winstree	Wigborough		6	

folio	Philli-more	Holder	Hundred	Manor	TRE	1086	Total
	9,14		Thurstable	Tollesbury		2	8
20	11,18	St Edmund's	Tendring	Wrabness		1	1
25v	18,43	Bishop of Bayeux	Tendring	Thorrington		1	1
28	20,19	Count Eustace	Winstree	Langenhoe		1	
32	20,57		Thurstable	Tolleshunt	12	5	
	20,62		Thurstable	Tollesbury		1	7
48	24,64	Swein of Essex	Tendring	Elmstead	1	1	1
54	27,16	Hugh de Montfort	Thurstable	(Little) Totham	1	3	
54v	27,17		Thurstable	Goldhanger	½	1½	4½
56v	28,17	Hamo, the Steward	Thurstable	(Great) Totham		2	2
59v	30,18	Geoffrey de Mandeville	Tendring	Moze		3	3
67v	32,38	Robert Gernon	Tendring	(Great) Oakley		2	
68v	32,45		Thurstable	Tolleshunt (D'Arcy)		1	3
70v	33,16	Ralph Baynard	Tendring	Ramsey		1	
71v	33,23		Thurstable	Tolleshunt		5	6
75v	34,36	Ranulf Peverel	Thurstable	Tolleshunt (D'Arcy)	1	1	1
77v	35,9	Aubrey de Vere	Tendring	(Great) Bentley		1	
	35,11		Tendring	Beaumont		2	3
83v	39,7	Roger of Raismes	Tendring	Bradfield		1	
	39,9		Tendring	Jacques Hall		1	2
86	41,12	Robert, son of Corbucion	Thurstable	Tolleshunt (Major)		1	1
94v	66,1	William, the deacon	Winstree	Peldon		1	1

KENT

folio	Philli-more	Holder	Hundred	Manor	1086	Render	Total
2v	P,19	Canons of St Martin's, Dover	Robert of Romney deprives them of		1		
	1,3	King	Milton	Milton	27	27s	
	1,4		Faversham	Faversham	2	3s 2d	29
3	2,11	Archbishop of Canterbury	Maidstone	Maidstone	2		
3v	2,13		Reculver	Reculver	5	64d	
	2,14		Reculver	Northwood (Whitstable)	7	25s 4d	
	2,18		Boughton	Boughton under Blean	1	16d	
	2,21		Wingham	Fleet	1 + fishery	30d	
	2,22		Longbridge	Mersham	2	5s	
4	2,35		Boughton	Graveney	4	4s	
4v	2,43		Langport	Langport	7	8s 9d	
4v–5	3,7	(archbishop's monks)	Thanet	Monkton	1	15d	
5	3,14		Chart	Chart Magna	1	6d	
	3,17		Eastry	Eastry	3	4s	34
9	5,115	Bishop of Bayeux	Milton	Tunstall	1	12d	
	5,122		Bridge	Bekesbourne	1	30d	
	5,124		Downhamford	Wickhambreux	2	32d	
9v	5,128		Folkestone	Folkestone	1	30d	
10	5,141		Faversham	Oare	1	28d	
	5,145		Faversham	Ospringe	1	4d	
	5,147		Faversham	Arnolton	2		
10v	5,175		Newchurch	Bilsington	10	100d	19
12	7,8	Church of St Augustine	Thanet	Thanet Minster	1 +2 fisheries	3d	
	7,9		Chislet	Chislet	47	50 *summae salis*	48
13	9,10	Hugh de Montfort	Worth	Eastbridge	8⅓	20s	8⅓

SUSSEX

folio	Philli-more	Holder	Hundred	Manor	1086	Render	Total
17	5,1	Abbot of Fécamp	Guestling	Rye	100	£8 15s	100
	6,1	Bishop Osbern	Bosham	Bosham	1	2s	1
18	9,1	Count of Eu	Ninfield	Hooe	30	33s	
	9,3		Ninfield	*Medehei*	5	64d	
	9,6		Foxearle	Wartling	3	7s	
	9,7		Foxearle	Ashburnham	3	58d	
18v	9,23		Netherfield	Netherfield	8	8s	49
20v	10,2	Count of Mortain	Eastbourne	Eastbourne	16	£4 40d	
	10,3		Totnore	Beddingham	4	40d	
21	10,27		Willingdon	Willingdon	11	35s	
	10,30		Willingdon	Charlston	3	10s 4d	
	10,34		Willingdon	(?West) Dean	4	8s	
	10,36		Willingdon	Ratton	fourth part	10d	
	10,37		Willingdon	Ratton	fourth part	10d	
22	10,67		Pevensey	Wootton	5	41s 8[d]	
	10,68		Pevensey	Hailsham	2	7s	
			Pevensey	Hailsham	11 kept	24s 6d	
	10,77		Ninfield	Hooe	4	20s	
	10,83		Pevensey	Bowley	4	22s 4d	
	10,86		Shiplake	Ripe	8	20s	
22v	10,93		Shiplake	Laughton	16	25s	77+
24	11,43	Earl Roger	Stockbridge	Hunston	2		
24v	11,59		Poling	Lyminster	2	20d	
	11,63		Poling	'Nunminster'	2	30d	
	11,69		Poling	(East) Preston	3	30d	9
26	12,4	William of Warenne	Holmestrow	Rodmell	11	26s	
27	12,33		Poynings	Saddlescombe	*de sale*	15d	11
28	13,9	William of Braose	Steyning	Washington	5	9s 2d, or 110 ambers of salt	
	13,10		Steyning	Steyning	3	30d	
	13,14		Steyning	Wappingthorne	*de sale*	20d	
28v	13,19		Steyning	Coombes	*de salinis*	50s 5d	
	13,20		Steyning	Applesham	2	5s	
	13,28		Aldrington	Kingston	6	20s, and 10 ambers of salt	
	13,29		Aldrington	Kingston	3	22d	
29	13,38		Brightford	Sompting	8	13s	

folio	Philli-more	Holder	Hundred	Manor	1086	Render		Total
			Brightford	Sompting	1	2s		
	13,43		Brightford	Lancing	7	20s	3d	
			Brightford	Lancing	11	12s	6d	
	13,44		Brightford	Lancing	5	12s	6d	
	13,45		Brightford	Cokeham	1		40d	
	13,46		Brightford	Hoe	6	7s	6d	58+

HAMPSHIRE

folio	Philli-more	Holder	Hundred	Manor	1086	Render		Total
38	1,10	King	Portsdown	Cosham	1			
38v	1,19		Broughton	(Nether) Wallop	1		5d	
	1,27		Redbridge	Eling	1	*sine censu*		3
43	3,27	Monks of Winchester	Bosmere	Havant	3		15d	3
	6,4	St Peter's, Winchester	Portsdown	Bedhampton	2	37s	8d	2
43v	10,1	St Peter's of Jumièges	Bosmere	Hayling Island	1	6s	8d	1
44	15,4	Romsey Abbey	Redbridge	Totton	1	10s		1
	18,1	Count Alan	Titchfield	Crofton	2		100d	2
44v	21,1	Earl Roger	Portsdown	Boarhunt	2	22s	4d	2
46v	28,2	Robert, son of Gerald	Portsdown	Copnor	1		8d	1
49v	68,5	Ansketel	Portsdown	Cosham	1		14d	1
51	NF,5,1	Ralph of Mortimer	Rowditch	Hordle	6		15d	6
51v	NF,9,2	Odo	Redbridge	Dibden	1			1
52	IoW,1,7	King		Bowcombe	1	*sine censu*		1
52v	IoW,5,1	St Mary of Wilton		Watchingwell	1	*sine censu*		1
53	IoW,6,14	William, son of Stur		Whitefield	1	14s	8d	1

DORSET

folio	Philli-more	Holder	Hundred	Manor	*salinae*	*salinarii*	Render	Total
77v	8,6	Glastonbury Abbey	Whitchurch Canonicorum	Lyme		(13)	13s	(13)
78	12,13	Milton Abbey	Rowbarrow	Ower		(13)	20s	(13)
79	26,15	Count of Mortain	Cullifordtree	Weymouth	12			
80	26,61		Rowbarrow	Studland	32		40s	
	26,67		Whitchurch Canonicorum	Charmouth		(16)		44(16)
85	57,14	William Belet	Whitchurch Canonicorum	Lyme		(14)		(14)

DEVON

folio	Philli-more	Holder	Hundred	Manor	*salinae*	*salinarii*	Render	Total
100v	1,23	King	Ermington	Ermington	1			
	1,24		Coleridge	Blackawton	1			
	1,26		Exminster	Kenton		(8)	20s	
101v	1,71		Coleridge	Ashprington	1			3(8)
	2,4	Bishop Osbern	Exminster	Bishopsteignton	24		10s	
102	2,18		Haytor	Paignton	1		10d	25
104	7,3	Abbot of Horton	Colyton	Seaton (*Fluta*)	11	(11)†	11d	
	7,4	(taken by Count of Mortain)	Colyton	Beer	4††			15
	10,1	St Mary of Rouen	E. Budleigh	Ottery St Mary	1		30d	1
	11,1	Abbot of St Michael's Mount	E. Budleigh	Otterton		(33)		(33)
	12,1	St Étienne, Caen	Shebbear	Northam	2		10s	2
104v	15,23	Count of Mortain	Axminster	Honiton		(2)	30d	
105	15,44		Ermington	Bigbury	1		30d	
	15,46		Roborough	Bere Ferris	7		10s	
105v	15,65		Ermington	Orcherton	1		5s	
	15,66		Ermington	Hollowcombe	4		40d, & 2 *summae salis*	17(2)

folio	Philli-more	Holder	Hundred	Manor	*salinae*	*salinarii*	Render	Total
503*			Axminster	Honiton	4*			
108	16,157	Baldwin, the sheriff	Teignbridge	Whiteway	1		12d	1
109v	17,69	Judhel	Roborough	Egg Buckland	1		2s	
110	17,105		Plympton	Woodford	1			2
	19,10	William Cheever	Exminster	(Nether) Haccombe	1			1
111v	21,20	William de Poilley	Roborough	Buckland Monachorum	1			1
114	34,11	Ralph of Pomeroy	Exminster	(Lower) Holcombe	4	(4)*	6s 5d	4(4)*
414*	35,20	Roald	Braunton	Lobb	1*			
115v	35,27		Plympton	Alfelmerston (Train)	1			2
	36,9	Tetbald, son of Berner	Fremington	Hollowcombe		(3)	4s 9d, & 5 *summae salis*, 1 *piscium*	
	36,10		Braunton	Saunton	1		30d	1(3)
116	39,19	Alfred, the Breton	Roborough	Tamerton Foliat	1		5s	
	39,20		Roborough	Blaxton	1		30d	2

* *Exon.* entry.
† *Exon.* has *salinarias*, which Finn (in Darby and Finn, *South-West England*, 271, n. 2) reads as 'salt-workers' rather than as a scribal error for *salinas*.
†† The 4 salt-works taken by the Count of Mortain, are those held by Drogo, attached to the manor of Honiton, *Exon.*, fo. 503.

CORNWALL

folio	Philli-more	Holder	Hundred	Manor	*salinae*	*salinarii*	Render	Total
121v	5,1,3	Count of Mortain		Stratton	10		10s	

THE WELSH ALLIANCES OF EARL ÆLFGAR OF MERCIA AND HIS FAMILY IN THE MID-ELEVENTH CENTURY

K. L. Maund

The 1050s must have looked bleak in prospect to Ælfgar, the son of the earl of Mercia, Leofric. While the decade had opened with a possibility of great power for him and for his family, with the fall of the house of Godwine in 1051,[1] this soon vanished as Godwine and his sons regained their former status within a year of that date.[2] Ælfgar, who had briefly enjoyed the position of earl of East Anglia, lost his newly gained lands to their former owner, Harold Godwinesson, and while that earldom was again to become his in 1053, it was only in the wake of a greater position for Harold, rising to become Earl of Wessex in the wake of Godwine's death.[3] The family of the Mercian earldom had had influence and power: in the earlier 1050s it must have begun to look to Ælfgar as though this was beginning to end, as the last few checks upon the power of the house of Godwine began to fall away.

The balance of power between the great families of the major earldoms, and those others who enjoyed royal favour, was never sure in the reign of Edward the Confessor.[4] Certainly, in the earlier part of his reign there appear to have been fears that the Normans whom he had brought with him from France were in possession of too great an influence over the king, and indeed Godwine's rebellion of 1051 was in the most part sparked off by the resentment and anxiety caused by Edward's foreign favourites.[5] But with the overthrow of these favourites, such as Robert of Jumièges, the most powerful group at Edward's court became that of Earl Godwine and his sons, especially Harold. Godwine himself died in 1053 and Harold succeeded to his earldom. And then, two years later (in 1055), another of the three great earls of Cnut's reign, Siward of Northumbria, died, and his young son Waltheof was passed over in favour of Harold's brother, Tostig Godwinesson.[6] To Ælfgar it must have seemed as though he and his father were hemmed in on all sides by the house of Godwine, and perhaps he even feared that on the death of his father he himself would be passed over, and the earldom of Mercia be bestowed on yet another of the sons of Godwine. The tensions no doubt generated by this situation came to a head and, later in that same year, Ælfgar was banished and stripped of his earldom.[7] The reasons for this banishment are shrouded in

---

[1] ASC (C) s.a. 1051; ASC (D) s.a. 1051; ASC (E) s.a. 1051.
[2] ASC (C) s.a. 1052; ASC (D) s.a. 1052; ASC (E) s.a. 1052.
[3] ASC (C) s.a. 1053; ASC (D) s.a. 1053; ASC (E) s.a. 1053.
[4] On this, see especially Frank Barlow, *Edward the Confessor*, London 1970, chapters 4–6.
[5] Barlow, *Edward the Confessor*, 104–15.
[6] ASC (E) s.a. 1055.
[7] ASC (C) s.a. 1055; ASC (D) s.a. 1055; ASC (E) s.a. 1055; ASC (F) s.a. 1055.

mystery: even his contemporaries seem not to have known them, or not to have wanted to record them. The issue is much additionally complicated by the problems presented by our sources at this point: the family of Godwine seems to have generated strong feelings in others; and our surviving texts, the C and E versions of the *Anglo-Saxon Chronicle*, are quite clear in their biases. The conflict generated by the C-text's desire to blacken Godwine and his sons, and the E-text's desire to show them to advantage, have completely obscured the facts behind Ælfgar's exile (and doubtless have blurred many other events of Edward's reign).

This banishment might have marked the effective end of Ælfgar's career: but in fact it did not. Following perhaps in the footsteps of Harold God-winesson before him, the exiled Ælfgar went overseas to Ireland, and thence to Wales; and, also like Harold, within a matter of months he was back in England and holding his former position. He was never to be a truly major power in England: indeed, he was again to suffer banishment later in the same decade,[8] but this first exile marked a turning-point in his political life, a turning-point indeed not simply for him, but for his sons, Eadwine and Morkere, and, perhaps more significantly, for one of the major powers beyond England's borders: Gruffudd ap Llywelyn, king – sole king – of Wales.

Gruffudd ap Llywelyn had first come into prominence in Wales in 1039, when he succeeded to the rulership of Gwynedd on the death of its former king, Iago ap Idwal.[9] He had rapidly established himself as the power in North Wales, and in the 1040s had turned his attention south, conducting lengthy and ultimately successful campaigns against two kings of Dyfed, first Hywel ab Edwin[10] and later Gruffudd ap Rhydderch.[11] In 1055, the year of Ælfgar's banishment, Gruffudd ap Llywelyn had finally conquered the South: his rival, Gruffudd ap Rhydderch, was dead and he had become the first – indeed the only – king ever to hold sway throughout the whole of Wales,[12] a position he was to maintain until his death in 1063.[13]

Gruffudd ap Llywelyn holds a position of considerable importance not only in the history of Wales but in that of England also. Throughout his reign he appears to have had a strong and expansionist policy, both towards his fellow Welsh men and towards his English neighbours: indeed, he opened his reign

---

[8] ASC (D) s.a. 1058. This incident is also recorded by Worcester s.a. 1058.

[9] Ed. John Williams ab Ithel *Annales Cambriae*, London 1860, B text s.a. [1038] C text s.a. [1040]; Thomas Jones, transl. *Brut y Tywysogion, or the Chronicle of the Princes: Peniarth ms. 20 version*, Cardiff 1941, s.a. 1037, *recte* 1039; Thomas Jones, ed. & transl. *Brut y Tywysogion, or the Chronicle of the Princes: Red Book of Hergest Version*, 2nd edition, Cardiff 1973, s.a. [1039]; Thomas Jones, ed. and transl., *Brenhinedd y Saesson, or The Kings of the Saxons BM Cotton ms. Cleopatra B.v and The Black Book of Basingwerk; NLW ms. 7006*, Cardiff 1971, s.a. 1037, *recte* 1039.

[10] On this see K. L. Maund, *Ireland, Wales and England in the Eleventh Century*, Woodbridge, forthcoming, chapter 2.

[11] Maund, *Ireland, Wales and England*, chapter 2.

[12] *Annales Cambriae* (B) s.a. [1055]; *Annales Cambriae* (C) s.a. [1057]; *Brut y Tywysogion* (Pen. 20) s.a. 1054, *recte* 1056; *Brut y Tywysogion* (RB) s.a. [1056]; *Brenhinedd y Saesson* s.a. 1054, *recte* 1056.

[13] ASC (D) s.a. 1063; ASC (E) s.a. 1063; *Annales Cambriae* (B) s.a. [1061]; *Annales Cambriae* (C) s.a. [1064]; *Brut y Tywysogion* (Pen. 20) s.a. 1061, *recte* 1063; *Brut y Tywysogion* (RB) s.a. 1060, *recte* 1063; *Brenhinedd y Saesson* s.a. 1061 *recte* 1063.

by striking both at Deheubarth and at the English in the vicinity of the River Severn.[14] However, his attitude towards the English was not purely hostile: through much of his career Gruffudd was to demonstrate a marked ability to exploit the political troubles of the English polity to his own ends and to his own advantage.[15] In 1055, with the South at last under his control, it is not at all surprising that he should look eastwards over his borders and in particular in the direction of Herefordshire. The exiled Ælfgar and the newly triumphant Gruffudd must have seemed like godsends to one another, as they joined in alliance to sack Hereford and defeat the army of its earl, Ralf the Timid.

I do not propose to discuss here in very great detail the career and apparent policies of Gruffudd ap Llywelyn, but it should be pointed out that this alliance was not the first which Gruffudd had formed with an English noble-man. In 1046 he had had a seemingly short-lived connection with Swegn, the eldest of Earl Godwine's sons, and at that time an earl with lands bordering on Wales.[16] Swegn Godwinesson had at best a chequered career (and never seems to have found much favour in England, especially in comparison with his brother Harold and his cousin Beorn), and his known actions appear to indicate a rather freebooting and belligerent nature.[17] At around the same time as the alliance with Swegn, and probably a little before,[18] Gruffudd ap Llywelyn had suffered something of a reverse in his attempts to overthrow Gruffudd ap Rhydderch of South Wales: his warband was heavily defeated by the South Welsh of Ystrad Tywi, according to our extant Welsh sources, *Annales Cambriae*[19] and the *Brutiau*.[20] Later in the same year Gruffudd launched a punitive raid upon both Ystrad Tywi and its neighbour Dyfed. The Welsh texts place this event *c.* 1047; the C-text of the *Anglo-Saxon Chronicle*, our sole witness to Swegn's and Gruffudd's alliance, places their joint activities in 1046. Sir John Lloyd considered the massacre in Ystrad Tywi to be a result of the alliance, which is not implausible.[21] However, it must be pointed out that, as far as chronology goes, in this period the Welsh texts and the *Anglo-Saxon Chronicle* are frequently out of step by one or two years. Given this, I should favour the theory that Gruffudd's punitive raid, and the joint raid by Gruffudd and Swegn described by the C-text of the *Anglo-Saxon Chronicle*, are one and the same. Both parties stood to gain: Gruffudd in acquiring extra forces to bring to bear against his enemy, and Swegn by keeping in check a possible threat on his own borders (the brother of Gruffudd ap Rhydderch, Caradog, had been put to death by the English in 1035, probably because he was proving to be a problem for them). In addition, Swegn no doubt gained financial resources and an outlet for his belligerence

---

[14] See note 9.

[15] Maund, *Ireland, Wales and England*, chapter 3.

[16] ASC (C) s.a. 1046.

[17] On the character of Swegn, see Barlow, *Edward the Confessor*, 90–1 and 99–103.

[18] Maund, *Ireland, Wales and England*, chapter 3.

[19] *Annales Cambriae* (B) s.a. [1046]; *Annales Cambriae* (C) s.a. [1048].

[20] *Brut y Tywysogion* (Pen. 20), s.a. 1045, *recte* 1047; *Brut y Tywysogion* (RB) s.a. [1047]; *Brenhinedd y Saesson*, s.a. 1045, *recte* 1047.

[21] J. E. Lloyd, *A History of Wales from the Earliest Times to the Edwardian Conquest* 3rd edition, 2 vols, London 1939, ii, 361.

and marauding spirit (indeed he was to crown this raid, on his return to England, by carrying off the abbess of Leominster).[22]

The alliance of 1046/7 was shortlived. In the wake of this raid Swegn was exiled, as punishment for his abduction of the abbess, and perhaps as a warning against forming too close links with the Welsh.[23] However, neither in this exile nor in his later exile with his family in 1051 is Swegn known to have turned towards Wales for support. It was a relationship formed for purposes of the moment and, those purposes served, it ceased.

The relationship which was to develop between Earl Ælfgar and the powerful Welsh king was somewhat different, and, indeed, as I said earlier, it was to play a major rôle in the lives of both men. Their joint activities in 1055 were to prove very successful. Having sacked Hereford, Gruffudd and Ælfgar returned to Wales while Harold Godwinesson busied himself in the collection of a large army. He led this force into Wales itself but did not manage to meet up with Gruffudd and Ælfgar. These two simply marched off into Gruffudd's new territory of South Wales and very shortly afterwards Harold let his army disband. Messengers passed between the two sides and eventually a meeting was arranged at Billingsley.[24] The outcome of this was the reinstatement of Ælfgar, and Professor Brooke has made a very good case for Gruffudd having achieved some territorial gains in Ergyng as a result of the same meeting.[25] Three years later, events were almost to repeat themselves. According to the D-text of the *Anglo-Saxon Chronicle*, in 1058 Ælfgar once more found himself exiled – again for no stated reason. The account is brief in the extreme, but it again shows Ælfgar turning to Wales in time of need, and enlisting the aid of Gruffudd ap Llywelyn to win reinstatement for himself. The alliance was to prove a success on this occasion also, and fairly swiftly if the words of the *Chronicle* are to be believed:

> Her man ytte ut Ælfgar eorl: ac he com sona inn ongean mid strece þurh Griffines fultum.

The immediate results of the alliance are fairly clear, and its ramifications were to prove quite lengthy, as will be seen later. First, however, I wish to return to the question of its origin. As has been mentioned, the 1050s were a time of considerable turbulence in England, and in their early part Ælfgar gained, lost and regained the East Anglian earldom, all within the space of about three years. The decade also saw the steady rise of Harold Godwinesson to power in England, and the deaths of Godwine and Earl Siward.[26]

The Welsh were not inactive on the English border in this period. In 1052, at the height of Godwine's rebellion, Gruffudd ap Llywelyn launched a raid into Herefordshire, exploiting to his own benefit, as he was often to do, the

[22] ASC (C) s.a. 1046.

[23] Maund, *Ireland, Wales and England*, chapter 3.

[24] ASC (C) s.a. 1055; ASC (D) s.a. 1055; ASC (E) s.a. 1055; ASC (F) s.a. 1055; the Welsh Chronicles omit all reference to Ælfgar but not the raid: *Annales Cambriae* (B) s.a. [1055]; *Annales Cambriae* (C) s.a. [1058]; *Brut y Tywysogion* (Pen. 20) s.a. 1054, *recte* 1056; *Brut y Tywysogion* (RB) s.a. [1056]; *Brenhinedd y Saesson* s.a. 1054, *recte* 1056.

[25] C. N. L. Brooke, *The Church and the Welsh Border in the Central Middle Ages*, Woodbridge 1986, 10–11.

[26] Godwine in 1053 and Siward in 1055.

troubles besetting the English polity.[27] (There is some doubt that this raid was led by Gruffudd ap Llywelyn and not by his southern rival, Gruffudd ap Rhydderch: however, as I have argued elsewhere, there is a very strong case indeed for accepting the raid as the work of the northern Gruffudd, and I shall do so here.[28])

It is my view that this raid played a rôle in the development of Gruffudd's and Ælfgar's alliance. It occurred at much the same time as Ælfgar lost East Anglia to Harold, and it seems possible that, seeing Harold's successful use of mercenaries in his bid for reinstatement, and also the success of Gruffudd's attack, Ælfgar was alerted to the existence of a powerful neighbour – and a possible political resource for himself. He was very probably in need of forceful support: the family of Godwine moved rapidly back into favour and soon gained the additional resources of Northumbria to add to their existing possessions.

It has generally been held that Ælfgar's alliance with Gruffudd was formed in 1055, during his exile – largely, perhaps, as a matter of expediency.[29] Ælfgar was in need of an army, and Gruffudd ap Llywelyn was perhaps wanting to show his strength after vanquishing the South Welsh. Both the latter points may be correct, but I beg leave to question the accepted timing of the formation of the alliance, following a suggestion first made over a century ago, by J. R. Green.[30] I should suggest that Ælfgar was making overtures to Gruffudd ap Llywelyn *before* he was exiled for the first time, and indeed that the exile may have resulted at least in part from this attempt to forge a relationship: after all, Ælfgar was likely to succeed his father as earl of Mercia, and thus to hold an important political position; and Gruffudd ap Llywelyn, who was known to be gaining in power in Wales, was likely to be a neighbour of his. In the alliance were the seeds of a formidable power-bloc and, with the ever increasing influence of the house of Godwine, something of this nature was what Ælfgar needed. He was very probably looking for a source both of power and of military strength – and Gruffudd's raid in 1052 had been a demonstration of both. Gruffudd himself stood to gain too: in Ælfgar he was acquiring a voice, and an ear, and a protector, at the English court.

This view is not uncontroversial. Sir John Lloyd argued against Green's suggestion on the ground that '. . . the sources imply that Ælfgar and Gruffudd did not come to terms until the former had returned from Ireland . . .'.[31] It is the case that those texts which mention Ælfgar's going to Ireland place the journey before his arrival in Wales, but it should be remembered, first and less important, that this Irish visit is not mentioned in all our sources,[32] and secondly, *pace* Lloyd, that there is nothing in the phrasing of any of the sources which can be taken as definitely indicating whether or not Gruffudd and Ælfgar had any prior contact. Moreover, there is no evidence that looking to Wales for support was a standard course of action in this period: unlike the

[27] Maund, *Ireland, Wales and England*, chapter 3.
[28] Maund, *Ireland, Wales and England*, chapter 3.
[29] Lloyd, *A History* ii, 364.
[30] J. R. Green, *The Conquest of England*, 3rd edition, 3 vols, London 1899.
[31] Lloyd, *A History* ii, 364, n. 19.
[32] The trip to Ireland is absent from ASC (E) and ASC (F).

Hiberno-Scandinavians, who seem to have acted regularly as mercenaries for whoever could offer sufficient incentive,[33] the Welsh on the whole appear to have been less a resource for the English than a threat. I find it somewhat difficult to imagine that, barring accidents of weather or tide, an exile from England (and a member of a family which had lost at least one member to Gruffudd's aggression), even with mercenaries accompanying him, would have risked an encounter with a powerful and potentially hostile Welsh ruler, on that ruler's own territory, unless he was sure of a moderately amicable reception. Some previous communication between the two seems more probable.

The alliance was above all a move in the power-game between the English noble families. Ælfgar was not alone in looking for political connections outside the English polity. Tostig Godwinesson had married a daughter of the Count of Flanders,[34] while Siward of Northumbria had involved himself in the fortunes of Malcolm Canmore in Scotland. Ælfgar's alliance with Gruffudd might have begun in 1053, when the house of Godwine perhaps suffered a temporary setback with the death of its head – such a setback seems likely, if only because Edward the Confessor chose to replace Harold Godwinesson as Earl of East Anglia with Ælfgar rather than with one of Harold's brothers. It seems more likely, however, that the alliance began early in 1055, when the earldom of Northumbria was given to Tostig, an event almost certainly threatening to Ælfgar, as it showed the ever increasing strength of the family of Godwine.

Whatever the motives behind the alliance may have been, its results can still be traced, at least in part. It was to prove effective, as is demonstrated both by Ælfgar's fairly rapid reinstatement and by Harold's having recourse to negotiation rather than force in 1055. Gruffudd and Ælfgar had presented a serious threat. This is demonstrated by the events of the next year.[35] Harold had succeeded in having his personal chaplain, one Leofgar, appointed as the new bishop of Hereford; and in the very year of his consecration, 1056, Leofgar had launched an attack upon Gruffudd ap Llywelyn. His force was defeated and Leofgar himself was slain. A negotiating party was sent out, led by Harold and by Ealdred, bishop of Worcester, and peace was made. Gruffudd swore a vow to be underking to Edward, but the incident above all else demonstrates that the English magnates of the time recognised Gruffudd as a significant power and as one it was necessary either to destroy or to bring in some formal way into the English polity.

Ælfgar himself seems to have wanted to formalise this relationship also. We learn from the *Historia Ecclesiastica* of Orderic Vitalis[36] that Ælfgar married his daughter Ealdgyth to his Welsh ally. The date of the marriage is not known. Sir John Lloyd appears to have thought that it was around 1057, the year in which Ælfgar succeeded his father as earl of Mercia, and the year prior

---

[33] They can be seen acting thus with Harold Godwinesson in 1053, and with the South Welsh king Hywel ab Edwin in 1044, to give but two instances.

[34] ASC (D) s.a. 1051.

[35] ASC (C) s.a. 1056; ASC (D) s.a. 1056.

[36] Orderic ii, 138, 216. There is also a mention of this in Orderic's interpolations into Jumièges, chapter 31.

to the year of his second exile.[37] It is not possible to reach an exact date, but there is some support for Lloyd's view in Giraldus Cambrensis's *Journey through Wales*.[38] Giraldus tells us that the Norman marcher lord, Bernard of Neufmarché, was married to Nest, a granddaughter of Gruffudd ap Llywelyn. Nest's mother was also named Nest, and was herself the wife of another border-lord, Osbern fitz Richard, who was still living in 1086. Osbern's wife Nest is usually taken to be Gruffudd's daughter by Ealdgyth, and the chronology of the two Nests seems to support Lloyd's date for the marriage of Ealdgyth and Gruffudd. It is unlikely, however, that Ealdgyth could have been the mother of Gruffudd's known sons, Maredudd and Ithel and possibly Owain. Owain died in 1059 at an unknown age: Maredudd and Ithel both fell in battle, probably in early manhood, in 1069.[39]

It is possible to glean further information about the alliance from the so-called Foundation-Charter of Coventry Abbey.[40] This text is a twelfth-century forgery, purporting to have been granted by Earl Leofric in 1043. The land to which it makes a claim is a place named Eaton, 'Eatun iuxta aminem que dicitur De in Cestre prouincia'.[41] This place can be identified as Eaton-on-Dee in the hundred of Maelor Cymraeg. The Cheshire Domesday tells us that in the time of King Edward this estate was the property of St Chad's, Chester.[42] However, it goes on to say:

> Rex E. dedit regi Griffino totam terram quae iacebat trans aquam quae De uocatur. Sed postquam ipse Griffin forisfecit et abstulit ab eo hanc terram, et reddidit episcopo de Cestre et omnibus suis hominibus qui antea ipsa tenebat.

In some measure at least this is a part of the settlements negotiated between Gruffudd ap Llywelyn and the English in 1055 and 1056. As was mentioned, in 1086 this land belonged to the bishop of Chester, not to Coventry Abbey. It has been persuasively argued by Dr Lancaster than Coventry Abbey made the claim to Eaton as a result of the links which developed between Coventry and Chester in the early twelfth century.[43] However, none of the other estates claimed in the charter was Chester episcopal land, and Lancaster's argument seems not to explain the claim completely. I should suggest that it was prompted by something else: the connection with Gruffudd ap Llywelyn. Coventry Abbey was founded by Leofric, and its first two abbots were related to his family, the same family which, in the persons of Ælfgar and his children, was closely linked to Gruffudd. It is not inherently unlikely, therefore, that the family's abbey should reflect the link also. There is further support for this

[37] Lloyd, *A History* ii, 369.

[38] Lewis Thorpe, transl., *Gerald of Wales: The Journey Through Wales and The Description of Wales*, Harmondsworth 1978, 88–9.

[39] *Annales Cambriae* (B) s.a. [1057], [1069]; *Annales Cambriae* (C) s.a. [1060], [1071]; *Brut y Tywysogion* (Pen. 20) s.a. 1057, *recte* 1059, 1068, *recte* 1069; *Brut y Tywysogion* (RB) s.a. [1059], [1069]; *Brenhinedd y Saesson* s.a. 1057, *recte* 1059, 1068, *recte* 1069.

[40] J. G. Lancaster, ed., 'The Coventry Forged Charters: a Re-appraisal', *BIHR* 27, 1954, 113–41.

[41] Lancaster, 'The Coventry Forged Charters', p. 141.

[42] John Morris, gen. ed., *Domesday Book*, 40 vols, Chichester 1975–1986, 17, Cheshire, 236 ra, where the modern spelling is 'Eyton'.

[43] Lancaster, 'The Coventry Forged Charters', p. 131.

theory in the Warwickshire Domesday.[44] Among the abbey's holdings is listed an estate (unmentioned in the foundation-charter) at *Bilvaie*, modern Binley, near Coventry. This had been purchased by the abbot from Osbern fitz Richard, the husband of Gruffudd's daughter Nest. Before Osbern, moreover – Domesday tells us – this estate was the property of 'Aldgid uxor Griffin' – Ealdgyth, Ælfgar's daughter, Gruffudd ap Llywelyn's wife. In 1086 the link between the Mercian house and the North Welsh king was still well remembered. This latter entry is, in addition, further support for the idea that Osbern fitz Richard's wife, Nest, was Gruffudd's daughter by Ealdgyth, since it is not improbable that Osbern came by Binley through his wife, and she may have inherited it from her mother.

It is not known exactly when Ælfgar died. He disappears from our records in 1062, but no obit is known. In the following year occurred an event which again reflects on the alliance: Harold Godwinesson and his brother Tostig moved two forces – one by sea and one by land – against Wales in what must have been a major campaign.[45] It seems very possible that one of the stimuli for this was the death of Ælfgar: as a result, the political climate had probably changed in such a way as to make a campaign possible. Moreover, it seems highly likely that Harold wanted to try to stop the Mercia-Gwynedd alliance from continuing beyond Ælfgar's lifetime to the advantage of his two young sons, Morkere and the new earl of Mercia, Eadwine. The campaign was successful in part only: it was to provoke the downfall and death of Gruffudd ap Llywelyn, showing perhaps how significant his alliance with Ælfgar had been. Harold, however, failed in one respect: he eliminated Gruffudd, but he did not put a stop to the alliance.

The effects on England of the death of Gruffudd were very interesting for, in the period after Gruffudd's fall, Harold Godwinesson can be seen making overtures to the sons of Ælfgar. This demonstrates Harold's political common sense – as a contender for ultimate royal power it was in his interest to gain the support of his noble peers. But it also demonstrates that Leofric's family had been by no means disempowered: even in the persons of two very young men, the house was a significant element in English politics. The events immediately following on Gruffudd's death were exploited by Harold to the full: he associated himself with the accession to power in Gwynedd of Bleddyn and Rhiwallon, the sons of Cynfyn and Gruffudd's half-brothers.[46] He also made a concerted attempt to ingratiate himself with Eadwine and Morkere. We learn from Orderic Vitalis that Ealdgyth – first used by her father to cement his Welsh alliance – now became the symbol of Harold's attempt to ally with Ælfgar's sons.[47] The earl of Wessex took the Welsh king's widow as his wife, thus tying her important English kin to him through the marriage-bond. In addition he may have held out as an incentive the possibility of a second crown for Ealdgyth and an accompanying high position for her brothers.

His overtures did not cease there. In 1065 there was a rebellion against Tostig Godwinesson in Northumbria, as a result of which Tostig was ex-

---

[44] *Domesday Book*, Warwickshire, 238 vb.
[45] ASC (D) 1063; ASC (E) s.a. 1063.
[46] ASC (D) s.a. 1063.
[47] Orderic, ii, 138, 216.

pelled.[48] Harold does not seem to have tried to get his brother reinstated: far from it. He gave his support to the young Morkere as candidate for the earldom. It seems clear that Harold was aware at last of the potential for political power vested in the Mercian house; and he was also aware that in the overthrow and death of Gruffudd ap Llywelyn, he had done the sons of Ælfgar an injury. It is not impossible that he was trying to woo them away from Wales and towards himself. Had he survived Hastings, the success of this policy might be discernible. As it was, the sons of Ælfgar were to continue their father's association with Wales.

In 1065, as I have already remarked, Morkere was appointed earl of Northumbria. He marched North and was shortly followed by his elder brother Eadwine, who brought with him an army consisting in part of Welshmen.[49] The source from which this Welsh aid was gained becomes more apparent in the aftermath of the battle of Hastings. From 1066 to 1071 the brothers were in almost continuous rebellion against the new king, William of Normandy. Both had been involved in the battle of Stamford Bridge: indeed their armies had borne the brunt of Harald Hardrada's invasion. However, neither fought at Hastings and both initially made submission to William. Their fealty did not last. In 1068 or thereabouts, the two came out in favour of the young Edgar Ætheling and went into rebellion. Orderic relates:[50]

> Tempore Normannicae cladis quae nimis oppressionibus Anglos immoderate conquassauit, Blidenus rex Gualorum ad auunculos suos suppetias uenit, secumque multitudinem Britonum adduxit.

Orderic is in slight error here: there was no blood-relationship between Ælfgar's sons and Bleddyn, except through Gruffudd and Ealdgyth's marriage. In calling Eadwine and Morkere Bleddyn's uncles, Orderic is repeating a mistake which he had made earlier, when he stated that Bleddyn was the son of Gruffudd and Ealdgyth.[51] However it is clear that people remembered a tie of some kind between the rulers of North Wales and the family of Leofric at this time, and that Orderic was aware of this. His account is testimony to the survival of the links built up by Ælfgar and Gruffudd – in their time of need, Ælfgar's sons turned to the successor of their father's friend, and the help which they sought was given. Bleddyn ap Cynfyn for his part was almost certainly aware of his half-brother's carefully constructed policy and saw the advantages inherent in continuing it. The house of Leofric might now be in a precarious situation, but if their rebellion succeeded they might not remain so and he might stand to gain a great deal. In addition, the Normans were almost certainly being noted as a potential threat by the Welsh, and Bleddyn was no doubt anxious to keep them from his lands. Like his half-brother before him, Bleddyn had exploited local troubles to his own ends (he supported the rebellion of Eadric Cild in 1067).[52] He had much to gain by continuing his

---

[48] ASC (C) s.a. 1065; ASC (D) s.a. 1065; ASC (E) s.a. 1064.
[49] See note 48.
[50] Orderic, ii, 214–16.
[51] Orderic, ii, 138.
[52] ASC (D) s.a. 1067; Orderic, ii, 228.

brother's alliance. For Ælfgar's sons the Welsh king who had helped one of them to noble estate in 1065 must have looked in 1068 like a heaven-sent resource.

Their rebellion was not to succeed, and in 1071 Eadwine was murdered, while his brother met with life-imprisonment.[53] Bleddyn ap Cynfyn concentrated on his Welsh kingdom and made no more moves towards the English – now Anglo-Norman – polity. Ælfgar's alliance was finally over. Its effects were not. In later years other Cambro-English and Cambro-Norman alliances were to form, notably that of the de Bellême family with Bleddyn's sons in 1102.[54] For something like fifteen years the earl of Mercia had demonstrated that it was possible to find more in Wales than merely a threat, and his actions left a legacy to both the Welsh and the English in the years which followed.

---

[53] ASC (D) s.a. 1072; ASC (E) s.a. 1071.
[54] *Brut y Tywysogion* (Pen. 20) s.a. 1100, *recte* 1102; *Brut y Tywysogion* (RB), s.a. 1100, *recte* 1102; *Brenhinedd y Saesson* s.a. 1100, *recte* 1102.

DOMESDAY SLAVERY*

John S. Moore

1. *Introduction*

If it is tedious to begin by defining one's terms, then it must inevitably be even more tedious to begin by defining one's translation of terms. More tedious, doubtless, but undoubtedly necessary. Certainly by the thirteenth century *servus* may be regarded for many purposes as synonymous with *villanus* and *nativus*[1] and the first two are commonly translated as 'serf' and 'villein'. But most historians would hesitate to translate *villanus* as 'villein' in an eleventh-century context, and Sir Frank Stenton approved the more neutral term 'villager', quite rightly emphasising that 'The *servi* and *ancillae* of Domesday Book are undoubtedly male and female slaves'.[2] Other historians were inconsistent: both Maitland and Vinogradoff in one of their works referred consistently to 'slaves' and 'slavery', in another, still dealing with the Anglo-Norman period, to 'serfs' and 'serfage'.[3] More recently, H. C. Darby moved in the opposite direction: having rendered *servus* as 'serf' throughout the regional volumes of his Domesday Geography, 'following the practice of the VCH' he changed to 'slave' in his concluding summary.[4] The major objection to

---

* As a 'new boy' at the Battle Abbey Conference, I should like to thank the 'old lags' for the welcome they so readily extended to me, and for demonstrating the continued truth of *Multum de cervisia biberunt Angli*. I particularly wish to thank Dr David Roffe and Dr David Pelteret for discussions of some difficult points before I read my paper, and to Dr Emma Mason and Dr Ann Williams for useful discussions afterwards. It is my hope that Dr Pelteret may yet revise for publication his University of Toronto Ph.D thesis on 'Anglo-Saxon Slavery', of which a very brief summary is given in 'Slavery in Anglo-Saxon England', in J. D. Woods, D. A. E. Pelteret, *The Anglo-Saxons: synthesis and achievement*, Waterloo (Ontario) 1985, 117–33, a work sadly little known in England.

[1] P. Vinogradoff, *Villainage in England*, Oxford 1892, 45, 47.
[2] F. M. Stenton, *Anglo-Saxon England*, Oxford, 3rd edn, 1971, 477. This translation of *villanus* has been adopted in the series of Domesday translations published by Messrs Phillimore.
[3] F. Pollock, F. W. Maitland, *History of English Law before the time of Edward I*, Cambridge, 2nd edn, 1898, I, 35–7, 424, 428; II, 472, 529; F. W. Maitland, *Domesday Book and Beyond*, Cambridge 1897, 26, 31–3, 328; P. Vinogradoff, *The Growth of the Manor*, London 1905, 202–3, 229–30, 332–3, 335; P. Vinogradoff, *English Society in the Eleventh Century*, Oxford 1908, 429, 460, 463–6.
[4] H. C. Darby, *Domesday Geography of Eastern England* [hereafter Darby, *DGEE*], Cambridge 1952, 47, n. 1; H. C. Darby, *Domesday England* [hereafter Darby, *Dom.Eng.*], Cambridge 1977, 9, 59, 63, 72–9, 337–45.

191

translating *servus* as 'serf' before the reign of Henry II is that it confuses two distinct historical processes: the decline of slavery, effectively complete in Henry I's reign, and the linked rise of serfdom and common-law villeinage from Glanvill's time.[5]

In settling this dreary question of translation it has already been necessary to refer to authorities other than Domesday Book. As Maitland had himself remarked,

> Of the legal position of the *servus* Domesday Book tells us little or nothing; but earlier and later documents oblige us to think of him as a *slave* (my italics).[6]

We do need to consider the Domesday evidence in the light of other sources and in the context of known or suspected economic, social, political and religious trends, not only because Domesday Book is not comprehensive but also because Domesday Book is otherwise not fully comprehensible. It is my belief that some at least of the questions about the Domesday (Anglo-Saxon, Anglo-Norman) slaves are capable of fuller answers than have usually been given if non-Domesday sources are laid under contribution. Having said that, I am well aware that, particularly in the matter of the sources for religious ideas and thinking, my knowledge is much less complete than it ought to be. Perhaps, by way of compensation, the particular insights of one who has specialised in economic and social history may be of some value. What, then, are the questions we ought at least to be asking? First, of course, *quot servi*? How many slaves were there in 1086? Second, where were they mostly to be found? Third, what was the nature of slavery, not just in legal terms but also in occupational, economic, social and residential terms? A full treatment of the subject would also need to enquire how people became slaves and why and how both domestic slavery and the associated external slave-trade finally disappeared, in other words to supply a broader context for the structures revealed by Domesday Book at one point in time.

2. *The extent and distribution of slavery in 1086*

Let us then begin with this apparently simple matter of the number of slaves recorded in Domesday Book for 1086. For nearly one hundred and fifty years, historians repeated an estimate of 25–26,000 slaves, derived from an addition

---

[5] H. R. Loyn, *Anglo-Saxon England and the Norman Conquest* [hereafter Loyn, *ASE&NC*], London 1962, 349; R. W. Finn, *An Introduction to Domesday Book* [hereafter Finn, *Introduction*], London 1963, 118; H. B. Clarke, 'Domesday Slavery (Adjusted for Slaves)', *Midland History* 1, pt 4, 1972, 40, 42; to the references cited in n. 24 should now be added E. Miller, 'England in the Twelfth and Thirteenth Centuries: An Economic Contrast?', *Economic History Review* [hereafter *Econ.Hist.Rev.*], 2nd ser., 24, 1971, 1–14; E. Miller, 'Farming of Manors and Direct Management', *Econ.Hist.Rev.* 2nd ser., 26, 1973, 138–40; P. D. A. Harvey, 'The English Inflation of 1180–1220', *Past & Present* 61, 1973, 3–30; P. D. A. Harvey, 'The Pipe Rolls and the Adoption of Demesne Farming in England', *Econ.Hist.Rev.*, 2nd ser., 27, 1974, 345–59; A. R. Bridbury, 'The Farming Out of Manors', *Econ.Hist.Rev.*, 2nd ser., 31, 1978, 503–20; P. R. Hyams, *King, Lords and Peasants: the common law of villeinage in the twelfth and thirteenth centuries*, Oxford 1980, esp. pt IV.

[6] Maitland, 27. This makes his use of 'serf' in this work quite inexplicable.

Table 1   Distribution of recorded Domesday slaves in 1086

County	Number of slaves	Percentage of total population	Total recorded population
England			
Bedfordshire	480	13.4	3,591
Berkshire	793	12.9	6,139
Buckinghamshire	845	16.6	5,103
Cambridgeshire	541	11.1	4,868
Cheshire	141	9.2	1,528
Cornwall	1,149	21.4	5,368
Derbyshire	20	0.3	2,836
Devonshire	3,318	19.2	17,246
Dorset	1,244	16.9	7,382
Essex	1,809	12.9	14,004
Gloucestershire	2,140	26.1	8,191
Hampshire	1,765	18.0	9,780
Herefordshire	722	16.7	4,326
Hertfordshire	591	13.0	4,556
Huntingdonshire	0	0.0	2,500
Kent	1,160	9.9	11,753
Lancashire (South)	20	7.7	260
Leicestershire	402	6.3	6,423
Lincolnshire	0	0.0	21,462
Middlesex	112	5.1	2,177
Norfolk	973	3.7	26,309
Northamptonshire	737	9.6	7,663
Nottinghamshire	24	0.4	5,608
Oxfordshire	1,002	14.9	6,713
Roteland	0	0.0	859
Shropshire	918	19.5	4,709
Somerset	2,120	16.3	12,991
Staffordshire	240	7.9	3,028
Suffolk	892	4.7	19,070
Surrey	503	12.3	4,105
Sussex	416	4.3	9,600
Warwickshire	781	12.4	6,277
Wiltshire	1,588	16.0	9,944
Worcestershire	718	15.6	4,604
Yorkshire	0	0.0	7,566
Sub-total:	28,164	10.5	268,539

County	Number of slaves	Percentage of total population	Total recorded population
Wales			
Cheshire	44	13.6	324
Gloucestershire	7	12.1	58
Herefordshire	10	66.7	15
Shropshire	10	20.8	48
Sub-total:	71	16.0	445
Total:	28,235	10.5	268,984

done with pen and paper either by Sir Henry Ellis and his clerks or by Adolphus Ballard,[7] until H. C. Darby with the aid of the University of London computer substituted a significantly higher figure of 28,200.[8] The geographical distribution of slaves and their proportion of total recorded rural population of each Domesday county is given in Table 1.[9] The distribution of Domesday slaves can also be seen on Map 1.[10]

From this table and the map it is immediately apparent that there are considerable anomalies in this distribution, both at county and at sub-county level. No slaves whatever are recorded in the Exchequer text for Huntingdonshire, Lincolnshire, *Roteland* or Yorkshire, and virtually none for Derbyshire and Nottinghamshire. These counties together are thought to comprise Circuit VI,[11] and it is fairly obvious that the commissioners for that circuit, for whatever reason, faced difficulties in ascertaining the presence of slaves. Dr David Roffe tells me that my instinct is not at fault here: the almost complete absence of slaves is only one of the marked peculiarities in 'diplomatic' which distinguish Circuit VI from other Domesday circuits.[12]

With the possible exception of Yorkshire, we are not entitled to assume that slavery no longer existed in these counties: Stenton asserted that 'There was a considerable amount of downright slavery in the Danelaw',[13] and specialist

---

[7] H. Ellis, *A General Introduction to Domesday Book*, London 1833, repr. 1971, II, 514; Maitland, 26; A. Ballard, *The Domesday Inquest*, London 1906, 264; P. Vinogradoff, *English Society in the Eleventh Century*, 463; A. L. Poole, *Obligations of Society in XII and XIII Centuries*, Oxford 1946, 12; M. M. Postan, 'The *Famulus*: the estate labourer in the twelfth and thirteenth centuries', *Econ.Hist.Rev.*, Supplement, 2, 1954, 5; Loyn, *ASE&NC*, 350; Finn, *Introduction*, London 1963, 120. It should be noted that Ballard's total, which was higher than Ellis', was the result of an independent calculation; all subsequent historians until Darby have based their figures, usually without acknowledgement, on Ellis or Ballard.

[8] Darby, *Dom.Eng.*, 63, 337; J. C. Holt (ed.), *Domesday Studies*, Woodbridge 1987, 110.

[9] Darby, *Dom.Eng.*, 338, 345.

[10] Darby, *Dom.Eng.*, 76, fig. 25.

[11] Ballard, 12–13; C. Stephenson, 'Notes on the Composition and Interpretation of Domesday Book', *Speculum* 22, 1947, 1–15; V. H. Galbraith, *The Making of Domesday Book*, Oxford 1961, 7–8.

[12] G. Black, D. Roffe, *The Nottinghamshire Domesday*, Nottingham 1986; D. Roffe, *The Derbyshire Domesday*, Derby 1986; see also his 'Domesday Book and Northern Society', *EHR* forthcoming.

[13] Stenton, 515.

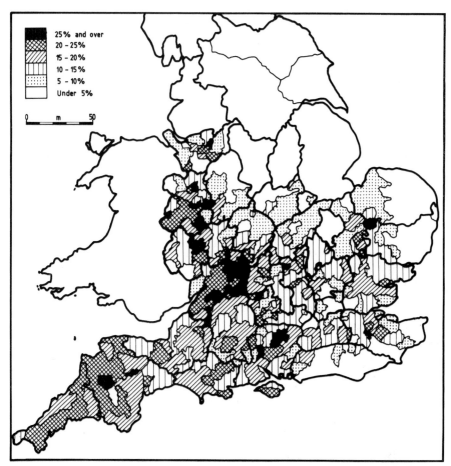

Map 1: The distribution of recorded slaves in Domesday England (H. C.
Darby, *Domesday England* (1977), fig. 25) [South Lancashire should
probably be added to the 10–15 per cent class, and Derbyshire,
Huntingdonshire, Lincolnshire and Nottinghamshire to either the
5–10 per cent or the 10–15 per cent class]

studies of Viking society have also emphasised the important role of the *thraell* in Danish and Norse areas of settlement. Both in Lincolnshire and Yorkshire there are still villages called Lazenby, 'the village of freedman', as well as the lost village of 'Laysingthorpe' in Lincolnshire, 'the outlying settlement of freedmen', which can only have been so named after the freeing of substantial numbers of *thraells* to become *leysings*.[14] Indeed, some of these freedmen had risen to become manorial lords by 1066. The Yorkshire Domesday reveals that one or more men called Le(i)sing or Le(i)sinc had held manors at Acklam, Great Busby, Faceby, Guisborough, Kirkleatham, Newham Hall, Normanby, Tanton, Tollesby and Tunstall in the North Riding (fo. 300a, *1 N*, 12; fo. 300b, *1 N*, 26–30; fo. 320c, *11 N*, 1–2) and at Allerton Mauleverer in the West Riding (fo. 301c, *1 W*, 37). In Lincolnshire also a man called Lesinc had been lord of Bag Enderby before 1066 (fo. 359c, *28*, 33). In the case of Huntingdonshire, a summary at the end of the *Inquisitio Eliensis* tells us that there were slaves on all the Ely Abbey manors in the county, though as a result of either scribal error or deliberate policy they are omitted both from the main body of the *IE* and from the Exchequer text of Domesday Book.[15] Reintegrating the slaves with the other inhabitants of the Ely Abbey estates in Huntingdonshire (*DB*, fo. 204a, *4*, 1–5) produces the reconstruction shown in Table 2.

Other scholars have also come to the conclusion, based on the above figures, that 10 per cent is a reasonable allowance for the slave-population of Huntingdonshire as a whole, since this is comparable to the proportion of slaves in the surrounding counties of Bedfordshire (13.4 per cent), Cambridgeshire (11.1 per cent) and Northamptonshire (9.6 per cent); in addition, the improbability of Ramsey Abbey, apparently, having slaves on its demesnes in six adjacent counties, but not in Huntingdonshire where 43 out of its 88 demesne plough-teams were found, was also stressed.[16] Consequently, the total recorded population of Huntingdonshire (2,500) should be estimated to be 90 per cent of the real total, i.e. 2,777, of which 277 slaves would form the estimated 10 per cent. Similarly, the total recorded population of *Roteland* (859) should be increased to 954, of which 95 would constitute the estimated 10 per cent of slaves.

Nottinghamshire presents a greater puzzle. Slaves are only mentioned intermittently, on the estates of three tenants-in-chief in the middle of the county folios, on eight manors, all of which are in just three out of the eight wapentakes in the whole county. On these eight manors the proportion of slaves to total recorded population ranges from 6.1 per cent at Bulcote to 44.4 per cent at Bilborough, but is, apart from these two manors, between 11.1 per cent and 22.2 per cent; the overall proportion of slaves is 14.5 per cent as can be seen from Table 3.

[14] A. H. Smith, 'English Place-Name Elements, pt II', *English Place-Names Society*, 26, 1956, 24; H. P. R. Finberg, *Agrarian History of England and Wales*, I, pt 2, Cambridge 1972, 474.

[15] Darby, *DGEE*, 331; Finn, *Introduction*, 120; R. W. Finn, *The Norman Conquest and its effects on the economy, 1066–86* [hereafter Finn, *Norm.Conq.*], London 1971, 226–7; Holt, 110.

[16] R. V. Lennard, *Rural England, 1086–1135*, Oxford 1959, 91; Finn, *Norm.Conq.econ.effects*, 227; Darby, *Dom.Eng.*, 73; Holt, 110.

Table 2 Recorded population on Ely Abbey estates in Huntingdonshire

Manor	Villagers (Villani)	Smallholders (Bordarii)	Priests	Slaves (Servi)	Total
Colne	13	5	0	3	21
Bluntisham	10	3	1	3	17
Somersham	32	9	0	4	45
Spaldwick	50	10	0	6	66
Little Catworth	7	0	0	0	7
Total:	112	27	1	16	156
Percentage of total	71.8	17.3	0.6	10.3	

Table 3 Recorded population on Nottinghamshire manors with slaves

Manor	Sokemen	Villagers (Villani)	Smallholders (Bordarii)	Priests	Slaves (Servi)	Total
Lands of William Peverel						
Colwick	0	7	6	0	2	15
Stapleford	0	6	0	1	2	9
Bilbrough	2	3	0	0	4	9
Lands of Walter of Aincourt						
Bulcote	8	11	12	0	2	33
Lands of Geoffrey Alselin						
Laxton	0	22	7	0	5	34
Stoke Bardolph and Gedling	0	15	21	1	6	43
Burton Joyce	1	5	1	1	1	9
Total:	11	69	47	3	22	152
Percentage of total:	7.2	45.4	30.9	2.0	14.5	
Percentage for entire county:	30.6	46.9	21.1	1.0	0.7	

It is, however, impossible to claim that these eight manors in any way form a representative sample from which a correction factor can be calculated with confidence for the entire county. A comparison of the distribution of the categories of the rural population for the county with the distribution of the eight manors with slaves in Table 3 shows that sokemen are relatively very scarce (30.6 per cent for the county) and that there is an above-average number of smallholders (21.1 per cent for the county). But the proportion of villagers in the eight manors is extremely close to the county average of 46.9 per cent.[17] It is clearly unrealistic to accept that the 22 slaves on these manors were the only slaves in Nottinghamshire, the more so as none of these manors had large demesnes. Stapleford had 3 demesne plough-teams, and Stoke Bardolph had 2, but on all the other manors (apart from Burton Joyce which had none) there was only one demesne plough-team. If we look at the Nottinghamshire demesnes with 3 or more plough-teams, we shall find little support for a theory that the slaves have been replaced by smallholders (*bordarii*). Assuming that each plough-team required two ploughmen (a ratio generally accepted, as we shall see), we can classify these demesnes in three groups, as in Table 4.

Overall, there is clearly a massive deficiency of ploughmen even if they are included amongst the smallholders, and this further supports the probability that most slaves have not been recorded in the Nottinghamshire Domesday. On the other hand, it is unlikely that the unrecorded slaves constituted 14.5 per cent or thereabouts of the total county population. Perhaps, in the light of the slave-ratio of 6.3 per cent for Leicestershire to the south, also a Danelaw county, a *minimum* estimate of 5 per cent for Nottinghamshire slaves may be thought acceptable. A *maximum* proportion could be 15 per cent as suggested by Table 3. Indeed, 10 per cent would by no means be an unacceptable correction-factor as in the counties of the southern Danelaw.

The situation with regard to Derbyshire is even less satisfactory: '13 out of the total of 20 were in the fief of Henry de Ferrers, and 10 of these were in the manor of Duffield'.[18] Again, it is difficult to believe that there were only 20 slaves in the whole of Derbyshire, and this is borne out by an analysis of those Derbyshire demesnes with more than 3 plough-teams given in Table 5. Again, there is a massive deficiency of demesne ploughmen even if they were included among the smallholders.

The situation is similar in Lincolnshire as Table 6 demonstrates; in a majority of manors with large demesnes in Lincolnshire, Nottinghamshire and Derbyshire it is simply impossible for the demesne ploughmen to have been recruited from the smallholders (Group (a) in Tables 4, 5 and 6). Attention may in particular be drawn to the manors where there are neither smallholders nor slaves recorded: Addlethorpe, Alkborough, Barrow on Humber, Brampton, West Bytham, Covenham, Culverthorpe, Denton/Wyville, Donington, Exton, Fillingham, Hale, Hibaldstow, Little Imber, Killingholme, Louth, Ludford, Lusby, Maidenwell, Normanby by Spital, Owmby, Rasen, Sturton by Stow, and Little Sturton in Lincolnshire; Cropwell Butler, Elton, Leake,

---

[17] H. C. Darby, I. B. Terrett, *Domesday Geography of Northern England*, Cambridge 1962, 253.
[18] Darby, Terrett, 299.

Table 4 Nottinghamshire demesne plough-teams and smallholders

[Manors (36) with 3 or more demesne plough-teams]

[Demesne plough-teams entered first, then smallholders]

---

a. Manors with smallholders less than double the plough-teams

'Newbold' (3:3), Gotham (3:2), Laneham (4.5:6), Newark (7:4), Tuxford (4:2), Perlethorpe (4:4), Gunthorpe (4:7), Plumtree (3:0), Wysall (3:0), Bingham (4:5), E. Bridgford (3:3), Elton (3:0), Wheatley (4:0), Stapleford (3:2 slaves), Linby (3:2), Toton (3:3), Staunton (3:2), N. Muskam (3:2), Costock (3:4), Cotgrave (3:4), Cropwell Butler (3:0), Kneesall & Kersall (3:4), Hickling (3:1), Leake (4:0)

Number of manors: 24 (67%)

b. Manors with smallholders double the number of plough-teams

Gringley on the Hill (3:6), Langar (3:6), Barnstone (3:6), Kirkby in Ashfield (3:6), Ossington (3:6), Granby (4:8)

Number of manors: 5 (14%)

c. Manors with smallholders more than double the plough-teams

Orston (3:11), Southwell (10:23), Warsop (3.5:11), Granby (4:9), Epperstone & Woodbrough (3:10), Whatton (3:12), Bradmore (3:8)

Number of manors: 7 (19%)

Table 5 Derbyshire demesne plough-teams and smallholders

[Manors (29) with 3 or more demesne plough-teams]

[Demesne plough-teams entered first, then smallholders]

---

a. Manors with smallholders less than double the plough-teams

Bakewell (7:9), Ashford (4:0), Mickleover (5.5:10), Brassington (3:2), Catton (3:2), Aston (3:4), Sutton on the Hill (3:0), Spondon (3:2), Youlgrave (3:0), Burnaston, etc. (3:1), Radbourne (3:5), Edensor (4:7), Codnor, etc. (3:2), Alvaston, etc. (3:0), Ripley & Pentrich (3:3), Drakelow & Hearthcote (4:0), Beighton (4:2)

Number of manors: 17 (59%)

b. Manors with smallholders double the number of plough-teams

Weston upon Trent (3:6), *Bolun* (4:8)

Number of manors: 2 (7%)

c. Manors with smallholders more than double the plough-teams

Sawley (3:13), Tissington (3:8), Doveridge (3:10), Scropton (7:26), Barton Blount (3:11), Duffield, etc. (3:8; also 10 slaves), Etwall (3:8), Barlborough & Whitwell (3:36; also 1 slave), Staveley (3:7), Ilkeston, etc. (3:7)

Number of manors: 10 (34%)

Plumtree, Wheatley and Wysall in Nottinghamshire; Alvaston, Ashford, Drakelow & Hearthcote, Sutton on the Hill and Youlgrave in Derbyshire. Here the case for the omission of slaves seems irrefutable; that ploughmen were at least not always drawn from the smallholders is further supported by the case of Duffield in Derbyshire where the smallholders are additional to the ten slaves who are already more than was needed to operate 3 demesne plough-teams. The late Rex Welldon-Finn also called attention to the labour-requirements of the lead mines mentioned in Domesday Book as already in existence by 1086.[19] Later evidence, however, suggests that lead-mining was generally carried out by peasants as a bye-occupation,[20] so this is probably not a material factor. A comparison with the slave-ratios for the adjoining counties of Staffordshire (7.9 per cent) and Leicestershire (6.3 per cent) suggests that the *minimum* correction in Derbyshire too is 5 per cent, and, as in the cases of Huntingdonshire and Nottinghamshire, 10 per cent seems a reasonable estimate for the slaves not recorded in Domesday. For Lincoln-shire also, given the absence of any factors which would explain a total disappearance of slaves before 1086, the same correction may be applied, by comparison with Bedfordshire (13.4 per cent), Cambridgeshire (11.1 per cent), Leicestershire (6.3 per cent) and Northamptonshire (9.6 per cent), averaging 10.1 per cent overall. Consequently, the Domesday totals for the counties of Derbyshire, Huntingdonshire, Lincolnshire and Nottinghamshire have been adjusted to allow for an additional 10 per cent of unrecorded slaves.

For Yorkshire, we may perhaps wish to echo Maitland's famous expos-tulation: 'never a *theow* in all Yorkshire is hardly credible';[21] nevertheless, Yorkshire may indeed be an exceptional case because of the special circum-stances of the 'harrying of the North' in 1069–70, after which, according to Symeon of Durham, the countryside remained empty and uncultivated for nine years.[22] Although Bishop and Kapelle differ in their accounts of the recolonisation of Yorkshire, which was still far from complete in 1086, both agree in stressing the role of manorial lords in repopulating partly or totally deserted villages.[23] In these circumstances it is more than likely that any

[19] Finn, *Norm.Conq.econ.effects*, 185; R. W. Finn, *Domesday Book: a guide*, Chichester 1973, 35.
[20] N. Kirkham, *Derbyshire Lead Mining throughout the Centuries*, Truro 1968, 24–5, 99; I. Blanchard, 'Derbyshire Lead Production, 1195–1505', *Derbyshire Archaeological Journal* 91, 1971, 119–40; I. Blanchard, 'The Miner and the Agricultural Community in Late Medieval England', *Agricultural History Review* 20, 1972, 93–106; I. Blanchard, 'Labour Productivity and Work Psychology in the English Mining Industry', *Econ.Hist.Rev.*, 2nd ser., 31, 1978, 1–24. Lead mining did not begin in the West Riding of Yorkshire until the mid-twelfth century: A. Raistrick, B. Jennings, *History of Lead Mining in the Pennines*, London 1965, 21–32; D. E. Greenway, *Charters of the Honour of Mowbray, 1107–1191*, London 1972, xlix, 37, 76–7, 79; A. Raistrick, *Lead Mining in the Mid-Pennines*, Truro 1973, 18; A. Raistrick, *The Lead Industry of Wensley-dale and Swaledale*, Buxton 1975, I, 18.
[21] Maitland, 35. Pedants will doubtless wish that Maitland had written 'Never a *thraell . . .*' Slavery was far from exotic in pre-Norman Yorkshire: W. E. Kapelle, *The Norman Conquest of the North: the region and its transformation, 1000–1135*, London 1979, 99, notes that in 1065 the Yorkshire rebels against Earl Tostig enslaved hundreds of people in Northamptonshire; see also the references to freedmen in n. 14 and to manumissions of slaves in the Durham area in nn 78–9.
[22] T. Arnold, 'Symeonis Monachi Opera Omnia', *Rolls Series*, 75, pt 2, 1885, 188, cited in Kapelle, 144.
[23] T. A. M. Bishop, 'The Norman Settlement of Yorkshire', *Studies in Medieval History presented to Frederick Maurice Powicke*, Oxford 1948, 1–14, esp. 6–9; Kapelle, 169, 176–8.

Table 6 Lincolnshire demesne plough-teams and smallholders

[Manors (105) with 3 or more demesne plough-teams]

[Demesne plough-teams entered first, then smallholders]

---

a. Manors with smallholders less than double the plough-teams

Sturton by Stow (4:0), Laceby, etc. (3:5), Welton (5:4), Brampton (4:0), Elsham (3:5), Worlaby (4:5), Louth (3:0), Fiskerton (3:3), Scotton (3:5), Waltham (4:1), Hough on the Hill (4:7), Fulbeck, etc. (6:4), Long Bennington (5:5), Donington (3:0), Tathwell (6:4), Maidenwell (3:0), Ketsby (3:1), Haugham (3:3), Tetney (6:7), Normanby by Spital (4:0), Hibaldstow (4:0), Alkborough (3:0), Killingholme (3:0), Little Imber (3:0), Appleby, etc. (4:2), Binbrook (4:4), Ludborough (4:0), Denton/Wyville (3:0), North Kyme (3:2), Ludford (3.5:0), Kirmond le Mire (4:4), Covenham (3:0), Owmby (3:0), Scampton (4:6), Baumber (5:6), Lusby (5:0), Edenham (5:4), Culverthorpe (5:0), Hale (3:0), Driby (3:5), 'Holme' (4:3), Folkingham (5:9), Aswarby (4:3), Cammeringham (4:2), Fillingham (4:0), Swaton (3:2), Redbourne (3:4), Little Sturton (5:0), Barrow on Humber (4:0), West Bytham (3:0), Blankney (4:6), Flixborough (4.5:6), Killingholme (3:1), Nocton (5:3), Melton Ross (5:9), Rasen (4:0), Thornton Curtis, etc. (5:7), Caythorpe (8.5:7), Thornton (3:5), Scrivelsby (6:11), Addlethorpe (3:0), Ranby (3:2), Wilsford (3:2), Whissendine (5:7), Exton (3:0), Fishtoft (3:1), Barrowby (5:2), Sedgebrook (4:5), Westborough (5:6)

Number of manors: 69 (66%)

b. Manors with smallholders double the number of plough-teams

Audleby (3:6), Greetham (4:8), Donington on Bain (3:6), Carlton Scroop (3:6), 'Greetwell' (3:6), Candlesby (5.5:11), Burwell (3:6)

Number of manors: 7 (6%)

c. Manors with smallholders more than double the plough-teams

Nettleham (3:12), Kirton in Lindsey (4:37), Bishop Norton (3:21), New Sleaford (4:11), Quarrington (3:15), Scotter (4:13), Brant Broughton (3:20), Mumby (3:8), Mumby (3:12), West Halton (4:9), Barnetby le Wold (3:10), Waddington (4:9), Belchford (5:15), Benniworth (3:10), Spalding (4:33), Immingham (4:14), Winteringham (4:10), Barton on Humber (7:83), Edlington (4:14), Skendleby (3:9), Bonby (3:7), 'Laythorpe' (4:10), Branston (5:23), Ulceby (4:10), Irnham (3.5:9), Helpringham (3:9), Market Overton, etc. (3:8), Burton Pedwardine (5:12), Welbourn (3:8)

Number of manors: 29 (28%)

---

surviving slaves would have been transmuted into smallholders (*bordarii*) if not villagers, especially as there were relatively far fewer demesnes in York-shire with three or more plough-teams at work in 1086 (Table 7). But the proportion of such demesnes whose labour-requirements could not be met by utilising local smallholders is very similar throughout the North, as can be seen by comparing section (a) in Tables 4–7: Nottinghamshire, 67 per cent; Derbyshire, 59 per cent; Lincolnshire, 66 per cent; Yorkshire, 69 per cent. Given the close correspondence of these ratios, a case could well be made for an omission of Yorkshire slaves of the same order of 10 per cent, and it is only the special circumstances of the 'harrying of the North' that appear to make the continued existence of slaves in Yorkshire in 1086 rather improbable.

At sub-county level, there are also some apparent or real anomalies in the numerical distribution of slaves recorded in 1086. I say 'apparent or real anomalies' because what may seem to be anomalous to an outsider may result only from his ignorance of the local history of the area concerned. I propose only to look at some of the major anomalies in the distribution of Domesday slaves; almost every county has some minor variations from the county average, and some counties, notably Kent, need more attention than I have been able to give them. I have therefore confined myself to counties whose overall proportion of slaves appeared out of line with those of surrounding counties, notably Middlesex and Sussex, or where the internal contrasts, as in Norfolk and Suffolk, seemed to be so marked that they were arguably depressing the county-average as a whole.

Although Lancashire is marked on Map 1 as having under 5 per cent of slaves, this is a little misleading. The small sample of satisfactory evidence for the area 'between the Ribble and the Mersey' yields 20 slaves (7.7 per cent) and 12 oxmen (4.6 per cent) – we will discuss the position of the oxmen shortly – out of a total recorded population of 260, a combined figure of 12.3 per cent. In view of the very small sample-size for south Lancashire, this ratio does not seem too far out of line with the servile ratios in Cheshire to the south: slaves 9.3 per cent, oxmen 10.6 per cent; slaves and oxmen 19.9 per cent.[24] In Staffordshire slavery was much more evident in the south and west that in the north-eastern uplands, for good geographical reasons;[25] in Leicestershire, slaves were more common in the south and east than in the north and west; Holly does not comment on this distribution, but much of the latter region in 1086 was heavily wooded as well as naturally infertile, with the average size of settlement being small; the lower Soar valley, though more attractive, was liable to flooding and its population-density was low.[26]

Similarly in Norfolk and Suffolk, Map 1 shows slaves to be more con-centrated in the west of each county. Darby offers no explanation, and, especially in Norfolk and to a lesser extent in Suffolk, slavery was apparently more common where natural fertility, and as a result plough-team and population-densities per square mile, were lower, the opposite of what one might expect.[27] The real explanation for this apparent anomaly may lie with

[24] H. C. Darby, I. S. Maxwell, *Domesday Geography of Northern England*, Cambridge 1962, 350 (Cheshire), 407 (Lancashire).
[25] Darby, Maxwell, 185, 188.
[26] Darby, Terrett, 352–3.
[27] Darby, *DGEE*, 113, 117, 150–1, 167, 173, 204–6.

Table 7 Yorkshire demesne plough-teams and smallholders

[Manors (49) with 3 or more demesne plough-teams]

[Demesne plough-teams entered first, then smallholders]

---

a. Manors with smallholders less than double the plough-teams

Everingham, etc. (3:0), Welton, etc. (6:3), Acklam, etc. (3:0), Bramham (3:0), Moulton (3:4), Scorton (3:0), Catterick, etc. (9:16), Ainderby Mires (3:4), Newton le Willows (3:0), North Dalton (4:3), Kirby Misperton (3:0), Buckton Holms (4:6), Barwick in Elmet (12:12), Sturton Grange (5:3), Whitwood (3:1), South Elmsall, etc. (3:5), Campsall (4:3), Womersley (3:4), Glass Houghton (3:4), Wheldale, etc. (3:1), Laughton en le Morthen, etc. (12:23), Wadworth (4:1), Dadsley, etc. (9.5:12), High Melton (3:1), South Cave (4:0), Clifton (4:0), Nafferton (3:0), Seamer (5:0), Thirtleby, etc. (4:6), Kirk Ella (3:0), Coxwold, etc. (4:0), Cottingham, etc. (4:3), Langton, etc. (6:4), Scrayingham (5:0)

Number of manors: 34 (69%)

b. Manors with smallholders double the number of plough-teams

Darrington (3:6), Tanshelf (4:8), Hunmanby (3:6)

Number of manors: 3 (6%)

c. Manors with smallholders more than double the plough-teams

Sherburn in Elmet (25.5:104), Saxton (3:7), Kirk Smeaton (6:20), Featherston, etc. (3:15), Maltby, etc. (5:18), Sprotbrough (3:10), Conisbrough (5:11), Warmsworth (5:16), Tadcaster (3:11), Topcliffe, etc. (3:14), Kirk Ella (5:16), Thorp Arch (3:7)

Number of manors: 12 (25%)

---

the numerous sokemen and freemen holding small acreages of land in East Anglia,[28] who may have appeared to new landlords in the more fertile areas as a better labour-force than slaves, for reasons to be discussed later.

Although Campbell and King noted that slaves in the south-eastern counties

> amounted to between about 10 and 20 per cent of the recorded population of every county but two; the exceptions were Sussex and Middlesex where they formed only about 5 per cent,

they offered no suggestions why this should be so. Miss Campbell at least noted that the majority of the Middlesex slaves were concentrated in the two hundreds of Elthorne and Spelthorne, but Mr King dismissed the Sussex slaves as presenting 'no special features of interest for our purpose'.[29] Yet Map 2 clearly shows that the major concentration of slaves in Sussex was in the hundreds of Bosham, Dumpford, Easebourne and Westbourne in Chichester Rape and the hundreds of Binsted and Rotherbridge in Arundel Rape immediately to the east. There were less significant concentrations in Bramber and Lewes Rapes, but only four manors in Pevensey Rape and one manor in

---

[28] Darby, *DGEE*, 114–5, 168–70.
[29] H. C. Darby, E. M. J. Campbell, *Domesday Geography of South-East England*, Cambridge 1962, 117–8, 439, 566–7.

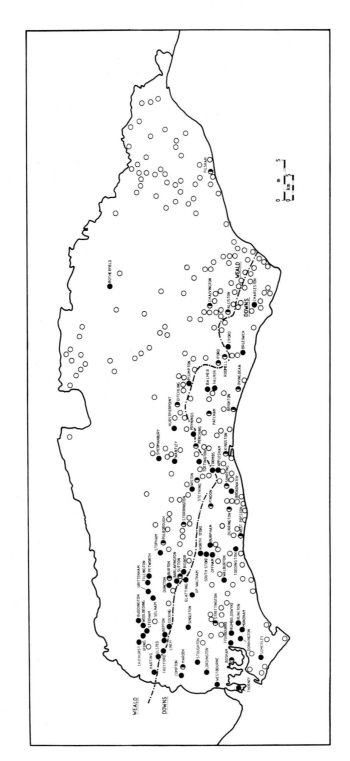

Map 2: The distribution of recorded slaves in Domesday Sussex
● Vills where slaves were recorded in every manor
◐ Vills where slaves were recorded in some manors
○ Vills where no slaves were recorded in any manor

Hastings Rape still had slaves in 1086. Again, this is hardly an expected distribution, since some of these hundreds (Dumpford, Easebourne, Rotherbridge and Rotherfield) and about a third of all the manors were partly or totally in the Weald, which was less advanced and less fertile than the Downland and coastal regions.

The anomalous distribution of slaves in the Middlesex folios probably reflects the special situation of an area adjoining the major trading-centre in England where one would expect the effects of a cash-nexus in the local labour-market to be displayed first. There are only eight manors where the number of slaves was even approximately twice the number of demesne plough-teams: Hanwell (1:2), Harmondsworth (3:6), Colham (3:8), Feltham (1:2), Kempton (1:2), Stanwell (3:8), Kensington (4:7), Tottenham (2:4). In addition there are four manors where the number of cottagers alone or in combination with slaves was approximately double the number of demesne plough-teams: Fulham (4:8 cottagers), Hendon (3:6 cottagers, 1 slave), Ickenham (4:4 cottagers, 3 slaves), Tollington (1:1 cottager, 1 slave). But most Middlesex manors fell into one of two other categories: either they had few or no smallholders, cottagers and slaves to serve the demesne plough-teams (e.g. Harlesden, Rug Moor, Ashford, East Bedfont), in which case they presumably had to buy-in labour from outside, or they had greatly in excess of the necessary number (e.g. Stepney, Islington, Stoke Newington, Westminster, Enfield) and doubtless sold their surplus labour elsewhere. We may also note, in this connection, as Map 3 demonstrates, that the demesnes with slaves are generally further away from London than those without slaves. In short, so far as we can judge, the apparently anomalous distribution of Middlesex is *not* a scribal aberration but reflects the early operation of the 'money economy' in eleventh-century England.

Closer examination of the distribution of Domesday slaves in Sussex also reveals that what appears to be an anomalous geographical distribution in reality reflects the different policies towards demesne-exploitation on the part of manorial lords, a factor recently explored on a national scale by Sally Harvey.[30] Even in hundreds with a high concentration of slaves, there were manors with no slaves, e.g. Treyford and Trotton in Dumpford hundred, Graffham and Todham in Easebourne hundred, Racton in Westbourne hundred, East Lavington and two out of three unnamed holdings in Rotherbridge hundred, and Mayfield in Rotherfield hundred. More significantly, there are vills with two (or more) manors of which one (or more) has slaves where the rest do not, e.g. two of the Marden manors have eight slaves between them, whilst two others have none; two out of the three manors in Burton had two slaves each; Alciston, Bosham, Ditchling, Iford, Patcham, West Preston, Pulborough, Rodmell, Singleton, Storrington and Sutton all had two manors, one with slaves, the other without.

The determining factor in the presence of slaves in Sussex in 1086 was landlord policy, for the variation between manors with or without slaves was 'feudal'. Certain lords, certain subtenants favoured demesne-agriculture with

[30] S. P. J. Harvey, 'The Extent and Profitability of Demesne Agriculture in England in the Eleventh Century', *Social Relations and Ideas*, ed. T. H. Aston *et al.*, Cambridge 1983, 45–72; Holt, 254.

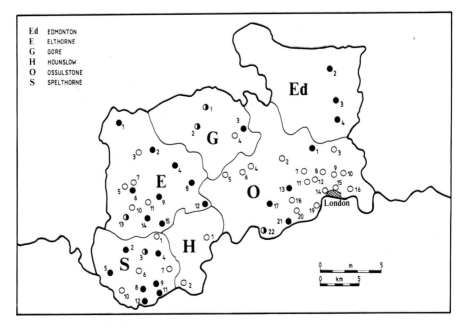

Map 3: The distribution of recorded slaves in Domesday Middlesex
- ● Vills where slaves were recorded in every manor
- ◑ Vills where slaves were recorded in some manors
- ○ Vills where no slaves were recorded in any manor

Map 3: Edmonton Hundred (Ed)   2 Enfield. 3 Edmonton. 4 Tottenham. *Not mapped:* South Mimms [details not recorded separately from Edmonton]

Elthorne Hundred (E)   1 Harefield. 2 Ruislip. 3 Ickenham. 4 Northolt.
5 Cowley. 6 Colham. 7 Hillingdon. 8 Greenford. 9 Hayes. 10 West Drayton.
11 Dawley. 12 Hanwell. 13 Harmondsworth. 14 Harlington. 15 Cranford

Gore Hundred (G)   1 Stanmore. 2 Harrow. 3 Hendon. 4 Kingsbury

Hounslow Hundred (H)   1 Isleworth. 2 Hampton

Ossulstone Hundred (O)   1 Tollington. 2 Hampstead. 3 Stoke Newington.
4 Willesden. 5 Twyford. 6 Harlesden. 7 Rug Moor. 8 Islington. 9 Hoxton.
10 Haggerston. 11 Tottenham Court. 12 St Pancras. 13 Lisson. 14 Holborn.
15 Bishopsgate. 16 Stepney. 17 Kensington. 18 Tyburn. 19 Westminster.
20 Ebury. 21 Chelsea. 22 Fulham. *Not mapped:* Nomansland, *Stanestaple*
[not located]

Spelthorne Hundred (S)   1 Hatton. 2 Stanwell. 3 Bedfont. 4 Feltham.
5 Staines. 6 Ashford. 7 Hanworth. 8 Charlton. 9 Kempton. 10 Laleham.
11 Sunbury. 12 Shepperton

slave-labour, others did not. Both the royal manors of Bosham and Rotherfield had slaves, though in the latter case a deficiency of four slaves would have necessitated calling on most of the six smallholders. Earl Roger de Montgomery, lord of Arundel and Chichester rapes, is known to be one of the few major exponents of intensive farming in Norman England, along with Arnulf of Hesding, Henry de Ferrers and Richard Fitz Gilbert;[31] his involvement is in conspicuous contrast to the disinterest of every other major tenant-in-chief in Sussex. All his major manors retained in hand had demesnes with slaves (Harting, Singleton, Stoughton, and Westbourne with Warblington); amongst the larger manors only Poling with four demesne plough-teams had no slaves, which was also true of his two smaller manors of Binderton and Trotton. Of his subtenants, Robert son of Theobald, sheriff of Arundel, clearly shared his master's agrarian enthusiasm: all his manors had slave-run demesnes; among the lesser knights, Geoffrey had slaves on his demesnes at Bepton and Compton but not Angmering, as did Morin at Burton and Chithurst and Arnold at Strettington and Upwaltham. 'William', if the same man throughout, had slaves on his demesnes at *Borham*, Lordington and Walberton but not on those of Birdham, Hunston and Todham; all Earl Roger's other subtenants apparently ploughed their demesnes by paying smallholders or cottagers.

In the rest of Sussex slaves are mostly confined to the Downs and the Greensand vale and the coastal plain immediately to their north and south in Bramber, Lewes and Pevensey rapes. No consistent policy can be discerned in Lewes rape: Earl William de Warenne, for example, retained four manors in hand; Iford and Patcham had slaves, Ditchling and Rodmell did not. This comital inconsistency is highlighted by the presence of slaves on the subinfeudated sections of both these last manors. Similarly in Bramber rape, Findon is the only demesne manor of William de Braose to retain slaves; of his subtenants, Ralph had slaves at Shermanbury, Sompting, Wantley and Wiston but not at Heene and Kingston. Apart from Rotherfield in the High Weald, slave-run demesnes were infrequent in Hastings and Pevensey rapes: only Alciston, which was to remain the home farm to Battle Abbey for most of the Middle Ages, was held by a tenant-in-chief. All the other manors with slaves were held by small lords who apparently resided on them and fed themselves from their produce. Although it has been objected that the absence of slaves from the estates of magnates such as the archbishop of Canterbury is a result of scribal omission,[32] this conclusion is unwarranted: to operate his 24 plough-teams at Lavant, South Malling, Pagham, Patching, Tangmere, West Tarring and Wotton, Archbishop Lanfranc or his steward could pick and choose from 185 smallholders on these manors. Statistically, the omission of slaves in either Middlesex or Sussex looks dubious if one compares the distribution of rural population as a whole in the south-east (see Table 8).[33]

It will be observed that the addition of the percentages for the two groups below the villagers produces comparable figures throughout the region:

[31] Harvey, 55-7.
[32] Finn, *Norm.Conq.*, 40, 63; R. W. Finn, *Domesday Book: a guide*, 34.
[33] Calculated from recorded population figures for *modern* counties in Darby, Campbell, 118, 382, 438, 513.

Table 8 Distribution of rural population in south-east England

Category	Percentage in Middlesex	Percentage in Surrey	Percentage in Kent	Percentage in Sussex
Sokemen/Freemen	0.0	0.0	0.4	0.0
Villeins	53.4	58.2	58.1	61.3
Smallholders/ Cottagers	38.0	29.5	31.3	34.2
Slaves	5.1	12.3	9.9	4.3
Miscellaneous	3.4	0.02	0.3	0.2

Middlesex, 43.1 per cent; Surrey, 41.8 per cent; Kent, 41.2 per cent; Sussex 38.5 per cent. There was no vast omission of slaves in either Middlesex or Sussex; all that has happened is that slaves in these two counties have progressed further into the free labouring groups in 1086 than their fellows in Kent and Surrey.

A further problem in connection with the distribution of slaves is the possibility that some may have been included in other Domesday categories. We have already seen that slaves cannot have been included within the smallholders (*bordarii*) in Derbyshire, Lincolnshire and Nottinghamshire, though as we have just seen in Sussex, demesne ploughmen must often have been drawn from that group. But it has specifically been suggested by Round and others that the oxmen (*bovarii*) who appear in large numbers in the counties along the Welsh border were in fact slaves, indeed that in these counties the scribal choice between 'slave' and 'oxman' was of little significance, one of Domesday's 'pleonastic vagaries'. In particular, the occasional use of *libri bovarii* was interpreted as proving that other *bovarii* were, by definition, unfree, i.e. slaves.[34] But Round's characteristic dogmatism was, as so often, not based on a thorough knowledge of the evidence: since *bovarii* and *servi* can be found appearing in the same entry at, for example, Grafton (Worcs.), Orleton (Herefs.) and Weaverham (Ches.),[35] they cannot be synonymous terms. Although, in the entry for Huntingdon (Salop.), *bovarii* is interlined above *servi*, this was not to provide more precise definition but to correct the original term used. The mention of a *liber bovarius* at Upton Cresset (Herefs.) was not to point a supposed contrast with an unfree *bovarius*; rather, it was to differentiate him from the *servi* in the same entry.[36] Tait therefore suggested that the *bovarius* was essentially a *servus casatus*, a *cotarius* in Domesday terminology,[37] and Nelson correctly points out that even by Henry I's reign the *bovarius* was not invariably free: in the Peterborough

[34] VCH *Herefordshire*, I, 288; VCH *Shropshire*, I, 302–3; VCH *Worcestershire*, 274–5; L. H. Nelson, *The Normans in South Wales, 1070–1171*, Austin, Texas 1966, 53–5; Finn, *Introduction*, 119.

[35] Darby, Maxwell, 79.

[36] W. J. Slack, 'The Shropshire Ploughmen of Domesday Book', *Trans. Shropshire Arch. & Nat. Hist. Soc.* 1 (1939), 31–5.

[37] J. Tait, 'The Domesday Survey of Cheshire', *Chetham Society*, 1916, 67–70.

Abbey estate-survey of 1125–9 he pays 1d a year if free, but nothing if unfree.[38] Since we shall see later that there are grounds for supposing that slaves generally could be cottagers, and it is generally accepted that most slaves were demesne ploughmen, it does seem to be reasonable to follow Nelson in amalgamating the *servi* and *bovarii* in the Welsh Marches.[39] It is, finally, possible that some of the people entered in Domesday as *cotarii* or even *bordarii* may have been slaves; given the short time-scale within which the basic information was collected in the counties for the Domesday inquest – from mid-January to mid-July 1086[40] – many mistakes may have occurred in social classification, especially at the lowest level of all. But we have already seen there is no justification, except in Circuit VI, for widespread correction of the Domesday statistics relating to slavery.

We can now present revised estimates for the extent and distribution of slavery in Domesday England (Table 9). The basis is the calculation made by Darby which was summarised in Table 1; this has been amended in two ways as a result of the above discussion. The first change concerns the counties in Circuit VI where, apart from the special case of Yorkshire, there is good reason to suppose that slaves have been almost, if not entirely, omitted. The total recorded populations of Table 1 have therefore been adjusted upwards on the assumption that slaves amounting to 10 per cent of an assumed total were for some reason not recorded in the Domesday inquest for Derbyshire, Huntingdonshire, Lincolnshire, Nottinghamshire and *Roteland*. The second alteration is the inclusion of the oxmen (*bovarii*) in the totals of slaves for the counties of Cheshire, Herefordshire, Lancashire, Shropshire, Warwickshire and Worcestershire.

Both these series of alterations are recorded within square brackets in cols 1 and 4 of Table 9. Col. 3 expresses col. 1 as a percentage of col. 4. Although it is necessary to start with the exact figures given in Domesday Book, their continued repetition to the last digit is liable to give the misleading impression to unwary readers that they are as accurate as a modern census, although that may well have an error-factor of 1–2 per cent.[41] But the error-factor in the case of Domesday Book must be very much larger: the implications of our increased knowledge of 'the making of Domesday Book'[42] are that figures, like other data, were recopied and summarised several times, each time increasing the cumulative probability of scribal error. Moreover, the use of roman numerals would increase the chance of miscopying (e.g. xl for xj, xj for vj or *vice versa*) but except where a 'satellite' text survives no independent check on Domesday statistics is possible. To avoid any spurious impressions of statis-

[38] Nelson, 55.

[39] Nelson, 51–3.

[40] Professor Holt and I have independently reached the same conclusion that the 'Salisbury Oath' in August 1086 marked a significant stage in the inquest: J. S. Moore, 'Post-Mortem of an Invasion', *Domesday: 900 Years of England's Norman Heritage*, ed. H. R. Loyn, R. Smith, London 1986, 69, 71; Holt, 41–64.

[41] T. H. Hollingsworth, *Historical Demography*, London 1969, 32–3.

[42] Galbraith, *passim*; R. W. Finn, *The Domesday Inquest and the making of Domesday Book*, London 1961; P. H. Sawyer, *Domesday Book: a reassessment*, London 1985, chaps 1, 5; Holt, 1–13.

Table 9 Distribution of estimated Domesday slaves in 1086

County	Number of slaves/oxmen		Percentage of total population	Total estimated population	
Column	(1)	(2)	(3)	(4)	(5)
England					
Bedfordshire	480	(500)	13.4	3,591	(3,600)
Berkshire	793	(800)	12.9	6,139	(6,150)
Buckinghamshire	845	(850)	16.6	5,103	(5,100)
Cambridgeshire	541	(550)	11.1	4,868	(4,900)
Cheshire	[302]	(300)	[19.8]	1,528	(1,550)
Cornwall	1,149	(1,150)	21.4	5,368	(5,400)
Derbyshire	[315]	(300)	[10.0]	[3,151]	(3,150)
Devonshire	3,318	(3,350)	19.2	17,246	(17,250)
Dorset	1,244	(1,250)	16.9	7,382	(7,400)
Essex	1,809	(1,800)	12.9	14,004	(14,000)
Gloucestershire	2,140	(2,150)	26.1	8,191	(8,200)
Hampshire	1,765	(1,800)	18.0	9,780	(9,800)
Herefordshire	[835]	(850)	[19.3]	4,326	(4,350)
Hertfordshire	591	(600)	13.0	4,556	(4,600)
Huntingdonshire	[277]	(300)	[10.0]	[2,777]	(2,800)
Kent	1,160	(1,200)	9.9	11,753	(11,800)
Lancashire (South)	[32]	(50)	[12.3]	260	(300)
Leicestershire	402	(400)	6.3	6,423	(6,450)
Lincolnshire	[2,385]	(2,400)	[10.0]	[23,847]	(23,850)
Middlesex	112	(150)	5.1	2,177	(2,200)
Norfolk	973	(1,000)	3.7	26,309	(26,300)
Northampton- shire	737	(750)	9.6	7,663	(7,700)
Nottinghamshire	[623]	(650)	[10.0]	[6,231]	(6,250)
Oxfordshire	1,002	(1,000)	14.9	6,713	(6,750)
Roteland	[95]	(100)	[10.0]	[954]	(950)
Shropshire	[1,307]	(1,300)	[27.8]	4,709	(4,700)
Somerset	2,120	(2,150)	16.3	12,991	(13,000)
Staffordshire	240	(250)	7.9	3,028	(3,050)
Suffolk	892	(900)	4.7	19,070	(19,100)
Surrey	503	(500)	12.3	4,105	(4,100)
Sussex	416	(450)	4.3	9,600	(9,600)
Warwickshire	[782]	(800)	[12.5]	6,277	(6,300)
Wiltshire	1,588	(1,600)	16.0	9,944	(9,950)

County	Number of slaves/oxmen		Percentage of total population	Total estimated population	
Column	(1)	(2)	(3)	(4)	(5)
Worcestershire	[797]	(800)	[17.3]	4,604	(4,600)
Yorkshire	0		0.0	7,566	(7,600)
Sub-total:	32,570	(32,600)	12.0	272,234	(272,250)
Wales					
Cheshire	[46]	(5)	[13.6]	324	(350)
Gloucestershire	7	(10)	12.1	58	(60)
Herefordshire	10	(10)	66.7	15	(20)
Shropshire	[12]	(15)	[25.0]	48	(50)
Sub-total:	[75]	(100)	[16.9]	445	(450)
Total:	32,645	(32,700)	12.0	272,679	(272,700)

Notes:
1. Figures within [ ] are corrected estimates discussed in the text.
2. Figures within ( ) are preferred approximations.
3. Estimated totals and sub-totals are both rounded from the calculated totals and sub-totals in cols 1 and 4, *not* from the sum of estimates in cols 2 and 5. The sum of estimates in col. 2 is 385 higher than the total given, and the sum of estimates in col. 5 is 680 higher than the total given, because of rounding errors.

tical precision, I have put in cols 2 and 5 within round brackets what Maitland rightly termed 'some rounder and therefore more significant figures'.[43] All I would claim for my estimates is the hope that they are of the right order of magnitude, and if anything err on the side of caution. The number and distribution of slaves before and after 1086 can be most usefully considered in the context of the decline of slavery, since the situation of 1086 portrayed in Domesday Book is one point in time within a long process. But this question of how, why and when slavery disappeared from England is itself a major problem worthy of full treatment elsewhere.

3. *The nature of slavery*

It is difficult to avoid the obvious starting-point of Aelfric's ploughman:[44]

> I work hard, I go out at daybreak, driving the oxen to the field, and I yoke them to the plough. Be it never so stark winter, I dare not linger at home for fear of my lord; but having yoked my oxen, and fastened share and coulter, every day must I plough a full acre or more. I have a boy,

[43] Maitland, vi.
[44] G. N. Garmonsway, *Aelfric's Colloquy*, London 1939, 20-1, lines 22–35.

driving the oxen with a goad-iron, who is hoarse with cold and shouting. Mighty hard work it is, for I am not free.

Clearly Aelfric believed that the contrast between freedom and slavery in his time was critical, and this is echoed in the judgements of modern historians, both in relation to Old English and Viking society. We should perhaps bear in mind the shift of opinion over the years from the position taken by Stenton and others, for whom the 'free peasant' was the essential basis of pre-Conquest economic and social structures[45] to the stance of Aston and Finberg who saw the landlord and his estate as the organising principle of the Anglo-Saxon economy,[46] and then recall the trenchant words of Henry Loyn: 'Right to the end of its days, Anglo-Saxon England was a slave-owning community . . . the Anglo-Saxons were avowedly, almost aggressively, slave-owners.'[47] Nor was the situation in the Danelaw any better, for the position of the Old English *theow* was virtually identical to that of the Scandinavian *thraell*.[48] *Thegn, socman, freoman, ceorl* and *bondr* were all indubitably free in personal status, and amongst their freedoms was the freedom to own, exploit and oppress their slaves.

Slavery is pre-eminently a personal condition or status; any connection with land, through tenure, or with a particular task or occupation, was incidental rather than fundamental to the definition of a slave. Whether or not slavery persisted from Roman times in Britain on estates whose structures continued into and beyond the fifth century is not a question we need to consider, though the Welsh law-codes suggest that slavery had been common in pre-Norman Wales, whilst in Wessex the Old English *wealh* could mean either 'welshman' or 'slave'.[49] Nevertheless, the legal position of the Anglo-Saxon slave, whatever his or her race, was little different from that of his Romano-British predecessor: he was a chattel, a thing rather than a person,[50] in Maitland's phrase 'in the main a rightless being'.[51] To avoid a tedious recitation of legal texts, let me quote a recent summary by one of our greatest living authorities on the Anglo-Saxon period:[52]

> Death, mutilation, reduction to slavery, savage corporal punishment lie behind bland statements sometimes made about discipline . . . The safeguards of a slave were tenuous . . . he could be punished or even killed without penalty.

Amongst the punishments were branding, castration, flogging and being stoned to death (or in the case of female slaves burnt to death) by fellow-

---

[45] Stenton, 277–80, 414.
[46] H. P. R. Finberg, *passim*; T. H. Aston, 'The Origin of the Manor' *with* 'A Postscript', *Social Relations and Ideas*, 1–44.
[47] Loyn, *ASE&NC*, 86; H. R. Loyn, *The Governance of Anglo-Saxon England*, London 1984, 5.
[48] For the *thraell*, see G. Jones, *A History of the Vikings*, Oxford 1968, 145, 147, 149; P. M. Foote, D. M. Wilson, *The Viking Achievement*, London 1970, 67–71, 73–4, 78; Finberg, 472–3; H. R. Loyn, *The Vikings in Britain*, London 1977, 15, 29, 129–30.
[49] Finberg, 47, 299–300, 364, 395.
[50] W. W. Buckland, *The Roman Law of Slavery*, Cambridge 1908.
[51] Maitland, 32.
[52] Loyn, *The Governance of Anglo-Saxon England*, 5, 49, 52.

slaves.[53] It is not surprising that in Domesday Book slaves were frequently grouped not with other people but with things, manorial appurtenances such as churches, mills and meadows, even being lumped together with hawks and hunting-dogs.[54]

As a 'manorial appurtenance' it is hardly surprising that the Domesday slave was essentially a rural labourer, though not completely so. Although Darby neglects to mention their occurrence in his 'Statistical Summary of Boroughs', there was a minority of just over one hundred urban slaves, though in some cases (e.g. Clifford (Herefs.), Okehampton (Devon), Steyning (Sussex)) it is unclear whether the slaves inside rural manors with an urban element were rural or urban labourers.[55] For the most part the male slave was a ploughman on a lord's demesne, both in and before 1086: this is the unanimous conclusion of all those who have considered the subject.[56] The female slaves (*ancillae*) present more of a problem; their presence on the ground (and in bed) is not reflected by Domesday Book, where the bulk of the total number of 706 are mentioned only in Circuits IV and V.[57] Obviously the commissioners on these two circuits were either more conscientious or more attuned to feminine sensibilities than their colleagues on other circuits, or indeed Professor Darby, whose analysis of Domesday rural population totally excludes women, slave or free. Presumably these female slaves were recorded as individuals, since, even if male slaves were heads of households – a matter still to be discussed – it can hardly be the case that so many households mainly in seven counties were headed by female slaves. Since the male and female slaves are often entered under a combined total (*inter servos et ancillas*), Darby and his colleagues in their analysis of recorded slaves were forced to assume a 50:50 sex-ratio and halve these combined totals before incorporating them in their calculations of county totals of slave-population.[58] It is generally assumed that these female slaves were domestic servants, dairymaids, etc.[59]

Slaves in the Exchequer Domesday rarely shared in the plough-teams of the manorial peasantry, and thus were certainly not substantial peasant land-holders. Indeed, it is sometimes said that they never shared in such teams,[60] but this is untrue: in a minority of entries slaves alone are recorded as holders of plough-teams or land.[61] The Exton text shows six slaves at Moortown in Somerset holding a virgate (Exon DB, fo. 429b) and one slave at East Buckland in Devon living on a ferling (Exon DB, fo. 129b2). The Devon texts

[53] H. G. Richardson, G. O. Sayles, *Law and Legislation from Aethelbert to Magna Carta*, Edinburgh 1966, 10, 16, 20–1.

[54] Darby, Campbell, 311; Loyn, *ASE&NC*, 349–50.

[55] Darby, *DGEE*, 111, 169, 225; Darby, *Dom.Eng.*, 364–8; Darby, Campbell, 88–90, 178–9, 352, 438; H. C. Darby, R. W. Finn, *Domesday Geography of South-West England*, Cambridge 1967, 284; Darby, Terrett, 48, 102–3, 206. Slavery was not incompatible with urban life in the eleventh century; Ipswich had a slave burgess in 1086: Darby, *Dom.Eng.*, 72.

[56] Maitland, 34–6; Ballard, 151, 213; Vinogradoff, *English Society in the Eleventh Century*, 464–5; Postan, 6–16, 31–2, 35–6; Loyn, *ASE&NC*, 349–50; Finn, *Introduction*, 118; Nelson, 52–7; Stenton, 477; Clarke, 41; Harvey, 60–3.

[57] Darby, *Dom.Eng.*, 86.

[58] Darby, Maxwell, 389, n. 2; Darby, Terrett, 17, 48, 74, 125, 234.

[59] Vinogradoff, *English Society in the Eleventh Century*, 464.

[60] Vinogradoff, *English Society in the Eleventh Century*, 463.

[61] Ballard, 151–2; Darby, Finn, 163, 250; Darby, *Dom.Eng*, 72.

of Domesday are most useful for elucidating the question of slave landholding. At Worthy and Wilson a villager and a slave in each place together held half a virgate (Exon DB, fo. 310b2–3); at Horton (fo. 102b, *3*, 11) and Stedcombe (fo. 108c, *16*, 169) in Devon, the Exchequer text mentions slaves whom Exon DB (fos 122b1, 313b4) terms 'villagers' holding a half-virgate and 2 virgates respectively, whilst at Mowlish the apparently landless '2 villagers and 2 smallholders' of the Exchequer DB (fo. 114a, *34*, 13) are designated as 2 villagers and 2 slaves 'who have a ferling' in Exon DB (fo. 336b3). The Exchequer DB entry for Raddon (fo. 103d, *5*, 9) refers to '1 villager with 1 plough-team and 1 slave'; Exon states that 'the villagers (unambiguously *villani*) have one ferling and half a plough-team' (fo. 179b1), and this is not the only instance where Exon refers to 'slaves' which the Exchequer text terms 'villagers': this is also true of the unambiguous '7 slaves with 1 plough-team' at Boasley (DB, I, fo. 105d, *16*, 6; Exon DB, fo. 288bl); the '1 villager, 1 slave' of Bradley (DB, I, fo. 103b, *379*) is rendered 'the villagers have half a plough-team' in Exon DB, fo. 133b3; at Widey '3 slaves with 1 villager have a half plough-team' replaces 'The villagers have half a plough-team' (DB, I, fo. 113b, *28*, 16; Exon DB, fo. 421b3); '1 villager and 2 slaves at Heavitree', unequipped in DB, I, fo. 114d, *34*, 56, have replaced 'the other plough is the villagers' (*villanorum*) of Exon DB, fo. 343b4). Finally, at Buckfast, 'A smith and 10 slaves have 2 plough-teams' (DB, I, fo. 104a, *6*, 13). The Summary of the 'lands of St Petroc' in Cornwall (Exon DB, fo. 528bl) also suggests that slaves can share in tenants' plough-teams.[62]

In other counties also slaves are recorded amongst various groups of peasants who certainly share plough-teams. At Ditchling in Sussex, in the sub-manor held by five men, probably knights, from Earl William de Warenne, there were '29 smallholders, 3 villagers and 10 slaves with 3 plough-teams' (fo. 26b, Sussex, *12*, 6). Even in apparently almost slave-free Nottinghamshire two entries for Geoffrey Aselin's estates suggest the same possibility: at Stoke Bardolph and Gedling he had '15 villagers, 6 slaves and 21 smallholders who have 8 plough-teams' and at Burton Joyce he had '1 freeman with 5 acres; 5 villagers, 1 smallholder, 1 male and 1 female slave; together they have 2 plough-teams' (fo. 289b, Notts., *12*, 16, 18). It is of course always possible to explain away entries such as the last three cited on the grounds that the slaves have been 'misplaced' from their 'proper place', but this assumes that the 'normal' position is the only possible position; it is an unprovable assertion unless a 'satellite' text exists. But Exon DB reveals that the 'normal' position of slaves after the demesne plough-teams is largely a convention of the Exchequer scribe, for Exon DB usually places the slaves with the other manorial tenants.[63] Indubitably, therefore, slaves could on occasion, though not of course by any means invariably, hold land and parts of a plough-team.

Though we have noted that slaves were usually demesne ploughmen, we have just established that they could in fact be cottagers. The corollary usually assumed from their occupation on the demesne that they were fed and housed in the lord's court is no more than an unproven hypothesis, probably relying

---

[62] R. W. Finn, *Domesday Studies: the Liber Exoniensis*, London 1964, 126.
[63] Finn, *Introduction*, 82.

HYDROGRAPHIC AND SHIP-HYDRODYNAMIC ASPECTS OF THE NORMAN INVASION, AD 1066

J. Neumann[1]

The purpose of this study is to re-examine the effects of hydrographic factors (tides and tidal streams) and to explore the ship-hydrodynamic aspects of sailing of the fleet of William, Duke of Normandy, from St-Valéry-sur-Somme to Pevensey in the autumn of 1066.

Earlier studies involving the hydrographic factors include a paper by Laporte[2] and a more recent and critical paper by Gillmor.[3] As to hydrography, we shall use tidal data newly computed for us for the Somme estuary by the Hydrographic and Oceanographic Service of the French Marine for the last (Julian) days of September 1066. The main difference of our study from earlier ones is, however, in the attention paid to problems of ship hydrodynamics and our attempt at estimating the speed of winds in the English Channel during the Invasion sailing and some characteristics of the Norman ships.

The day when the wind in the Channel shifted to blow from the south (after a wait said to have been fifteen days long) and made it possible for William's fleet to sail from St Valéry in the Somme estuary to Pevensey, was either 27 or 28 September (Julian dates; 3 or 4 October on the Gregorian calendar) 1066. Version 'D' of the ASC says that the Duke arrived at Pevensey on Michaelmas Eve (28 September), while Version 'E' states that he landed at Hastings on Michaelmas Day, i.e. 29 September.[4] The nineteenth-century British historian Freeman, a scholar of the Norman Conquest, argued that the two versions are not at variance: William landed at Pevensey on the 28th, and, after disembarking troops, horses and supplies, marched to Hastings, reaching it the next day. Modern historians tend to agree that the landing took place at Pevensey on the 28th, see e.g. Douglas.[5]

Table 1 lists the source of our data:

---

[1] Emeritus, Department of Atmospheric Sciences, The Hebrew University, Jerusalem, Israel; in 1986–89 visiting with the Department of Meteorology, University of Copenhagen, Copenhagen, Denmark.
[2] J. Laporte, 'Les opérations navales en Manche et Mer du Nord pendant l'année 1066', *Ann. Normandie* XVII, 1967, 3–42.
[3] C. M. Gillmor, 'Naval logistics of the cross-Channel operation 1066', *ante* VII, 1985, 105–31.
[4] *ASC*, 141–2.
[5] D. C. Douglas, *William the Conqueror*, London 1983, 396.

Table 1   Astronomical and hydrographic data for the English Channel for
27–9 September 1066 (OS) and dimensions of Viking ships

		September 1066 (Julian dates)			Sources and remarks
		27	28	29	
		GMT			
Sun	rise	05 57	05 59	06 00	Royal Greenwich Observatory (from
	set	17 29	17 26	17 24	data supplied by the Science and
Moon	rise	11 56	12 57	13 49	Engineering Research Council of the
	set	21 05	22 04	23 09	UK)

Phase of moon: First Quarter on the night 28/29 September	Goldstine.[6] Since the moon was near or at its First Quarter, the tides in the Channel were intermediate between spring and neap rates
Tidal data for St Valéry and Cayeux (Cayeux is approximately 8 km. to the west of St Valéry, in the Somme estuary)	Principal Establishment, Hydrographic and Oceanographic Service of the French Marine, Brest (Ing. B. Simon)
Times of High Water and Low Water at Pevensey	Within about 15 minutes of those at Dover, see Admiralty Manual of Tides[7]
Tidal streams in the English Channel	British Admiralty Publication NP250[8]
Dimensions of Viking ships	Olsen and Crumlin-Pedersen,[9] Crumlin-Pedersen,[10] Graham–Campbell[11] and Shetelig[12]

It is appropriate to devote some attention to the weather in September 1066.
According to chroniclers of the eleventh century, the first half of September
1066 was stormy in the English Channel. We have two indications for that: (i)
Version 'C' of the ASC[13] says that on 8 September, Harold, king of the
English, disbanded the fyrd and ordered his warships to sail to London (both
the fyrd and the navy were guarding Southern England) and 'many of the ships
perished before they reached London'. Presumably, the losses were caused by
stormy seas. (ii) Writing about the passage of the Norman fleet from the Dives

---

[6] H. H. Goldstine, *New and Full Moons, 1001 B.C. to A.D. 1651*, Philadelphia, Pa., 1973, 173.
[7] A. T. Doodson and H. D. Warburg, *A Manual of Tides*, London 1941, Fig. 24.10.
[8] *Admiralty Tidal Stream Atlas, The English and Bristol Channels*, 3rd ed., British Admiralty Publication NP250, London 1973.
[9] O. Olsen and O. Crumlin-Pedersen, *Five Viking Ships from Roskilde Fjord*, 2nd ed., translated by B. Bluestone, Copenhagen 1983, 101. See also the principal paper of these two authors 'The Skuldelev ships (II)', *Acta Archaeol.* XXXVIII, 73–174.
[10] O. Crumlin-Pedersen, 'Ships, navigation and routes in the reports of Ohthere and Wulfstan', translated by P. H. Sawyer, in: N. Lund (ed.), *Two Voyagers at the Court of King Alfred*, York 1984, 31, lower diagram.
[11] J. Graham-Campbell, *The Viking World*, London 1980, 46–7.
[12] H. Shetelig, The Viking ships, in A. W. Brøgger and H. Shetelig, *The Viking Ships, Their Ancestry and Evolution*, translated by K. John, Oslo 1971, 104.
[13] *ASC*, 142.

to St Valéry, which according to historians[14] began on 12 September, the chronicler William of Poitiers[15] (born *c.* 1020, d. *c.* 1090; archdeacon and chaplain to Duke William, though there is no indication that the chronicler travelled with the fleet) mentions the losses of life 'through waves'.

Apparently, towards the end of the third week of the month, an improvement took place in the weather, at least in the area of Northern England. Snorre Sturlason,[16] the Icelandic skald and historian (1178–1241), writes that when Harald Hardråda, king of Norway (a rival of William for the throne of the English), arrived with his fleet in the Humber estuary, Northern England, '. . . the weather was fine, and it was hot sunshine'. Date: 18 September 1066.

The improvement in weather conditions, that seems to have set in the third week, continued into the fourth. According to Guy,[17] bishop of Amiens (d. 1076), perhaps the contemporary author of the *Carmen de Hastingae Proelio*, William had to tarry 'three times five days for a favourable wind', and then the bishop goes on: 'He [God] drove the clouds from the sky and the winds from the sea and rid the heavens from rain . . . the sun shone forth with unwonted brilliance . . . the feast of Michael [St Michael, 29 September] was to be celebrated'.

If we accept Guy's effusion, then the weather must have been fine prior to the invasion night and, what is particularly important in the context of this study, *the winds were not excessive.* A quantitative assessment of the wind speed in the Channel will be made below.

Guy of Amiens and William of Poitiers give accounts of the departure and sailing of the fleet that have a number of features in common. Both write that the time of departure from St Valéry was about nightfall and that Pevensey was reached the next morning. Both say that the sailing over was executed in two stages: the first was from inside the Somme estuary to the 'open' Channel, and, after an interval of time, stage two: from the waters of the Channel near the estuary's mouth to Pevensey. In the following quotations the italics are ours.

William of Poitiers[18] writes as follows: 'The ships were loosened from their moorings, but *as William did not want to put in at the hostile coast* before daylight, he ordered the ships to anchor awhile in the more open waters and wait for his signal for sailing.' Guy[19] puts it in the following words: 'Already the day was waning, *already the setting sun was low*, when your [William's] ship, racing ahead, set the course . . . But after rosy dawn brightened the lands and the sun cast his beams over the world, you gave command to set course and made sail, ordering that the vessels should weigh anchor. *When you reached safe landing places, leaving the sea astern, the third hour of the day was rising over the Earth . . .*'

[14] Douglas, 396.

[15] *Gesta Guillelmi*, II-6.

[16] S. Sturlason, *The Heimskringla, A History of the Norse Kings*, translated by S. Laing, Vol. III, London 1906, 785.

[17] *Carmen*, lines 54–5 and 72–7. For the authenticity of this text, see R. H. C. Davis, *EHR* xciii, 1978, and *ante* ii, 1979.

[18] *Gesta Guillelmi*, II-7.

[19] *Carmen*, lines 105 and 119–24.

According to Goldstine,[20] on the Julian 27 and 28 September 1066, the moon was near its First Quarter. Hence the lunar-solar ocean tide must have been intermediate between the spring and neap rates, that is, not so excessively large as at the spring rate. Ing. B. Simon, of the Principal Establishment of the Hydrographic and Oceanographic Service of the French Marine (letter dated Brest, 9 January 1986), has kindly calculated the times of High Water (HW) and Low Water (LW) at St Valéry and at Cayeux, the latter being situated about 8 km. west of St Valéry along the Somme estuary, close to the exit to the Channel. The times of tides and their heights, as calculated by Ing. Simon, are listed in Table 2.

Table 2 Hours of HW (High Water) and LW (Low Water) and height of tides in the Somme Estuary towards the end of September 1066 (Julian dates)

Data computed by the Principal Establishment, Hydrographic and Oceanographic Service of the French Marine, Brest

Date (AD 1066)	tide	Hour (GMT)	Height (m.)
St Valéry			
27 September	HW	01 57	9.9
	HW	14 22	9.6
28	HW	02 49	9.3
	HW	15 17	9.0
29	HW	03 51	8.7
	HW	16 24	8.5
Cayeux			
27 September	HW	01 35	10.0
	LW	08 33	1.4
	HW	13 59	9.8
	LW	20 56	1.4
28	HW	02 25	9.4
	LW	09 19	1.8
	HW	14 51	9.1
	LW	21 44	1.9
29	HW	03 23	8.7
	LW	10 13	2.3
	HW	15 55	8.5
	LW	22 43	2.3

[20] Goldstine, 173.

The figures in the Table were computed on the assumption that the shape of the estuary bed was the same in 1066 as today. This is certainly not the case, both for natural and artificial causes. After some earlier man-made changes, works carried out in 1835 further modified the estuary's shape (letter of Ing. Simon dated 27 March 1986). For these reasons, the figures in the Table are no more than approximate values.

In Table 2 the lower values of HW and the higher values for LW for the 28th signify that the tides were on their way to neap tides. Furthermore, the figures for Cayeux suggest that, as far as the tides (and, by implication, the tidal streams) are concerned, a good time for departing from the estuary was between the hours from HW to LW, for, at least during the second half of that interval *the tidal streams are outward* (see next paragraph), *assisting exit from the Somme.* Even if the chroniclers would not have mentioned that the time of sailing from St Valéry was about nightfall (which on the 27th and, to a lesser extent, on the 28th occurred about midway between HW and LW), the figures in Table 2 and the facts that Pevensey was a relatively short sailing time *with favourable winds*, and that an early-morning arrival at Pevensey was desirable (to make landfall in daylight, to take advantage of daylight for disembarkation and to be able to face better any unexpected developments), suggest that *the period between the early afternoon HW and the evening LW was a most suitable time for setting out.* It is probably correct to assert that the Normans had experienced mariners who were well acquainted with the tidal conditions in the Somme estuary and in the Channel. Williamson[21] points out that William himself made the journey to London in the reign of Edward the Confessor and that *there was much cross-Channel traffic.* 'There were seamen in the Norman ports who knew the Sussex coastline in all its convolutions.'

With outflow currents being noteworthy only about three hours after HW, departure times between 17 and 18 GMT on the 27th, and between 18 and 19 on the 28th seem to have been 'optimal'. (We are using the term 'optimal' in a somewhat loose sense.) A later departure hour, closer to the time of LW, would have entailed the risk of ships getting stranded. The height difference between HW and LW is very considerable in the estuary (Table 2) and the depth of water is very small in some sections of the bed about LW. A detailed map of the Somme estuary, prepared in the seventeenth century (published as Plate VIII in Héraud[22]) shows water depths of between 0.1 and 4.8 m, based on actual measurements at times of LW. In 1066 the depths may have been different, but possibly not substantially different. Fig. 1 is a photographic copy (kindly supplied by Ing. B. Simon) of the above-mentioned seventeenth-century chart which shows the shallowness of water in the estuary at LW.

As to the velocity of tidal streams in the estuary during the hours of approach of LW, a publication of the Hydrographic Service of the French Marine[23] gives velocities of about 2 kn (2.4 kn at about HW, and 1.9 kn at

[21] J. Williamson, *The English Channel, A History*, London 1959, 80.

[22] M. G. Héraud, *Recherches hydrographiques sur le régime des côtes*. Dixiéme cahier *Rapport sur la reconnaissance de la Baie de Somme et ses abords en 1878*, Dépôt des Cartes et Plans de la Marine, No. 625, Paris.

[23] Service Hydrographique de la Marine Française, *Courants de marée dans la Manche et sur les côtes français de l'Atlantique*, Paris 1953, 56.

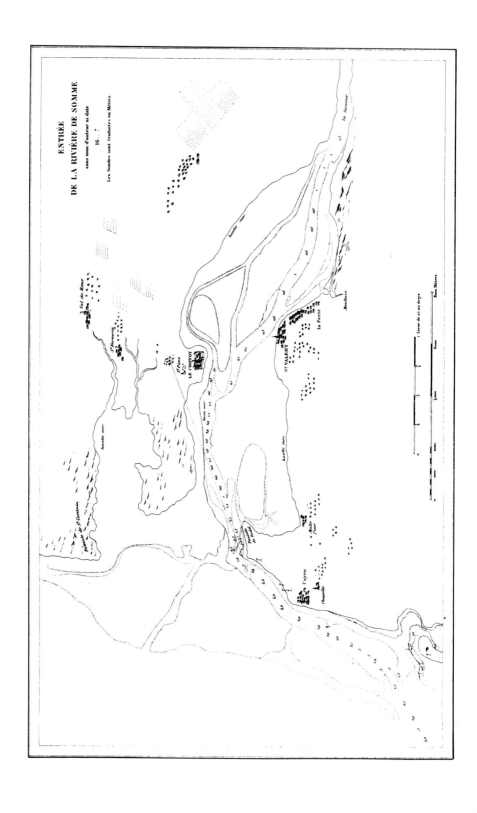

ENTRÉE
DE LA RIVIÈRE DE SOMME
sans nom d'auteur ni date
16...?
Les Sondes sont traduites en Mètres.

about LW) near the estuary's mouth ('devant l'embrochure de la Somme'), but it is reasonable to assume that the velocities are greater inside the estuary, e.g. near St Valéry, where the estuary bed is narrower. Héraud's[24] Plate XIII shows stream velocities of up to 5–6 kn, and a publication of the Seewarte in Hamburg, *Segelhandbuch des englischen Kanals*,[25] quotes figures of 6–7 kn inside the estuary three hours after LW. Ing. Simon suggests (letter of 27 March 1986) that a value somewhat short of 4 kn would be plausible for the hours approaching LW. Unless the winds were very strong on the 27th or the 28th (which we do not think to have been the case, see our remarks above where we discussed the weather) from an unfavourable direction, the above-quoted tidal stream velocities could have been helpful to get William's ships out of the estuary.

Table 3 quotes the directions and velocities of the lunar-solar tidal streams in the English Channel: near the mouth of the Somme, at mid-Channel and near Pevensey. They do not include any wind-generated currents, moreover the shape of the coastline near Pevensey is thought to have been quite different in 1066, see the diagram on p. 77 of Williamson[26] or the frontispiece in Beeler[27] or p. 38 in Ashley.[28]

The figures in Table 3 were extracted from a British Admiralty publication.[29] The hours are given as 'before' and 'after' HW at Dover (HWD). As to the difference between the hours of HWD, at the mouth of the Somme and near Pevensey, Fig. 24.10 in the *Admiralty Manual of Tides*[30] shows that the difference is no more than about ¼ hour, i.e. a difference that is immaterial in the present study.

[24] Héraud.
[25] *Segelhandbuch des englishen Kqnals*, Pt. III: *Die französische Küste*, Hamburg 1893, p. 1.
[26] Williamson, 77.
[27] J. Beeler, *Warfare in England, 1066–1189*, Ithaca, NY, 1966.
[28] M. Ashley, *The Life and Times of William I*, London 1973, 38.
[29] *Admiralty Tidal Streams Atlas*.
[30] Doodson and Warburg, 207.

Fig. 1   The Somme estuary at time of Low Water. This is a copy of a chart made in the seventeenth century, illustrating the measured depth of water which varies between 0.1 and 4.8 m. (0.3 and 16 ft). The particularly shallow water of 0.1 m. (0.3 ft) occurs 2 km. (just over 1 n.mi.) WNW of St Valéry. The shallowness of water emphasises the importance for the Norman fleet to leave the estuary before Low Water which during the last few days of September 1066 occurred about 21 (and 09) GMT, see the figures for Cayeux in Table 1.

The chart shown here is a copy of the seventeenth-century drawing, published as Plate VIII in a book by Héraud[22] on the Somme estuary. A photographic copy of the plate was made available to us by Ing. B. Simon, Principal Establishment, Hydrographic and Oceanographic Service of the French Marine at Brest. It is regretted that the figures for depth of water are in far too small print.

Table 3   Mean direction and speed of tidal streams in the English Channel (A) near the mouth of the Somme estuary (B) about mid-point between St Valéry and Pevensey and (C) near Pevensey

The figures were extracted from the British Admiralty Publication *NP 250 Tidal Stream Atlas, The English and Bristol Channels* (1973). As in the *Atlas*, in the Table the speed is given in tenths of a knot, the numbers before the comma relating to the neap rate, the numbers after the comma to the spring rate. Thus, at 6 hours before High Water Dover, 09 stands for 0.9 kn. The direction of stream is given as the direction *from* which it is coming. If at any given hour and area two sets of directions and speed are given, the first refers to the south side, the second to the north side of the area of concern.

HWD = High Water Dover

Hour		(A) Somme	(B) Mid-Channel	(C) Pevensey
Before HWD	6	NNE 09,17	NE 09,16	ENE 05,09
	5	NNNE 09,16	NNE 06,10	SSW 03,06; NE 05,09
	4	Slack; NNW 04,07	NNW 04,07	WSW 11,19; N 02,04
	3	SW 10,17; SW 03,06	WWSW 06,10	WWSW 15,26; WSW 04,08
	2	SW 08,14	WSW 07,12	WWSW 06,10
	1	SW 06,10; SSSW 09,16	WSW 07,12	WSW 07,13; WSW 04,08
HWD		SSW 03,06; SSSW 09,16	WSW 03,06	WWSW 01,02
After HWD	1	Slack	Slack	Slack
	2	Slack	S 03,05; slack	Slack
	3	NNE weak	E 03,06	ENE weak
	4	NNE weak	ENE 05,09	EENE 10,18; EENE 02,04
	5	NNE 07,12	NE 07,12	EENE 09,17; ENE 05,09
	6	NNE 09,17	NE 07,13	E 07,12; EENE 06,11

Note: NNNE means a direction between NNE and N, etc.

It is seen in the Table that, with very few exceptions, tidal stream velocities exceed 1 kn only at times of spring tides. Since we are dealing with conditions intermediate between spring and neap rates, and, assuming that in 1066 tidal steam velocities were not significantly different from those listed in the Table, we can say that on 27 or 28 September 1066, when the moon was nearing First Quarter, the tidal streams encountered by the Norman fleet were not in excess of 1 kn, except for one or two hours, about midway between the afternoon and the nocturnal HWD ('6 hours after HWD' and '6 hours before HWD', see Table 3 and then Table 2). If the departure was on the 27th, then the midpoint in time would have been about 20 GMT; if on the 28th, then about 21 GMT. If Guy of Amiens and William of Poitiers are right that the Duke ordered the fleet to ride at anchor in the Channel close to the Somme estuary, then these hours when the tidal stream velocities may have been somewhat above 1 kn, may well have coincided, at least in part if not wholly, with the hours when the ships were tarrying at anchor.

A quantitative estimate of the effect of tidal streams on the shape and length of the route of the fleet is made in Appendix A. But before quoting the results, we have to consider the speed capabilities of the Norman ships in the absence of tidal streams (and wind currents). In order to be able to estimate the shape and length of the route of the Norman fleet from the Somme to Pevensey, we have to look first at the speed capabilities of the Norman ships as *single* ships in favourable wind conditions, and then estimate the fleet speed.

Virtually nothing is known about the dimensions of the Norman ships, except for the uncertain estimates that one can derive from visual inspection of the Bayeux Tapestry. Some helpful hints can be obtained if we assume that the Norman shipwrights built on the Viking ship-building experience and tradition. This assumption seems to us reasonable as the Normans were, in part, descendants of Viking raiders-settlers who came 150 years earlier to the country that was to become Normandy.[31] But before taking quantitative note of some characteristics of Viking ships, we wish to make use of a result of basic ship theory.

According to basic ship theory (e.g. Rawson and Tupper[32]) ships have a 'limiting' speed. The fact that this speed is called 'limiting' does not mean that it cannot be exceeded at all, but, at and beyond that speed vessels encounter *a sharply increasing resistance against motion*. In case of ships whose length is large compared with their beam, to be referred to as 'slender' ships, the limiting speed has a simple relationship to the length of the ship. Strictly, the length and beam should be taken at the waterline, but, when we consider the *ratio* of the two, the use of the 'overall' length and beam, in lieu of the correct waterline quantities, is not very critical. In case of sailing ships, we mean the speed that can be attained with favourable winds.

Fig. 2 shows the relationship between the length of slender ships and their limiting speed. Actually, the relevant theoretical treatment assumes that the depth of water is great relative to ship length, but, if we bear in mind that of the waves ['gravity waves'] excited by a ship in motion relative to the water waves of a length about equal to or greater than the ship length are most disturbing to the ship and cause the generation of a limiting speed, then a point made by a Danish ship scientist (Halvard[33]) tells us that a water of depth equal to or greater than half the ship length is sufficient to render Fig. 2 valid for slender ships. If, however, the ship is not slender, then its limiting speed will be lower than what is indicated by Fig. 2. This very important point for our present study is further elaborated in the next few paragraphs.

---

[31] It is shown in the paper 'Viking weather-vane practices in mediaeval France' by S. Lindgrén and J. Neumann, *Fornvännen* 78, 1983, 197–202, that *throughout the Middle Ages* in Normandy the special Viking weather vane practices were preserved: the possession of weather vanes was restricted to outstanding personages, the vanes were gilded etc.

[32] K. J. Rawson and E. C. Tupper, *Basic Ship Theory*, Vol. 2; London 1984, 382–3.

[33] AA. S. Harvald, *Resistance and Propulsion of Ships*, New York 1983, 77.

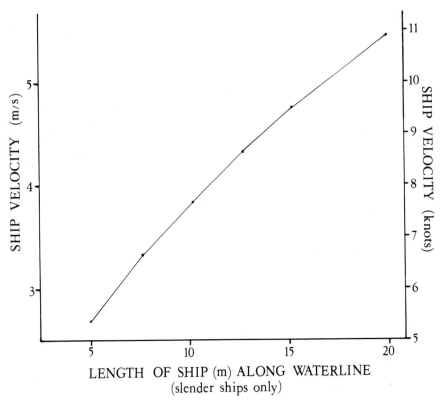

Fig. 2   The relationship between the length of *slender ships* and their limiting sailing speed. The curve is based on eq. (10) in Appendix B of this paper.

At least since the Antiquity, warships were of the slender type, unless speed was sacrificed for the sake of firepower. The Vikings called their warships 'longships' ('langskipin' in the Icelandic and Norse sagas). Undoubtedly, William's fleet must have included longships, i.e. warships; his scout ships, if any, must have been slender too, even though small in dimensions. If we knew the lengths of his warships (here and elsewhere, waterline length is the really significant datum), we could estimate their limiting speed with favourable winds from Fig. 2, whose simple theoretical background is described in brief in Appendix B.

But a knowledge of the limiting speed of William's longships does not help for the speed of a fleet is dictated by the speed of the slow ships. And, if we know this, a correction must be applied, for the speed of sailing in formation is less than the limiting speed of single ships.

It is reasonable to assume that the Norman troop and supply ships were not slender in order to increase the capacity of their hold. Now we have to get to grips with the problem of length(s) and beam(s) of William's slow ships.

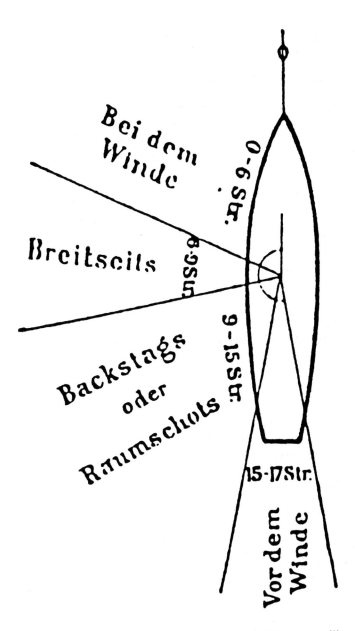

Fig. 3   Prager's four wind groups with respect to German sailing vessels.
The highest sailing speed is attained with the wind direction designated
'Backstags' or broad reach, i.e. winds somewhat *off* stern (and not with
winds blowing from stern). In this diagram the abbreviation 'Str.' stands for
'Strich(e)' or compass points. One Strich is equivalent to *c*. 11°.

C.   As Pevensey was a relatively short distance from St Valéry (*c.* 100 km; 90 km from the estuary's mouth) and as it was desirable to reach Pevensey early in the morning, it was advisable to depart from St Valéry *before the evening LW*. The relatively early departure hour from St Valéry, dictated by the approaching LW of the evening hours, suggested a short riding at anchor outside the estuary in order to take up fleet formation and in order not to arrive at Pevensey while it is still dark.

D.   With favourable winds, the speed of the fleet was determined by two factors: the limiting speed of the slow ships (troop and cargo ships), and the fact that sailing in fleet formation inevitably entails a reduction of the attainable speed. As to the slow ships, their length-to-beam ratio may have been about 4.5 if the Normans followed the Viking knowledge, experience and tradition of ship construction. If the ships were 12 m long, as estimated by Williamson, they may have had a limiting speed of about 6.5 kn with favourable winds. The fleet speed was bound to have been less than that.

E.   The tidal streams in the English Channel caused a curved sailing course of a length between about 100 and 110 km from the Somme's mouth to Pevensey, or about 110 to 120 km from St Valéry. The fleet speed is estimated at about 4.5 kn (= 8.3 km/hr = 2.3 m/s).

F.   It is estimated that the wind in the Channel during Invasion night may have had a force of 3, or 3½ at the most, on the Beaufort scale. Near Pevensey the wind speed was likely to be a little less due to the approach of an onshore wind to a land mass (frictional effect).

G.   Ship-hydrodynamic calculations indicate that ships of an overall length of 12.5 m and a length-to-beam ratio 4.5, and winds from a direction of 135° relative to the sailing course (the angle counted counterclockwise from the bow; note that the direction of wind but *not* its speed is assumed; moreover, a southerly wind forms an angle of about 135° relative to a WNW sailing course), may have required for a good sailing speed a square sail of 4 m × 4 m with a wind of force 4 and a sail of 5 m × 5 m with a wind of force 3½. It is estimated that the (single) mast may have been 7–8 m high, a height that accommodates a 5-m-high sail.

H.   The hours of HW and LW at Pevensey occur within about ¼ hour of those in the Somme estuary, i.e. at, respectively, about 0230 and 0920 GMT on 28 September and about 0320 and 1015 on the 29th. With the Norman fleet's arrival time between the hours of HW and LW, the tidal currents were bound to flow outward from the then existing 'Pevensey Bay' (or 'Baylet'). These currents were probably weak compared with the wind speed which is estimated at about 10 kn, or the Norman ships should not have experienced difficulties at reaching the coast, beaching the ships and disembarking. Danish experiments with the replica of what is thought to have been a Viking warship (the Ladby ship, see Table 3) indicate that the embarkation and disembarkation of horses posed no problems and required no auxiliary devices.

The Effect of the Tidal Streams on the Length of Sailing Course
of the Norman Fleet

Let V_{sw} denote the hypothetical velocity of the fleet solely due to the wind, v_t the tidal stream velocity and let α stand for the angle subtended by the two. Then, if V_s denotes the actual sailing velocity of the fleet,

$$V_s = + \sqrt{V_{sw}^2 + v_t^2 - 2\, v_t\, V_{sw}\, \cos\alpha} \,, \qquad (1)$$

$$V_s = V_{sw} \sqrt{1 + \frac{v_t^2}{V_{sw}^2} - 2\, \frac{v_t}{V_{sw}}\, \cos\alpha} \,. \qquad (1a)$$

Making the assumption that in 1066 the tidal stream directions and velocities were not appreciably different from those in Table 3, we estimate that the Invasion sailing covered the following 'tide hours' (HWD = High Water Dover):

In the Channel, near the Somme estuary . . . the hours '4 (or 5) after HWD'

About mid-Channel . . . the hours '6 to 0 before HWD'

The Channel close to Pevensey . . . the hours '1 to 4 (or 5) after HWD'

Looking at the tidal stream velocities in Table 3 for the above hours, we note that the speeds intermediate between the spring and neap rates (moon in the First Quarter) were less than 1 kn, with the exception of two hours: hour '6 After HWD' near the Somme and hour '6 Before HWD' about mid-Channel. Let us assume that $v_t = 1$ kn (1.9 km/hr), which is an overestimate for most of the time of concern. As to V_{sw}, earlier we have come up with the estimate for V_s that it is about 4.3 kn. Although what we need is V_{sw}, but for the order of magnitude estimate of the term (v_t^2/V_{sw}^2) we shall use the value of 4.3 kn, yielding that (v_t^2/V_{sw}^2) is roughly 1/20 which is negligibly small relative to the term 1 under the square root.

Turning to the term $\cos\alpha$, we note that the angle α subtended by v_t and the direction of sailing varies between 75° and 105° for which $\cos\alpha$ is between +0.25 and −0.25 (that is, the cosine values are rather small), where the positive values apply for the area near the Somme and the area off Pevensey, while the negative values hold for the intermediate region. Let us consider 0.25 as a kind of amplitude of a cosine wave, and then, to an approximation, the suggested cosine wave is of the form

$$\cos\alpha = 0.25\, \cos\frac{2\pi}{T}t \,, \qquad (2)$$

where T is the total time of crossing and t the time since the start just outside the Somme. Earlier we have justified the neglect of the quadratic term in eq. (1a). In view of this and of (2), we can put (1a) in the form

$$V_s = V_{sw} \sqrt{1 - 0.5 \frac{v_t}{V_{sw}} \cos \frac{2\pi}{T} t} \quad . \tag{4}$$

With 0.5 (v_t/V_{sw}) equal to about 0.1 ($v_t = 1$ kn and V_{sw} something like 4 kn), the second term under the square-root in (4) is small enough relative to the term 1 for expanding the square-root. On expanding and neglecting quadratic and higher terms, we obtain with $v_t = 1.9$ km/hr (= 1 kn, but now we revert to km/hr),

$$V_s = V_{sw} - 0.48 \cos \frac{2\pi}{T} Tt \quad . \tag{5}$$

The route length, λ say, is the integral with respect to time of eq. (5) from $t = 0$ to $t = T$, or

$$\lambda = \int_0^T V_s \, dt = \int_0^T V_{sw} \, dt - 0.48 \frac{T}{2\pi} \left[\sin \frac{2\pi}{T} t \right]_0^T . \tag{6}$$

We have pointed out a few lines above that the field of tidal-stream velocities between the Somme and Pevensey (at least during the recent decades) is such that the velocities in mid-Channel are oppositely directed to those near the Somme, on the one hand, and near Pevensey, on the other. The idealisation of this distribution through eq. (2) entails that the integral of the trigonometric term in eq. (6) drops out, or

$$\lambda = V_{sw} T \quad . \tag{7}$$

Assigning the values 11, 12 and 13 hours to T, and taking the fleet velocities 50%, 60% and 70% of the limiting speed of slow ships as single ships V_{sw}, assuming that $V_{sw} = 12$ km/hr (rounded off from 11.9 km/hr), we arrive at the following table for route length λ:

% of V_{sw}	Assumed fleet speed (km/hr)	T (hrs)	11	12	13
50	6		66 km	72 km	78 km
60	7.2		79	86	94
70	8.4		92	101	110

We reject all computed route lengths less than 90 km. Moreover, in view of Guy's 'statement' that 'the fleet arrived at safe landing places when the third hour of the day was rising', we suggest giving greater credence to the longer passage durations and, if so, the route length may have amounted between 94 and 110 km.

APPENDIX B

The 'Limiting Speed' of Slender Ships
(and some Remarks on Non-slender Ships)

We begin this Appendix by referring back to that part of the present paper where we discuss the limiting speed of slender ships and where this speed is illustrated in Fig. 2. We have pointed out that the speed that we have called 'limiting speed' of slender ships is, strictly speaking, not a ship speed but the speed of propagation of gravity waves of water of wave length L that are aroused by the ship in motion relative to the water. Ships in motion relative to the water excite (gravity) waves of many different wave lengths: waves of wave length L, L = length of the ships, interfere in a disturbing way with motion of the ships. If a slender ship of length L (to be strict again, L should be the waterline length of the ships) travels at a speed equal, or close to, the speed of propagation of gravity waves of wave length L, then these waves 'keep abreast' of the ship and represent for it a seriously disturbing factor. It is this fact that makes it possible to call the speed of propagation of gravity waves of wave length L as the limiting speed of travel of the ship itself. Gravity waves of shorter wave lengths lag behind the ship while gravity waves of wave lengths longer than the ship outrun the ship.

In texts of basic ship theory it is pointed out that what really happens is that the above-mentioned waves represent pressure systems and that both the bow and the stern excite such pressure systems. E.g., Rawson and Tupper[55] write as follows (hereunder L = overall length):

'Since at most speeds both the bow and stern systems are present aft of the ship, there is an interaction between the two transverse wave systems. If the systems are so phased that the crests are coincident, the resulting system will have increased wave height, and consequently greater energy content. If the crest of one system coincides with the trough of the other the resulting wave height and energy content will be less. . . . The distance between bow and stern pressure systems is typically 0.9 L. The condition that crests or troughs of the bow system should coincide with the first trough of the stern system is therefore

$$\frac{V^2}{0.9L} = \frac{g}{N\pi} \ . \tag{8}$$

For N = 1, 3, 5, 7, etc., the troughs will coincide and for N = 2, 4, 6, etc., the crests from the bow system coincide with the trough from the after system. . . .'

For N = 2 the relation between the speed of propagation of the wave, or that of the pressure system, is

$$\frac{V^2}{0.9L} = \frac{g}{2\pi} \ , \tag{9}$$

where, as in eq. (8), g is the acceleration of gravity. Another way of writing eq. (9) is

$$\frac{2\pi}{L} = \frac{0.9g}{V^2} \ . \tag{9a}$$

---

[55] Rawson and Tupper, 382.

Here on the left we have the important physical quantity *wave number*, $2\pi/L$ being the wave number of wave of length L.

Fig. 10.4, p. 383 in the Rawson and Tupper text, illustrates the interaction between the bow and stern pressure systems. It shows, among other things, that for N = 2 the pressure trough of the bow system coincides with the trough of the stern system, the resulting wave height (and energy content) being reduced. Fig. 10.5 of the same page shows the wave resistance (also called wave-making resistance) as a function of ship speed. The graph indicates that immediately beyond the point represented by N = 2, that is, at still higher ship speeds, *a very steep increase in the resistance of the waves is experienced by the ship*. Hence it is proper to call the ship speed at which this sharply augmented resistance sets in as 'limiting speed' *of the ship*.

With $2\pi = 6.28$, eq. (9) may be rewritten as

$$V = 0.38 \sqrt{gL} \ . \qquad (10)$$

This equation is represented by Fig. 2 of the present paper.

The non-dimensional quantity (= pure number) V^2/gL is an important quantity in fluid dynamics. It is called the Froude-number after the British physicist William Froude of the nineteenth century who made important water-tank experiments studying the relationship between the speed of model ships as a function of wave resistance.

When the ship is not slender, its limiting speed will be lower. Gravity waves of wave lengths shorter than ship length L will 'catch up' or keep abreast of the slow ship and disturb its motion. Determination of the limiting speed of non-slender ship requires somewhat involved procedures.

Acknowledgments

The writer is pleased to record his indebtedness to the following scientists for their ready assistance. Particular thanks are due to the first three who accompanied the preparation of this study with their comments and who read and commented on the draft of this paper:

Dr Ewan C. B. Corlett (Burness, Corlett & Partners, Naval Architects, Ramsey, Isle of Man, England) for his helpful comments and suggestions in matters of ship-hydrodynamics;

Prof. Sean McGrail (then National Maritime Museum, Greenwich, England; now at the Institute of Archaeology, University of Oxford, Oxford, England) for his useful comments on the speed of single ships and fleet speed of ancient sailing vessels;

Ing. B. Simon (Etablissement Principal, Service Hydrographique et Océanographique de la Marine Française, Brest, France) for the considerable amount of work he put in computing the tides in the Somme estuary the last few days of (Julian) September 1066, for his comments and for a photographic copy of a chart made in the seventeenth century showing the Somme estuary at time of Low Water. His tide calculations were made especially for the present paper;

Ing. K. Hanhirova (Ship-Hydrodynamic Laboratory, Technical University, Espoo (Helsinki), Finland, for computing the speed of winds and sail size as a function of sailing speed for a reduced-scale version of the Viking ship Gokstad;

Dr R. Whyman (Meteorological Office, Bracknell, England) for preparing statistical tables of nocturnal winds at Herstmonceux Castle, near Pevensey, and for copies of some papers on the land breezes of Southern England;

The following scientists have kindly helped with copies from relevant literature:

Dr D. E. Cartwright (Institute of Oceanographic Sciences, Godalming, Surrey, England)

Dr J. Darchen and M. H. Darnajoux, especially M. H. Darnajoux (Météorologie Nationale, Paris)

Dr G. Heise (Deutsches Hydrographisches Institut, Hamburg)

Mr M. Wood (National Meteorological Archive, Bracknell, England), for his frequent assistance.

Finally, the writer thanks the Royal Greenwich Observatory and the Science and Engineering Research Council of the UK for data of sun and moon rise and set for the last few days of (Julian) September 1066.

MONKS IN THE WORLD:
THE CASE OF GUNDULF OF ROCHESTER

Marylou Ruud

During the thirty-one years of his episcopal career, from 1077 to 1108, Gundulf of Rochester worked intimately with two celebrated archbishops of Canterbury, Lanfranc and Anselm, and under the Anglo-Norman kings, William I, William Rufus, and Henry I. He was an active participant in the post-conquest reform of the English Church, a vicar for Canterbury during vacancies and absences, and a moving force in several late-eleventh-century English building projects. Scholars today, however, tend to downplay this aspect of the monk-bishop's life and refer to Gundulf primarily in terms of his sanctity.[1] Frank Barlow, throughout his work on the English Church, presents glimpses of Gundulf that emphasise the saintly and monastic aspects of his life. In fact, Barlow openly admires how 'the saintly Gundulf, who had to act for Anselm during his exiles, managed to cope with Rufus' outbursts'.[2] C. N. L. Brooke, commenting on Gundulf's rôle in building the Tower of London, admits that 'this saintly monk seems to us a strange choice' for such a job.[3] Along that same line, R. A. L. Smith, whose 1943 *EHR* article provides the only detailed account of Gundulf's life, speaks of him as 'the saintly prelate who remained . . . aloof from the confused political turmoil of the times'.[4] And, implicitly construing fact from image, the index of David Knowles' *The*

I would like to thank the American Association of University Women Educational Foundation for providing support for this research; and C. Warren Hollister, Katharin Mack, and Cassandra Potts for their rigorous criticism and comments. I am indebted, as well, to Robin Fleming and Michael Burger for their constructive suggestions.

[1] Besides emphasising his sanctity, historiographical mention of Gundulf remains limited, often relegated to brief asides when he appears as an adjunct to other Anglo-Norman dignitaries. The first complete account of Gundulf's life is R. A. L. Smith, 'The Place of Gundulf in the Anglo-Norman Church', *EHR* 58 (1943), 257–72. Smith's focus is constitutional as he demonstrates the subordinate, or *chorepiscopus*, relationship Gundulf and the see of Rochester held in relation to Canterbury. Although the article covers Gundulf's entire life, it concentrates on his episcopal ties to the archbishop of Canterbury. David Knowles, *The Monastic Order in England*, 2nd edn, Oxford 1963, provides snippets of Gundulf's monastic activities and connections. Frank Barlow, *The English Church, 1066–1154*, London 1979, also presents glimpses of Gundulf, but again emphasises the saintly and monastic elements of his life. Recent studies that mention Gundulf in relation to other historical figures are: David Douglas, *William the Conqueror*, Berkeley 1964; Frank Barlow, *William Rufus*, Berkeley 1983; Margaret Gibson, *Lanfranc of Bec*, Oxford 1975; and Sally N. Vaughn, *Anselm of Bec and Robert of Meulan: The Innocence of the Dove and the Wisdom of the Serpent*, Berkeley 1987.

[2] Barlow, *English Church* 70.

[3] C. N. L. Brooke and Gillian Keir, *London 800–1216: The Shaping of a City*, Berkeley 1975, 31.

[4] Smith, 269.

Monastic Order in England lists Gundulf as 'Gundulf, St', even though he was never officially canonised.[5]

This picture of Gundulf accords with and, for the most part, has been drawn from the few contemporary narrative sources that provide direct information about him. Gundulf left no scholarly writings or collection of letters, and because the bishopric of Rochester was relatively insignificant, contemporary chroniclers did not dwell on activities there. Therefore, our main source is the *Vita Gundulfi*, written by a monk of Rochester who knew Gundulf well.[6] The Vita naturally emphasises Gundulf's monastic vocation and holiness, and it contains the requisite hagiographical criteria that mark the vitae of saintly men: a poignant conversion experience; a close relationship with other holy men – in this case Anselm; a reluctance to assume episcopal or 'worldly' office; and constant efforts to maintain the contemplative life. Similarly, other contemporary narrative sources that refer to Gundulf extol and emphasise his sanctity.[7]

There is, however, another dimension to Gundulf's life that is equally significant. The Vita itself incorporates this aspect and, upon closer inspection, tells us much more than its hagiographical overtones imply at first reading. For example, rather than accentuating Gundulf's miraculous powers or the rôle of the supernatural in his life, the Vita emphasises Gundulf's temporal accomplishments. So although the writer of Gundulf's life clearly affirms his subject's sanctity, he also depicts the bishop's activities in the world. In particular, the biographer lauds Gundulf's recovery of Rochester lands, even while attributing this accomplishment to the bishop's holiness. And even a brief examination of the extant diplomatic evidence confirms Gundulf's involvement and interest in Rochester's material needs.[8] Indeed, the *Textus Roffensis*, Rochester's twelfth-century cartulary, iterates his rôle in legal action and negotiated settlements to secure lands for St Andrew's. But despite this evidence, many historians interpret Gundulf's activities within the purview of his reputation as a holy monk-bishop and have not looked further to unravel the nature of his episcopal duties and how they were perceived by contemporaries. Even scholars such as R. A. L. Smith and Rodney Thomson, who acknowledge Gundulf's practical resourcefulness, take historical detours in order to reconcile the holy man with his worldly activities. Territorial bickering and real estate deals do not accord with today's notions of saintly behaviour. So, Smith readily accepts the Vita's viewpoint that Gundulf's holiness was the source of his competence: kings and barons were so impressed with his piety that they sought his counsel and donated generously to his see. Gundulf, from this perspective, is seen to achieve what he does

---

[5] Knowles, 769.

[6] *Vita Gundulfi*, ed. Rodney Thomson, in his *The Life of Gundulf Bishop of Rochester*, Toronto 1977. Thomson provides a reasoned evaluation of the anonymous biographer and his connections with Gundulf: *Vita Gundulfi*, Intro., 4–5.

[7] For example, *De gestis pontificum* 136: William of Malmesbury calls Gundulf a man 'religionis plenus'; *Vita Herluini* 103: Gilbert Crispin refers to Gundulf as a 'vir morum sanctitate admodum reverendus'; see also Eadmer, 39 and 75.

[8] The main printed collections of chartes are: Ernulf, *Textus Roffensis*, ed. Peter Sawyer in *Early English Manuscripts*, in Facsimile, vol. 11, Copenhagen 1962; *Registrum Roffense*, ed. J. Thorpe, London 1796; and *Regesta Regum Anglo-Normannorum*.

because he is first and foremost a saintly individual and because he somehow rises above the political milieu. Even Rodney Thomson, who labels Gundulf a 'hard-working diplomat', goes to some length to explain the bishop's involvement in the more material aspects of the Rochester community by suggesting that the Vita was composed as part of the Rochester monks' programme of forged land donations and 'campaign of "territorial aggression"' that culminated in 1145.[9] In the introduction to his edition of the *Vita Gundulfi*, Thomson posits that the Vita aimed at sanctifying the legal claims which the monks were advancing: the biographer used Gundulf's holiness to harness ascetic sanctity to the purposes of the Rochester monastic community.

I would suggest, however, that Gundulf was as concerned with Rochester's lands as the monks of 1145, and for that reason we need to re-evaluate his rôle in the post-conquest Church. We can best achieve this view by avoiding the issue of a dichotomy between saintly behaviour and the monk-bishop's activities in the world. It is fairer both to Gundulf and to our own understanding of the Anglo-Norman world to recognise that many monk-bishops not only possessed the abilities and skills to deal with 'worldly' responsibilities, but also were seen to be saintly for the very reason that they did. Just as it was important to the monks at Rochester that their abbot and bishop be a holy man, it was important that he be able to protect their material needs by securing lands and rents. The Vita repeatedly demonstrates that Gundulf's sanctity and practical abilities were a composite: one enhanced the other and both worked together for Rochester's benefit. Without a doubt, Gundulf represents the many Anglo-Norman bishops of whom Orderic Vitalis later spoke as 'prudent pilots and spiritual charioteers who have been entrusted by divine providence with holding the reins of the churches in the arena of this world'.[10]

The purpose of this paper, then, is to obtain a clearer picture of the daily needs and tasks that confronted late-eleventh-century Anglo-Norman monk-bishops. In Gundulf's case, this will allow us to examine our notions of saintly administrators and how their contemporaries perceived them. In general, it will enable us to reappraise the coexistence of saintly behaviour and effective management, a step that will lead to a revision of Thomson's interpretation and dating of the *Vita Gundulfi*.

Gundulf's life of responsibility and service began only a few years after he became a monk at Bec in Normandy around 1057.[11] When Duke William built his monastery at Caen and chose Lanfranc, then prior at Bec, to become its first abbot, Gundulf was one of the Bec monks who accompanied Lanfranc to Caen.[12] There, according to the Vita, because of Gundulf's sanctity and

[9] Thomson's assessment of Gundulf is in *Vita Gundulfi*, Intro., 13. For his interpretation of why the Vita was written see Intro., 9–10.

[10] Orderic, ii, 196. For a well-reasoned discussion of the active and 'worldly' rôle monks played during this period, see John Van Engen, 'The Crisis of Cenobitism', *Speculum* 61 (1986), 269–304.

[11] The Vita says that Gundulf assumed the monastic life after a conversion experience during a pilgrimage to the Holy Land: *Vita Gundulfi* 6; 7. 1–3. He accompanied William Bonne Ame and Maurilius, archbishop of Rouen, in whose cathedral church Gundulf was a clerk. Orderic, ii, 68, mentions the pilgrimage but does not include Gundulf as a participant.

[12] At this time, Gundulf was acting as warden and sacrist at Bec: *Vita Gundulfi* 7. 13–15. Thus, Lanfranc, as prior, undoubtedly had a sense of Gundulf's capabilities and had reason to select him to go to St Étienne.

prudence, he became Lanfranc's assistant.[13] We have no record of Gundulf's responsibilities at Caen, but we do know that Lanfranc, during his seven years there, worked for the growth and prosperity of St Étienne. He acquired property, exported stone for buildings, gathered tolls, and lent money.[14] Gundulf, in addition to his duties as Lanfranc's aide, must have been involved in many of these activities as well. According to the Vita, Lanfranc, after his election to the archbishopric of Canterbury, took Gundulf to England with him because his assistant had proved himself capable in external affairs.[15]

As coadjutor with Lanfranc at Canterbury for the next seven years, Gundulf's reputation for managing external matters grew. In fact, the Vita asserts that his fame increased both because of his sanctity and his ability to manage temporal business.[16] It was during this time that William I commissioned him to oversee the building of the White Tower in London, the first of Gundulf's many architectural projects in England.[17] Nowhere, of course, is Gundulf described as an architect or master mason, but he may have acquired experience at Caen during its early days of development, or even at Canterbury where Lanfranc had instigated the rebuilding of the cathedral and monastery, which were partly in ruins from a fire in 1067.[18] At any rate, the London project established Gundulf's reputation, for the *Textus Roffensis* states that later, in 1088, William Rufus negotiated for Gundulf to replace the timber castle at Rochester with one of stone because the bishop was known to be extremely knowledgeable and efficient in such endeavours.[19] As bishop, Gundulf also would rebuild the cathedral church at Rochester, a structure modelled on Christ Church, Canterbury; and he added the necessary domestic buildings for the restored monastery.[20] When that was completed, he built a convent at Malling along with a church dedicated to the Virgin Mary.[21] Some of these structures had similar and distinctive features, which has led to speculation that Gundulf inspired a 'style' and series of churches in his immediate area.[22] But more important, Gundulf's building projects denote his early and continuing involvement in the outside world and in the material provisions of the church.

Following his seven years at Canterbury, Gundulf was appointed bishop of Rochester in 1077 by Lanfranc, with King William's concurrence. The Vita

---

[13] *Vita Gundulfi* 9.6: 'in eiusdem coenobii gubernatione coadiutorem haberet'. Smith, 59, takes this to mean that Gundulf was made prior. See also *Lanfranc's Letters* 176–9. In the note preceding letter no. 61 to William, abbot of St Étienne, Caen, Gibson identifies the departing prior, spoken of in lines 5–6, as Gundulf. There is, however, no charter evidence from Caen to substantiate Gundulf as prior. I am indebted to Cassandra Potts, who recently has examined all the Caen *acta* and the unedited Caen cartulary, for this information.

[14] Gibson, *Lanfranc* 100 and citations. In particular see Lucien Musset, *Les actes de Guillaume le Conquerant et de la reine Mathilde pour les abbayes Caennaises*, Caen 1976, 14 and 30.

[15] *Via Gundulfi* 10. 4–5: 'et quia in rebus etiam exterioribus in industrius valde erat . . . '

[16] *Vita Gundulfi* 10. 5–8.

[17] *Textus Roffensis* 210v.

[18] Eadmer, 12, describes Lanfranc's building projects at Canterbury.

[19] *Textus Roffensis* 173v: 'Quia in opere cementarii plurium sciens et efficax erat . . . ' See also Eadmer, 15.

[20] *Vita Gundulfi* 7. 8–10.

[21] *Vita Gundulfi* 34. 1–9.

[22] Smith, 268.

reports that Gundulf accepted the office with great reluctance; yet his actions as bishop demonstrate only diligence and concern rather than unwillingness.[23] As bishop, Gundulf spent much time preaching, caring for the needs of his see, and fulfilling episcopal duties such as ordinations, consecrations and dedications. But even in his new rôle as spiritual shepherd, many of Gundulf's activities drew on his 'worldly' resourcefulness. One of his first accomplishments was to restore a monastic chapter at Rochester where the number of clergy had dwindled to five.[24] He then reconstructed the cathedral of St Andrew's and, the Vita explains, provided both the material and spiritual setting for the original number of twenty-two monks to increase to sixty.[25] To a great extent, Gundulf was able to achieve this growth by turning his considerable skills towards restoring and expanding Rochester's landed assets.

This project had begun under Lanfranc when William I's tenants-in-chief adjudicated between the archbishop and Odo of Bayeux regarding lands Odo had taken from the see of Canterbury. Lanfranc won the judgment and among the manors he received was Freckenham in Suffolk, which he held for the monks at Rochester and granted to Gundulf in 1087 after the bishop had re-established the monastic chapter there and decided to separate episcopal and monastic lands.[26] Earlier, Gundulf had made a claim to a Cambridgeshire estate which was 'of' Freckenham.[27] This led to a dispute with Picot, sheriff of Cambridgeshire, who had grabbed bits and pieces of land throughout the area. The *Textus Roffensis* account states that Picot confirmed the right of one of the king's men, Ulfkytel, to occupy the land which Gundulf claimed for Rochester.[28] The king interceded and asked his barons to decide the issue. They swore that the land belonged to the king because they feared Picot; but Gundulf denounced them all as perjurors and appealed to Odo of Bayeux, earl of Kent, to settle the matter. Odo's investigation revealed that the barons indeed had lied, and, after another hearing, he returned the land to Rochester. In light of current Domesday information, we can suppose that the incident was not so civilised and that a certain amount of bullying on the part of Picot and Odo was more likely to have occurred. But it is important to note Gundulf's rôle: he was willing to confront the wily Picot and to use Odo's influence to secure this land for Rochester. Similarly, Gundulf took on one of his own subtenants, the great Domesday magnate, Gilbert of Tonbridge,

---

[23] For the account of Gundulf's protests of unworthiness for episcopal office, see *Vita Gundulfi* 16. 6–7.

[24] *Vita Gundulfi* 17. 5–14. Eadmer, 15, estimates the number of clergy at four.

[25] *Vita Gundulfi* 17. 12–18, in particular 17. 17–18: 'his Martha necessaria procurando, his Maria intentae contemplationis se formam praebendo'.

[26] The details of the Penenden Heath trial are in *Textus Roffensis* 168r–170v; and *Registrum Roffense* 27–28. The charter in which William I originally granted this land to Lanfranc is in *Textus Roffensis* 171r; and *Regesta* i, 47. The original division of the Rochester lands was made in a charter dated 1089, which survives today only in a forged original: *Vita Gundulfi* 60, note 36/7. However, Henry I reconfirmed the division and donations in 1103: *Regesta* ii, 636; and *Registrum Roffense* 33–4. See also David Bates, 'The Land Pleas of William I's Reign: Penenden Heath Revisited', *BIHR* 51 (1978), 1–19; D. C. Douglas, *The Domesday Monachorum of Christ Church Canterbury*, London 1944, 30–1.

[27] *Textus Roffensis* 175v.

[28] The *Textus Roffensis* gives the king's man's name as 'Olchete': *Textus Roffensis* 175v.

concerning property rights.[29] Lanfranc presided over the case about which we have no details, and his judgment required that Gilbert pay Gundulf 50s per year for land he held from Rochester until he gave the bishop another piece of land of equal value.[30]

In order to secure Heddenham, the largest and most valuable of Rochester's holdings, Gundulf had to contend with King William Rufus. The manor had been held by Lanfranc and then Gundulf on a life tenancy from William I.[31] On the accession of William Rufus, the prelates sought reconfirmation of the grant, but William Rufus demanded £100 for the concession, an amount that both Lanfranc and Gundulf immediately and vehemently rejected. After serious negotiations between the king and the archbishop and bishop, which eventually required the mediation of Robert Fitz Hamon and Henry of Beaumont, Gundulf received the manor in return for building the royal castle of Rochester with his own funds.[32] Here, as well as in his contentions with Picot and Gilbert of Tonbridge, Gundulf's actions indicate that he regarded gaining and protecting property rights as essential ingredients in proper episcopal stewardship.

The Vita, of course, paints Gundulf's acquisition of property with saintly overtones, stating that because of his pious reputation and abilities as a mediator both William Rufus and Henry I lavished favours upon the bishop and the community of Rochester. Indeed, it establishes the relationship between Gundulf and William Rufus by stating that the king, because he had heard of Gundulf's sanctity, held the bishop in greater esteem than any of the other bishops, mercifully sparing the church of Rochester from the excessive demands of heavy exactions with which he oppressed many bishoprics.[33] R. A. L. Smith, swayed by this portrayal, infers that Gundulf had an 'essentially non-political character, intent only on the fulfilment of his spiritual office', and that is why William Rufus 'was prodigal in his gifts of manors and churches to the bishop and his monastic chapter'.[34]

The charter evidence, however, adds another dimension to this picture by depicting Gundulf as no mere saintly and passive recipient of William Rufus' favours. We know, for example, that Gundulf was at Rochester during the 1088 rebellion led by the king's uncles, Odo of Bayeux and Robert of Mortain. The Vita states that during this time Gundulf remained on friendly terms with both sides, negotiating and mediating, because all could profit by his goodness.[35] But, from an analysis of William Rufus' charters, Frank Barlow posits that Gundulf was allied with the king and was probably supervising defence preparations in Kent even before the Rochester siege.[36] If Gundulf did play a

---

[29] *Textus Roffensis* 197r.

[30] *Regesta* i, 450 indicates a later grant by Gilbert to St Andrew's. See below, note 47.

[31] For the original donation and Lanfranc's confirmation, see *Textus Roffensis* 212r–3v.

[32] The negotiations for Heddenham are recounted in *Textus Roffensis* 173r–4v. It is estimated that Gundulf spent £60 on the construction of Rochester castle: R. Allen Brown, *Rochester Castle*, English Heritage, London 1986, 7.

[33] *Vita Gundulfi* 27. 3–10.

[34] Smith, 269.

[35] *Vita Gundulfi* 28. 5–10. For other discussions of the 1088 rebellion, see Worcester, s.a. 1088; *ASC*, s.a. 1088, E; and Orderic, iv, 124–35.

[36] Barlow, *William Rufus* 67.

part in negotiating a settlement at Rochester, he probably represented the king's interests.[37] Even if he somehow remained neutral throughout the 1088 rebellion, that in itself demonstrates acute political acumen. The important point is that in either case Gundulf does not exhibit a 'non-political character'.

Although Gundulf served William Rufus well in this and other instances, there is no corroborating evidence for the *Vita*'s claim that the king held Gundulf as his holy model or Rochester as a special protectorate.[38] During the 1089–93 vacancy, Gundulf is not known to have been at court more than three or possibly four times; and there is no record of his attesting royal charters during Anselm's 1097–1100 exile.[39] If Gundulf indeed had held the king's highest respect, his curial activities might be more apparent.[40] Nor does the evidence support Smith's contention that William Rufus showered gifts on Gundulf and Rochester. Although eight royal notifications of grants and confirmations to St Andrew's remain from William Rufus' reign, the number alone gives a false impression about the king's generosity. For example, the first grant also is mentioned in the *Vita*, which states that the king allowed Heddenham to be bestowed on St Andrew's, and the manor of Lambeth he gave 'of his own bounty'.[41] But we have already seen that Heddenham, the first manor, cost Gundulf dearly. The £60 Gundulf spent on the construction of Rochester castle in order to acquire the manor certainly was less than what William Rufus first required, but it also shows that Heddenham was anything but a benefaction. Lambeth, the second manor, which the *Registrum Roffense* says originally came to Rochester from Goda, sister of Edward the Confessor, was restored to Rochester by the king.[42] It may appear to have been a royal gift but hardly constitutes excessive generosity on the king's part, since he gave it to Rochester to compensate for the damage which he did to the Church of St Andrew during the 1088 rebellion.[43]

In addition, the extant charters record seven other royal notifications of grants to St Andrew's during William Rufus' reign. The first, in conjunction with the grant mentioned above, bestows the church of St Mary of Lambeth on

---

[37] For a full account of the negotiations, see Orderic, iv, 129–35, which does not mention Gundulf. *ASC*, s.a. 1088, E, sheds no light on Gundulf's rôle during the siege, either. But considering that one of Odo's strategies during the rebellion was to raid Canterbury lands, Gundulf hardly could remain neutral: see below, note 53.

[38] William Rufus also had relied on Gundulf's aid in adjudicating an ecclesiastical rebellion that occurred at St Augustine's Canterbury shortly after Lanfranc's death in 1089: *Acta Lanfranci*, ed. J. Earle and C. Plummer in *Anglo Saxon Chronicle, Two of the Saxon Chronicles Parallel*, 2 vols, Oxford 1892, 1898, i, 287–92.

[39] Gundulf attested four royal charters during the 1089–93 vacancy: *Regesta* i, 315, 319, 325 and 328. No. 328 may have been issued in 1088, before the vacancy. After Anselm became archbishop, Gundulf attested three charters: *Regesta* i, 336, 338 and 348. But from 1094 to 1100 Gundulf does not appear on witness lists. This evidence, of course, must be measured in light of William Rufus' extensive use of writs, which are marked by brief attestation lists.

[40] In comparison to Gundulf's four attestations, it should be noted that during the 1089–93 vacancy Walkelin, bishop of Winchester, attested at least nine and perhaps as many as thirteen royal charters: *Regesta* i, 315, 319, 320, 326, 328, 329, 330, 332, 337, 355, 385, 395 and 402. And Remigius, bishop of Lincoln, appears in at least five witness lists during the vacancy: *Regesta* i, 315, 318, 319, 320 and 326; no. 406 also may have been attested by Remigius during this period.

[41] *Regesta* i, 301; *Vita Gundulfi* 27. 10–13; *Textus Roffensis* 212r–3r.

[42] *Registrum Roffense* 2; *Textus Roffensis* 177v; and *Regesta* i, 301.

[43] *Regesta* i, 301; *Domesday Book* i, 34a, gives Lambeth's TRW value as £11.

Rochester, also in consideration for any harm done to St Andrew's in 1088.[44] The second concerns land given to the monastery in return for Gundulf giving back land of equal value.[45] And the third probably involves a purchase of land by Gundulf from William Rufus. Although the *Regesta* states that the king gave the land to Bishop Gundulf and the church of Rochester, the *Textus Roffensis* claims that Ralph, the son of Gilbert of Heddenham, held the manor of 'Estona' in Heddenham, and he convinced Gundulf to buy it from the king so that Ralph could hold it from the bishop in order to avoid further excessive royal taxation.[46] The *Regesta* also includes three grants which the king confirmed: one from Gilbert of Tonbridge, one from sheriff Hamon, and one from Roger Bigod.[47] Finally, there is a confirmation of Gundulf's work and alms at Malling, where he recently had built a convent.[48] Again, none of these grants implies overwhelming prodigality by William Rufus.

As for the Vita's reference to William Rufus sparing Rochester from heavy exactions, we must keep in mind that the see, with a Domesday value of £220, was one of the poorest in England and could offer little to the king's treasury.[49] It could be argued that William Rufus, in an attempt to fill the royal treasury, would exact money from all sees, even the poorest. But recent studies of William Rufus' ecclesiastical policies indicate that the king was selective, pressing the more wealthy sees and monasteries.[50] Also, the length of Gundulf's tenure – 1077–1108 – overlapped that of William Rufus and left the king no opportunity to exploit a vacancy or to collect an entry fee.

When Henry I became king in 1100, Rochester, like many other sees, fared better in terms of royal grants. The king realised early in his reign that he needed ecclesiastical support in his confrontation with his brother, Robert Curthose, and in his attempt to secure the throne. To this end, Henry called Anselm home from exile, and in the early months of 1101 he issued a flurry of charters confirming grants and privileges to monasteries and churches across southern England.[51] Bishop Gundulf and St Andrew's received a number of churches and tithes at this time.[52] It was an advantage gained for the king, because while Henry camped at Pevensey in June awaiting Robert's invasion, both Anselm and Gundulf joined the field along with the Canterbury knights.[53] The Vita, in tones echoing the description of Gundulf's influence at Rochester

---

[44] *Regesta* i, 302.

[45] *Regesta* i, 355.

[46] *Regesta* i, 400; *Textus Roffensis* 213v–4r.

[47] *Regesta* i, 450, 451 and 452. On no. 450, see above, note 30, that Gilbert had been required to make such a donation to Rochester.

[48] *Regesta* i, 485.

[49] Martin Brett, *The English Church under Henry I*, Oxford 1975, 103, note 1. Only the sees of Chichester and Chester had lower Domesday values than Rochester (York, Durham and Hereford were not included in these valuations).

[50] C. Warren Hollister, 'William Rufus, Henry I and the Anglo-Norman Church', *Peritia*, forthcoming. In addition, I would like to thank Lauren Helm Jared for use of her unpublished paper, 'English Ecclesiastical Vacancies During the Reigns of William II and Henry I', which provides a statistical analysis of vacancies under William Rufus.

[51] For Anselm's recall, see *Vita Gundulfi* 35. 6; and Eadmer, 119.

[52] *Regesta* ii, 516, 517.

[53] Rochester owed its knight service directly to Canterbury, so was represented in that number: Smith, 262.

in 1088, once more praises the bishop's actions as a mediator: Gundulf himself went to the rebels and, because of his 'innocence and sanctity', caused them to promise to remain in unity and concord with the king.[54] Naturally, Eadmer gives credit not to Gundulf but to Anselm for saving Henry's throne. He says that without the archbishop's loyalty and devotion all would have been lost.[55] Very likely, both men were involved in negotiations: it would have been to their advantage not to have their lands and security threatened by war. And if they were involved, their success can doubtless be attributed to their political and diplomatic skills no less than to their 'innocence and sanctity'.

Praising Gundulf's diplomatic skills, the Vita claims that the bishop's role in the negotiations earned for him such love from Henry and his barons that they valued him as 'their superior and father'.[56] Furthermore, it says that when Gundulf was at court, he often approached the king and queen on behalf of those who asked his help.[57] Likewise, Henry's queen, Matilda, frequently sought Gundulf's advice and had such affection for him that she requested that Gundulf be the one to baptise her son.[58] In short, Gundulf's biographer depicts Gundulf as a saintly intermediary who earned the king's highest respect and unwavering devotion. But the charter evidence does not point to Gundulf as a regular at Henry's court. During the first three years of Henry's reign, Gundulf attested several royal charters; but as was the case during Anselm's first exile, Gundulf did not attest, with one exception, during the archbishop's second absence from England, 1103–1106.[59] After Anselm's return to England, Gundulf again appears in witness lists for the brief period before his death in 1108.[60] As for Henry's benefactions to Rochester, the *Regesta* lists, besides the aforementioned grants issued in 1101, only two others to Rochester between Henry's accession and Gundulf's death, 1100–1108: one confirms a land grant from Geoffrey Talbot, and the other, from the king, allows a yearly fair to be held in Rochester on the eve and day of St Paulinus.[61] Although the donations were more freely given during this period than during William Rufus' reign, they did not constitute the kind of over-whelming support that the Vita would tie to Gundulf's saintly inspiration. Nor does this evidence support R. A. L. Smith's assertion that because of Henry's

---

[54] *Vita Gundulfi* 35. 10–28.
[55] Eadmer, 127.
[56] *Vita Gundulfi* 35. 25–8.
[57] *Vita Gundulfi* 37. 8–13.
[58] *Vita Gundulfi* 37. 1–8. Anselm, as archbishop of Canterbury and because of his close relationship with Matilda, naturally would have baptised the child had he been in England. But William was born during the 1103–6 exile: *Sancti Anselmi Cantuariensis archiepiscopi opera omnia*, ed. F. S. Schmitt, Stuttgart-Bad Canstatt 1963–8, 305. (Hereafter, *SAE.*) Pope Paschal wrote this letter after 23 November 1103, and in it he speaks of William's recent birth.
[59] The royal charters Gundulf witnessed between 1100 and 1103 are: *Regesta* ii, 488, 524, 544, 547, 548, 549, 636 and 645. It should be noted that of these eight charters, six were issued in 1101 during Henry's honeymoon with the English Church. The one charter Gundulf attested during Anselm's 1103–6 exile is 677, dated 1104.
[60] *Regesta* ii, 832, 833, 834; the first two also are attested by Anselm and are probably concurrent.
[61] *Regesta* ii, 647, 634 and 868. Both 634 and 868 refer to the fair at Malling. The granting of markets and fairs was fairly common at this time, often being a confirmation of existing rights: *Regesta* ii, Intro., xxiv. Consequently, it is difficult to establish to what extent this grant was an act of Henry's beneficence to Rochester.

affection for the pious bishop, Gundulf and his see received generous benefactions and support that allowed Rochester 'to become a centre of peace and
order in a much disturbed kingdom'.[62] Instead, as we have seen, Rochester's
monastic chapter expanded and achieved some measure of security because of
Gundulf's skills and perseverance.

Furthermore, Gundulf's capabilities were not limited to guarding Rochester's
needs. During Lanfranc's achiepiscopate, the see of Rochester had developed
a direct dependence upon the see of Canterbury, and by the time of Gundulf's
episcopate the bishop of Rochester was regularly summoned to exercise
Canterbury functions, either with the archbishop or in his absence.[63] A
document compiled by the monks of Rochester in the mid twelfth century sets
out the traditional obligations that Rochester owed Canterbury and the
compensation to be given for fulfilling them. Moreover, it specifies that if the
archiepiscopacy was vacant or if the archbishop was unable to exercise his
office, the bishop of Rochester 'should fulfil his [the archbishop's] functions
both in consecrating kings and bishops and in all other episcopal duties . . .'[64]
Consequently, the bishop of Rochester had to be ready and willing to act as
Canterbury's deputy at any time. After Lanfranc died in 1089, two years after
William Rufus had succeeded William I, the see of Canterbury remained
vacant for over four years, and Gundulf became a full-time vicar for Canterbury. The Vita reports that he did so 'by the king's order and as was the
custom of the church of Rochester'.[65]

Specific examples of Gundulf's involvement in Canterbury's interests appear
in letters to the bishop written by Anselm during his 1103–1106 exile. The
archbishop consistently instructs Gundulf to protect Canterbury's property
rights against encroachment by barons or by King Henry himself. In one
letter, Anselm spoke of 'the quarrel between our men and the men of Robert
of Montfort', which Gundulf was to solve by seeking the king's help.[66] And
when William Calvellus attempted to transfer a market from Canterbury lands
to another location, Gundulf received instructions to meet sheriff Hamon and
to advise him not to permit this injustice to happen.[67] Once, King Henry
demanded money from the monks and prior of Christ Church, money which
Anselm claimed the monks could not possibly have, and the archbishop urged
Gundulf to persuade the king to desist from 'such an unheard of and
unaccustomed thing'.[68] In another effort to keep Canterbury money out of the
king's hands, Anselm advised Gundulf to have the keeper of Canterbury's
revenues give the chrism pennies to the monks.[69] Since the king had seized the
archbishop's revenues, one way to deny him this money was to grant it to the
monks for the work of the monastery.[70]

---

[62] Smith, 269.

[63] Smith, 261–70, gives a full analysis of the Rochester–Canterbury relationship.

[64] *Registrum Roffense* 140. For a full analysis of the claims Rochester made regarding its bishop's rôle as Canterbury's vicar, see Irene Churchill, *Canterbury Administration*, 2 vols, London 1933, i, 179–84.

[65] *Vita Gundulfi* 30. 5–9.

[66] *SAE* 299.

[67] *SAE* 359.

[68] *SAE* 293.

[69] *SAE* 359.

[70] For a discussion of the chrism pennies, see Brett, 164 and note 4.

Such encounters and machinations, even when handled with saintly tact, hardly could have allowed Gundulf to rise coolly above political statesmanship and the 'turmoils of the time'. Additionally, he had to have been fully aware of the extent and implications of the issues separating his sovereign and his archbishop since he was responsible for delivering messages between Anselm and Henry, negotiating with the king, and tracking papal correspondence and legations.[71] Overall, Gundulf appears to have been adept in these matters, not piously aloof.

Yet we should not dismiss Gundulf's monastic and holy qualities as presented in the narrative sources. There is no reason for us to doubt the account that he struggled to preserve his humility and often experienced moments of spiritual ecstasy that caused him to weep uncontrollably.[72] Also, it is important to remember that Gundulf's episcopate spanned the early years of reform in the English Church, a time when the purity and ability of the clergy were given special consideration. These issues were apparent in Archbishop Lanfranc's seven reforming councils, which issued legislation condemning simony and clerical incontinence, and advocating proper pastoral care for the laity. The standards were rigorous, and few bishops or priests fully measured up. Remigius, who held the see of Lincoln, had to battle accusations of simony.[73] And Osmund of Salisbury, celebrated for his chastity and care with money, had his reputation darkened by rumours of his 'grasping' and having succumbed to a dreadful illness because of it.[74] But Gundulf, according to all the narrative sources, met the standards and surpassed them. In particular, the Vita states:

> How worthy was he to teach, for he did as he taught others to do in order that they might follow his example. How worthy was he to be a bishop, for he obtained his office by tears, not by money.[75]

Thus the Vita indicates an active concern about simony and makes every effort to separate Gundulf from its perceived wickedness. In addition, the Vita emphasises Gundulf's pastoral qualities by indicating that he preached and celebrated the mass frequently and had small oratories built on each of his manors for his use, an act denoting regularity in visitations.[76] And Gundulf consistently demonstrated great concern for the poor, even to the extent of sending his own meals to those in need.[77] The Vita describes that on one occasion the bishop, travelling near Rochester, noticed that some property belonging to the monastery was overgrown with weeds; he returned later with a group of monks and together they cultivated the land so the produce could be sent to the poor.[78] And earlier, even before he became bishop, when a plague

---

[71] *SAE* 291, 299, 314 and 316.
[72] *Vita Gundulfi* 33. 43–53.
[73] *De gestis pontificum* 65–6.
[74] *De gestis pontificum* 183–4.
[75] *Vita Gundulfi* 33. 59–62.
[76] *Vita Gundulfi* 33. 47–51; 21. 22–6.
[77] *Vita Gundulfi* 29. 6–21. See also *SAE* 300, which indicates Gundulf's care of the poor at Canterbury while Anselm was in exile.
[78] *Vita Gundulfi* 29. 25–39.

had gripped most of England, Gundulf procured money from Lanfranc and went to London where he fed and cared for those in need.[79]

In addition to his pastoral duties, we know that Gundulf participated actively in formal ecclesiastical functions. He was present at Anselm's 1102 reform council, and he took part in several dedications and translations.[80] He participated at the opening of Edward the Confessor's grave in 1073, the dedication of Battle Abbey in 1094, and in 1092, during the Canterbury vacancy, he carried out the ceremony of translation of the body of St Augustine.[81] The Vita contends:

> At that time in England, whenever there were any dedications of special importance or translations of holy relics to be carried out, as if by established custom Gundulf was immediately called upon so that the sacred rites might be administered by one who had clean hands.[82]

As a pastor and as a holy leader, then, the bishop was seen as worthy.

On the other hand, it should not be surprising that the Vita also praises Gundulf's desire to provide St Andrew's with a proper material setting. Certainly his successes towards this end enhanced his perceived sanctity and made him even more worthy of acclaim.[83] Many of his contemporaries received similar praise for their 'worldly' accomplishments. Both Lanfranc and Anselm worked to gain and guard lands for Canterbury, activities which William of Malmesbury later commented on and signalled as vital elements in proper episcopal and monastic care.[84] And the *Vita Wulfstani* praises Gundulf's contemporary, the monk-bishop Wulfstan, for his activities in church building, his rôle as a mediator, and his struggle to regain contested lands for Worcester.[85] Even Gundulf's decision to separate Rochester's episcopal and monastic lands, highly lauded by the Vita, was indicative of the time. Rochester, in fact, followed Canterbury's model in this effort; and throughout England, as Margaret Howell has shown, there was a growing trend in the eleventh century towards this kind of separation.[86] In sum, the Vita portrays many of Gundulf's legal and administrative accomplishments,

---

[79] *Vita Gundulfi* 10. 13–20. The plague referred to here may be the one of 1070: *ASC*, s.a. 1070, D'E.

[80] *Councils and Synods, with Other Documents Relating to the English Church* 1, *AD 871–1204*, ed. Dorothy Whitelock, Martin Brett and C. N. L. Brooke, Oxford 1981, part 2, 674, shows Gundulf as a participant of the 1102 council.

[81] For the opening of Edward's tomb, see *Memorials of St Dunstan*, ed. William Stubbs, RS, vol. 63, 413; Gundulf's presence at the Battle dedication is recorded in *Battle Chronicle*, 96; and the translation of St Augustine is reported in *Vita Gundulfi* 31. 1–5.

[82] *Vita Gundulfi* 31. 10–14.

[83] *Vita Gundulfi* 38. 1–8.

[84] *De gestis pontificum* 70, 83 and 106.

[85] *The Vita Wulfstani of William of Malmesbury*, ed. R. R. Darlington, London 1928, 21–5.

[86] Margaret Howell, 'Abbatial Vacancies and the Divided *Mensa*', *Journal of Ecclesiastical History* 33 (1982), 173–7. David Knowles has argued that separation of property between the abbot (and in Gundulf's case, bishop) and monks was done to protect it from the king, so that in times of vacancies the king would administer only the abbatial estates: Knowles, 405, 435–6, 613 and 757. This view is questioned by Howell, who sees the separation as more than a contrivance to avoid royal control; she posits that it represented a need in the monastic economy to provide for the food and clothing of the monks.

even while tempering them with pious inflections. What it shows us is a bishop who, with many outside obligations, was able to use his skills to incease Rochester's spiritual and material standing while at the same time maintaining a relationship with his king and archbishop that would not threaten what he had built up.

Rodney Thomson readily agrees that the Vita portrays Gundulf as a deeply spiritual man and also as an able administrator. But he argues that the writer of the Vita tied these two elements in a deliberate attempt to serve the interests of the Rochester community in their relationship with their bishop.[87] For, although the monks enjoyed an amicable relationship with Gundulf and his immediate successors, by the mid twelfth century they were in litigation with Bishop Ascelin concerning the manors of Lambeth and Heddenham.[88] The inadequacy of sources from the period preceding the trial makes it difficult to pinpoint precisely when the relationship between the monks and the bishop soured, but Archbishop Theobald's notification regarding the adjudication suggests that it was under Ascelin's predecessor, John II.[89] John purportedly usurped Lambeth for his own use, and Ascelin then added that manor to his possessions upon becoming bishop; further, he exacted an annual rent of ten marks for Heddenham.

When, in 1145, the monks presented their case to the papal legate, Imar of Tusculum, they produced full documentation of the donations of Lambeth and Heddenham to Rochester cathedral, and Gundulf's grants of these manors to the Rochester monks, along with the confirmations of Henry I, Stephen, and Anselm for the same lands. Some of these documents, particularly those concerning Lambeth, were forgeries and had been created as early as the 1120s.[90] Thomson welds this evidence to the fact that the *Vita Gundulfi* prominently features both of the contested manors, Heddenham and Lambeth. He then posits that these possessions, the most valuable that the monastery held, were being threatened in the early 1120s and that the Vita and forging programme became complementary evidence for the monks' campaign to save their property. Thomson states:

> The manufactured charters supplied legal evidence of Gundulf's grants; the *Vita* sanctified the same grants by presenting them as the solemn and deliberate acts of a particularly holy individual. In other words the purpose of the charters, and one of the aims of the *Vita*, was to render the alleged donations inviolate.[91]

Here Thomson neatly explains the Vita's emphasis not only on Gundulf's sanctity but on his abilities to acquire donations for Rochester cathedral. For

---

[87] *Vita Gundulfi*, Intro., 8–10.

[88] *Vita Gundulfi*, Intro., 8; *Registrum Roffense*, 8–10; Avrom Saltman, *Theobald, Archbishop of Canterbury*, New York 1969, 134.

[89] Saltman, 450, no. 223. The report of the papal legate, Imar of Tusculum, who presided at the hearing is in *Councils and Synods*, 812–3. It is even more nebulous in providing answers to the root of the estrangement. Nor does a letter from Ascelin, dated 1143–4 and returning property stolen from the monks, allow insight into the genesis of the struggle: Kent County Archives, DRC L1.

[90] Thomson discusses the Lambeth forgeries in *Vita Gundulfi*, Intro., 9.

[91] *Vita Gundulfi*, Intro., 10.

this explanation to hold, the Vita's composition must be dated in the early 1120s. Thomson interprets the Vita's internal evidence to indicate that it was composed between 1114 and 1124; he then presses for the period between 1122 and 1124, which coincides with his conclusion that the Vita abetted the monks' forgery programme.[92]

In some ways, Thomson is correct. The *Vita Gundulfi*, like much other hagiography, is ascetic propaganda, aimed at edifying posterity. It is difficult, however, to accept his argument for the Vita's purpose and, consequently, its date of composition. First of all, the internal evidence itself points more readily to a terminus date of 1122 than of 1124. The latest event mentioned in the Vita is Ernulf's succession to the bishopric of Rochester in 1114.[93] Since there is no mention of his death, which was in 1124, it seems likely that the Vita was completed before then. But more importantly, the Vita also includes references to Ralph of Séez becoming bishop of Rochester and, later, archbishop of Canterbury.[94] Ralph died in 1122 and since the biographer neither notes his death nor refers to Ralph as 'our bishop of holy memory' as he most likely would have done had he been writing after 1122, Thomson's suggestion seems even more fragile. In fact, the only 'final' date that the internal evidence fixes assuredly is 1114, when Ralph became archbishop of Canterbury and Ernulf bishop of Rochester.

Why, then, Thomson asks, did the author wait six or more years after Gundulf's death to write the Vita? This question has no ready answer, but a possible suggestion is that it was done because Ralph, a bishop of Rochester, in 1114 had just become archbishop of Canterbury and primate of all England. The commemoration of his predecessor in a vita, particularly since that predecessor had been an intimate of the great Canterbury archbishops, Lanfranc and Anselm, could further connect the two sees and heighten Rochester's importance as a bishopric governed by saintly and capable leaders.[95] Gundulf's biographer poignantly details the connection as he describes how Gundulf, as he was dying, placed his episcopal ring on Ralph's finger.[96] When Anselm later selected Ralph as bishop of Rochester, the Vita states that Gundulf, while he was still alive, had foreknown who should succeed him. The very next sentence then relates how, only six years later, Ralph was translated to the archbishopric.[97] This account comes very near the end of the Vita and seems a fitting tribute to Rochester's link to the new archbishop.

Thomson's particular concern with the rift between the monks and bishop at Rochester also presents problems. He posits that difficulties may have been brewing as early as the 1120s, but provides no substantiating evidence. In fact, he reads back onto an earlier period the problems of John II's episcopate,

---

[92] *Vita Gundulfi*, Intro., 3: 'the life might have been written before then [1122], although this is more doubtful'.
[93] *Vita Gundulfi* 48. 12–17.
[94] *Vita Gundulfi* 48. 1–15.
[95] For example see the biographer's portrayal of Gundulf's especially close relationship with Anselm: *Vita Gundulfi* 18, 19 and 20.
[96] *Vita Gundulfi* 45.
[97] *Vita Gundulfi* 48. 1–15.

which began around the year 1139. But what evidence we do have indicates that all was well at least through the pontificate of Ernulf, who died in 1124: the *Registrum Roffense* reports that in an attempt to emulate his predecessors Ernulf did many good things for the monks.[98] The main accomplishment attributed to Ernulf was the compiling of the *Textus Roffensis*, a corpus of both genuine and spurious legal and historical texts relating to Rochester.[99] But, Thomson postulates, since the *Textus* emphasises the rights and privileges of the monks, it was probably initiated by the priory, not the bishop.[100] Here again he hints at problems between the episcopal and monastic interests at Rochester. We should remember, however, that the main portion of the *Textus* appeared in late 1122 and early 1123, which coincides with the death of Archbishop Ralph and the emergence of powerful pressures to prevent the election of another monk to Canterbury.[101] The chapter of Christ Church reluctantly chose William of Corbeil, who was a learned canon but not a monk, and Rochester's relations with Canterbury immediately took on an entirely new complexion.[102] Because of this change and Rochester's subordinate position to Canterbury, it seems more likely that Bishop Ernulf of Rochester, who was a monk, would work with the cathedral monks to protect the community's rights and privileges.

Is it possible, then, that the Vita was composed at the same time, as Thomson suggests, to bolster this effort? Three arguments against this interpretation present themselves. First, as mentioned, the Vita's internal evidence points to a terminus of 1122, prior to the compilation of the *Textus*, rather than 1124. Second, Thomson himself argues that the Vita follows what Sir Richard Southern has called the 'commemorative model', in which the subject's spiritual qualities and temporal prosperity are the main focus.[103] Clearly, the Vita's writer patterned his work on this model and context, which dilutes Thomson's theory that the Vita emanated from a monastic-episcopal struggle at Rochester.

---

[98] *Registrum Roffense* 7: ' . . . antecessores suos in bono emulari studens, innumera bona monachis contulit'.

[99] Included in the *Textus Roffense* were the documents discussed above that related to the 1145 litigation concerning Heddenham and Lambeth. Although C. N. L. Brooke has demonstrated that some of the Lambeth documents were forgeries, Thomson himself admits that Gundulf's charters separating episcopal and monastic property 'lack suspicious features': *Vita Gundulfi*, Intro., 9.

[100] *Vita Gundulfi*, Intro., 17.

[101] *Vita Gundulfi*, Intro., 17, gives the dates for the completion of the main portion of the *Textus Roffensis*. For a discussion of the pressures to prevent the election of a monk to Canterbury, see Barlow, *English Church*, 85.

[102] Barlow, *English Church* 85, adds that William was an austere man and perhaps avaricious. Further, Barlow notes that Henry of Huntingdon, who 'was not likely to have been unnecessarily severe in his judgments', claimed that of the five archbishops of Canterbury from Lanfranc to Theobald, only William 'could not be praised "because there is nothing to praise"', 89. See also Denis Bethell, 'William of Corbeil and the Canterbury York Dispute', *Journal of Ecclesiastical History* 19 (1969), 154 and note 5. A non-monk as archbishop of Canterbury could be threatening, as Smith, 262–3, points out: 'in the purely administrative sphere . . . the bishop of Rochester looked to the archbishop [of Canterbury] as his immediate lord'. We must also remember that it was the archbishop who held the right to name the bishop of Rochester: Smith, 264. In 1125, Archbishop William named John I, who was not a monk, to Rochester.

[103] *Vita Gundulfi*, Intro., 15. For Southern's complete discussion of the models used by early twelfth-century biographers, see Sir Richard Southern, *St Anselm and His Biographer*, Cambridge 1963, 320–8.

Finally, and most important for our understanding of early twelfth-century perceptions of spirituality, we need not go to such lengths to explain the combination of Gundulf's holiness with his abilities in restoring church lands. Gundulf's biographer needed no impetus such as monastic-episcopal rivalries for his interest in the bishop's land acquisitions, because the activities he described were compatible with twelfth-century spiritual ideals. Good monk-bishops were holy men and they were also good stewards. In this light, the Vita's specific inclusion of Gundulf acquiring Lambeth and Heddenham is not curious since they were the most important and highly valued manors that Rochester held. William of Malmesbury, like the writer of the Vita, praises Gundulf's abilities in helping Rochester recover its lands; in particular, he mentions the bishop's rôle in providing the manor of Heddenham for the needs of the monks.[104] William's inclusion of a specific mention of Heddenham does not appear to tie him to Rochester's campaign of 'territorial aggression' any more than it should when Gundulf's biographer discusses it. Of course the Vita does not fully and accurately portray the extent of Gundulf's involvement in procuring and restoring Rochester's lands, but prefers to concentrate on the bishop's sanctity as a conduit for those accomplishments. However, even this selective and idealised picture can help reverse our incorrect notions of this early-twelfth-century monk-bishop: Gundulf was not perceived as being holy despite his functions in the world; his sanctity was inseparable from them.

The most striking example of this balance comes from the latter part of the Vita itself. During the final days of his life, the Vita relates, Gundulf retreated to the monastery so he could die not as a bishop in a grand house, but humbly as a monk.[105] He ordered generous alms to be given to all his manors, but earlier had reserved plenty for his successor because he had heard Anselm say that no dying bishop ought to divide the church's property but should save it for use by the next bishop.[106] 'Thanks be to God', Gundulf proclaimed, 'for giving me such abundance that I can relieve the needs of the poor and yet leave my successor with sufficient rents should he have as many as thirty men with him.'[107] And so, after thirty-one years in the episcopacy, as he died, Gundulf summed up the two complementary and compatible attributes of a good bishop: holiness and wise stewardship.

---

[104] *De gestis pontificum* 137. Lanfranc likewise receives accolades from William of Malmesbury for recovering church lands and enriching the clergy and monasteries: *De gestis pontificum* 70.
[105] *Vita Gundulfi* 42. 1–5.
[106] *Vita Gundulfi* 39. 14–17.
[107] *Vita Gundulfi* 39. 17–20 J. B. Hall presents a somewhat different interpretation for the latter part of this passage: ' . . . leave my successor with enough to tide him over until the new year's rents come in, even if he brings thirty men with him': J. B. Hall, 'Critical Notes on Three Medieval Latin Texts: "Vita Gundulfi", "Carmen de Hastingae Proelio", "Vita Merlini" ', *Studi Medievali*, 3rd series, 21 (1980), 901.

ROYAL SERVICE AND REWARD:
THE CLARE FAMILY AND THE CROWN, 1066–1154

Jennifer C. Ward

Landed reward in return for loyal service was expected in mediaeval feudal society, and the importance of the king's powers of patronage has been emphasised by many historians. In particular, under the Norman kings, the appearance of 'new men' at court as *curiales* and their advance into landed society have been stressed, as has the fact that men who were already magnates also received rewards. Kings and barons were dependent on each other; peace and order in the realm depended on the existence of a good relationship between the two, with the barons providing military service, aid and counsel, and the kings security and protection as well as reward. In addition to the general support given by the baronage as a whole, every king needed his own circle of close advisers, both magnates and *curiales*, who would serve in the hope and expectation of reward. The backing of such a group would be especially necessary in the early years of a reign when the king was establishing his position.

The Clare family provide a prime example of the rise of a baronial family over three generations, largely as a result of royal service, and it is possible to make an assessment of the comparative significance of royal patronage as against other means of increasing power, to see the variety of service performed, and to gauge how far there was a correlation between service done and reward gained. The family built up their estates largely as a result of their connections with William I and Henry I; they were somewhat in eclipse under Rufus. Before 1066, the family were of little importance among the Norman magnates, but, by the time of the Domesday Survey, Baldwin son of Count Gilbert of Brionne and more particularly his brother Richard were powerful barons, and by 1130 five members of the Clare family ranked among the tenants-in-chief of the Crown, with most of their lands being situated in England and Wales. Throughout their history, the Clares had an insatiable appetite for land and wealth, and were always ready to put forward their demands; the *Brut* refers to Henry I's statement that Gilbert of Tonbridge had often pestered him for land, and at the beginning of Stephen's reign Richard fitz Gilbert made what the king regarded as excessive requests.[1] Although the

---

[1] *Brut y Tywysogyon, Red Book of Hergest Version*, ed. T. Jones, Board of Celtic Studies, University of Wales, History and Law Series, xvi, 1955, 70–1. *Brut y Tywysogyon*, Peniarth ms. 20 Version, ed. T. Jones, Board of Celtic Studies, University of Wales, History and Law Series, vi, xi, 1941 and 1952, i, 53, ii, 34. *Brenhinedd y Saesson*, ed. T. Jones, Board of Celtic Studies, University of Wales, History and Law Series, xxv, 1971, 114–17. *Gesta Stephani*, ed. K. R. Potter, London 1955, 10–11.

The Clare Family, 1066–1154

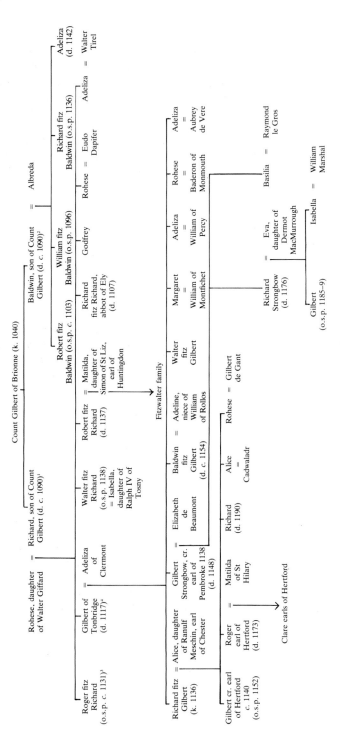

Notes

[1] Richard was also known as Richard of Bienfaite, Richard of Tonbridge, and, once, as Richard of Clare.

[2] Baldwin was also known as Baldwin of Meules, Baldwin the sheriff, and Baldwin of Exeter.

[3] Roger was also known as Roger of Bienfaite.

[4] Gilbert was also known as Gilbert fitz Richard.

Clares suffered some serious losses of land in Wales, they were on the whole successful in exploiting their rewards.

A comparison between Richard and Baldwin, the sons of Count Gilbert, points to a close correlation between service and reward under the Conqueror, service being seen as the best way in which their family fortunes could be revived. After their father's murder in 1040 during Duke William's anarchic minority, they had been taken to Flanders, only returning to Normandy after the duke's marriage.[2] They entered William's service at the time when the duke was building up his following of loyal supporters; they made good marriages and received grants of land, Baldwin being granted Le Sap and Meules, and Richard, Orbec and Bienfaite.[3] Neither of them, however, was given Count Gilbert's castle of Brionne or the title of count. They probably welcomed the invasion of England because of the prospect of gaining plunder and land; it gave them the opportunity to become powerful and influential and to gain compensation for the loss of Brionne.

Both men continued to serve William after the Conquest, but to different extents, and with contrasting rewards. They were often present at William's councils and helped to crush rebellions, but Richard was more frequently employed as counsellor and envoy, and his estates by 1086 were correspondingly greater than his brother's. Baldwin attended the larger assemblies of the court, both in Normandy and England.[4] He served at the siege of Exeter in 1068, and on the city's surrender a new castle was begun which was handed over to Baldwin.[5] Baldwin was also made sheriff of Devon, an office inherited by his sons.[6] Henceforth the power of Baldwin and his sons was centred in the South-West; in 1086, most of his lands lay in Devon where he was the most important landholder, but he also held some estates in Dorset and Somerset.[7] In Devon, his estates were mainly concentrated round Exeter and Okehampton, where a castle had been built for the *caput* of his honour, and it is likely that they had been granted to Baldwin shortly after the Exeter rising.[8] As a result of the Conquest and his subsequent service, Baldwin had undoubtedly bettered himself and his family, but he had not reached the highest echelons of the nobility.

Richard, on the other hand, was one of William's intimate counsellors. Like his brother, he played his part in the suppression of rebellions; he acted as one of William's representatives in England during the king's absence in Normandy in 1075 when the rebellion of the three earls broke out, and Richard and William of Warenne were responsible for defeating Ralph Gael, earl of East Anglia, at the battle of 'Fagaduna', and subsequently took part in the siege of Norwich.[9] The fact that Richard was one of those left in charge during William's absence indicates how much he was trusted by the king, and it is likely from the number of writs addressed to him that he was one of those

[2] Orderic, iv, 208.
[3] Orderic, iv, 208, 212. Fauroux, no. 231.
[4] *Regesta*, i, nos 76, 125, 135, 147, 206, 220, XXXII.
[5] Orderic, ii, 214. *ASC*, 146.
[6] *Regesta*, i, no. 58. *Monasticon*, iii, 377.
[7] *Domesday Book*, i, fo. 81; iv, fos 288–315, 495–506 *passim*.
[8] *Domesday Book*, iv, fo. 288.
[9] Orderic, ii, 316.

again left in charge of affairs two years later.[10] The close relationship between Richard and the king is also borne out by the fact that Richard not only attended great councils, but was also present at court on many other occasions, witnessing the king's orders with a few other officials or trusted lords.[11] The practice of witnessing charters with a small group is a sure indication of royal favour. Furthermore, he sometimes acted in a judicial capacity, as over the loss of lands by the abbey of Bury St Edmunds, and the abbey's quarrel with the bishop of Thetford.[12] In all these respects, Richard was acting in the same way as William's other intimate counsellors, such as Archbishop Lanfranc, Odo bishop of Bayeux and Roger of Montgomery. There is however one point of contrast. Most of the close counsellors attended William's court in Normandy as well as in England, but it appears from the surviving documents that Richard was rarely in Normandy; he witnessed only one charter there, some time between 1079 and 1082.[13]

Richard's services were more onerous and his duties more responsible than Baldwin's, and being more frequently with the king he was in a better position to know what lands were available. He certainly received a much greater reward than his brother. According to Domesday Book, Richard was one of the wealthiest tenants-in-chief in England, and his importance at William's court had resulted in his gaining lands worth over twice as much as his brother's.[14] He held land in ten counties, and his wife Rohese was a tenant-in-chief in Hertfordshire and Huntingdonshire. The barons who were most often at court were generally the ones who held land in the largest number of counties, but in six of the counties where Richard held land (Devon, Wiltshire, Bedfordshire, Cambridgeshire, Middlesex and Sussex) his holdings were negligible and his most valuable estates were concentrated in Kent, Surrey, Essex and Suffolk. It appears likely that he received his Kent and Surrey lands shortly after 1066; his castle of Tonbridge, an appropriation from the Canterbury lands, may well have been part of William's arrangements for the defence of South-East England, and the low values of the Surrey manors when Richard received them indicate that they were still suffering from waste. The king probably considered that Richard had to perform further service before more land was granted, and there are signs in Domesday Book that Richard's most important concentration of lands in Essex and Suffolk, which was to give the family its name, were obtained later; both of Richard's predecessors, Wihtgar son of Aelfric and Finn the Dane, continued to hold most of their lands after the Conquest.[15] Clare itself, which was to become the *caput* of all the estates,

---

[10] *Regesta*, i, nos 50, 100, 102.

[11] *Regesta*, i, nos 22, 26, 128, 162, 209, 212, 220, XXXII, 260.

[12] *Regesta*, i, no. XL. *Feudal Documents from the Abbey of Bury St Edmunds*, ed. D. C. Douglas, British Academy Records of the Social and Economic History of England and Wales, viii, 1932, no. 10. *Ungedruckte Anglo-Normannische Geschichtsquellen*, ed. F. Liebermann, Strasbourg 1879, 253.

[13] *Regesta*, i, no. 169.

[14] J. C. Ward, 'The Lowy of Tonbridge and the Lands of the Clare Family in Kent, 1066–1217', *Archaeologia Cantiana* xcvi, 1980, 119–26. J. C. Ward, 'The Place of the Honour in Twelfth-Century Society: the Honour of Clare, 1066–1217', *Procs. of the Suffolk Institute of Archaeology and History* xxxv, 1983, 191–2. R. Mortimer, 'The Beginnings of the Honour of Clare', *ante* iii, 1980, 119–41.

[15] *Domesday Book*, ii, fos 393b–394a, 448a.

was a prosperous manor in 1086 and developing as a small seignorial borough, and a castle was built there by 1090.[16]

Certainly the Norman Conquest of England brought about a major change in the status, wealth and importance of the Clare family. It must be stressed, however, that the Clares of the next generation would want to extend their fathers' lands, partly through sheer ambition and acquisitiveness, and partly because none of them succeeded to all his father's estates. On the deaths of Richard and Baldwin about 1090, their Norman and English lands were divided between their two eldest sons, as was common practice among tenants-in-chief. Thus Robert fitz Baldwin gained Le Sap and Meules, while William fitz Baldwin took over the estates in South-West England;[17] the third son, Richard, was not provided for. After William's death in 1096, it is possible that Robert took over the English lands; his presence at Henry I's court in England in 1101 and 1103 is an indication that he had English interests.[18] When he died, probably soon after 1103, his brother Richard succeeded him. With Richard son of Count Gilbert's sons, Roger fitz Richard inherited the hereditary lands of Orbec and Bienfaite, while Gilbert of Tonbridge took over the honour of Clare. Richard's other three sons were not provided for on the family lands. Walter and Robert had to make their own fortunes as knights, while Richard became a monk at Bec which had received several grants of land and tithes from the family.[19]

The main question facing the Clares in the 1090s was how their lands and wealth were to be increased. Outright seizure of land was not an option. Richard son of Count Gilbert had made fairly extensive encroachments on the lands of the Church and of freemen and sokemen for which Gilbert of Tonbridge had to make compensation.[20] Attempts to gain land by force or rebellion were dangerous gambles which might well result in the forfeiture of estates as the families of some of the wealthiest Anglo-Norman barons discovered. A marriage alliance could be useful politically and might lead to landed gain, but this could well be in the long term rather than immediately; Richard son of Count Gilbert's marriage to Rohese Giffard brought the eldest line of the Clare family half the Giffard inheritance in 1189.[21] Claims for land held in the past by the family offered the prospect of more immediate gain. Both lines of the family are found putting in their claims for Brionne which had fallen into Duke William's hands after the murder of Count Gilbert in 1040 and been part of the ducal demesne from 1050 until 1087, when Roger of Beaumont succeeded in gaining it from Duke Robert in exchange for Ivry.[22] Count Gilbert's grandsons, Roger fitz Richard and Robert fitz Baldwin,

---

[16] *Domesday Book*, ii, fo. 389b. *Stoke by Clare Cartulary*, ed. C. Harper-Bill and R. Mortimer, Suffolk Record Society, Suffolk Charters, iv–vi, 1982–4, nos 136, 137.

[17] Orderic, iv, 204–10. *Regesta*, i, nos 378, 401. *Brut, Red Book of Hergest*, 34–5. *Brut, Peniarth ms. 20*, i, 26; ii, 19–20. *Brenhinedd*, 86–7.

[18] *Regesta*, ii, nos 544, 552, 636.

[19] J. C. Ward, 'Fashions in Monastic Endowment: the Foundations of the Clare Family, 1066–1314', *Journal of Ecclesiastical History* xxxii, 1981, 427–37.

[20] *Textus Roffensis*, ed. T. Hearne, 1720, 149. *Registrum Roffense*, ed. J. Thorpe, London 1769, 590–1. *Feudal Documents from the Abbey of Bury St Edmunds*, no. 170.

[21] *Cartae Antiquae, Rolls 11–20*, ed. J. Conway Davies, Pipe Roll Society, ns xxxiii, no. 564.

[22] Orderic, iv, 114.

clearly considered that they had the better claim; according to Robert of Torigni, Richard son of Count Gilbert had been given Tonbridge as compensation for the loss of Brionne, but this would have benefited Gilbert of Tonbridge and not Roger.[23]

Roger fitz Richard laid his claim to Brionne before Duke Robert on grounds of inheritance; it was refused, largely because of the intervention of Roger of Beaumont's son, Robert Count of Meulan. The count urged that Roger should be given land at Le Hommet in the Cotentin to satisfy his demand; this would be some return for the large sum of money which Roger had brought the duke in order to strengthen his claim.[24] Orderic's story of Robert fitz Baldwin is far more colourful and dramatic. Robert was ordered to occupy Brionne when trouble arose between the duke and Robert Count of Meulan in 1090, and he refused to give it up when Count Robert regained the duke's favour, on the grounds that he would be handing over his inheritance. In the end, the duke had to besiege the castle, and Robert fitz Baldwin was forced to surrender when the besiegers succeeded in setting fire to the roof of the great hall, a stratagem which the defenders did not notice until the fire was blazing fiercely. Brionne was then handed back to the Beaumonts, but Robert fitz Baldwin was not punished for his action; he was given his father's lands in compensation. Possibly this was at least partly the result of the strength of his support; Orderic stressed that he had plenty of backing from his friends and relatives, and that he had supporters in the duke's own circle as well.[25]

These claims indicate the importance attached to inheritance in the late eleventh century, and also the crucial rôle played by king or duke. The fact that Brionne was not secured by the Clares shows the number of competing pressures on royal or ducal patronage. To gain the inheritance of a distant relative it was necessary to obtain the ruler's consent, and it was essential for the Clares to be on good, and preferably close, terms with the ruler if they were to gain more estates. However, there is no sign of a close relationship between the second generation of the Clares and either Duke Robert of Normandy or William Rufus. Neither the demands made from Duke Robert for Brionne nor the Clares' involvement in the 1088 rebellion in his support presuppose the sort of relationship between him and the Clares which Richard son of Count Gilbert enjoyed with the Conqueror. The succession of Robert in Normandy and William in England in 1087 posed serious problems of allegiance for baronial families who found that some of their members owed homage to one overlord, some to the other, and some to both.

It is possible that William fitz Baldwin was on better terms with William II than the sons of Richard son of Count Gilbert, but this may simply be because he was in the right place at the right time. He took part in the advance into Dyfed in the 1090s, where he built the castle of Rhyd-y-gors, and it is said that

---

[23] Jumièges, 289.
[24] *William of Jumièges, Historiae Northmannorum*, in *Patrologiae Latinae Cursus Completus*, ed. J.-P. Migne, cxlix, col. 890. The edition of the chronicle by J. Marx omits the name of Le Hommet. Roger had been one of Duke Robert's companions during his rebellion against William I in 1077 or 1078; Orderic, iii, 100–1.
[25] Orderic, iv, 204–10.

he was acting with the king's licence.[26] This may indicate that he was on good terms with Rufus, or, more likely, that his estates in Devon made him an obvious baronial leader to cross the Bristol Channel to South Wales. Subsequent events show that royal licence was not sufficient to keep a reward. Although William held out during the Welsh rebellion of 1094, the garrison abandoned the castle on his death two years later.[27]

As for the sons of Richard son of Count Gilbert, their loyalty to William II can best be described as suspect, and in view of their activities they were lucky to survive with their estates intact. There is very little evidence of attendance at court by members of the family, and, although Gilbert of Tonbridge may have acted as a royal steward in 1091, there is no definite reference to him as a witness of charters after that date.[28] Gilbert and probably Roger were implicated in the widespread baronial revolt of 1088, when Gilbert held Tonbridge against William who took only two days to capture it.[29] The rebels were lucky in that few were punished severely. Gilbert was again implicated in rebellion in 1095, but he must either have lost his nerve at the last moment, or seen that the rebels' cause was hopeless, for on Rufus' march north he disclosed full details of the plot to the king.[30] He thus succeeded in saving himself and his lands, for on this occasion Rufus was by no means lenient with the rebels. In view of this evidence, it appears unlikely that Gilbert was given the Norfolk estates of Rainald son of Ivo in William's reign, even though some of these manors are named in the charter concerned with the foundation of Stoke by Clare Priory in 1090; quite possibly, Gilbert spread his gifts to Stoke over a number of years, and they were later grouped for convenience under one date.[31]

The events of William II's reign point to the potential risks for the Clares of implication in rebellion, and the vital importance of securing royal favour. Under Henry I, they found that royal contacts and royal service led to great reward; as J. H. Round put it, they owed to Henry I 'an immense accession of wealth and consequently of power'.[32] It was Henry I's reign as much as the Conqueror's that put the Clares in the forefront of the Anglo-Norman baronage. Yet it would be an over-simplification of events to see the relationship between Henry I and the Clares as a repetition of the situation under William I.

In the first place, it is not clear in 1100 whether the Clares still had hankerings after Duke Robert as king. The events surrounding William II's death in the New Forest have led some writers to suggest that the Clares were again plotting against the king: Gaimar stated that Roger fitz Richard and Gilbert of Tonbridge were among the group of barons hunting close at hand,

---

[26] *Brut, Red Book of Hergest*, 34–5. *Brut, Peniarth ms. 20*, i, 26; ii, 19–20. *Brenhinedd*, 86–7. I. W. Rowlands, 'The Making of the March: Aspects of the Norman Settlement in Dyfed', *ante*, iii, 1980, 148–9.

[27] *Brut, Red Book of Hergest*, 34–5. *Brut, Peniarth ms. 20*, i, 26; ii, 19–20. *Brenhinedd*, 86–7.

[28] *Regesta*, i, nos 290, 301, 318–20.

[29] *ASC*, 167. Worcester, ii, 21–3. Orderic, v, 208.

[30] Orderic, iv, 280.

[31] *Stoke by Clare Cartulary*, nos 136, 137.

[32] J. H. Round, 'The Family of Clare', *Arch. Journ.* lvi, 1899, 223.

and Walter Tirel, alleged to have shot the king, was their brother-in-law.[33] However, Gaimar's information cannot be relied on, and no word of a plot was breathed by the chroniclers: Walter Tirel later asserted that he was not responsible for the king's death.[34] If the Clares had been plotting with Henry, they would have been present at court from the early days of the reign. In fact there is no direct evidence of the Clares taking part in the military campaign against Duke Robert in the summer of 1101.[35] Henry's grant of the abbey of Ely to Richard, the youngest son of Richard son of Count Gilbert, could well be interpreted as a 'bribe' to secure their support, rather than as gratitude for their backing since the beginning of the reign.[36]

Whatever the case in 1100–1, it is clear that after that the Clares' loyalty was unquestioned. Yet there are strong contrasts in the amount and type of service performed by individual Clares and in the extent to which they were rewarded. There is not the same correlation between service and reward as was found under William I. The evidence from the witnessing of royal documents indicates that Henry I only felt the need for a 'Clare presence' at particular times in the reign; the Clares were most often with the king in the early years before the battle of Tinchebrai when Henry was in especial need of support, and in the years immediately after the White Ship disaster in 1120. At other times, chronicle evidence shows that they were performing military service, but this did not necessarily mean that they were in the close circle round the king. Of the various members of the family, it was Roger fitz Richard and Gilbert of Tonbridge who were particularly close to the king.

Looking at the evidence in more detail, the Clares were present in force at great councils. After the threat of Duke Robert's invasion was over in September 1101, many of the family were present at a large baronial gathering at Windsor; all but one of the sons of Richard son of Count Gilbert were there, together with Robert fitz Baldwin.[37] That Christmas, Roger fitz Richard, Gilbert of Tonbridge, and Robert and Richard fitz Baldwin were with the court at Westminster.[38] What is more significant in the early years of the reign is that the Clares often witnessed with only a small group of barons and officials; this can be taken as a strong indication of a close relationship with the king, and Roger fitz Richard and Gilbert of Tonbridge enjoyed this favoured position. Of their brothers, Walter occasionally witnessed with a small group, but was more often present at formal gatherings.[39] The other two are rarely mentioned, and it is difficult to see why Robert, who was well rewarded by the

---

[33] *L'Estoire des Engleis by Geffrei Gaimar*, ed. A. Bell, Oxford 1960, 201. Worcester, ii, 44–5. Huntingdon, 232. *De gestis regum*, ii, 378. Orderic, v, 290–2. C. W. Hollister, 'The Strange Death of William Rufus', *Speculum* xlviii, 1973, 637–53.

[34] *Suger, Vie de Louis le Gros*, ed. A. Molinier, Paris 1887, 8. *Joannis Saresberiensis Vita Sancti Anselmi Cantuariensis*, in *Patrologiae Latinae Cursus Completus*, ed. J.-P. Migne, cxcix, col. 1031.

[35] Gilbert of Tonbridge was one of the sureties for Henry I in his treaty with the count of Flanders in March, 1101; *Regesta*, ii, no. 515.

[36] *ASC*, 176. *Liber Eliensis* ed. E. O. Blake, Camden, 3rd series, xcii, 1962, 225.

[37] *Regesta*, ii, nos 544, 547–8. Robert fitz Richard was the only one of Richard's sons not mentioned among the witnesses.

[38] *Regesta*, ii, no. 552.

[39] *Regesta*, ii, nos 544, 683–5, 828, 877, 1015a, 1057, 1283–4, 1303, 1466, 1715.

king, rarely attested charters. In the case of Richard this is understandable as he was deposed as abbot of Ely in 1102, and, although probably reinstated, died in 1107. During his short time at Ely, he proved an energetic abbot, continuing the building of the new monastic church, recovering abbey lands, and working towards the conversion of Ely into a bishopric, an achievement finally secured by his successor.[40]

Once Henry had become duke of Normandy in 1106, he could consolidate his rule in England and the duchy, and signs of change were soon apparent at court. The Clares did not disappear from court completely, and they fought in the royal armies, as when Gilbert of Tonbridge led a Cornish and South Welsh contingent on Henry's expedition against Gwynedd in 1114.[41] They were not however with the king as often as before. It could be argued that this impression is due to the accidental survival of charters and writs, but it seems too much of a coincidence that less frequent attendance at court comes just after the time when Henry had overcome Duke Robert. Gilbert of Tonbridge's absence after 1110 is partly to be explained by the grant to him of Ceredigion and the need to secure it by conquest, and he suffered from growing ill-health in the years before his death in 1117.[42]

During the period after 1106, it was Roger fitz Richard who was most often with the king, probably because, with his lands in the duchy, he was more closely involved in Norman affairs than his brothers; Gilbert and Walter, who held no lands in the duchy, made no attestations in Normandy, and this also applies to Gilbert's eldest son Richard. Roger may have been with the king on the Tinchebrai campaign; he was at a great council at Rouen in 1106 or 1107.[43] He was with Henry, at least for a time, during the fighting in Normandy between 1111 and 1113.[44] With his brother Robert fitz Richard and his cousin Richard fitz Baldwin, he was at the court at Rouen in June 1119, when peace was made with Anjou.[45] The following August, Henry's forces defeated the French decisively at Brémule in the Vexin; according to Orderic, Roger and William of Warenne urged Henry to join battle with the French, and Roger saved the king's life during the fighting.[46]

This triumph over the French was closely followed by a tragedy which temporarily brought the Clares back into greater prominence at court. On the return journey to England, in November 1120, the White Ship with Henry's only legitimate son William on board was lost. The feeling of crisis was such that for the next three years the Clares were more often with the king; the picture that emerges from the charters and writs is very similar to the early years of the reign. Roger had been with the court at Barfleur before it embarked for England.[47] In the spring of 1121, Roger, Walter and Robert fitz

[40] *Regesta*, ii, nos 726, 1204, 1246, 1283. *Liber Eliensis*, 225, 227, 228–36. *De gestis pontificum*, 119, 325. Worcester, ii, 52. Eadmer, 142, 185–6.
[41] Instances of their attendance at court are found in *Regesta*, ii, nos 875, 877, 1057. *Brut, Red Book of Hergest*, 78–9. *Brut, Peniarth ms. 20*, i, 59; ii, 37. *Brenhinedd*, 120–1.
[42] *Brut, Red Book of Hergest*, 70–3, 90–5, 100–1. *Brut, Peniarth ms. 20*, i, 53–4, 68–70, 76; ii, 34, 41–4, 46. *Brenhinedd*, 114–17, 128–33, 136–7.
[43] *Regesta*, ii, no. 809.
[44] *Regesta*, ii, no. 1015.
[45] *Regesta*, ii, nos 1203–4.
[46] Orderic, vi, 234–8.
[47] *Regesta*, ii, no. 1233.

Richard were with the king at Winchester, together with two of the sons of Gilbert of Tonbridge, Richard and Baldwin.[48] During the next two years, Roger was especially often at court.[49]

The panic had somewhat subsided by 1123, and from then until the end of the reign the attendance of the Clares was much less frequent. Like other barons, they may have been reluctant to accept Matilda as heir to the throne at Christmas, 1126. When the oath of fealty to her was renewed five years later, Roger and Walter fitz Richard and Richard fitz Gilbert (the eldest son of Gilbert of Tonbridge) were among those present.[50] This council virtually brought to an end the part played by the Clares at court under Henry I, and marked Roger's last appearance, for he died soon afterwards.[51]

It is clear from the attestations that the Clares played an important rôle in the early years of the reign and immediately after 1120. Roger fitz Richard enjoyed the closest relationship with the king, while his younger brothers were much less significant, as were the sons of Gilbert of Tonbridge. The Clares' service differed in some respects from that performed by Richard son of Count Gilbert under William I. They were no longer needed to help run the kingdom while the king was in Normandy, and they did not serve on judicial commissions, although Gilbert of Tonbridge acted as a local justiciar in Kent in 1103.[52] The main part of the family's service comprised military support and counsel.

Not only are differences to be found in the service performed by individual Clares, but also in the rewards received. It is an oversimplification to say that a greater amount of service led to greater reward. Henry did not have the same amount of land available for reward as his father, and his use of forfeitures shows a desire to extend his power and reward his followers at as small a cost as possible to the royal demesne; many of his followers had a long wait for their rewards. At the same time, the clamour for grants must have been considerable; Gilbert of Tonbridge is said often to have asked the king for land before receiving Ceredigion.[53] The rewards made show how closely king and barons were interdependent, as they had been under the Conqueror. Henry ensured that he gained loyal men in the localities while giving them the means of increasing their status; payment for rewards, as for the marriage of heiresses, could be an added bonus for the king. The Welsh grants furthered Norman penetration to the mutual benefit of baron and king; here, barons were doing service to the king at the same time as reaping their reward, and the Welsh revolt of 1136 showed how much the survival of their lordships depended on the reputation of Henry I. Baronial ambitions in Wales were however subject to Henry's overall policy; Richard fitz Baldwin apparently

[48] *Regesta*, ii, nos 1283–4.

[49] *Regesta*, ii, nos 1270, 1319, 1383.

[50] *Regesta*, ii, no. 1715.

[51] The only later attestations by the Clares under Henry I are found in *Regesta*, ii, nos 1736, 1900–1.

[52] *Regesta*, ii, no. 635.

[53] *Brut, Red Book of Hergest*, 70–1. *Brut, Peniarth ms. 20*, i, 53; ii, 34. *Brenhinedd*, 114–17.

had to give up his claims in Eastern Dyfed, because of Henry's intentions of building up royal power in the region.[54]

All these considerations have to be borne in mind when the Clare gains are examined. If there had been a clear correlation between service and reward, Roger fitz Richard would have made the greatest gains, but this did not turn out to be the case. This may explain Orderic's story that in 1110, when Roger journeyed to Germany with Henry's daughter Matilda, he hoped to make his fortune in the emperor's service; Henry V however distributed presents and sent the Normans home. It was in 1110 that Gilbert of Tonbridge had been given the lordship of Ceredigion, and, although Roger was granted land in England, it was insignificant compared with his brothers'.

According to the Pipe Roll of 1130, Roger fitz Richard's demesne lands in England comprised forty-five hides – seven each in Cambridgeshire and Huntingdonshire, six in Bedfordshire, twenty in Essex, and five in Suffolk.[55] Only a few references survive as to the places where Roger's land lay; he is known to have had a demesne manor at Everton in Bedfordshire, and one of his knights held land at Birdbrook in Essex.[56] Nevertheless, these details, together with information about lands held by Roger's successors, the Clare and Marshal earls of Pembroke, indicate that Roger was given most of the Domesday estates of Ranulf brother of Ilger by Henry I.[57] Ranulf's lands were worth about £116 in 1086, the most important group in Essex being valued at about £58.

The English lands granted to Gilbert of Tonbridge were of similar value. Apart from the Norfolk lands of Rainald son of Ivo which have already been mentioned, Gilbert received estates in Northamptonshire which had been held by Geoffrey bishop of Coutances.[58] These possessions formed a valuable addition to the honour of Clare, but Gilbert was probably far better pleased with the grant of Ceredigion in 1110.[59] Here was a new area to conquer and exploit. By doing this, Gilbert was furthering Henry's policy of Anglo-Norman rule in Wales, as well as benefiting himself and his family. The region was difficult to control, being remote and isolated; communications were poor and there were few harbours. These problems explain why Henry chose to grant the region to one of his supporters in return for an annual payment; in 1130, Richard fitz Gilbert accounted for £43 6s 8d for his land in Wales.[60] Gilbert

---

[54] Richard had begun to re-establish himself in Eastern Dyfed, and may have been given the office of sheriff of Devon in return for abandoning his Welsh claims, a post which he held between 1107 and 1128. *Regesta*, ii, nos 649n, 1486. *Brut, Red Book of Hergest*, 44–5, 48–51. *Brut, Peniarth ms. 20*, i, 33, 37–8; ii, 24, 26–7. *Brenhinedd*, 100–3. Rowlands, 152–3.

[55] *Pipe Roll, 31 Henry I*, ed. J. Hunter, Record Commission, 1833, 46, 49, 59, 99, 104.

[56] BL Cotton ms. Faustina A iv, fo. 46a. Everton lay in both Bedfordshire and Huntingdonshire in 1086, and it is likely that the 1130 Pipe Roll references to these two counties apply to Everton. *Stoke by Clare Cartulary*, no. 137.

[57] As well as the counties mentioned, Ranulf also held lands in Middlesex, Hertfordshire and Norfolk.

[58] 'The Northamptonshire Survey', ed. J. H. Round, VCH *Northamptonshire*, i, 1902, 365–6, 377. *Facsimiles of Early Charters from Northamptonshire Collections*, ed. F. M. Stenton, Northamptonshire Record Society, iv, 1930, no. XVIII. *Monasticon*, ii, 601, 603. *Domesday Book*, ii, fos 230a–234b.

[59] *Brut, Red Book of Hergest*, 70–3. *Brut, Peniarth ms. 20*, i, 53–4; ii, 34. *Brenhinedd*, 114–17.

[60] *Pipe Roll, 31 Henry I*, 53.

maintained strong rule in Ceredigion until his death, and Richard fitz Gilbert probably continued his father's methods of control and exploitation. For both, the prestige of Henry I was essential; once the king had died, the Welsh rose in successful rebellion, and deprived Richard of his life and lands.[61]

In comparison with Roger and Gilbert, Walter and Robert fitz Richard received the greater reward. At first sight this is surprising, as they made relatively few attestations of royal documents, and they appear to have had little connection with the court. Possibly they received greater estates than their elder brothers simply because they were landless, and therefore would be completely dependent on Henry I's generosity. Henry may have felt that they would best serve him by dominating the regions where their lands lay. The king may have been influenced by the fact that they belonged to a loyal family, and their rewards certainly strengthened Clare influence both in Wales and in Eastern England. The presence of Gilbert and more particularly Roger at court may have helped in securing rewards for their brothers; those with a close court connection were in the best position to know what estates were available and to put in their demands for them. Family solidarity may well have been a significant factor in securing reward.

Most of Walter fitz Richard's lands in England and Wales had been held in 1086 by William of Eu who had forfeited them for his part in the rebellion of 1095. According to Domesday Book, William was farming much of Lower Gwent for £55, and this area must have been granted to Walter some time before 1119, the year that Pope Calixtus II ordered the restoration of lands seized by Walter and other nobles from the bishopric of Llandaff.[62] Unfortunately, little is known of Walter's activities in the area; he is best known for his foundation in 1131 of the Cistercian abbey of Tintern in the Wye valley.[63] The *caput* of the lordship was situated at Chepstow, then known as Striguil. The lands were less extensive than Ceredigion, but, being nearer to England and on the Bristol Channel, were easier to defend, and the Clares continued to hold them until 1189.

In 1086, William of Eu held land in nine English counties to a total value of nearly £394, and much of this was also granted to Walter; it is likely that Walter was also given the important manor of Tidenham in Gloucestershire which in the later twelfth century formed part of the honour of Striguil. According to the Pipe Roll of 1130, Walter's demesne holdings amounted to 106 hides, more than twice as much as Roger's; twenty-one hides lay in Hertfordshire, eleven in Bedfordshire, twenty-five in Wiltshire, and forty-nine in Gloucestershire.[64] Walter's main concentration of lands lay in the West, in Gloucestershire and Lower Gwent.

Robert fitz Richard received estates which had been held by Ralph Baynard in 1086 soon after they had been forfeited when his grandson William rebelled against Henry I in 1110.[65] Robert gained widespread lands in Norfolk, Suffolk

[61] *Gesta Stephani*, 10–11. *Brut, Red Book of Hergest*, 112–3. *Brut, Peniarth ms. 20*, i, 86; ii, 51. *Brenhinedd*, 144–5. Worcester, ii, 97. *Giraldi Cambrensis Opera*, ed. J. S. Brewer, J. F. Dimock and G. F. Warner, RS, 1861–91, vi, 47–8, 118.
[62] *Text of the Book of Llan Dâv*, ed. J. G. Evans and J. Rhys, Oxford 1893, 93.
[63] J. C. Ward, 'Fashions in Monastic Endowment', 440.
[64] *Pipe Roll, 31 Henry I*, 23, 62, 80, 104.
[65] Huntingdon, 237.

and Essex, together with a few lands in Hertfordshire, and the stronghold of Baynard's Castle in London.[66] It was especially important for Henry to have a loyal vassal on the west side of London, and Robert would be backed up by his Clare kindred. The honour had its *caput* at Little Dunmow in Essex, and in 1086 had been worth about £440. On these lands Robert enjoyed the usual franchises accorded to barons, sac and soc, toll and team, and infangenetheof; according to the charter, his brothers enjoyed similar privileges on their estates.[67] Robert's marriage to Matilda, daughter of Simon of St Liz, earl of Huntingdon, further secured his place among the Anglo-Norman baronage.

The lands thus granted by Henry I to the sons of Richard son of Count Gilbert added immeasurably to the family's power and standing. Even in this generation, however, Henry did not reward the Clares indiscriminately, and in the next generation, among the sons of Gilbert of Tonbridge, there is little sign of special treatment or a close relationship. It would appear that for preference Henry looked to the Clares who were his own contemporaries and whom he had known from at least the early years of the reign. Henry occasionally made gestures of favour towards the younger generation, as when he advanced Richard fitz Gilbert 200 marks to pay his debts to the Jews, but such moves were slight compared to his treatment of Richard's father and uncles.[68] Three of the sons of Gilbert of Tonbridge, however, made good marriages, and it is likely that Henry I had a say in these. Richard's marriage to Alice, daughter of Ranulf Meschin earl of Chester, strengthened his position in the Marches. Gilbert Strongbow's marriage to Elizabeth, daughter of Robert of Beaumont, count of Meulan and earl of Leicester, probably took place before 1135; his son and heir, Richard Strongbow, witnessed the treaty of Westminster at the end of 1153, and this probably implies that he was of age. Gilbert's marriage must have strengthened his position at court early in Stephen's reign when his brothers-in-law, Waleran Count of Meulan and Robert earl of Leicester were prominent.[69] Baldwin fitz Gilbert served as one of Henry I's knights, and secured the marriage of Adeline, the niece and heiress of William of Rollos, lord of the honour of Bourne in Lincolnshire. In 1130, he owed the king £301 16s 4d for the marriage and lands.[70]

As far as the Clare family are concerned, the reign of Stephen can be regarded as the transitional period, illustrating the gradual change from a reliance on royal grants for advancement in the earlier period, to the increasing use of claims to inheritances which were the usual way of increasing the estates in the later twelfth and thirteenth centuries. Royal favour continued to be vital for family advancement, but after Roger fitz Richard no member of the Clare family enjoyed as close a relationship with the king.

Like many of the families who had been highly rewarded by Henry I, all the Clares supported Stephen at the beginning of his reign, and the older generation were assiduous in attending the king's court until their deaths. Quite possibly, they had been on good terms with Stephen in Henry I's lifetime, but

---

[66] *Monasticon*, vi, 147. *Domesday Book*, i, fos 132, 138a–b; ii, 68b–71, 247b–253b, 413b–415b.

[67] *Cartae Antiquae, Rolls 1–10*, ed. L. Landon, Pipe Roll Society, ns xvii, no. 182.

[68] *Pipe Roll, 31 Henry I*, 53, 148.

[69] Jumièges, 327. Elizabeth was sometimes known as Isabella.

[70] *Pipe Roll, 31 Henry I*, 110.

the only evidence of a connection is Roger fitz Richard's witnessing at Rouen of Stephen's charter founding the abbey of Furness in 1127.[71] Robert and Walter fitz Richard probably attended Henry I's funeral at Reading on 4 January 1136, as did Baldwin fitz Gilbert.[72] Robert accompanied the king on his journey to the North in February when a treaty was concluded with King David of Scotland.[73] Robert and Walter both attended the great Easter court when Robert acted as royal steward.[74] This was the last time that Walter attended (he died in 1138), but Robert was present at the siege of Exeter during the summer.[75] There is no indication that he accompanied Stephen to Normandy in 1137, but he was with him again after his return.[76] Altogether in the two years between 1135 and his death about the end of 1137, he witnessed twenty-nine charters, eighteen of which were attested by eight people or less, a total far in excess of the four surviving documents he witnessed under Henry I.

Clearly, Stephen valued Robert's support, but the help of the next generation of Clares would be worth very much more to the king. Richard fitz Gilbert was ready to make the most of Stephen's generosity, but his gamble ended quickly in death. According to the *Gesta Stephani*, he came to court, but the king refused to grant his high demands. Richard therefore went away, as was said, to stir up war against him.[77] On his journey to Ceredigion, Richard was warned of the Welsh rising, but took no notice, was caught in a Welsh ambush, and slain in April 1136.[78] Ceredigion was lost to the Welsh, and Richard's eldest son Gilbert succeeded to a diminished inheritance. He was still an important baron, as seen in his creation as earl of Hertford *c*. 1140, but he is an obscure figure, and seems to have taken no action to recover Ceredigion.

Richard fitz Gilbert's death left his younger brother Gilbert Strongbow as head of the Clare family. Gilbert was highly ambitious and eager for rapid advancement, and an interesting comparison can be drawn between him and his father and uncles. As a younger son, he had to make his own way, and chose to do this by service to Stephen, but rewards were heaped on him far more quickly than would have happened under Henry I. Moreover, as was becoming increasingly common at the time, Gilbert made good use of claims to lands by right of inheritance to a far greater extent than his predecessors had been able to do.

The *Gesta Stephani* describe Gilbert as a poor knight raised in honour and wealth by King Stephen.[79] In fact, Gilbert may have risen from poor knight to earl in the three short years between 1135 and 1138 and his relationship with the Beaumonts may well have helped his advancement. He first took over the lands of his uncle, Roger fitz Richard, who died childless in 1131.[80] It is

---

[71] *Regesta*, ii, no. 1545.
[72] *Regesta*, iii, no. 387.
[73] *Regesta*, iii, nos 99, 832, 904.
[74] *Regesta*, iii, nos 46, 944–7, 949.
[75] *Tintern Chronicle*, in *Monasticon*, v, 270. *Regesta*, iii, nos 337, 952.
[76] *Regesta*, iii, nos 288, 827.
[77] *Gesta Stephani*, 10–11.
[78] *Brut, Red Book of Hergest*, 112–13. *Brut, Peniarth ms. 20*, i, 86; ii, 51. *Brenhinedd*, 144–5. Worcester, ii, 97. *Giraldi Cambrensis Opera*, vi, 47–8, 118.
[79] *Gesta Stephani*, 133–4.
[80] Jumièges, 326.

unlikely that his enrichment was begun by Henry I, as there is no record of Gilbert at Henry's court, and it is far more probable that this grant was made at the beginning of Stephen's reign. Robert of Torigni asserted that Gilbert gained these lands by hereditary right and with Roger's consent, but rules of inheritance were still fluid, and the arrangement must have been made with the full knowledge and agreement of the king. By this acquisition, Gilbert gained some lands in England, and Orbec and Bienfaite in Normandy; Le Hommet in the Cotentin, granted to Roger by Robert Curthose, apparently reverted to the ducal demesne. At the beginning of Stephen's reign, Gilbert supported the king in Normandy, and was involved in the fighting in which the duchy was engulfed. In 1136, he made an unsuccessful expedition against Exmes which had been taken by Geoffrey of Anjou, and at about the same time his brother Walter was defending the castle of Le Sap against Geoffrey.[81]

It seems likely that it was the death of Walter fitz Richard in 1138 and his succession to Walter's lands which led Gilbert Strongbow to take a serious part in English affairs. From that time, no references survive concerning his fighting in Normandy or any attempt to defend his lands against the Angevin conquest, and in 1138 he was occupied with fighting in England.[82] Robert of Torigni wrote of his succession to Walter at the same time and in the same terms as his succession to Roger, although a few years may have elapsed between the two grants.[83] Certainly the arrangements must again have been sanctioned by the king, and Stephen was undoubtedly piling rewards on Gilbert. It was probably in 1138 that Stephen gave him the rape and castle of Pevensey; this grant especially illustrates Stephen's reliance on his loyalty in view of the key role often played by Pevensey in defence of the south coast.[84] To these lands must be added the honour of his nephew, Gilbert of Montfichet, since, for at least part of Stephen's reign, Strongbow was acting as his guardian and was in charge of his estates.[85]

It was presumably because of his powerful connections at court, and his wide possessions, including the lordship of Striguil in the Welsh Marches, that Gilbert Strongbow was created earl of Pembroke in 1138.[86] He was the only earl with a Welsh title. He had no estates in Pembroke before becoming earl, and the choice of the area appears to have been due both to royal policy and Gilbert's own ambition. As has been seen under Henry I, service and reward were intertwined. Stephen probably desired to have at least one prominent supporter acting in his name in South Wales, for the great majority of Marcher lords, notably Robert earl of Gloucester, adhered to the party of the Empress. Gilbert, on the other hand, would wish to prosecute family claims.

In view of the military nature of the earl's duties, Gilbert's main responsibility would be to reconquer areas taken by the Welsh in 1136, and to prevent further rebellion. How active he could be as earl of Pembroke is not clear, but a series of documents in the cartulary of Worcester cathedral priory indicates

---

[81] Orderic, vi, 462, 470.
[82] Orderic, vi, 520.
[83] Jumièges, 326. *Tintern Chronicle*, in *Monasticon*, v, 270.
[84] J. H. Round, *Studies on the Red Book of the Exchequer*, London 1898, 7.
[85] Round, *Studies*, 8–9. *The Letters and Charters of Gilbert Foliot*, ed. A. Morey and C. N. L. Brooke, Cambridge 1967, 416–17.
[86] Orderic, vi, 520. *Regesta*, iii, nos 275–6, 634.

that he was making interventions in the affairs of the county.[87] Pembroke made an excellent centre for campaigns into the former Clare lands of Ceredigion and Eastern Dyfed. Gilbert's primary interest was in Eastern Dyfed where he tried to stake a claim to the Welsh lands held for a short time by William and Richard fitz Baldwin, and surrendered to the Crown by Richard early in Henry I's reign. In 1144, Gilbert came to Dyfed, rebuilt Carmarthen castle, and constructed another castle at Dinwileir in Mabudryd.[88] Both strongholds fell to the Welsh the following year. However, the fact that Gilbert had been able not only to hold Gwent but also to mount an attack on Dyfed was significant, and suggests that, although he was the king's official, he enjoyed at least the neutrality of the supporters of the Empress in the Marches; quite possibly, this may have aroused Stephen's suspicions against him.

Gilbert's career illustrates the importance of royal service and reward and the prosecution of inheritance claims; it also shows the dangers of being overambitious and overreaching oneself in a period of instability and civil war. The political situation had continuously to be assessed to decide whether to remain loyal to Stephen or to gamble on gaining more by joining the Angevins. After Stephen's defeat at the battle of Lincoln, Strongbow joined the Empress, at least for the summer of 1141.[89] Like many of Stephen's leading supporters who changed sides at this point he probably considered that Stephen's cause was hopeless and it would be more politic to switch his loyalty to Matilda. He returned to his allegiance to Stephen before the end of the year, and was present, along with Baldwin fitz Gilbert and Gilbert earl of Hertford, at Stephen's Christmas court at Canterbury.[90] The events of 1141 may well have changed Stephen's attitude towards Strongbow, as may Gilbert's temporarily successful campaign in Dyfed three years later; according to the *Gesta Stephani*, the king was unsure of him before his revolt in 1147. Strongbow also had a grievance against the king as a result of the loss of his Norman lands due to the Angevin conquest.[91] However, with the main part of his estates in England and Wales, it would have been folly for him to desert Stephen in an attempt to save his Norman inheritance.

It was in the defence of Clare family rights in England that he overreached himself. His action stemmed from the knock-on effects of Stephen's arrest of Ranulf earl of Chester. When Ranulf was freed and subsequently revolted, he endangered the position of his nephew, Gilbert earl of Hertford, who had given himself and his castles as a guarantee of Ranulf's good behaviour. Stephen kept Gilbert a prisoner until he had handed over all his castles; Gilbert was then freed and joined Ranulf in disturbing the peace.[92] This surrender by Gilbert gave his uncle Strongbow the opportunity to claim the

[87] *The Cartulary of Worcester Cathedral Priory*, ed. R. R. Darlington, Pipe Roll Society, ns xxxviii, pp. xxxi–iii, nos 252–5.
[88] *Brut, Red Book of Hergest*, 120–1. *Brut, Peniarth ms. 20*, i, 91; ii, 54.
[89] *Regesta*, iii, nos 275, 634.
[90] *Regesta*, iii, no. 276.
[91] *Gesta Stephani*, 133. By 1154, the honour of Orbec was in the hands of Robert de Montfort.
[92] *Gesta Stephani*, 133. *Radulfi de Diceto Opera Historica*, ed. W. Stubbs, RS, 1876, i, 255–6. *Symeonis Monachi Opera Omnia*, ed. T. Arnold, RS, 1882–5, ii, 324.

castles for himself, arguing that they were his by hereditary right. This claim can be compared with a charter of the Empress of 1141 when she granted to William of Beauchamp the inheritances of his kinsmen who opposed her in the war.[93] On Stephen's refusal, Gilbert Strongbow joined the revolt, but was taken by surprise by Stephen's rapid moves against his castles. His gamble to gain his nephew's castles failed, and indicates the dangers to a magnate of rebellion, since his successors never again held Pevensey. Gilbert himself was reconciled to the king, but died soon after in 1148.[94]

In looking back over Gilbert Strongbow's career, it is clear that he was driven solely by his own ambitions. He was primarily loyal to Stephen because that was where he felt his interests lay. Unlike his father and uncles in the time of Henry I, he had succeeded in obtaining valuable lands without undergoing a lengthy period of royal service. Again in contrast to them, he was able to put pressure on Stephen to grant him lands by right of inheritance, for, like other barons, he had a tenacious memory for any estates previously held by his family. Before 1135, the only claim made by the Clares on hereditary grounds was that to Brionne, and it was a failure; under Stephen, Gilbert Strongbow acquired the estates of his uncles Roger and Walter, cast greedy eyes on the Welsh lands held earlier by the Clares, and finally in a gamble which did not pay off demanded the castles of his nephew on the grounds of his rebellion against the king.

Throughout the period of the Norman kings, the Clares' rise to power was dependent on royal favour. The Clares were fortunate that, except for William II's reign, they were on good terms with the king for whom they provided military service and counsel. The relationship between Richard son of Count Gilbert and William I, and between Gilbert of Tonbridge and Roger fitz Richard and Henry I involved more than the normal ties of homage and service between king and tenant-in-chief, and their close connections with the court were especially important for the Clare family. Service was undoubtedly an important factor in the gaining of rewards, but, after the first generation of the Clares in England, there is little sign of correlation between service and reward. Political circumstances changed, and other factors besides service became significant, such as the policy of expansion into Wales, family solidarity, and a knowledge of what lands were available for possible distribution. The presence of younger sons ready to carry out Henry I's policies undoubtedly also contributed to the family's growing importance at this time. Whether they could take advantage of their gains was very much up to the Clares themselves, but even here continuing royal power and favour were vital, as is seen in the effects of the Welsh rising of 1136, and the Angevin conquest of Normandy eight years later.

Disloyalty and rebellion in the Norman period often resulted in forfeiture. It is remarkable that in an age when many of the wealthiest Anglo-Norman families lost their estates in this way, the Clares went from strength to strength. The author of the *Liber Eliensis* extolled the power of the Clares and

---

[93] J. H. Round, *Geoffrey de Mandeville*, London 1892, 314.
[94] *Regesta*, iii, nos 845–7. *Tintern Chronicle*, in *Monasticon*, v, 270. In 1153, Pevensey was in the hands of Richer of L'Aigle; *Foedera, Conventiones, Litterae*, ed. T. Rymer, Record Commission, 1816–69, i, part 1, 18. *Gesta Stephani*, 133–5.

the fear which they inspired. He described how they overawed the other magnates at the royal court, and imposed their will in lawsuits; according to him, even Henry I trembled at their power.[95] The passage referred to an episode early in Henry's reign, in connection with Richard fitz Richard, abbot of Ely, but it is likely that the author was influenced by the position of the family at the time he was writing in the mid-twelfth century. Quite clearly, he was concerned to praise a family once connected with Ely, and it is therefore interesting to find the writer of the *Gesta Stephani*, who had no special bias towards the Clares, making a similar comment; he described Richard fitz Gilbert as supported by very wealthy relations and men, and endowed with countless lands and castles.[96]

The achievement of the Clares under the Norman kings can be summed up in the number of adventurers between 1066 and 1154 who through their own efforts and royal favour achieved baronial rank – Richard and Baldwin sons of Count Gilbert under the Conqueror, Walter and Robert fitz Richard and Baldwin fitz Gilbert under Henry I, and Gilbert Strongbow under Stephen. In addition, there were those who like Roger fitz Richard and Gilbert of Tonbridge augmented their holdings through royal service. From this period four baronial families emerged – the earls of Hertford of the eldest Clare line, the Fitzwalter family descended from Robert fitz Richard, the Strongbow earls of Pembroke, and the lesser barony of Bourne which passed from Baldwin fitz Gilbert to the Wake family. The lands and wealth which they gained in the Norman period made the Clares a force to be reckoned with down to the fourteenth century.

---

[95] *Liber Eliensis*, 226.
[96] *Gesta Stephani*, 10.

A VICE-COMITAL FAMILY IN
PRE-CONQUEST WARWICKSHIRE

Ann Williams

'We are ignorant even of the names of most pre-Conquest sheriffs.' Thus Eric John, in a recent survey of the late Old English kingdom, sums up one of the major problems facing any detailed study of its administration: the identification of its agents of government. The magnitude of this deficiency can be seen by comparing the scope of the present paper with Judith Green's splendid study, delivered to this conference a few years ago, on the sheriffs of William the Conqueror.[1] I should dearly love to present a companion piece on the sheriffs of Edward the Confessor, but the groundwork for such an essay has not yet been laid. One of the purposes of this paper is to suggest one line of enquiry by which more information on the Confessor's sheriffs (and indeed the Confessor's thegns) might be obtained. The subject of this exercise is a pre-Conquest sheriff whose name is known, and better-known than most, at least in his progeny; Æthelwine, the ancestor of the Arden family.[2] A summary of what has already been established concerning him is, nevertheless, both short and superficial. It is generally assumed that he was sheriff of Warwickshire in the reign of Edward, and possibly in the early years of William the Conqueror. He was living in 1072, when he attested, as sheriff, a charter of Robert of Stafford, granting two hides at Wrottesley, Staffs, to Æthelwig, abbot of Evesham.[3] Two of his sons, Thorkil and Ketilbiorn, attested the same charter, and a third, Guthmund, held Great Packington, Warks, in 1086.[4] All three sons have Norse names, which suggests that their mother was of Scandinavian origin, either from one of the Anglo-Danish kindreds long established in eastern England, or a connection of one of the Scandinavians who settled in the west midlands during the reign of Cnut.[5] We have no information on

---

[1] Eric John, 'The end of Anglo-Saxon England', *The Anglo-Saxons*, ed. James Campbell, Oxford 1982, 237; Judith Green, 'The sheriffs of William the Conqueror', *ante 1982*, 5, 1983, 129–45.

[2] This paper could not have been written without the generous help of Dr David Crouch, who allowed me to use his as yet unpublished material on the Arden family. Thanks are due to him and to Dr C. P. Lewis, who read a draft of this paper and corrected many errors. Those which remain are my own responsibility.

[3] R. W. Eyton, 'The Staffordshire Cartulary', *Collections for a history of Staffordshire* 2, 1881, 178. The charter now exists only in an English translation of the sixteenth century and its authenticity is hard to gauge. The tenement of Wrottesley was in Robert of Stafford's hands in 1086, and no Evesham interest is recorded (*Domesday Book* i, fo. 249).

[4] *Domesday Book* i, fo. 241.

[5] Ann Williams, ' "Cockles amongst the wheat": Danes and English in the western Midlands in the first half of the eleventh century', *Midland History 11* 1986. Earl Leofric, with whom Æthelwine's family was connected, had Danes in his entourage, see p. 286 below.

279

The Kinsmen of Æthelwine

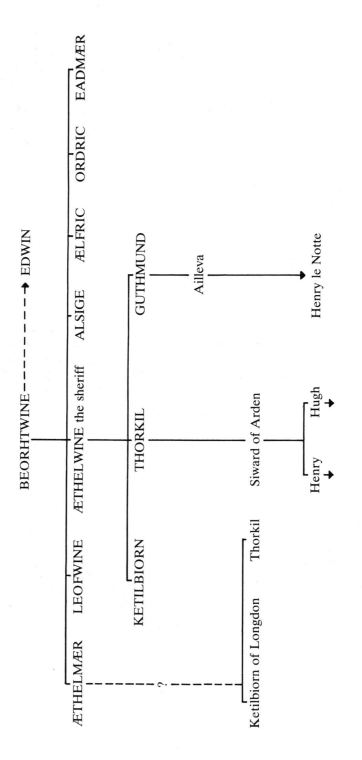

CAPITALS indicate a reference in Domesday Book.
Only those descendants mentioned in the text are included.

Æthelwine's marriage, however, and his sons' names may merely represent current fashions in nomenclature. Æthelwine was dead by 1086, when his lands were held by his son, Thorkil.[6] He probably died in the abbacy of Æthelhelm of Abingdon (1071–1083), for it was during Æthelhelm's time that Thorkil gave to the abbey three manors described as being of his patrimony.[7] Æthelwine himself had been a benefactor of Coventry Abbey, to whom he gave Clifton-on-Dunsmore, Warks, 'with the consent of King Edward, and of his (own) sons, for his soul and in the witness of the shire'.[8] He had a brother, Leofwine, still living in 1086, and holding two manors which had belonged to Æthelwine.[9]

To discover any other members of this kindred is no easy task. The problems of identifying individuals in pre-Conquest sources are well known, the main difficulty being the absence of heritable and consistently used family names to qualify the Christian names. For this the structure of English families and the customs of inheritance are to blame. Yet these very structures may hold the key to the identification both of individuals and of kindreds. If a man's estate was divided at death amongst his heirs, as we know that it was, then some of the vills which Domesday Book displays split up into several manors may be the result of such a partition, and the pre-Conquest tenants of these manors may be the groups of kinsmen who have shared out their common inheritance. It should be emphasised that this explanation will in no way cover the origins of all divided vills recorded in Domesday Book; there are numerous factors contributing to this phenomenon. But some divided vills, notably the small vills, with more or less equal holdings spread between two or more individuals, may be the result of such a process. The hypothesis can be tested only on a wide basis. For this paper, the divided vills of Warwickshire have been analysed, along with those of Worcestershire, Gloucestershire, Oxfordshire, Shropshire and Staffordshire. The group relevant to the family of Æthelwine is shown in Table I for ease of reference.

Before I describe the results of this exercise, something should be said about the treatment of Old English names in Domesday. The English seem to have been particularly fond of names with the first elements *Ælf-* and *Æþel-*. It is therefore particularly unfortunate that Domesday does not regularly discriminate between the two elements. Æthelwine, for instance, appears in Domesday only as Alwine (*Aluuin, -us*), a form which could also represent Ælfwine. The correct form of Æthelwine's name is known only from Robert of Stafford's charter. This applies to all names of the type. Confusion is therefore prevalent. The Old English name Ælfric, one of the commonest in the eleventh century, appears in Domesday both as *Aluric, -us*, which gives Ælfric, and as *Alric, -us*, which could also represent Æthelric. Only occasionally does Domesday unequivocally represent *Æþel-* by using such forms as *Ail-* or *Aiel-*. The muddle is compounded in Æthelwine's case by Domesday's

---

[6] *Domesday Book* i, fos 240v–241v.
[7] *Chronicon monasterii de Abingdon*, ed. J. Stevenson, RS 1858, ii, 8.
[8] *Domesday Book* i, fo. 238v. It had been seized by Aubrey de Couci and is entered again under his fief (fo. 239v). Thorkil and his son Siward were also connected with Thorney and appear in the Thorney *Liber Vitae* (BL Add ms. 40,000 fo. 3r). I owe this reference to Cecily Clark.
[9] See below, note 11.

tendency to confuse the second element *-wine* for the element *-wig*; thus in Gloucestershire the name of the pre-Conquest sheriff appears both as Alwin (*Aluuin, -us*) and as Alwig (*Aluui, -us*). The first is probably correct, but still leaves open the question whether the man was called Ælfwine or Æthelwine. In the discussion which follows I have tried to use the *Ælf-* and *Æþel-* forms only where other evidence suggests that they are the correct ones; in ambiguous cases, the *Al-* form has been used.[10]

In the search for Æthelwine's kinsmen, which can now begin, the starting-point is the vill of Flecknoe, where there were four manors in 1086. One was held by Leofwine, who had bought it from his brother Alwine and another by Thorkil, in succession to his father Æthelwine. It seems reasonable to conclude with both Round and Freeman (and what an amazing concord is there represented) that Leofwine's brother and Thorkil's father were one and the same. Round further suggested that the Leofwine who held a manor at Fillongley of the bishop of Coutances, in succession to a man called Alwine, was the same Leofwine, succeeding once again his brother Æthelwine.[11] Here John Horace lost interest in two obscure Englishmen, but we can, I think, go a little further. Leofwine (the same Leofwine) held a second manor in Flecknoe in 1086. He claimed to hold it of the bishop of Worcester, but 'the bishop failed (to support) him in his plea, so that Leofwine is in the king's mercy'.[12] Now it happens that another Warwickshire manor was in dispute between the bishop of Worcester and a man called Leofwine in 1086. It was one of two lying in the vill of Alvestone, and in King Edward's day it had belonged to Beorhtwine, but the soke was held by Archbishop Ealdred, formerly bishop of Worcester. The six sons of Beorhtwine, Leofwine, Eadmær and four others unnamed, did not dispute the bishop's rights of soke, but said they did not know from whom their father had held the land, 'whether from the church or from Earl Leofric (d. 1057) whom he served'. They themselves, however, had held it from Earl Leofric 'and could go where they would with the land'. Since the manor was entered in the name of the bishop of Worcester, he presumably had other ideas on the subject.[13]

Leofwine is, of course, a common name, but the coincidence of two occurrences, in the same shire, both relating to 1086, and both concerned in disputes with the bishop of Worcester, tends to suggest that both relate to the same man. If so, then Leofwine, Æthelwine's brother, had five brothers living in 1086, four unnamed. Æthelwine was certainly dead by this date, but there

---

[10] Olof von Feilitzen, *The pre-Conquest personal names of Domesday Book*, Uppsala 1937, 142, 182, 412, 415.

[11] VCH *Warwickshire* i, 283; E. A. Freeman, *The history of the Norman Conquest of England* iv, Oxford 1871, 189 note 2.

[12] *Domesday Book* i, fos 238v, 244v. As in many disputes, the manor is entered twice, in the names of both parties.

[13] Another manor in Alvestone was the subject of a dispute between the bishop of Worcester and the former holders, Beorhtnoth and Alwig, but a court of four shires, under the presidency of Queen Matilda (before 1083), had found for the bishop. This dispute and the one concerning Beorhtwine are treated together in Domesday, in an additional entry inserted at the foot of the first column on folio 238, with interpolation marks to indicate the correct place in the sequence of manors. It seems likely that Beorhtnoth and Alwig belong to the same kindred as Beorhtwine, but this possibility has not been fully investigated.

are certain clues to the identity of the survivors. As we have seen, the Leofwine who held a manor at Fillongley of the bishop of Coutances in 1086 can be identified with the brother of Æthelwine. There were three other manors at Fillongley. One was held in 1086 by Alsige as a king's thegn; he had also held it before the Conquest. Another belonged to Coventry Abbey, the house to which Æthelwine had given Clifton-on-Dunsmore, and which was, of course, founded by Earl Leofric, of whom Beorhtwine's sons had claimed to hold Alvestone. The fourth was held in 1086 by Robert *dispensator* in succession to Æthelmær. Were Alsige and Æthelmær two of the unnamed brothers of the Alvestone entry?

Supporting evidence can be adduced in support of Æthelmær. His successor, Robert *dispensator*, held four manors in Warwickshire in 1086, one at Lea Marston, in succession to Alwine, another in the same vill, in succession to Æthelmær, a third at Fillongley, also Æthelmær's, and a fourth at Barston, which had been sold by Æthelmær, with King William's permission, to Æthelwine the sheriff. This pattern suggests that the Alwine of Lea Marston was Æthelwine the sheriff also, and the appearance of Æthelmær in conjunction with Æthelwine at Barston and Lea Marston, and with Æthelwine's brother Leofwine at Fillongley, seems sufficient to establish kinship.[14] Further confirmation comes from the second entry for Barston in the Warwickshire folios. It is clear that the estate was disputed in 1086 between Robert *dispensator* and the Domesday sheriff of Warwickshire, Robert d'Oilly. Robert d'Oilly claimed to hold as the tenant of Æthelwine's son, Thorkil. He held only one manor in chief in Warwickshire, which lay at Lea Marston, where Æthelwine had held land; Robert's predecessor, however, was called Ælfric, from whom he had bought the manor, with King William's permission. Another manor in Lea Marston was held by Robert d'Oilly as Thorkil's tenant; it had belonged to Earl Leofric's son and successor, Earl Ælfgar.[15] As we have seen, the other manor in Lea Marston had belonged to Æthelmær.

The name of Ælfric, Robert d'Oilly's predecessor at Lea Marston, is one of the commonest personal names in pre-Conquest England. However, it is perhaps significant that a man of this name appears to be connected with Leofwine. At Harbury, Leofwine and Alric held an estate which they 'could sell but not depart with the land'. The formula implies dependence, but no lord is recorded. However, a second manor in this vill belonged to Coventry Abbey, founded by Earl Leofric, and it may therefore be suggested that it was he who was the lord of Leofwine and Alric. Another manor at Harbury belonged to Thorkil, son of Æthelwine the sheriff, and a fourth manor in the vill was held in 1086 by William Bonvalet in succession to Alwine. Since William Bonvalet can be identified with Thorkil's tenant at Coughton, this Alwine may be Æthelwine the sheriff.[16] The charter of Robert of Stafford, already mentioned, provides further evidence of a connection between Æthelwine and a man called Ælfric. The attestations of Æthelwine the sheriff, his son Thorkil and Thorkil's brother Ketilbiorn are immediately followed by that

---

[14] *Domesday Book* i, fos 238v, 242v, 244v (Fillongley); 242v (Lea Marston).
[15] *Domesday Book* i, fos 241, 242v (Barston), 241v, 242 (Lea Marston).
[16] *Domesday Book* i, fos 239, 239v, 241v, 243v (Harbury); for William Bonvalet, see *Domesday Book: Warwickshire*, ed. Judy Plaister, Chichester 1976, 17, 69 note.

of Ælfric (*Aluricus*) 'the king's knight'. The original of this charter was probably drawn up at Evesham Abbey (the beneficiary) and therefore on the English model, and it is thus of relevance that in Old English witness-lists kinsmen tend to attest charters in groups. The appearance of Ælfric's name in this position, taken with the other evidence presented here, suggests that he was a member of Æthelwine's family. It is likely that he is the Ailric (Æthelric) who held Æthelwine's manor of Flecknoe as Thorkil's tenant in 1086.

Another of Thorkil's tenants in 1086 was Ordric, who held the manor of 'Walcote' with its appurtenances at Willoughby and Calcutt which had belonged to him before the Conquest. He can probably be identified as Thorkil's predecessor at Harbury (discussed above) and at Ratley, which was held of Thorkil by a man called Almær in 1086. This Almær is probably, though not certainly, the Æthelmær whose connection with Æthelwine's family has already been proposed. Almær and Ordric are associated again at Ettington, where each held a manor before 1066; Ordric retained his estate as a king's thegn in 1086, but that of Almær was held of Thorkil by Ermenfrid.[17] Ordric also preceded Thorkil at Fenny Compton, which he had held in conjunction with Alwine (possibly Æthelwine) and Wulfsige; a man called Roger held it of Thorkil in 1086, and a second manor in the same vill, whose pre-Conquest tenant was probably Ordric, was held of Thorkil in 1086 by Almær, or Æthelmær. The third manor at Fenny Compton, held in 1086 by the Count of Meulan, had belonged to Ælfric in 1066.[18] It seems we may add the name of Ordric to those of Alsige, Æthelmær and Ælfric as the four unnamed brothers of Leofwine, himself the brother of Æthelwine the sheriff.

Another member of the family may be seen in Edwin, who before the Conquest held the only manor in Flecknoe not belonging to Leofwine and his brother Æthelwine the sheriff; it was held by Oslac of Thorkil in 1086. He is probably the same Edwin who held nine other manors which were in Thorkil's hands in 1086, four at Ladbroke, two at Calcutt (where Ordric held land), two at Cawston and one at Rugby.[19] One of his Ladbroke manors had an outlier at Radbourne, and it is therefore of considerable interest to find that in 998, Æthelred II granted land at Southam, Ladbroke and Radbourne to Ealdorman Leofwine, father of Leofric, earl of Mercia. Southam was subsequently used for the endowment of Coventry Abbey, in whose possession it is found in Domesday Book; which might suggest that Edwin's land at Ladbroke and Radbourne may have come in the first instance from the earls of Mercia.[20] He may be the Edwin who had held the manor at Radford Semele, sold by Thorkil's brother Ketilbiorn to Ermenfrid, the tenant in 1086; this Ermenfrid held other manors of Thorkil in 1086, including, as we have seen, Almær's manor at Ettington, and two manors at Ladbroke and Calcutt which had

---

[17] *Domesday Book* i, fos 241 ('Walcote'), 241v (Ratley), 241v, 244v (Ettington).
[18] *Domesday Book* i, fos 240v, 24lv. The two entries for Fenny Compton on folio 24lv are contiguous and the information on the pre-Conquest tenants seems to relate to both.
[19] *Domesday Book* i, fo. 241.
[20] P. H. Sawyer, *Anglo-Saxon Charters, an annotated list and bibliography*, London 1968, no. 892 (hereinafter cited as S.) The hidages of the charter do not agree with those of Domesday, so that some rearrangement has taken place between 998 and 1066.

belonged to Edwin.[21] It is also tempting to identify this Edwin with Edwin the sheriff, who held Thorkil's manor of Marston Green and also Beausale, which had passed by 1086 to the bishop of Bayeux.[22] Edwin does not appear to hold any land in 1086 and was probably dead by this date; he may belong to the generation of Æthelwine's father Beorhtwine rather than to that of Æthelwine himself.[23]

Since all the kinsmen (assuming that that is what they are) have common names, further identifications are necessarily speculative. Even Æthelwine himself presents certain problems, unless he is specifically described as Thorkil's father, or appears with the designation of *vicecomes*. He is certainly Thorkil's predecesor at Bericote and Ryton-on-Dunsmore, and probably at Nuneaton and Little Lawford as well.[24] He may be the tenant of half a hide at Kemerton, Glos., for another half-hide in the same place was held by Leofwine. Both tenements were berewicks of Deerhurst, a great multiple estate belonging in 1086 to Westminster Abbey. Its previous owner, Odda, was earl of Worcestershire from 1053 to 1056. Given the association of Æthelwine's family with the earls of Mercia, a connection with one of the other holders of comital authority in the west midlands would not be surprising.[25] Whether Æthelwine is also to be identified with Alwine the sheriff, whose lands in Gloucestershire passed, with his widow, to Richard *iuvenis*, must remain uncertain. Richard's Domesday successor, William *Goizenboded*, has an English by-name ('cursed, or foretold, by a witch') but we do not know whether he was the half-brother of Thorkil or not. His lands, like Thorkil's, passed to the earls of Warwick, which may indicate a connection of some kind.[26]

Of Æthelwine's putative brothers, Ælfric can probably be identified as Thorkil's predecessor at Bickenhill. Given that he attests Robert of Stafford's charter for Wrottesley, Staffs, he may be Robert's tenant at Ilmington, Bearley and Bubbenhall, all of which he had held in King Edward's time.[27] Much of Robert's land in Warwickshire had belonged to thegns connected with Earl Leofric. Vagn, who attests a St Albans lease as the chief of Earl Leofric's *barones*, held seven of Robert's twenty-eight manors in the shire, including the four most valuable at Tysoe, Churchover, Wolford and Wooton

---

[21] *Domesday Book* i, fo. 241v. Ketilbiorn's name appears as *Chetelbert*, which should represent the Anglo-Scandinavian hybrid 'Ketilbeorht', but this is a scribal error, understandable with two such rare names. A similar mistake occurs in the Worcestershire folios (fo. 174v, Powick).

[22] *Domesday Book* i, fos 238v (Beausale), 241v (Marston Green).

[23] Unless he is the Edwin who held Whitacre of Thorkil in 1086 (fo. 241) but the name is common.

[24] *Domesday Book* i, fos 240v, 241v.

[25] *Domesday Book* i, fo. 166. Leofwine held another berewick of Deerhurst, at Oridge. For Odda, see Ann Williams, 'An introduction to the Gloucestershire Domesday' *The Gloucestershire Domesday*, ed. R. H. W. Erskine and Ann Williams, forthcoming.

[26] Feilitzen identified Æthelwine not only with Alwine *vicecomes* of Gloucestershire, but also with the Alwine *vicecomes* who appears in Herefordshire, holding Wolferlow, and in Huntingdonshire, holding Offord; manors assessed at eight hides and three hides respectively ('Pre-Conquest personal names' 190 note 8; *Domesday Book* i, fos 183v, 185, 206v). See however the counter-arguments of C. P. Lewis, 'English and Norman government and lordship on the Welsh borders, 1039–1087', Oxford D.Phil. 1985, 101–2.

[27] *Domesday Book* i, fo. 242v.

Wawen; the last of these preserves his name.[28] One of Vagn's manors lay at Ullenhall, where Thorkil's descendants held land in the twelfth century, but it is difficult to trace any clear connection between Vagn and Thorkil's kindred in the eleventh century.[29] Another thegn of Earl Leofric, Sigmundr the Dane, held Robert of Stafford's manor at Wolverton. Like Leofwine, Sigmundr had been in dispute with the bishop of Worcester over the episcopal manor of Crowle, Worcs, which he had seized with the help of his lord, Earl Leofric.[30]

Since Ælfric attests Robert of Stafford's charter as 'the king's knight' (the original reading was probably *miles*, which can also mean 'thegn'), we should expect to find him among the king's thegns in Domesday Book, and indeed a thegn called Ælfric held a manor at Barcheston in 1086. Only five Englishmen, in fact, held land as king's thegns in Warwickshire in 1086, and four of them – Ælfric at Barcheston, Alsige at Fillongley, Ordric at Ettington and Leofwine at Flecknoe – are certainly or probably Æthelwine's brothers. Among the king's thegns in Staffordshire is an Ælfric, holding a ploughland at Cannock, who may be our man, since another manor in this vill belonged to Earl Ælfgar, the son of Earl Leofric.[31] Leofwine must be the pre-Conquest tenant of Cubbington, Warks, for his co-tenant was Ketilbiorn, the rarity of whose name allows us to identify him with Thorkil's brother; another manor in the same vill belonged to Coventry Abbey.[32] Ordric is possibly the pre-Conquest tenant of two manors at Hodnell, one of which passed to Thorkil and the other to the count of Meulan.[33] Tables II and III show the lands which may be assigned with some degree of certainty to Æthelwine and his kinsmen. The totals, though interesting in themselves, cannot be pressed too far, since there is no way of knowing what other estates belonged to the family, nor what proportion of their land the manors actually identified represent.

It might be thought that exercises such as these are of purely local interest, but if the conclusions reached above have any validity, some points of general interest emerge. The reconstruction of his family and (in part) their holdings throws light on the position of Thorkil himself in 1086. The Abingdon Chronicle describes Thorkil as 'a great nobleman . . . dwelling in the region of

---

[28] *Domesday Book* i, fo. 242v; for Vagn's attestation see S. 1425 and M. Gelling, *Early charters of the Thames Valley*, Leicester 1979, 189. Vagn also witnessed the spurious foundation charter of Coventry Abbey (S. 1226).

[29] Ullenhall belonged to Thorkil's grandson, Henry of Arden (*Sir Christopher Hatton's Book of Seals*, ed. L. C. Loyd and D. M. Stenton, Oxford 1950, no. 56 p. 32). There were two other manors in Churchover in 1086, one belonging to Earl Aubrey's fief, in succession to Alric (fo. 239v) and another held by Thorkil, no previous tenant being named (fo. 241v). At Wolford there were four tenements apart from that held by Vagn; in 1086, one belonged to the bishop of Bayeux's fief, no previous tenant being named (fo. 238v), another, held by the count of Meulan, had belonged to Ælfric (fo. 240v); and the other two, both held in 1086 by Robert of Stafford, had belonged to Alwig and Alwine respectively; Alwine was still holding as Robert's tenant in 1086 (fo. 242v).

[30] *Domesday Book* i, fo. 242v; for Sigmundr and his connection with Earl Leofric, see Williams, 'Cockles amongst the wheat', 13–14.

[31] *Domesday Book* i, fos 244v, 250v.

[32] *Domesday Book* i, fos 238v, 240v.

[33] *Domesday Book* i, fos 240, 241. Thorkil had two manors in Hodnell, the other being held by Wulfnoth before the Conquest. A fourth manor in the vill was held by William fitzCorbucion in succession to Alwig (fo. 243).

Arden', an assessment amply confirmed by his substantial fief of 127 hides in Warwickshire and 5 hides at Drayton, Oxon.[34] Thorkil's wealth is exceptional for an Englishman in 1086; Stenton maintained that he and Colswain of Lincoln were the only two Englishmen to hold fiefs of baronial dimensions in 1086, though Edward of Salisbury should perhaps be added to the list.[35] Freeman regarded Thorkil's unusual eminence with suspicion:

> the one loyal man, the one prudent man, the one traitor, as he would be called in the mouths of his more stout-hearted countrymen, reaped his rewards in retaining his wealth and honours and adding to them . . . at the cost of men better than himself.[36]

These strictures assume that Thorkil's fief had been built up out of lands forfeited by men who had taken part in the Mercian risings of 1067–71. The accusation might in part be true, but the evidence set forth above suggests that nearly half Thorkil's fief (some 62 hides out of 132) had belonged to members of his own family, some of whom were still his tenants in 1086. Nor do we know how much of the remainder had been held by men commended to his father and uncles. Some of it certainly was held by *commendati* for Domesday itself records that Arnketil and Ceolred, the pre-Conquest holders of Baddesley Ensor, were Thorkil's men. Moreover the lands at Hill and Chesterton which Thorkil gave to Abingdon are described as his patrimony, but do not appear in Æthelwine's possession in 1066. No tenants at all are recorded for Hill, but the two estates at Chesterton were held by Alweald and by three men called Alnoth, Beorhtwine and Thuri respectively.[37] They were all probably the men of Æthelwine. The numerous cases of men holding of Thorkil the lands which they themselves possessed before the Conquest need not imply that his wealth was gained at the expense of his 'stout-hearted' comrades who resisted the Norman settlement. It could just as well suggest that Thorkil was in a position to support and protect, rather than to despoil, his neighbours.[38]

Of even more interest is the dominant position of Thorkil amongst his surviving kinsmen. The lands which Ælfric, Ordric, Leofwine and Alsige held of the king were inconsiderable, a hide or two at the most, and Eadmær and Æthelmær seem to have nothing in chief at all. Æthelmær, however, held some 12½ hides as Thorkil's tenant, consisting of the lands at Ladbroke and Cawston, which had belonged to Edwin, Ratley, which had belonged to Ordric, Fenny Compton, which he may have held himself, since no pre-Conquest tenant is named, and Longdon, which had belonged to Earnwulf. Longdon is of particular interest. In the twelfth century one Ketilbiorn

---

[34] *Chron. Abingdon* ii, 8; *Domesday Book* i, fos 160v, 240v–241v.

[35] F. M. Stenton, *Anglo-Saxon England*, Oxford 3rd ed. 1971, 626; for Edward of Salisbury see VCH *Wiltshire* ii, 99.

[36] Freeman, 'Norman Conquest', iv, 189.

[37] *Domesday Book* i, fos 239, 241v. Coventry Abbey held a manor at Chesterton (fo. 239).

[38] Henry of Arden, Thorkil's grandson, confirmed the grant of Binley to Combe Abbey made by Thurbert son of Æthelwulf (BL Cotton Vitellius A, i, fo. 45). Æthelwulf is presumably the 'Hadulfus' who held Binley of Thorkil in 1086, and had held himself before the Conquest (*Domesday Book* i, fo. 241v). Another manor there had belonged to Ealdgyth, daughter of Earl Ælfgar (fo. 238v). 'Hadulf' seems to have done quite well out of his association with Thorkil.

(*Ketelbern*) of Longdon and his brother Thorkil (*Turchill*) attest charters of Siward of Arden, Thorkil's son, and Siward's son, Hugh of Arden.[39] If Ketilbiorn's name was rare in the eleventh century, it was rarer still in the twelfth, and its appearance here, especially in conjunction with that of Thorkil, must, on prosopographical grounds, suggest that the holders were kinsmen of Thorkil and Ketilbiorn, sons of Æthelwine. Perhaps they were the sons, or more likely the grandsons, of Thorkil's uncle, Æthelmær. Two more uncles, Ordric at 'Walcote' and Ælfric at Flecknoe, appear among Thorkil's tenants in 1086.

Thorkil's brother Ketilbiorn seems not to have any land at the time of Domesday and may have been dead. Guthmund, however, held Great Packington as his brother's tenant in 1086. Since his name is relatively uncommon, he can probably be identified with the Guthmund who held Aston of William fitzAnsculf, for the estate had formerly belonged to Edwin, earl of Mercia and grandson of Leofric.[40] Guthmund was the ancestor of the Le Notte family, who held estates belonging to William fitzAnsculf, as well as Great Packington itself, which belonged to them as tenants of the Ardens. In 1210, Henry le Notte claimed lands at Bushbury and Penn, both in Staffs, in right of his great grandmother *Ailleva* (Æthelgifu) daughter of Guthmund.[41] There were two manors at Penn in 1086, both held by William fitzAnsculf; one belonged to Earl Ælfgar and another to his mother, Godgifu. A virgate at Bushbury was attached to Godgifu's manor at Essington, Warks, which appears twice in the Domesday folios, once in Warwickshire and once in Staffordshire. This estate and another at Bushbury, held by Wulfric in King Edward's time, belonged in 1086 to William fitzAnsculf.[42]

The interest of these tenurial arrangements is that such relationships between the members of a family, whereby the main holdings are concentrated in the possession of one man, of whom the rest hold as tenants, conforms to continental rather than to English practice. It is as if Æthelwine's family had made a deliberate decision to channel the remnants of their inheritance through Thorkil, adjusting at the same time the amounts of land which each of them held of him. Some intentional rearrangement is surely indicated by the number of sales in which members of the kin were involved; Æthelmær's sale of Barston to Æthelwine, Æthelwine's sale of Flecknoe to Leofwine, Ælfric's sale of Lea Marston to Robert d'Oilly, Ketilbiorn's sale of

---

[39] Ketilbiorn of Longdon attests a charter of Siward of Arden, and is probably identical with Ketilbiorn *dapifer* who appears in two other witness-lists (Shakespeare Birthplace Trust ms. ER1/68 fos 78–78v, Bodleian ms. Dugdale 13 p. 464; CUL ms. Add 3021 fo. 238; Bodleian ms. Dugdale 21 fo. 49); his brother Thorkil appears in the first reference. Ketilbiorn of Longdon also witnesses a charter of Siward's son Hugh (*Sir Christopher Hatton's Book of Seals*, no. 138). I am indebted to Dr Crouch for these references.

[40] Ketilbiorn had sold his manor of Radford Semele to Ermenfrid, and Cubbington, which he held in conjunction with Leofwine, had passed to the count of Meulan; his only other manor in the shire was Church Lawford (five hides), held in 1086 by Earl Roger of Shrewsbury (fo. 239). For Aston, see fo. 243.

[41] For the le Notte family, see Colin Watson, 'The cartulary of Kenilworth' London PhD 1966, 161–2; *Feet of Fines, Warwickshire* no. 25, p. 5; *Curia Regis Rolls vi 11–14 Jn*, London HMSO 1932, 72.

[42] *Domesday Book* i, fos 249v, 250.

Radford Semele to Ermenfrid. Perhaps it was this adjustment to Norman customs of land tenure and inheritance which enabled the family to preserve their patrimony and transmit it to another generation.

In this, they were unusual but not unique. The fortunes of many English families were wrecked in the storms of the Norman Conquest and settlement, but some survived. One such family, in Gloucestershire, has much in common with Æthelwine's kindred. In 1086, William Leofric held a fief extending over Gloucestershire, Oxfordshire, Berkshire and Essex, all of which (with the possible exception of his single Oxfordshire manor) came from a predecessor called Asgot. William is unusual in having no other named predecessor. Since one of his manors was Hailes, Gloucs, this predecessor can be identified as Asgot (Osgod) of Hailes, who attests a grant of Ealdred, bishop of Worcester, in the 1050s, with 'the better men of the shire'.[43] Domesday nowhere implies that William Leofric and Asgot of Hailes were related, but it is significant that William is said to have freed twelve slaves at Hailes. This piece of information is unique in Domesday, and the freeing of slaves was a pious duty often imposed on heirs by testators in pre-Conquest England. This and William's English by-name suggests that he was of mixed blood (like Orderic Vitalis) and it seems not unlikely that Asgot was his father. Asgot's manors in Berkshire were interlinked with those of two other thegns, Beorhtric and Edmund, in a pattern resembling that which we have seen for Æthelwine's kin in Warwickshire, and which suggests that they were co-heirs and kinsmen.[44] Beorhtric was living in 1086 and holding as a king's thegn two pieces of land at Leckhampton, Gloucs. One piece had belonged to him before the Conquest, and the other had been held by a thegn called Ordric, but 'King William, when he went into Normandy, assigned both (holdings) to this Beorhtric.'[45] The date of the king's visit to the duchy is not specified, but one naturally thinks of his triumphal tour in 1067, after the meeting at Barking in January when the English 'bought back' their lands. Perhaps Beorhtric was one of the western thegns who, by speedy submission to the new king, salvaged some part of his family's fortunes. Interestingly enough, a very early charter of William, dated before his departure to Normandy in 1067 and relating to lands in Wiltshire and Gloucestershire, includes a Beorhtric in its address.[46] Though Beorhtric does not appear as William Leofric's tenant in 1086, there is still a certain similarity between the position of this little family and that of Æthelwine. Another, more famous, parallel can be found in the kindred of Wigod of Wallingford. Wigod himself was dead by 1086, but had managed to retain much of his estate well into the Conqueror's reign. His son Toki was killed at the battle of Gerberoi, seemingly acting as one of the king's squires.[47] The family lands, however, passed to Toki's sister Ealdgyth and her Norman

---

[43] S. 1408 (1052 × 1056).
[44] For William Leofric, Asgot, and their family, see Williams, 'An introduction to the Gloucester-shire Domesday', forthcoming.
[45] *Domesday Book* i, fo. 170v.
[46] *Regesta* i, no. 9.
[47] *ASC* 'D' 1079. The standing of the family, at least in English eyes, is shown by this notice of Toki's death in the Anglo-Saxon Chronicle. See also Marjorie Chibnall, *Anglo-Norman England 1066–1166*, Oxford 1986, 35.

husband, Robert d'Oilly, and to their son-in-law, Miles Crispin. Wigod's nephews, Thorvald and Alfred, continued, however, to hold land but in small amounts, Thorvald as a tenant of Earl Roger of Shrewsbury and Alfred of the king.[48]

Adaptation to Norman customs of inheritance, tenure and even names was the key to survival. Another important factor seems to have been experience in the royal administration. Wigod of Wallingford had some official position in Oxfordshire at the end of King Edward's reign, Beorhtric (as we have seen) is addressed in an early writ of William I, and Æthelwine was a sheriff.[49] It has been assumed that he was sheriff of Warwickshire and that Thorkil succeeded him in this office, though there is no direct evidence on either point. Circumstantial evidence nevertheless tends to support the traditional view. It has been remarked that many of the Englishmen who survived and even prospered through the vicissitudes of William's reign were named after towns.[50] In this context the fact that Domesday Book refers to Thorkil as Thorkil of Warwick, though elsewhere he is known as Thorkil of Arden, is surely crucial. Thorkil's connection with the shrievalty of Warwickshire is presumably the reason why he, and not some other kinsman, was the dominant landholder in 1086. He may indeed have been the third member of his family to hold the office if Edwin is, as suggested above, identical with Edwin the sheriff. Thorkil's relationship with the Domesday sheriff of Warwickshire, Robert d'Oilly, suggests that the latter stepped into the former's shoes. The only Warwickshire manor which Robert held in chief was Lea Marston, bought from Ælfric. But he held six manors in the shire as a mesne-tenant, one from the bishop of Bayeux and five from Thorkil. Two of these had previously belonged to Æthelwine.[51] Robert also appears as Thorkil's neighbour in Oxfordshire, where he held ten hides at Drayton.[52] Thorkil was also sheriff of Staffordshire at the beginning of King William's reign, an office in which he had been succeeded by Robert of Stafford, whose links with Thorkil and Æthelwine have already been remarked.[53]

The reconstruction of Æthelwine's family and its possessions throws some light on the kind of men who held shrieval office in King Edward's reign. They appear as substantial local thegns, of middling wealth, but conclusions about the size of their tenures cannot be drawn, for we have no means of knowing what other estates they possessed, nor what proportion of their wealth is represented by those manors which can be assigned to them. For the same reasons, no firm conclusions can be drawn about the comparative wealth of

---

[48] Thorvald nephew of Wigod held Meysey Hampton, Gloucs, of Earl Roger and can be identified as the earl's tenant at Easton Mewsey, Wilts, Penton Mewsey and North Houghton, Hants, Loseley, Surrey, and probably Burpham and Worpledon, Surrey, as well; see Lewis 'English and Norman government', 216–7. Alfred, Wigod's nephew, held Littlestoke and Checkendon, Oxon, of the king, and is probably the Alfred who held Cuxham in the same shire of Miles Crispin (*Domesday Book* i, fos 159v, 160).

[49] For Wigod see F. E. Harmer, *Anglo-Saxon Writs*, Manchester 1952, no. 104.

[50] James Campbell, 'Some agents and agencies of the late Anglo-Saxon state', *Domesday Studies*, ed. J. C. Holt, Woodbridge 1987, 210.

[51] *Domesday Book* i, fos 238v,.241, 241v, 242.

[52] *Domesday Book* i, fo. 158v.

[53] *Regesta* i, no. 25; Green, 'Sheriffs of William the Conqueror', 130–1

individual members of the family; Tables II and III illustrate the positions before and after the Conquest as far as can be determined. It is unlikely that these totals represent all the possessions of the family. If this conclusion seems rather disappointing for the amount of work, another is more striking and more innovative. This is the connection between Æthelwine's kindred and the earls of Mercia. Æthelwine, unlike his brothers, is nowhere said to hold of the earls, but his gift of Clifton-on-Dunsmore to Earl Leofric's church at Coventry resembles a vassal's donation to his lord's foundation. A similar significance may attach to the tenure by St Mary's, Warwick, of land at Myton as Thorkil's tenant, for the land had belonged to Earl Edwin; it might be a gift for the soul of Thorkil's former lord.[54] If this is the case, it is of considerable interest. We are used to thinking of the pre-Conquest sheriffs as king's men, who 'within the territory of even the greatest earls . . . stood for the executive power of the crown'.[55] The relationship between the earls of Mercia and the family of Æthelwine suggests that this was not the case, and that in Warwickshire, the sheriff was the earl's man. In Worcestershire also, the pre-Conquest sheriff, Cyneweard of Laughern, belonged to the family of Archbishop Wulfstan of York, *quondam* bishop of Worcester, and he and his kindred were in the *mouvance* of the bishops of Worcester just as much as (or more than) that of the king.[56] It would appear that powerful lords, lay and ecclesiastical, were drawing royal officers, no less than king's thegns, into the circles of their own patronage.

The relationship of Æthelwine's family and the Mercian earls has some bearing on the eventual fate of their descendants. In about 1088, William II granted the lands of Thorkil of Arden to Henry de Beaumont, as part of the newly formed fief of the earldom of Warwick.[57] Some previous connection between the Beaumonts and the Ardens is shown by the count of Meulan's tenure of Myton, which had belonged to Thorkil's fee, for the count was, of course, Robert de Beaumont, Henry's brother.[58] Robert of Meulan also held the manors of Cubbington, which had belonged to Leofwine and Ketilbiorn, Fenny Compton, which had belonged to Ælfric, and Harbury, which Leofwine and Alric had held, probably of the earls of Mercia. Other estates in Robert's hands in 1086 may have come from the family of Æthelwine, for the names Alwine, Ordric, Alsige, Ælfric and Leofwine appear among his predecessors, and a Leofwine was his tenant at Shuttington in 1086.[59] When Thorkil's heirs,

---

[54] *Domesday Book* i, fo. 241v. Another manor in Myton, also held by Earl Edwin, had passed to Thorkil, as had land at Lea Marston held by Edwin's father, Earl Ælfgar.

[55] Stenton, *Anglo-Saxon England* 549.

[56] See Ann Williams, 'An introduction to the Worcestershire Domesday', *The Worcestershire Domesday*, ed. R. W. H. Erskine and Ann Williams, London 1989, 24–6.

[57] *Chron. Abingdon* ii, 20.

[58] *Domesday Book* i, fos 239v, 241v. The manor is entered both in Thorkil's name and in that of the count, which would suggest a dispute.

[59] *Domesday Book* i, fos 239v–240v. Alwine held Whitchurch, Alsige held Astley and Ælfric held Wolford; Leofwine preceded the count at Milverton, Bourton-on-Dunsmore and Shuckborough, the latter a vill where Thorkil held land in 1086. Leofwine also appears as the count's tenant at Shuttington, held before the Conquest by Ceolred and Godric. Ceolred's name is rare and he may therefore be identical with Ceolred, Thorkil's man, who held land at Baddesley Ensor (fo. 241). The Ordric who preceded the count at Hodnell is almost certainly Thorkil's uncle, see note 33 above.

the Ardens, became tenants of the earls of Warwick, the wheel had come full circle and they were in the same position as their pre-Conquest forebears *vis-à-vis* the earls of Mercia; a most remarkable example of survival through adaptive ingenuity. The study of Æthelwine's kindred thus illuminates not only what a pre-Conquest shrieval family was like, but also how one of them managed to weather the storms of the Norman Conquest and settlement.

Table I   Some divided vills in Warwickshire

Vill		Pre-Conquest tenants	Tenants in 1086
ALVESTONE	7½ h	Beorhtwine of Earl Leofric	Bishop of Worcester
	7½ h	Beorhtnoth and Alwig	Bishop of Worcester
BARSTON	9/10 h	Æthelmær	Æthelwine/Robert *dispensator*
	½ h	Thorkil	Robert
CALCUTT	½ h	Edwin	Thorkil
	½ h	Edwin	Thorkil
	—	Ordric	Ordric
ETTINGTON	1 h	Æthelmær	Thorkil
	1 h	Baldwin son of Herlwin	Hugh de Grandmesnil
	17 h	[not given: ?Siward Barn]	Henry de Ferrers
	1 h	[not given: ?Ordric]	Ordric
FENNY COMPTON	4¾ h	Ælfric	Count of Meulan
	3¼ h	Ordric, Alwine and Wulfsige	Thorkil
	2 h	(?Ordric, Alwine and Wulfsige)	Almær of Thorkil
FILLONGLEY	½ h	Coventry Abbey	Coventry Abbey
	½ h	Æthelwine	Leofwine of the bishop of Coutances
	½ h	Æthelmær	Robert *dispensator*
	½ h	Alsige	Alsige
FLECKNOE	2h ½v	Leofwine	Bishop of Worcester
	1½ h	Æthelwine	Leofwine
	1h ½v	Æthelwine	Æthelric of Thorkil
	2½ h	Edwin	Oslac of Thorkil
HARBURY	1¼ h	Coventry Abbey	Coventry Abbey
	4½ h	Leofwine and Alric	Count of Meulan
	4 h	Ordric	William of Thorkil
	3 v	Alwine	William Bonvalet
	2 h	Siward Barn	Henry de Ferrers
LEA MARSTON	1 h	Earl Ælfgar	Robert d'Oilly of Thorkil
	2 h	Ælfric	Robert d'Oilly
	9 h	Æthelmær	Robert *dispensator*
	1 h	Æthelwine	Robert *dispensator*

Table II   Lands belonging to Æthelwine and Edwin

	Manor	*Hides*	*Virgates*
1. ÆTHELWINE	Flecknoe	1	½
	Flecknoe	1	2
	Fillongley		2
	Barston	10	
	Lea Marston	1	
	Harbury		3
	Ryton-on-Dunsmore	3	2
	Bericote	2	
	Clifton-on-Dunsmore	5	
	Nuneaton	3	
	Little Lawford	2	
	Kemerton (Gloucs.)		2
		30	3½
2. EDWIN	Flecknoe	2	2
	Ladbroke	1	1
	Ladbroke	2	1
	Ladbroke		1
	Ladbroke with Radbourne	1	2
	Calcutt		2
	Calcutt		2
	Cawston	1	2
	Cawston	1	
	Radford Semele	5	
	Marston Green	3	
	Beausale		2
	Rugby	2	2
		22	1

Table III   Lands belonging to Ælfric, Æthelmær, Ordric and Leofwine

	Manor	*Hides* (TRE)	*Virgates* (TRE)	*Hides* (1086)	*Virgates* (1086)
1. ÆLFRIC	Lea Marston	2			
	Fenny Compton	4	3		
	Bickerhill	2			
	Ilmington	1		1	

	Manor	Hides Virgates (TRE)		Hides Virgates (1086)	
	Bubbenhall	5		5	
	Bearley	1		1	
	Barcheston			1	½
	Flecknoe			1	½
	Cannock [Staffs]	1		1	
		16	3	11	1
2. ÆTHELMÆR	Fillongley		2		
	Lea Marston	9			
	Ettington	1			
	Barston	10			
	Fenny Compton	2		2	
	Longdon			2	2
	Ladbroke			1	2
	Cawston			1	2
	Ratley			5	
		22	2	12	2
3. ORDRIC	Calcutt	2		2	
	Harbury	4			
	Ettington	1		1	
	Fenny Compton	3	1		
	Ratley	5			
	Hodnell	1			
	Hodnell	4			
		20	1	3	
4. LEOFWINE	Flecknoe	1	2	1	2
	Flecknoe			2	½
	Fillongley		2		2
	Kemerton [Gloucs]		2		
	Oridge [Gloucs]		2		
			3	4	½

Notes
1. Leofwine and Ælfric held 4½ hides at Harbury TRE.
2. Leofwine and Ketilbiorn held 3 hides at Cubbington TRE.
3. Alsige seems to have held only at Fillongley (½ h) and Eadmar is mentioned only in connection with Alvestone.